JOURNAL FOR THE STUDY OF THE OLD TESTAMENT SUPPLEMENT SERIES
212

Editors
David J.A. Clines
Philip R. Davies

Executive Editor
John Jarick

GENDER, CULTURE, THEORY
2

Editor
J. Cheryl Exum

Sheffield Academic Press

The Prostitute and the Prophet

Hosea's Marriage in Literary-Theoretical Perspective

Yvonne Sherwood

Journal for the Study of the Old Testament
Supplement Series 212

Gender, Culture, Theory 2

This book is dedicated to my parents,
who have given me many things,
but none so precious as the freedom to be myself.

Copyright © 1996 Sheffield Academic Press

Published by Sheffield Academic Press Ltd
Mansion House
19 Kingfield Road
Sheffield, S11 9AS
England

Printed on acid-free paper in Great Britain
by Bookcraft Ltd
Midsomer Norton, Bath

British Library Cataloguing in Publication Data

A catalogue record for this book is available
from the British Library

ISBN 1-85075-581-7
ISBN 1-85075-777-1 pa

CONTENTS

ACKNOWLEDGMENTS

No work is complete without acknowledgment to those who have helped the author and generally made her task easier and more enjoyable than it might otherwise have been.

This book is a slight revision of my doctoral thesis and I consider myself lucky to have been part of a lively group of postgraduates so that I did not have to spend more time than was necessary in the 'not-so-splendid' isolation usually associated with doctoral work. In memory of times spent in seedy hotels in Dublin and Münster, of coffee in the Plaza, and of Friday nights at the Star and Garter, this book is a tribute to Mark Love, Ruth-Anne Reese, Noel Bailey, Todd Klutz, Froo Signore, Helen Duckett and all the 'class of 91–94'.

I would also like to thank David Clines, my supervisor, for giving me initial momentum when I was more than slightly daunted by the task ahead, for allowing me freedom to develop my own thoughts, and for providing an intriguing 'metacommentary' on my ideas. I am grateful to Robert Carroll and Cheryl Exum for being such attentive readers of my manuscript and for offering advice, additions and above all enthusiasm. Thanks also must go to Steve Barganski and the team at Sheffield Academic Press for a job well done and particularly for hunting down the Marc Chagall print for the front cover.

The bulk of the proofreading and editing was done prior to submission by my own 'in-house' (actually 'live-in') editor, Richard Davie, who spent many hours deciphering my idiosyncratic housestyle and punctuation. No statement, I think, could possibly be as rewarding to you as the one that I am about to make: that I sincerely promise to use commas properly in future.

ABBREVIATIONS

AB	Anchor Bible
AJSL	*American Journal of Semitic Languages and Literatures*
ANET	*Ancient Near Eastern Texts Relating to the Old Testament* (ed. J.B. Pritchard; 2nd edn 1955)
AT	The Alexander Text of *William Shakespeare: The Complete Works* (ed. P. Alexander)
AV	Authorised Version
BBB	Bonner biblische Beiträge
BI	*Biblical Interpretation*
Bib	*Biblica*
BSac	*Bibliotheca Sacra*
BTB	*Biblical Theology Bulletin*
BW	*Biblical World*
BZ	*Biblische Zeitschrift*
BZAW	Beihefte zur *Zeitschrift für die alttestamentliche Wissenschaft*
CAT	Commentaire de l'Ancien Testament
CBQ	*Catholic Biblical Quarterly*
CI	*Critical Inquiry*
CTA	*Corpus des tablettes en cunéiformes alphabétiques* (ed. A. Herdner)
DBSup	*Dictionnaire de la Bible, Supplément*
EC	Epworth Commentaries
EncJud	*Encyclopaedia Judaica* (ed. G. Roth and C. Wigoder)
EvT	*Evangelische Theologie*
FS	*Feminist Studies*
GNB	Good News Bible
HAT	Handbuch zum Alten Testament
Herm	Hermeneia
HUCA	*Hebrew Union College Annual*
IBS	*Irish Biblical Studies*
ICC	International Critical Commentary
ISBE	G.W. Bromiley (ed.), *International Standard Bible Encyclopaedia*, rev. edn
JAAR	*Journal of the American Academy of Religion*
JBL	*Journal of Biblical Literature*
JNES	*Journal of Near Eastern Studies*

JNT	*Journal of Narrative Technique*
JSOT	*Journal for the Study of the Old Testament*
JSOTSup	*Journal for the Study of the Old Testament*, Supplement series
JSS	*Journal of Semitic Studies*
KAT	Kommentar zum Alten Testament
KTU	*Keilalphabetischen Texte aus Ugarit* (ed. M. Dietrich, O. Loretz and J. Sammartin)
LB	*Literature and Belief*
LivB	Living Bible
LUÅ	Lunds universitets årsskrift
MLN	*Modern Language Notes*
MT	Masoretic Text
NEB	New English Bible
NJB	New Jerusalem Bible
NLH	*New Literary History*
NRSV	New Revised Standard Version
NRT	*La nouvelle revue théologique*
OED	*Oxford English Dictionary*
OTG	Old Testament Guides, JSOT Press
OTL	Old Testament Library, SCM Press
OTWSA	*Die Oud Testament Werkgemeenskap in Suid-Afrika*
RevExp	*Review and Expositor*
RevScRel	*Revue des sciences religieuses*
REB	Revised English Bible
RHPR	*Revue d'histoire et de philosophie religieuses*
RSV	Revised Standard Version
SBL	Society of Biblical Literature
SBLDS	SBL Dissertation Series
SEÅ	*Svensk exegetisk årsbok*
Sem	*Semitica*
SJOT	*Scandinavian Journal of the Old Testament*
TBT	*The Bible Today*
TLS	*Times Literary Supplement*
TOTC	Tyndale Old Testament Commentaries
TQ	*Theologische Quartalschrift*
VSpir	*Vie spirituelle*
VT	*Vetus Testamentum*
WBC	Word Biblical Commentary
WC	Westminster Commentaries
ZAW	*Zeitschrift für die alttestamentliche Wissenschaft*

Introduction

PROBLEM TEXTS AND PROBLEM PLAYS

Si in explanationibus omnium prophetarum sancti Spritus indigemus
aduentu (ut cuius instinctu scripti sunt, illius reuelatione pandantur)...
Quanto magis in explanatione Osee prophetae orandus est Dominus, et
cum Petro dicendum: *Edissere nobis parabolam istam.*

If we have need of the help of the Holy Spirit in the interpretation of all
the prophets... how much more, when we come to the interpretation of
the prophet Hosea, should we pray to the Lord and say with Peter:
'Explain unto us this parable' (Jerome).[1]

From centuries of critical debate only one consensus on the book of
Hosea emerges: that this is a disturbing, fragmented, outrageous and
notoriously problematic text. Many texts pose ethical and/or semantic
difficulties, but the difficulty of Hosea is defined by superlatives: Gélin
and McCurdy observe (only veering slightly towards hyperbole) that
'tout le monde a remarqué le caractère décousu et fragmentaire du
livre' ('*everyone* has remarked on the disconnected and fragmentary
nature of the text'),[2] and that ch. 1 is the most diversely interpreted
chapter in all prophetic literature.[3] With Ezekiel and Samuel, Hosea is
classed by Gélin as the most 'defective' book in the Massoretic Text,[4]
while Andersen and Freedman judge that it 'competes with Job for the
distinction of containing more unintelligible passages than any other
book of the Bible'.[5] Statements of bewilderment unite critics across

1. Jerome, *Commentaria in Osee prophetam*, in J.P. Migne [ed.], *Divinae
Bibliotheca Pars Prima: Hieronymi Opera*, 9 [Patrologia: Series Latina, XXV; Paris:
Vrayet de Surcy, 1845], col. 823.
2. A. Gélin, 'Osée', in L. Pirot and F. Vigouroux (eds.), *Dictionnaire de la
Bible, Supplément*, VI (Paris: 1960), pp. 926-40 (932).
3. J.F. McCurdy, 'Hosea', in *The New Schaff-Herzog Encyclopaedia of
Religious Knowledge*, V (Grand Rapids: Baker Book House, 1908), p. 371.
4. Gélin, 'Osée', p. 932.
5. F.I. Andersen and D.N. Freedman, *Hosea: A New Translation with*

chronological and theological divides: Jerome found the text 'cryptic' (*commaticus*);[6] Lowth compared it to *sparsa quaedam Sybillae folia* ('scattered pages of the Sybil');[7] and G.W. Ewald found it 'dark and enigmatical'.[8] Twentieth-century critics similarly deem the text 'mangled',[9] 'tormented',[10] 'turbulent'[11] and, more reservedly, 'vexing'.[12]

I find it intriguing that the only unanimous definition of Hosea is based not on its 'theme' or 'content' (both of which are highly controversial) but on the complex responses experienced by its readers. The way in which this text has become known, informally, as a 'problem text' is analogous to the way in which certain Shakespearean texts have been defined, more formally, as 'problem plays' and set apart from the rest of the canon. As the range of critical verdicts suggests, the statement that Hosea is a problem text can mean anything from 'the text is emotionally or ethically disturbing' (that is, 'dark' and 'tormented'), to 'the text is linguistically corrupt' (that is, 'mangled' and 'defective'). In this book I want to move beyond vague and impressionistic verdicts that the text is 'problematic' and ask what particular features in the text, and complexities in the relationship between the text and reader, conspire to produce such a disturbing and disorientating effect.

Just as critics and reviewers of the 'problem plays' of Shakespeare have explored in some detail what they mean when they term a text 'problematic', I want to begin by exploring some specific features of

Introduction and Commentary (AB; New York: Doubleday, 1980), p. 166.

6.   Jerome, cited by H. Fisch, 'Hosea: A Poetics of Violence', in Fisch (ed.), *Poetry With a Purpose: Biblical Poetics and Interpretation* (Bloomington: Indiana University Press, 1990), pp. 136-57 (141; Fisch does not state his source and I have been unable to trace the reference).

7.   R. Lowth, cited by Gélin, 'Osée', p. 932 (Gélin gives no reference and I have been unable to trace the original statement).

8.   G.W. Ewald, *Commentary on the Prophets of the Old Testament*. I. *Joel, Amos, Hosea and Zechariah* (trans. J.F. Smith; London: Williams & Norgate, 1875), p. 210.

9.   T.H. Robinson, 'Hosea', in T.H. Robinson and F. Horst (eds.), *Die zwölf kleinen Propheten: Hosea bis Micha* (HAT; Tübingen: Mohr, 1954), pp. 1-54 (1).

10.   Fisch, 'Hosea: A Poetics of Violence', p. 141.

11.   Andersen and Freedman, *Hosea*, p. 140.

12.   H.H. Rowley, *Book List of the Society of Old Testament Study*, 1951, p. 46, cited by R. Gordis, 'Hosea's Marriage and Message: A New Approach', *HUCA* 25 (1954), pp. 9-35 (9).

their definition, and to ask how, and to what extent, they can be applied to a text like Hosea. A review of major definitions of the 'problem plays' suggests that what distinguishes *All's Well That Ends Well*, *Measure for Measure* and *Troilus and Cressida* from the rest of the canon is their capacity to shock and perplex the reader on a linguistic, generic, ethical and conceptual level. The difficulty of the language is not only attributed to awkward constructions but to 'unexpected words', 'daring and resonant images',[13] and a verse structure that encompasses 'the stress of conflicting emotions'.[14] Generically, the plays 'defy absorption into the traditional categories of romantic comedies, histories, tragedies and romances';[15] poised between 'tragedy' and 'comedy', and subverting both, they might be defined, as Polonius would put it, as 'comical–tragical'.[16] Already points of intersection between the problem plays and the problematic biblical text begin to emerge, for the book of Hosea is not only characterized by awkward structures and 'broken construct chains'[17] but also uses the hapax legomenon אֵשֶׁת זְנוּנִים[18]—an exceedingly 'daring and resonant image'.[19] The disjointed rhythm has been seen by some critics as reflecting a divided emotional state; while responding to the text as a whole, commentators have struggled to categorize it as 'comedy' or 'tragedy',[20] *Heilsgeschichte* or prophecies of doom.

13. P. Ure, *Shakespeare: The Problem Plays* (London: Longman, 1970), p. 4.

14. V. Thomas, *The Moral Universe of Shakespeare's Problem Plays* (London: Croom Helm, 1987), p. 21.

15. Thomas, *The Moral Universe*, p. 21.

16. Polonius invents several comical new genres when he announces that the players are 'The best actors in the world for tragedy, comedy, history, pastoral, pastoral–comical, historical–pastoral, tragical–historical, tragical–comical–historical–pastoral, scene individable, or poem unlimited' (*Hamlet*, II.ii, ll. 392-95, in the Alexander Text of *William Shakespeare: The Complete Works* [ed. P. Alexander; Glasgow and London: Collins, 1985]; I use the Alexander Text throughout this thesis).

17. Andersen and Freedman, *Hosea*, p. 67.

18. 'Wife of harlotry'; for a discussion of the meanings of this phrase see Chapter 1, n. 4.

19. Ure, *Shakespeare: The Problem Plays*, p. 4, cf. n. 13.

20. Traditionally, the critical tendency has been to class Hosea as tragedy *or* comedy, but recently Martin Buss has proposed that 'positive and negative impulses' are held together in an 'ironic tension', as in the problem plays (M.J. Buss, 'Tragedy and Comedy in Hosea', in J.C. Exum [ed.], *Tragedy and Comedy* [*Semeia* 32; Atlanta: Scholars Press, 1985], pp. 71-82 [71]).

Morally as well as generically, the problem plays are said to elicit a 'radically schizophrenic' response.[21] The plays begin 'with a moral problem presented in such a manner that we are unsure of our moral bearings';[22] and, set among 'civilization[s] that are "ripe unto rotten-ness"', they focus on 'intricate cases of conscience [that] demand a solution by unprecedented methods'.[23] 'Sexuality, sexual disgust and bawdy have full and frank presentation':[24] in *Measure for Measure*, for example, a noviciate (Isabella) frees her brother from imprisonment by co-operating in the sordid substitution games of a bed-trick. Sex and religion merge with disturbing inappropriateness: thus a noviciate con-templates acting like a whore, and the proceedings are sanctioned and orchestrated by a 'friar' who is not all that he seems. Again, the analo-gies with Hosea 1–3 are clear: set among an (allegedly) apostate and 'rotten' nation (Hos. 5.12),[25] the prophet proposes a solution to the problem of the national conscience by a radical and 'unprecedented' method. The harlotry of Israel is enacted, and presumably counteracted, by taking a 'wife of harlotry'; the audience's response is divided, how-ever, as the accuser of Israel places himself, confusingly, in what seems to be a morally compromising position. The audience's sympathies are confused as Hosea and Yhwh, the two key characters with whom they might be expected to sympathize, do not, as in *Measure for Measure*, 'fully gratify conventional expectations'.[26] The spokesmen of morality continue to act in an ethically questionable manner as in ch. 2 the 'husband' threatens to strip his wife (2.5, 11), to parade her in front of

21. E.M.W. Tillyard, *Shakespeare's Problem Plays* (London: Chatto & Windus, 1950), p. 2.

22. E. Schanzer, *The Problem Plays of Shakespeare: A Study of Julius Caesar, Measure for Measure, Antony and Cleopatra* (London: Routledge & Kegan Paul, 1963), p. 3.

23. F.S. Boas, *Shakespere and His Predecessors* (London: Murray, 1896), p. 345.

24. C. Watts, *Shakespeare: Measure for Measure* (Harmondsworth: Penguin, 1986), p. 42.

25. To compound the sense of difficulty provoked by this text, Hosea casts Yhwh as the cause, as well as the cure, of national 'rottenness'. The statement 'I am like a moth to Ephraim, and like dry rot to the house of Judah' (Hos. 5.12) suggests that if something is rotten in the life of the nations, that something is, on one level, Yhwh himself.

26. Watts, *Measure for Measure* , p. 42.

her lovers (2.12), and to subject her to violence and imprisonment (2.5, 8; 3.3).

Conceptually, the problem plays encompass a kind of 'shiftingness' in which 'all the firm points...are felt to be fallible'.[27] The plot follows a disorientating path of 'inversion, deflation and paradox', and a permanent sense of disillusionment is achieved by the relentless commentary of 'cynical spokesmen or cynical points of view'.[28] The plays 'throw [such] opposed or contrary views into the mind'[29] that it is hard to believe that all ends well, and theatregoers tend to 'choke on the... consummation which they readily accept in Shakespeare's romantic comedies'.[30] In Hosea, similarly, the dream of reconciliation in Hos. 2.16-17 is undercut by the preceding text, for the fantasy of the seduction in the wilderness is ironically placed at the end of a passage of intense conflict and a misogynistic diatribe against the 'woman' Israel.

Like the problem plays, Hosea 1–3 does not give the reader an ending to believe in: the 'happy ever after' is neither 'happy' nor comforting, and the reader is left with a 'peculiar sense of perplexity or open-endedness'.[31] As it provides no unambiguous solution, so the text provides no stable point to cling on to; instead, Yhwh himself plays the part of cynical commentator and begins by snatching away the foundations of Israel's identity by questioning the assumption that the nation is loved by, or belongs to him (Hos. 1.6, 8). 'Inversion' follows 'deflation', and curses are converted to blessing, but this creates a paradox in which the two uneasily co-exist. In this text even names and identities are liable to change (Hos. 1.3-8; 2.3, 25) and the reader is left with no univocal point of view that has not already been subverted and interrogated by the text.

The analogy between Hosea and the problem plays provides a brief outline of some of the textual effects that readers may find disorientating or disturbing, and anticipates some of the directions in which this book shall progress. Linguistic, generic, ethical and conceptual tensions permeate this study, which focuses on four major problem areas in the text. In the four main sections of this book I shall be examining the ethical dilemmas arising from Hosea's marriage; the linguistic problems created

---

27. A.P. Rossiter, *Angel with Horns* (London: Longman, 1971), p. 117.
28. Watts, *Measure for Measure*, p. 42.
29. Rossiter, *Angel with Horns*, p. 117.
30. Thomas, *The Moral Universe*, p. 11.
31. Thomas, *The Moral Universe*, p. 8.

by audacious and unexpected images; the conceptual tensions created by the text's tendency to comment on and subvert its own arguments; and the tensions that inevitably arise between the text and the twentieth-century feminist reader. In each case I shall be taking as my text Hosea 1–3, which may be considered a self-contained unit,[32] and which, with its complex analogies between the domestic and the divine, and its disturbingly explicit imagery, has been the focus of a large proportion of critical study and the source of much 'perplexity'.

As the analogy between the problem plays and the book of Hosea might suggest, this book treats Hosea 1–3 not as a theological document but as a literary text. Each of the four studies is shaped and illuminated by a particular dimension of literary theory: the first study, which investigates commentators' responses to Hosea's marriage, is placed in the context of reader-response criticism and Fredric Jameson's theory of 'metacommentary'; and the second study, which considers the text's audacious sign-language, situates the prophetic signs within the wider field of semiotics. The text's propensity to undermine itself, the subject of the third chapter, draws on strategies of deconstruction, and in particular the work of Jacques Derrida. The fourth and final chapter, the feminist analysis, is a kind of methodological *bricolage*,[33] which draws on the principles of feminist approaches but, like most feminist theories, fuses feminist concerns with other branches of literary theory, such as deconstruction and reader-response. Each of the approaches merits an explanation in itself, and so although the distinctions are not always rigidly maintained, each chapter comprises two elements, which might roughly be termed 'theory' and 'practice'. In the theory section I attempt to provide an accessible definition to the approach that I shall be using, and to suggest ways in which it might be applicable to the wider

32. The critical consensus is that the book of Hosea can be divided into two distinct units: chs. 1–3 and 4–14 (see Andersen and Freedman, *Hosea*, p. 57). Yehezkel Kaufmann concludes, somewhat extremely, that because the two sections are so distinct, they must result from two distinct authors and two radically different time frames (*The Religion of Israel: From its Beginnings to the Babylonian Exile* [trans. M. Greenberg; London: George Allen & Unwin, 1961], pp. 370-71).

33. The term *bricolage* was first applied to method by Claude Levi-Strauss and means 'the adaptation of given materials to a specific task'. The *bricoleur* (or 'handyman') is the type of theorist who lacks tools 'conceptualised and procured specifically for his project', but who resourcefully adapts existing methods to the task; the feminist theorist is, by extension, a *bricoleuse* (C. Levi-Strauss, *The Savage Mind* [Chicago: Chicago University Press, 1961], p. 24).

field of biblical studies. In the second section I read Hosea 1–3 through the filter of this approach.

One of the fundamental premises of this book is that problems are not confined to the text but result from the interaction between the text and reader. To reflect this dual emphasis I shall be using text- and reader-based theories. Chapters 1 and 4 foreground the role of the reader, but semiotics and deconstruction are, in contrast, essentially text-based theories in which the reader is virtually invisible. The two theoretical approaches are not incompatible but are modified by their co-existence: thus the focus on text in Chapters 2 and 3 is literally framed by an awareness that a text is never a 'brute fact'[34] outside the consciousness of the reader.

Although the text is divided into four distinct sections, these are designed to overlap with, extend, and comment on one another. Chapter 2, for example, lays the theoretical foundations for Chapter 3, since semiotic theory is the basis of deconstruction, and Chapter 4, similarly, fits into this methodological continuum, as it takes issue with Derrida's insistence that deconstruction is apolitical, and borrows deconstructive strategies for a feminist re-reading of the text. Chapter 4 is also a development and a reply to Chapter 1, because it re-considers responses to Hosea's marriage from the point of view of gender as well as ideology. As the title 'Gomer's Marriage' might suggest, this chapter considers the text and related commentaries from a woman's point of view, and proposes a female reader's response to the text.

A Note on the Text

Throughout this book I shall be using the verse numbering of the Masoretic Text (MT). This differs slightly from the numbering in English translations, which number Hosea 2.1 and 2.2 as 1.10 and 1.11. All translations are taken from the RSV unless otherwise specified. Where no other indication is given, translations from foreign language texts are my own.

As this book falls into the category of 'final form' analysis of the text, it is detached from what Walter Vogels terms 'the quest for the

---

34. E. Freund, *The Return of the Reader: Reader-Response Criticism* (London: Methuen, 1987), p. 149.

"historical Hosea"'.[35] 'Hosea', 'Yhwh' and 'Gomer', therefore, are simply references to characters in a text and no epistemological or historical statement is implied. Any similarity to any persons, living or dead, is, as they say, entirely coincidental.

35. W. Vogels, ' "Osée–Gomer": *car* et *comme* "Yahweh–Israël", Os 1–3', *NRT* 103 (1981), pp. 711-27 (712).

Chapter 1

THE STRANGE CASE OF THE MISSING PROSTITUTE:
A RESPONSE TO SOME RESPONSES TO HOSEA 1.2

What is wrong with this play? Evidently something is wrong, since critics so entangle themselves in apologies and interpretations.[1]

When the Lord first spoke to Hosea, the Lord said to Hosea 'Go, take to yourself a wife of harlotry and have children of harlotry, for the land commits great harlotry by forsaking the Lord' (Hos. 1.2).[2]

I begin my analysis of Hosea 1–3 as a problem text with a study of the text's most notorious problem, Gomer-bat-Diblayim or the אֵשֶׁת זְנוּנִים. The marriage of the prophet[3] to a promiscuous woman[4] has been the focus

---

1.   A. Quiller-Couch on *Measure for Measure*, cited by W.W. Lawrence, *Shakespeare's Problem Comedies* (New York: Ungar, 1960), p. 4.

2.   RSV (I have amended the translation of אל הושע from 'through Hosea' to 'to Hosea').

3.   Most commentators assume that Hosea marries the promiscuous woman, since the verb לקח ('to take') is a common Hebrew idiom for marriage. However, some interesting alternatives have been proposed, most recently by G.I. Davies, who argues that since לקח can also be used interchangeably with שכב עם (for example in Lev. 20), Hos. 1.2 may be a command to 'lie with' the prostitute. If this is the case, Davies argues, it is possible that Hosea is called to represent not Yhwh, but Baal, 'one of Israel's clients or "lovers" ' (G.I. Davies, *Hosea* [OTG; Sheffield: JSOT Press, 1993], p. 90). While I find this a provocative suggestion, I shall be using the term 'Hosea's marriage' throughout this chapter because (1) this is the assumption made by all the commentaries that I shall be analysing, and (2) the issue at stake is the *relationship* between a prostitute and a man of God. Critics who object violently to the marriage would also, I suspect, react similarly to the idea of any kind of sexual relationship between the prophet and a promiscuous woman.

4.   The phrase אשת זנונים has been variously translated 'wife of harlotry' (RSV); 'whore' (NJB); 'a wife of whoredoms' (AV); 'a wife of whoredom' (NRSV); 'a girl who is a prostitute' (LivB); and 'your wife will be unfaithful' (GNB). In this chapter I shall use the translations 'promiscuous woman', 'prostitute' and 'wife of harlotry' in order to do justice to Gomer's ambiguous status in the text. Following Phyllis Bird I

of a large proportion of articles on Hosea; the purpose of this study is
not to add my own solution to the many solutions that have been proposed (although I shall outline my own reading at the end of the
chapter), but rather to analyse the ideological objections that are implied
in the act of solving the text. Some critics, such as H.W. Wolff
or Andersen and Freedman, openly declare that they find the MT
'atrocious'[5] in its implications, or see Yhwh's command as 'one of the
most startling divine allocutions recorded in the Bible',[6] but most critics
imply their objections in the act of diluting or devising an intricate
apologetic for the text. In this analysis I want to show how the types of
solutions proposed consistently point to a refusal to tolerate the 'wife of
harlotry', and I shall be drawing some inferences from this about critics'
expectations of a biblical text.

For Quiller-Couch, 'apologies and interpretations' point to a problem
in the text, but in this study I suggest that attempts to alter or correct
the text also highlight a point of dissonance between the text and reader.
As the study progresses, it becomes clear that the point of contention is
almost invariably the אֵשֶׁת זְנוּנִים, who is toned down by commentators as a
woman who became harlotrous, an adherent of the Canaanite cult, a
'woman of idolatry' or a 'lazy wife', and is even eradicated altogether.
Many critics spirit the offensive woman out of the text by consigning
her to a later redaction, arguing that she is just a metaphor, or claiming

assume that the stem זנה refers, more widely than נאף, to all pre- or extra-marital
intercourse, and that the abstract plural noun points to habitual behaviour and inclina-
tion rather than profession. However, as Bird also observes, Hosea is the first text to
develop the term figuratively, and it broadens its usage in two ways. First, it uses it
to include a sense of betrayal, usually limited to נאף, since the woman is promiscuous
away from (מאחרי) her husband. Secondly, it blurs the role of the אשת זנונים with that
of the professional prostitute, since in ch. 2 the 'wife of harlotry' receives presents
for her services. Though 'promiscuous woman' probably does most justice to the literal denotative sense, 'woman of harlotry' and 'prostitute' are included in the connotative sense. In using all three terms interchangeably, I want to reflect the way in
which patriarchy does not discriminate between the three roles in this text, and to
underline in the strongest possible terms the perceived threat of Gomer's sexuality
(see P.A. Bird, ' "To Play the Harlot": An Enquiry into an Old Testament
Metaphor', in P.L. Day [ed.], *Gender and Difference in Ancient Israel* [Minneapolis:
Fortress Press, 1989], pp. 75-94).

5.   H.W. Wolff, *A Commentary on the Book of Hosea* (trans. G. Stansell;
Herm; Philadelphia: Fortress Press, 1974), p. 15.

6.   F.I. Andersen and D.N. Freedman, *Hosea: A New Translation with
Introduction and Commentary* (AB; New York: Doubleday, 1980), p. 116.

that the 'wife of harlotry' is a symbolic role, played by the prophet's otherwise virtuous wife. As she is often removed from the text, or adjusted beyond recognition, this study is, effectively, an investigation of the case of the missing prostitute that examines in detail how the prostitute is removed from the text, and proposes potential motivations for her removal.

My enquiry into the critical treatment, and ultimately the disappearance of Gomer-bat-Diblayim, is divided into five sections. In the first section I outline the theoretical basis of my approach, drawing on ideological criticism, the field of reader-response, and Fredric Jameson's definition of metacommentary. In the second, third and fourth sections I look at a variety of responses to Hosea's marriage that range from the second to the twentieth centuries, that represent Jewish and Christian exegetical traditions, and that include ostensibly objective, and self-consciously creative reactions to the text. In the second section I examine so-called 'pre-critical' interpretation, from midrash to the theologians of the Reformation; in the third section I dwell chiefly on nineteenth- and twentieth-century interpretation, and in the fourth section I look at self-consciously 'artful' reworkings of the marriage theme in art, poetry, drama and prose. As Stephan Bitter observes in the preface to *Die Ehe des Propheten Hosea*, this chapter is written 'ohne Anspruch auf Vollständigkeit' ('without any claim to being exhaustive'),[7] but I have tried nevertheless to include a wide range of sources that are colourful and sometimes idiosyncratic, but at the same time representative of trends in interpretation. In the fifth and final section I tie these diverse strands together and draw some general conclusions about critical responses to Hos. 1.2; I also propose my own interpretation of the marriage which exploits, rather than solves, the motif of the collision of opposites.

1. Theories of (Mis)Reading

1.1. A Manifesto for Metacommentary: Fredric Jameson

> You are not such wiseacres as to think or say that you can expound scriptures without assistance from the divines and learned men who have laboured before you in the field of exposition. If you are of that opinion, pray remain so, for you are not worth the trouble of conversion, and, like

7. S. Bitter, *Die Ehe des Propheten Hosea: Eine auslegungsgeschichtliche Untersuchung* (Göttingen: Vandenhoeck und Ruprecht, 1975), p. 13.

a little coterie who think with you, would resent the attempt as an insult to your infallibility (Charles Spurgeon).

Insidious Questions (*Hinterfragen*): When we are confronted with any manifestation which someone has permitted us to see, we may ask: what is it meant to conceal? what is it meant to draw our attention from? What prejudice does it seek to raise? and again, how far does the subtlety of the dissimulation go? (Nietzsche, *The Dawn of Day*).

We need to interpret interpretations more than to interpret things (Montaigne).

The self-consciousness of postmodernism, particularly over the last two decades, has erupted in the development of a whole new metagenre. The prefix *meta* has been added, as a·kind of question mark, to the most influential and powerful institutions, resulting in metafiction, metapolitics, metarhetoric, metahistory, metatheatre. The insertion of the *meta*, for example in metafiction, is an indication of a heightened self-awareness and a refusal to accept any institution as a given. In metafiction, such as Thomas Pynchon's *Gravity's Rainbow* or B.S. Johnson's *A Few Selected Sentences*, the author problematizes his or her own profession, and exposes the artifice involved in the writing process.[8]

Recently another *meta* has been proposed for the rapidly expanding meta-industry, metacommentary. Commentary is a candidate because like politics, rhetoric, fiction and theatre it exerts a strong, and often unquestioned, persuasive force. Because it appears to be a real or accurate exposition of the text, commentary can become virtually synonymous with the text, and it is possible not only for texts but for commentaries (as surrogate texts) to be canonized. Orthodox and assimilated commentaries set the parameters within which acceptable readings must operate, and texts are habitually read through the filter of their assumptions.

The first critique of this situation came, appropriately, from Fredric Jameson, a critic well-known for his capacity to perceive and expose imbalances of power in critical as well as social structures.[9] In true Marxist fashion he argued for divesting commentary of its ruling class privileges (its capacity for judging without being judged) and for the

8.   For a more detailed description of fiction 'which self-consciously and systematically draws attention to its status as an artefact', see P. Waugh, *Metafiction: The Theory and Practice of Self-Conscious Fiction* (London: Methuen, 1984).

9.   Jameson's manifesto for metacommentary was not directed specifically at biblical commentary, but at criticism in general.

writer of commentary, like the author of metafiction, to comment on his[10] own comments with increased self-criticism. 'All thinking about interpretation', he wrote, 'must sink itself in the strangeness, the unnaturalness of the hermeneutic situation; or to put it another way, every individual interpretation must include an interpretation of its own existence, must show its credentials and justify itself: every commentary must be at the same time a metacommentary as well'.[11] Every commentator looks at the text from a certain angle and corners it in a particular way. Metacommentary is concerned with this act of textual cornering, which can also be a repression, and studies what the commentator omits as much as what he includes. Jameson argues for an act of criticism that examines itself and catches itself in the act of struggle and evasion. Whereas commentary 'struggle[s] with the object in question', metacommentary 'observes [its] own struggles and patiently set[s] about characterising them'.[12]

Jameson's manifesto envisaged the commentator himself in an act of self-criticism. Yet while some biblical commentators have briefly metacommentated on their own genre,[13] they have done so tentatively and apologetically. For example, Terence Fretheim's article, 'Old Testament Commentaries: Their Selection and Use',[14] raises some

10. Ideally, I would choose an inclusive pronoun for commentators, metacommentators and readers, but because no such pronoun is available in English, I shall be using the masculine pronoun for commentators, but the feminine pronoun for metacommentators and readers. This compromise avoids the awkwardness of s/he or he/she, but it is important to stress that no value-judgment is implied: the masculine pronoun is appropriate for commentators since all the commentators I am referring to are men, and the feminine pronoun seems appropriate for metacommentators and readers because it is a role in which I, as the female author of this book, envisage myself. For convenience, I shall be using the feminine pronoun for the reader throughout the rest of this book.

11. F. Jameson, 'Metacommentary', in *The Ideologies of Theory*. I. *Situations of Theory, Essays 1971–1986* (London: Routledge & Kegan Paul, 1988), pp. 3-16 (5).

12. Jameson, 'Metacommentary', p. 4.

13. A panel was devoted to 'Commentary: An Appraisal' at the 1982 meeting of the SBL, and in the same year an edition of *Interpretation*, edited by B.W. Anderson, was devoted to a discussion of 'The Problem and Promise of Commentary' (*Int* 36 [1982]). For other examples of commentators metacommentating, see R. Keiffer, 'Was heißt das, ein Text zu kommentieren?' *BZ* 20 (1976), pp. 212-16, and W. Schenk, 'Was ist ein Kommentar?', *BZ* 24 (1980), pp. 1-20.

14. T.E. Fretheim, 'Old Testament Commentaries: Their Selection and Use', *Int* 36 (1982), pp. 356-71.

tantalizingly provocative questions, but answers them prematurely, to forestall explosive conclusions. He confronts 'the dogmatic/philosophic overpowering of the text that has been (and still is) characteristic of religious and scholarly communities', but ultimately takes solace in the idea that the danger is alleviated by 'the publicly recognised canons of accountability with respect to theological statements'.[15] He confesses that 'commentary writing is a distiller's art',[16] but does not go on to suspect his own statement and ask why he 'distils' or what impurities he is trying to filter out.

Where commentators fail to press their own questions, the metacommentator becomes a secondary figure, a commentator on commentary, who extrapolates from the hints expressed by commentators themselves, using the resources of critical theory. For while commentators have been generally restrained in their self-questioning, literary criticism has become increasingly critical of its own critical strategies and increasingly self-knowing about the illusions and subterfuges involved in the seemingly innocent act of interpretation. Stanley Fish's theory of 'interpretive communities',[17] for example, can be seen as both a radical extension and a subversion of Fretheim's ideal of 'publicly recognised canons of accountability'. Whereas Fretheim regards consensus as a safe-haven, a guarantee against error, Fish regards communities as potential power-units, who may rewrite the text in the image of their beliefs and use the idea of the 'true text'[18] politically to enforce their domination. The commentator declares that 'commentary writing is a distiller's art': the metacommentator attempts to identify the ideological filter through which the text is being passed. The metacommentator asks 'insidious questions' about which aspects of the text the commentator is trying to obscure: as Jameson graphically puts it, she hunts out the

15. Fretheim, 'Old Testament Commentaries', p. 367.

16. Fretheim, 'Old Testament Commentaries', p. 369. I have taken this phrase slightly out of context here, as Fretheim is actually referring to the process of sifting through secondary material on the text and distilling the content for inclusion in commentary. However, in view of his earlier statement concerning the 'dogmatic/philosophical overpowering of the text', the image of distillation must surely raise the question, 'Have the secondary sources repressed any features of the primary text, and does the commentator in using these sources inevitably inherit these repressions and omissions?'

17. S. Fish, *Is There a Text in this Class? The Authority of Interpretive Communities* (Cambridge, MA: Harvard University Press, 1980).

18. Fish, *Is There a Text?*, p. 171.

'Censor which the message must slip past',[19] directed by the 'glance that designates, *in the process of avoiding*, the object forbidden'.[20]

A project of metacommentary involves a critique of 'ideology', but the definitions of ideology are so diverse that the term becomes, as Terry Eagleton puts it, ' "a text" in itself'.[21] In this study I shall be using 'ideology' in a non-pejorative sense, not as 'false consciousness' or an 'illusory'[22] misconception of the 'real', but as a filter that appears entirely natural yet shapes a commentator's perception of 'the world' and 'the text'. Because commentaries on Hosea have reinforced a particular set of beliefs and have assumed a status of orthodoxy, I am also using 'ideology' in the sense of 'ideas which help to legitimate a dominant political [and critical] power'.[23] The proposition that readings are ideologically conditioned is based on the premise that readings are not objective but are conditioned by the conscious and unconscious preferences of the reader—a proposition that I go on to examine in an analysis of reader-response criticism.

1.2. *What is Reader-Response Criticism and Why Are They Saying Such Terrible Things About It?*

In the popular imagination, reader-response criticism has become something of a stereotype, a nihilistic force that heralds the death of the author, the erasure of the text, and the triumph of the omnipotent and cavalier reader. Terry Eagleton's Marxist cartoon, 'The Revolt of the Reader', charts the rise of the RLM—the Reader's Liberation Movement—and describes how readers, 'brutally proletarianised as they have been by the authorial class',[24] have united in 'an all-out *putsch* to topple the text altogether and install the victorious reading class in its

---

19. Jameson, 'Metacommentary', p. 13.

20. Jameson, 'Metacommentary', p. 16 (my italics).

21. T. Eagleton, *Ideology: An Introduction* (London: Verso, 1991), p. 1.

22. The idea of ideology as 'false consciousness' was developed by Karl Marx and Friedrich Engels in *The German Ideology* (1846, cited by R.P. Carroll, 'Ideology', in R.J. Coggins and J.L. Houlden [eds.], *A Dictionary of Biblical Interpretation* [London: SCM Press, 1990], pp. 309-11 [309]); Louis Althusser similarly perpetuated the definition of ideology as a system of assumptions which represents 'the imaginary relationships of individuals to their real conditions of existence' ('Ideology and State Apparatuses', in *Lenin and Philosophy and Other Essays* [trans. B. Brewster; New York: Monthly Review Press, 1971], p. 162).

23. Eagleton, *Ideology*, p. 1.

24. T. Eagleton, 'The Revolt of the Reader', *NLH* 13 (1982), pp. 439-52.

place'.[25] In Eagleton's caricature of interpretative anarchy, the liberation left, represented by Stanley Fish, rebels against the more conservative positions of Roman Ingarden and Wolfgang Iser, and marches triumphantly under the slogan, 'The authors need us; we don't need the authors!'[26] Like a *Punch* cartoon Eagleton's parody both captures popular opinion and caricatures the caricature; in a similarly playful spirit Valentine Cunningham casts Fish as 'the big bad textual wolf-man who'd huff and puff until he blew your house down'.[27]

The stereotype of reader-response is, as Cunningham implies, overmelodramatic and reductive. It tends to focus exclusively on images of usurpation and revolution, and to imply that the central and indeed the only issue for the reader-response critic is whether, and to what extent, meaning is in the text, or is read into the text by the reader. The sensationalist emphasis on the struggle for control is also a denial of the two most powerful implications of reader-response theory: that '*all* interpretation is implicitly reader criticism'[28] and that readings are shaped by the reader's ideology. The term 'reader-response criticism' suggests a genre and a method, rather than a set of ideas that have implications for all acts of interpretation; similarly, the emphasis on the triumphant reader implies that critics subscribe to the idea of an autonomous self, completely unconditioned by social and cultural factors.

Readers familiar with the stereotype will find reader-response criticism less triumphalist and more heterogeneous than they have been led to expect. Even critics such as Roland Barthes, who are associated with the boldest slogans of reader-response such as 'the death of the author', do not simply delete the notion of author or text. Barthes, who envisions the author leaving off-stage right, 'diminishing like a figurine at the far end of the literary stage',[29] is haunted by the possibility of a final encore and finds it impossible to describe the act (or 'pleasure') of reading without appealing to the agency of the text. Paradoxically, his writings seem to support the unlimited freedom of the reader ('the theory of the

---

25. Eagleton, 'The Revolt', p. 451.

26. Eagleton, 'The Revolt', p. 439.

27. V. Cunningham, *In the Reading Gaol: Postmodernity, Texts and History* (Oxford: Basil Blackwell, 1994), p. 5.

28. M.G. Brett, 'The Future of Reader Criticisms', in F. Watson (ed.), *The Open Text* (London: SCM Press, 1993), pp. 13-31 (16; my italics).

29. R. Barthes, 'The Death of the Author', in *Image–Music–Text* (trans. S. Heath; London: Fontana, 1987), pp. 142-48 (145).

text removes all limits to the freedom of reading')[30] *and* the limitation of that freedom by textual constraints ('the text dislocates the reader's historical, cultural and psychological assumptions').[31]

Ambiguous descriptions of the relation between reader and text divide theorists from themselves. In the 1960s and 1970s Umberto Eco developed his theory of 'open' and 'closed' texts (analogous to Barthes's *scriptible* and *lisible* texts):[32] open texts, he argued, were written in the process of reading, and so gave the reader more freedom, and yet paradoxically, they constrained the reader more than 'closed texts' because they forced the reader to 'co-operate as a component of its structural strategy'.[33] More recently, as the chair of a roundtable on 'Interpretation and Overinterpretation', Eco has taken the position that 'the rights of interpreters' have been 'overstressed' at the expense of the 'rights of the text'.[34] However, as Richard Rorty points out, his attempt to impose a new standard, the 'intention of the text', between the reader and infinity, gets caught in the 'turns of the hermeneutical wheel':[35] for if the intention of the text is even partly constructed by the reader,

30. R. Barthes, 'Texte, Théorie du', *Encyclopaedia Universalis* (Paris, 1968–82), XV, pp. 1013-17 (1016).

31. R. Barthes, *The Pleasure of the Text* (trans. R. Miller; New York: Hill & Wang, 1975), p. 14.

32. For Eco's theory of 'open texts' see *The Role of the Reader: Explorations in the Semiotics of Texts* (Bloomington: Indiana University Press, 1979). For Barthes's theory of *scriptible* ('writerly') and *lisible* ('readerly') texts see *S/Z* (trans. R. Miller; Oxford: Basil Blackwell, 1990), pp. 4-5 (a full description is given in Chapter 2 of this book).

33. Eco, *The Role of the Reader*, p. 9.

34. U. Eco, 'Interpretation and History', in S. Collini (ed.), *Interpretation and Overinterpretation* (Cambridge: Cambridge University Press, 1992), pp. 23-43 (28). By advocating the 'rights of the text', Eco invokes the language of morality. He proposes, nobly, to defend the powerless text against the powerful reader, but this rhetorical flourish disguises the real issues of power in reader criticism. To introduce the intention of the text as standard is to revert to the situation in which readers construct different versions of the text's intention, and the definition of the dominant group prevails. The marginalization of the powerless text is a rhetorical device, while the marginalization of certain readers is a genuinely political issue: to sanction intention, in whatever form, is to return to a situation in which readers will be able to claim that their own objectification is more authoritative, and superior to, someone else's.

35. R. Rorty, 'The Pragmatist's Progress', in Collini (ed.), *Interpretation and Overinterpretation*, pp. 89-108 (97).

then how can it be used to restrain its creator?

As Eco's attempts to promote the *intentio operis* become entangled in the actions of the reader, so Rorty's promotion of the autonomous reader is undercut by a sense of the 'text'. Reducing reading to its lowest common denominator, Rorty takes up a pragmatic and anti-essentialist position, and argues that 'Interpreting something, knowing it, penetrating to its essence, and so on, are just various ways of describing some process of putting it to work'.[36] However, even as he tries to debunk the myth of 'What is Really Going On in the Text'[37] and to erase the contrast between 'interpretation' and 'use', he tries to establish another contrast between use and misuse. The pragmatist expresses the hope that readers would ultimately be 'enraptured or destabilised by the text';[38] ironically, he also expresses anxiety, as author, that readers might misunderstand his 'intention'.[39]

A close reading of Barthes, Eco and Rorty shows that, far from being triumphalist, reader-response criticism is inscribed with a sense of an unresolved struggle. Inconsistencies do not demonstrate the flaws of a particular argument, but illustrate, as Jonathan Culler puts it, the sheer impossibility of telling a story of reading using the reader as the only protagonist. Even Fish, the most famous and notorious 'champion of readers',[40] cannot fulfil the conjuring trick he promises, and 'mak[e] the work disappear in the reader's experience of it'.[41] The same critic who asserts that readers read the poems that they themselves have made presents a very different picture in his reading of *Paradise Lost*, *Surprised by Sin*. Despite his claims that the mighty reader can theoretically overpower the text, he describes a reader who is more manipulated than manipulating, tossed and turned by the textual vacillations, cornered by the text's trickery, until he is forced to acknowledge his own sinful condition.[42]

36. Rorty, 'The Pragmatist's Progress', p. 93.
37. Rorty, 'The Pragmatist's Progress', p. 103.
38. Rorty, 'The Pragmatist's Progress', pp. 106-107.
39. Rorty, 'The Pragmatist's Progress', p. 108.
40. Fish, *Is There a Text?*, p. 14.
41. S. Fish, *Surprised by Sin: The Reader in Paradise Lost* (London: University of California Press, 1971), p. ix.
42. Fish later glossed the paradoxes of his own texts. 'The argument in "Literature in the Reader" is mounted on behalf of the reader and against the self-sufficiency of the text, but in the course of it the text becomes more and more powerful and rather than being liberated, the reader finds himself more and more

Mark Brett describes Fish as a 'lover of paradox',[43] but I would suggest that the paradoxes in Fish's text cannot be purely accounted for by his love of them, and that, like all critics who try to describe the reading process, Fish is trapped in a central paradox from which he cannot escape. His work is invaluable because it foregrounds a function that has previously been denied: the reader 'comes out', and her active participation in criticism is foregrounded; but at the same time, the theorist needs to distinguish between reading a text, and reflecting in a vacuum. Though theory is structured around a single verdict (the text is in control/the text is made by the reader), as soon as the theorist starts to detail the reading process, she needs two participants: the interpreter and the interpreted. The story of the struggle between reader and text will, Culler claims, always haunt the pages of reader-response criticism, not only because it is a better adventure story, full of 'dramatic encounters, moments of deception and reversals of fortune',[44] but because reader-response critics, like critics of reader-response criticism, are acutely aware that 'the reader who creates everything learns nothing'.[45]

A close reading of Stanley Fish blows away some of the assumptions of the 'big bad wolf' stereotype. He does not dispense with 'the text' and 'intention' as redundant terms, but radically redefines our under-standing of what we are doing when we 'find' and 'describe' them: since 'perception is never innocent of assumptions',[46] he argues, inten-tion does not precede interpretation, but is the product of it.[47] He does not delete or transcend the text but debunks illusions of the text as a 'brute fact'[48] outside the consciousness of the reader; he does not deny the possibility of describing reading in a way that distinguishes between what is supplied by the text and what is supplied by the reader, but he does insist that 'the distinction itself is an assumption which, when it informs an act of literary description, will produce the phenomena it purports to describe'.[49] His most radical move, in my opinion, is not to

constrained in his new prominence than he was before' (*Is There a Text?*, p. 7).

43. Brett, 'The Future of Reader Criticisms', p. 16.

44. J. Culler, *On Deconstruction: Theory and Criticism after Structuralism* (London: Routledge, 1993), Chapter 2, §3, 'Stories of Reading', pp. 64-83 (72).

45. Culler, *On Deconstruction*, p. 72.

46. S. Fish, 'Why No One's Afraid of Wolfgang Iser', *Diacritics* 11 (1981), pp. 2-13 (8).

47. Fish, *Is There a Text?*, p. 163.

48. Freund, *The Return of the Reader*, p. 149.

49. Fish, 'Why No One's Afraid', p. 7.

replace the text with the reader, but to transfer to the reader terms that have been habitually associated with texts, and to argue that 'intention' and 'context' operate at the level of the text's reception, as well as at the level of its conception. Far from being transcendent, a reader, like a sentence is, 'never not in a context',[50] but is framed by a specific time and social situation. Reader-response, therefore, can perhaps be best understood not as the erasure of intention, but the doubling of it, since Fish maintains that the reader, like the author, puts words together 'in the light of some purpose'.[51] Reader-response criticism does not deny the theoretical actuality of 'the text', or 'the author's intention', but problematizes the act of accessing or describing them: the author's purpose is mediated and obscured by the reader's own purpose and assumptions so that, paradoxically, 'a sentence that seems to need no interpretation is already the product of one'.[52]

1.3. *The Reader's Progress: Reader-Response and Biblical Studies*

> Reader theory in literary studies is a Pandora's box into which we, infant literary critics of the Bible, have barely begun to peer. Opened more fully it might release some unsettling, but possibly timely, ways of reconceiving biblical interpretation.[53]

If critics like Fish are 'champions of the reader' and biblical commentators are 'champions of the text',[54] under close scrutiny this rigid dichotomy breaks down. For just as Fish cannot elide 'the text' from the reading process, so commentary betrays an implicit awareness of the role of the reader. The tradition, style, even the name of the genre, conceal the author's participation in it: a 'comment' poses as less ideologically committed than an opinion, and the way in which the commentator carefully examines each verse in sequence suggests that in ideology, as in structure, the commentator is the servant of the master-text. In a culture accustomed to media commentary, the implication is that

---

50. S. Fish, 'Normal circumstances, literal language, direct speech acts, the ordinary, the everyday, the obvious, what goes without saying, and other special cases', *CI* 4 (1978), pp. 625-44 (637).

51. Fish, 'Normal circumstances', p. 637.

52. Fish, 'Normal circumstances', p. 637.

53. S.D. Moore, *Literary Criticism and the Gospels: The Theoretical Challenge* (New Haven: Yale University Press, 1989), p. 107.

54. Fish, *Is There a Text?*, p. 14. Again, the connection between Fish's term and biblical commentary is made by myself and not by Fish.

commentary comes as close to the textual 'event' as possible, but this is an impression that several commentators are eager to modify. In his preface to his commentary on Hosea, J.L. Mays foregrounds the anxieties of the commentator (or self-conscious 'reader') when he writes:

> Once a commentary is in print, the opinions and judgments contained therein take on a certainty and finality which at places exceeds the confidence felt by the exegete who wrote them. The demands of a manuscript rob one of the luxury and honesty of remaining tentative and undecided before ambiguous problems.[55]

The impression of objectivity and authority associated with the commentary genre is subverted, less self-consciously, by other critics. As Fish, true to stereotype, pledges to erase the work in his reading of it, so C.R. North, conversely, attempts to erase all traces of himself from his commentary on Second Isaiah. 'The commentary', he asserts, 'is as objective and impersonal as I have been able to make it';[56] the qualification 'as I have been able to make it' is not only a clause of self-doubt, but an irony that subverts the critic's claim. Objectivity, paradoxically, is depicted as a product of the subject, something that the commentator makes.

When seen as a philosophy of criticism, rather than a distinct genre in which the critic *chooses* to be subjective, reader-response poses a challenge to biblical criticism. It explains the existence of competing, even contradictory, interpretations of the same text, all claiming to be 'objective', and foregrounds what many commentators are already aware of: the possibility for numerous interpretations, and the way in which their own preferences condition their reading of the text. However, in the critical environment of biblical studies, in which exegesis is commonly misinterpreted as the ability to extract meaning from a text in a kind of 'juice extraction process',[57] and eisegesis, its opposite, is

55. J.L. Mays, *Hosea: A Commentary* (OTL; London: SCM Press, 1969), p. vii.
56. C.R. North, *The Second Isaiah: Introduction, Translation and Commentary to Chapters 40–55* (Oxford: Clarendon Press, 1964), p. vii.
57. J. Barton, 'Eisegesis', in Coggins and Houlden (eds.), *A Dictionary of Biblical Interpretation*, p. 188. The idea that exegesis is interpretation legitimated by the text and that extracts meaning from the text is an interesting deviation from an earlier sense of 'exegesis'. As Barton points out, 'the object of the verb *exe*(diacrit)*gesthai* is originally not the text, but the reader for whose benefit interpretation is being carried out... The exegete is one who leads the reader out and explains the text to him' (p. 188).

a term of critical abuse, reader-response is in danger of being regarded only as a distinct literary genre. The danger is that it will come to represent merely the domain of the subjective as opposed to the objective, and be dismissed as critical irresponsibility, a modern day eisegesis.

The emphasis on the role of the reader is not merely a contemporary critical fashion but a vital aspect of the critical process, anticipated in much earlier descriptions of the biblical text. Eric Auerbach's famous description of Abraham and Isaac's journey through biblical lacunae, their 'silent progress through the indeterminate and contingent',[58] anticipates Wolfgang Iser's theory of the reading process published almost thirty years later. For Auerbach 'the decisive points of the narrative alone are emphasised, what lies between is non-existent'[59]: the text provides bare tools with which to construct a plot (an ass, two young men, a knife, wood for the offering) but provides no adjectives, and leaves time and place, thought and feelings undefined in a way that 'call[s] for interpretation'.[60] In Iser's theory, similarly, fixed points, or constellations, in the text direct the reader through the paths of indeterminacy. 'The stars in the literary text are fixed', but 'the lines that join them are variable',[61] and it is the task of the reader to form a coherent whole and produce her own personal *Gestalt*.

The role of the reader is not repressed but highlighted by a collection of texts that are notoriously 'fraught with background'.[62] Biblical texts are particularly elliptical, fragmentary and provocative, and it is the task of the reader, as Auerbach and Iser suggest, to 'supply what is not there'.[63] In the case of texts like the *Akedah* or Hos. 1.2, however, this description of the reading process is, at best, only partial. For when the fixed points of the text are difficult or offensive, the commentator does not merely fill in the gaps, but attempts to negotiate his way around the points that are given by the text. Kierkegaard's *Fear and Trembling*,[64]

58. E. Auerbach, *Mimesis: The Representation of Reality in Western Literature* (trans. W. Trask; Princeton: Princeton University Press, 1953), p. 11.

59. Auerbach, *Mimesis*, p. 11.

60. Auerbach, *Mimesis*, p. 15.

61. W. Iser, 'The Reading Process: A Phenomenological Approach', in D. Lodge (ed.), *Modern Criticism and Theory: A Reader* (London: Longman, 1988), pp. 212-28 (218; repr. from *NLH* 3 [1972]).

62. Auerbach, *Mimesis*, p. 12.

63. Iser, 'The Reading Process', p. 213.

64. S. Kierkegaard, *Fear and Trembling* (trans. H.V. Kong and E.H. Kong; Princeton: Princeton University Press, 1983).

for example, is a more active response than Auerbach anticipates, because the perplexed reader does not simply seek to supply the background, but wrangles and contends with the ethics at the foreground of the text.[65] Hosea 1.2, similarly, provokes a response that is far less passive than that described by Auerbach or Iser: although some critics do fill out the starkness of the narrative and describe what Gomer looked like and where she and Hosea met, most commentaries aim to contend with, adjust or explain the only fixed point in the verse, Yhwh's bizarre command.

1.4. *The Text and the Reader: 'Amicable' Relations?*

> No author who understands the just boundaries of decorum and good breeding would presume to think all: The truest respect which you can pay to the reader's understanding is to halve the matter amicably, and leave him something to imagine, in his turn, as well as yourself. For my own part, I am eternally paying him compliments of this kind, and do all that lies in my power to keep his own imagination as busy as my own.[66]

Like Laurence Sterne, Wolfgang Iser and Eric Auerbach imagine an 'ideal' reader who has come to an amicable compromise with the text. Only slightly less compliant than the ideal commentator, this reader takes her cue from the master-text, does not fill in gaps unless called upon to do so, and accepts the fixed points of the text as non-negotiable.[67] The ideal reader is provoked into action only when the text

---

65. For Kierkegaard, the *Akedah* raises three central ethical dilemmas: 'Is there a teleological suspension of the ethical?', 'Is there an absolute duty to God?', and 'Was it ethically defensible for Abraham to conceal his undertaking from Sarah and Isaac?'

66. L. Sterne, *The Life and Opinions of Tristram Shandy* (Harmondsworth: Penguin, 1987), p. 79.

67. The most recent and extreme manifestation of the ideal reader in biblical studies is in Meir Sternberg's *The Poetics of Biblical Narrative: Ideological Literature and the Drama of Reading* (Bloomington: Indiana University Press, 1985). As Mieke Bal points out, the subtext 'the drama of reading' is highly ironic, because Sternberg describes a reader who is constrained by an omniscient narrator, who functions as a kind of substitute deity and whose will must be obeyed. According to Sternberg's thesis, interpretation is circumscribed by given points that 'must be accepted', and the text can only be misread by an inferior class of reader, the 'underreaders'. The ideal reader (alias Sternberg) has, in contrast, no difficulty in following the text's 'foolproof composition'. (For a thorough critique of Sternberg, see M. Bal, 'The Bible as Literature: A Critical Escape', *Diacritics* 16 [1986], pp. 71-79 [72-73]).

fails to supply the information required and so 'engages the reader's imagination'.[68] But this arrangement is both too comfortable and theoretically untenable, because real readers are provoked not only by absences in the text but by 'fixed points' that they find offensive.

In a critique of Wolfgang Iser's balanced definition of reading, Fish argues that 'the stars in a literary text are not fixed; they are just as variable as the lines that join them'.[69] The important point is not what is given, but what the reader is prepared to *take* (as given): givenness is a product of interpretation, and it is the reader who decides what is determinate and what is not. One of the fixed points of the book of Hosea, for example, according to Iser's definition, seems to be Yhwh's command to Hosea to 'take a "wife of harlotry"', and yet critical consensus finds this statement ethically unviable. Commentators argue not only that it cannot be taken into account when defining the divine, or authorial intention, but even that it cannot be taken as part of the text: redaction critics are doing something rather more than gap-filling when they redefine textual boundaries in order to exclude part of the text.

In confronting Hos. 1.2, some critics are aware of conflict between their own expectations and Yhwh's command. Abraham Heschel, for example, confesses that he resists the text because the marriage of Gomer and Hosea would have a 'highly questionable...moral didactic effect',[70] while Georges Brillet consciously censors 'fleshy' physicality, which he deems grossly out of place in a religious text.[71] Readings in which readers consciously struggle with, and seek to alter, what they perceive as 'the text', highlight some limitations in reader-response theories. Most theories are too idealistic and exclude all sense of conflict: from Michael Riffaterre, who suggests that the text helps the reader to 'build a better self',[72] to Wolfgang Iser, who describes a perfect alliance in which both know their role, many critics present text and reader in productive mutual co-operation. The most provocative element in Fish's theory is not the main argument, that readers produce texts (and by inference that they presumably agree with them), but the narrative subtext in which the text 'troubles [the reader's] understanding' and

68. Iser, 'The Reading Process', p. 213.
69. Fish, 'Why No One's Afraid', p. 7.
70. A.J. Heschel, *The Prophets* (New York: Harper & Row, 1969), p. 54.
71. G. Brillet, *Amos et Osée* (Paris: Editions du Cerf, 1958), p. 76.
72. J.P. Tompkins (ed.), *Reader-Response Criticism: From Formalism to Poststructuralism* (Baltimore: Johns Hopkins University Press, 1980), p. xvi.

'displace[s]...discompose[s]...and disorder[s] the judgement'.[73] A more thorough examination of the dynamics of conflict is found beyond the conventional boundaries of reader-response criticism in Bloom's metaphors of struggle and warfare, Freud's description of textual murder and Sontag's images of usurpation and displacement.

1.5. *Power, Displacement and Criticism by Coercion: Some More Unsavoury Descriptions of what Critics do to Texts*

'Nothing is gained', writes Harold Bloom, 'by continuing to idealise reading, as though reading were not an art of defensive warfare'.[74] Bloom provides a far more sensationalist story of reading than mainstream reader-response theorists, and his reader (or 'critic') acts from far less noble motives: 'No critic', he claims, 'can evade a Nietzschean will to power over a text because interpretation is at last nothing else'.[75] Freud, similarly, provides a chilling tale of reading, in which the reader/commentator is the anti-hero, the murderer, and the metacommentator plays the detective at the scene of a textual crime. 'The distortion of a text', Freud writes, 'is not unlike a murder...The difficulty lies not in the execution of the deed but in the doing away with the traces.'[76]

Freud's famous discussion of the treatment of biblical texts in *Moses and Monotheism* is the first critical hint, to my knowledge, that criticism/redaction of biblical texts might not always be reverential, and may involve textual violence. 'Two mutually opposed treatments', he claims, have 'left their traces on the text': the one seeking to revise the text, to 'mutilate and amplify it, and even change[ ] it to its reverse', and the other presiding over it with a 'solicitous piety' that seeks to preserve everything in its original form.[77] Freud sees preservation and revision as two opposing aims that cannot be united in the same critical act. In 'Against Interpretation' Susan Sontag suggests that they may be allies

73. John Donne, cited by Fish, *Self-Consuming Artifacts: The Experience of Seventeenth Century Literature* (Berkeley: University of California Press, 1972), p. 380.

74. H. Bloom, *Kabbalah and Criticism* (New York: Seabury, 1975), p. 126.

75. H. Bloom, 'From J to K, or the Uncanniness of the Yahwist', in F. McConnell (ed.), *The Bible and the Narrative Tradition* (New York: Oxford University Press, 1986), p. 21.

76. S. Freud, *Moses and Monotheism* (Harmondsworth: Penguin, 1985), pp. 283-84.

77. Freud, *Moses*, pp. 283-84.

as well as opponents, and introduces the shocking possibility that '*Piety towards the ancient text*' may 'conceal an aggression.'[78]

Sontag's study of the ideological manipulation of religious texts starts from the assumption that all interpretation involves displacing the text. On one level this is a commonplace, because if criticism had no criticisms, it would, as Pierre Macherey puts it, 'run the risk of abolishing itself in satisfaction,'[79] but Sontag argues that while the replacement of the text can be an accident of the critical situation, it can also be a deliberate act of usurpation. Interpretation, she argues, can indicate 'a dissatisfaction (conscious or unconscious) with the work, a wish to replace it by something else'[80], and this leads to a provocative redefinition of criticism (particularly in the case of ancient and highly-prized texts) as 'a radical strategy for conserving an old text, which is thought too precious to repudiate, by revamping it'.[81] Commentary, she implies, may treat the text not in the sense of objective detachment, but in the sense of doctoring or altering it. Like plastic surgeons commentators huddle around the problem text, to change its appearance and make it acceptable for renewed life in society, according to the principles by which that society *operates*.

'The question that haunts post-mythic consciousness', argues Sontag, 'is that of the *seemliness* of religious symbols'.[82] Her example—the Stoics' revision of Zeus's adulterous liaison with Leto—is strikingly similar to critical treatment of the offensive marriage between a prophet and an אֵשֶׁת זְנוּנִים. Metacommentating on the Stoics, Sontag looks at the way in which they 'allegorised away the rude features of Zeus' to 'accord with their view that the gods had to be moral',[83] and created from divine adultery a more seemly, allegorical union between power and wisdom. Her conclusion, pertinently, is that a conservative position is not necessarily conservationist, and that a reader concerned with the text's reputation may 'revamp' or manipulate the text just as much as a

78. S. Sontag, 'Against Interpretation', in D. Lodge (ed.), *Twentieth Century Literary Criticism: A Reader* (London: Longman, 1972), pp. 652-60 (655; my italics); repr. from *Evergreen Review* (1964).

79. P. Macherey, *A Theory of Literary Production* (London: Routledge, 1989), p. 15.

80. Sontag, 'Against Interpretation', p. 657.

81. Sontag, 'Against Interpretation', p. 655.

82. Sontag, 'Against Interpretation', p. 654.

83. Sontag, 'Against Interpretation', p. 654.

'reader-response' or self-confessedly radical critic who foregrounds the effect of her own preferences.

1.6. *Conclusion: The Logic of the Dice Throw*

Sontag's and Freud's metaphors reflect a general paradigm shift in which romantic images of the critic as miner of deep meanings and plunderer of the text's rich secrets have yielded to more cynical metaphors of power struggles, usurpation and violation. Potentially, these changes in perceptions of reading also apply (perhaps even particularly apply) to readings of religious texts, but some critics, like Joseph Sitterson, have reacted by insisting that biblical critics are immune to such forces as the 'will to power'. Just as critics try to separate the prophet and the prostitute in Hos. 1.2, so Sitterson attempts to re-establish proper boundaries between sacred and secular, religion and Nietzsche. Perhaps he is stating explicitly a belief that many scholars express implicitly, when he advises that biblical critics should only draw from narratology, and should remain sceptical of what other 'recent secular theor[ies]' have to offer.[84]

Ironically, in trying to repress the political dimension of biblical interpretation, Sitterson draws attention to it in his determined act of resistance. As Hayden White observes, 'it is the privilege of devotees of dominant conventions either to pay attention or not to any new practice appearing on the horizon of a discipline'[85]—but defensive barricades against new critical proposals are revealing in themselves. If commentators are to argue effectively against intrusive secular theories, they need to adopt a more persuasive strategy than special pleading. Theoretically, the evidence for making commentary into a special case immune from less idealistic metaphors of reading is tenuous; if the will to power, which 'can manifest itself only against resistances', instinctively 'seeks that which resists it',[86] nowhere is this better demonstrated than in the sheer volume of criticism that proliferates, for example, around the recalcitrant text of Hos. 1.2.

Critics like Jameson, Fish, Iser, and Sontag offer some provocative

---

84. J.C. Sitterson, 'Will to Power in Biblical Interpretation', in V. Tollers and J. Maier (eds.), *Mappings of the Biblical Terrain: The Bible as Text* (Toronto: Bucknell University Press, 1990), pp. 134-41 (134).

85. H. White, 'Conventional Conflicts', *NLH* 13 (1981), pp. 145-60 (155).

86. F. Nietzsche, *Will to Power* (trans W. Kaufmann; New York: Vintage Books, 1968), p. 346.

insights into the politics of interpretation, but also, sometimes unwittingly, expose some of the possible pitfalls of this approach. For if readers of secondary texts, like readers of primary texts, are conditioned by their own perspective, no absolute standard of legislation can be enforced. Ironically, even as she exposes the way in which critics usurp the values of the text, Sontag displaces the standards of secondary critics with her own. Her argument flounders when she attempts to distinguish between good readings that 'liberate' and 'escape the dead past', and bad readings that are 'reactionary, impertinent, cowardly, stifling'.[87] Stripping the two definitions of their different connotations, of heroism and mean-mindedness, she asserts that good readings are good because they restrain the text and revise it, and bad readings are bad—because they restrain the text and revise it. The ultimate standard is the critic's own preference: the metacommentator, like the reader, has her own concept of the text and her own sense of when textual use disintegrates into textual ill-treatment.

I suggest that the metacommentator is a reader of readers in a pragmatic not a superlative sense. Having shown how the commentator allows his values to shape his definition of text, she cannot then pretend to transcend her own interests and cast herself as a policing authority, a member of the textual vice squad, or as a valiant defender of the true sense of the text. To act as lawyer for the victim text, to show how older readings are wrong, and to replace them with one's own more correct readings, is the rhetorical strategy not of metacommentary, but of conventional criticism. Traditionally, before introducing his new improved account, each commentator criticized and displaced the criticism of his predecessors, so creating a space for another contribution, but the metacommentator pursues a different strategy. In examining stories told about Hosea's marriage I shall not argue, as R.E. Wolfe does, that 'there is no other book in the Bible about which such a large percentage of what is written is untrue',[88] for metacommentary, as an ideological study, regards claims to 'truth' and 'error' with suspicion as potential polemical devices. I shall be attacking commentaries on Hos. 1.2 not because they are erroneous, but because they are dominant, and legitimate that dominance with untenable claims to 'objectivity'.

In his analysis of 'ideology' for the *Dictionary of Biblical*

87. Sontag, 'Against Interpretation', p. 655.

88. R.E. Wolfe, *Meet Amos and Hosea* (New York: Harper & Row, 1945), p. 81.

Interpretation, Robert Carroll argues that 'ideological factors should be part of the debate about the meaning and function of texts', and that the 'guild of [biblical] scholars may find itself having to recognise the political nature of its activities'.[89] To some extent the guild has always recognized the 'political nature' of reading, or more accurately, of other people's readings: an awareness of the 'dogmatic/philosophic overpowering of texts' is not merely a modern invention, and in relation to the book of Hosea, for example, J.L. Waterman noted the pressure of 'theological and sectarian' interests on (other) readings of Hos. 1.2 as early as 1918.[90] Then, as now, the danger is that ideology, 'like halitosis', will be defined as 'what the other person has'.[91] In this study I want to avoid the illusion that my reading is ideology-free: its value is not that it transcends ideological interest, but that it brings different ideological interests into play and relativizes the dominant (apparently natural) descriptions of Hos. 1.2 by introducing an alternative, more marginal perspective.

In another, rather earlier model of reading, Umberto Eco argues that readings are subject to a dice throw, being affected by 'private codes and ideological biases' and by '*aleatory factors*'.[92] A spectrum of readings of a text might be expected to give several permutations of that text and to represent different interpretative communities, but in the case of a text such as Hos. 1.2, critics throw with weighted dice and produce theological sixes every time. Despite the huge variety of interpretations, commentators are united in their assertion that Hosea could not possibly have married an אֵשֶׁת זְנוּנִים, and this reading has attained such ascendancy that critics rarely think, or dare, to suggest an alternative. Without suggesting that there is only one way to read the text, I find it suspicious that the most obvious interpretation, that the prophet did marry a wife of harlotry, is so studiously avoided, and in the next section I want to ask whether the dominant reading is indeed 'natural' or 'obvious', as critical rhetoric suggests, or whether it is necessitated by a particular ideology. In a close reading of the most popular responses to Hos. 1.2, I want to ask whether they merit the standard of orthodoxy that they have attained, or whether they represent, despite their illusion of naturalness, 'theological and sectarian interests'.

89. Carroll, 'Ideology', p. 311.
90. L. Waterman, 'The Marriage of Hosea', *JBL* 37 (1918), pp. 193-208.
91. Eagleton, *Ideology*, p. 2.
92. U. Eco, *A Theory of Semiotics* (Bloomington: Indiana University Press, 1976), p. 142.

2. *The Averted Gaze: 'Pre-Critical' Readings of Hosea 1.2*

Every interpretation has its blind spot, which I would like to think of not only as the spot or place from which the interpreter cannot see his or her own misreading of a text, but also as the spot or place in a text from which the interpreter averts his or her gaze.[93]

The interpreter, without actually erasing or rewriting the text, is altering it. But he can't admit to doing this. He claims only to be making it intelligible by disclosing its true meaning.[94]

To tame the text, I write a paper.[95]

If metacommentary is an attempt to locate, through the 'glance that designates in the process of avoiding', the 'object forbidden', it is not difficult to see from commentators' embarrassed glances in the opposite direction that the taboo object in this text is the אֵשֶׁת זְנוּנִים. In the next two sections, which examine older and then more contemporary strategies for coping with the difficult woman, I want to look at how commentators restyle Gomer-bat-Diblayim, specifically by improving, or by removing her. The collection of commentaries that I shall describe are colourful and creative, and blur the distinction between objectivity and subjectivity, commentary and storytelling. Because the collection of 'stories' looks like one huge adventure in midrashic storytelling, I shall begin with midrash proper, and three stories which attempt to dilute the pernicious effect of the 'wife of harlotry'.

2.1. *Midrash Rabbah: 'The Indulgent Husband', 'The Miscreant Schoolboy' and 'The Lethargic Queen'*

In *If on a Winter's Night a Traveller*, a parody of reader-response theory, Italo Calvino writes of a saturation of other stories he could tell which clamour for attention around the central narrative.[96] Midrash Rabbah, a rabbinic 'reader response', similarly assembles three stories

---

93. S. Rubin Suleiman, 'Pornography, Transgression and the Avant-Garde: Bataille's Story of the Eye', in N.K. Miller (ed.), *The Poetics of Gender* (New York: Columbia University Press, 1986), pp. 117-36 (122).

94. Sontag, 'Against Interpretation', p. 655.

95. D.M. Gunn, 'In Security: The David of Biblical Narrative', in J.C. Exum (ed.), *Signs and Wonders: Biblical Texts in Literary Focus* (Atlanta: Scholars Press, 1989), pp. 133-51 (133).

96. I. Calvino, *If on a Winter's Night a Traveller* (London: Picador, 1982), p. 88.

around Hosea's marriage, each reiterating the same theme, the enduring love of Yhwh. An amplitude of love seems to generate an amplitude of stories; Yhwh's love goes on forever, and can be infinitely redescribed: 'To what may this be likened...To what may this be likened...This may be illustrated by another parable.'[97] The question 'to what may this be likened?' produces three miniature narratives, which I shall refer to for convenience as 'The Indulgent Husband', 'The Miscreant Schoolboy', and 'The Lethargic Queen'.

In the tale of 'The Indulgent Husband' a king becomes angry with his wife and vows he will divorce her; he later relents, however, and gives her jewellery. In the second miniature a truant schoolboy is scolded and then forgiven, and invited to dine with his father. In the story of 'The Lethargic Queen' servants overhear a king lavishly praising his wife but are then surprised to see her 'looking disreputable, her house untidy, the beds not made'. The story ends with a moral exhortation to all negligent wives, and by inference all slothful servants of Yhwh: 'If he lavishes such praise on her when she is disreputable, how much more when she is at her best!'

Though the removal of Gomer's promiscuity in these midrashic analogies is desirable from a moral perspective, tampering with the text's offensive morality has unfortunate repercussions at the level of plot. 'The Indulgent Husband' suggests that inconstancy cannot be eradicated but merely transferred from one character to another: if the wife is not inconstant then the husband must be, since he seems to reject and accept her on the basis of a personal quirk. The narrative problem cannot be removed entirely but merely displaced, and attempts to censor the text produce a scene as ambiguous as the nunnery scene in *Hamlet* in which the erratic lover tells his beloved that she is loved and that she is not. In 'The Indulgent Husband' it is impossible to tell whether the woman has been unfaithful, or whether her husband is simply putting on a perverse 'antic disposition' and treating his wife as Hosea treats his children, whom he perceives alternately as 'loved' and rejected.

While the other narratives do not omit the offence altogether, they soften and domesticize it beyond recognition. In each case the story is censored, and the figure of the bad woman is morally adjusted. In the tale of 'The Miscreant Schoolboy' the very adult culpability of Israel is diluted beyond recognition to the cunning mischief of youth. In the tale of 'The Lethargic Queen' a far more subtle transition is effected

97. *Num. R.* 2.15.

between the prostitute, the audaciously bad wife, and the not-so-good wife. According to Proverbs the antithesis of the good wife who 'works with willing hands' to spin wool and flax is 'the adulteress with her smooth words,' whose lips drip with honey and whose speech is smoother than oil (Prov. 31.13; 2.16). An intermediate version of the evil woman is the negation of the good woman, whose house is untidy and her beds not made. From the stock of images of pernicious woman-hood the Midrash selects the milder figure, the wife of lethargy, as sur-rogate for the wife of harlotry. Like the mischievous crimes of youth, domestic torpor can be looked on with a certain indulgence, and perhaps most importantly, the husband/father figure can forgive the offence without suffering too much reduction in his dignity.

2.2. *Targum Jonathan: Figs (fig.)*

A midrashic rule of thumb would seem to be: whenever a prostitute crosses your path, circumnavigate her as widely as possible. The rabbis seem to be of the same persuasion as Judah, who, according to Midrash Rabbah, would have avoided Tamar altogether had not an angel of the Lord appeared on the scene and hinted that the presence of the prosti-tute was, regrettably, a key factor in the birth of the next generation.[98] Targum Jonathan shows a similar 'primness' and preference for 'circumlocution'[99] and does not simply swerve to avoid the offensive woman but erases her altogether. Disturbed, as Smolar and Aberbach infer, by the 'halachic-theological aspects of the case' and 'the manifest impossibility of God commanding anyone, least of all a prophet, to marry a harlot',[100] the targumist deftly removes her with a subtle change in pointing. By interpreting the strange dual form דִּבְלַיִם as a derivative of 'fig', דְּבֵלָה, the text depersonifies Gomer, and reduces her to the inoffensive whisper of falling fig leaves. Hosea 1.2-3 in the more refined version reads as follows:

> The beginning of the word of the Lord with Hosea: and the Lord said to Hosea, 'Go and prophesy against the inhabitants of an idolatrous city, who continue to sin. For the inhabitants of the land surely go away from the worship of the Lord'. So he went and prophesied concerning them

---

98. *Gen. R.* 85.8.

99. L. Smolar and M. Aberbach, *Studies in Targum Jonathan to the Prophets* (Baltimore: Ktav Publishing House, 1983), p. 50.

100. Smolar and Aberbach, *Studies*, p. 44.

that, if they repented, they would be forgiven; but if not they would fall as the leaves of the fig-tree fall.[101]

As in popular representations of Eden, fig-leaves are used as a cover-up, to cunningly obscure potential sources of offence. Gomer-bat-Diblayim, an overtly sexual figure, is concealed by the phrase 'as the leaves of the fig-tree fall', and the stark physicality of the MT is replaced by a pristine dialectic between righteousness and iniquity. In the MT marriage and intercourse lead to the conception of children (who are not mere symbols but are both born and 'weaned') but in the Targum real figures become abstract figures of speech. Reducing the players in the domestic drama to philosophical abstractions, the Targum insists on concepts, not conception, and so reduces the vivid novelty of Hosea 1 to a prophetic conventionality.

The transformation of the prostitute into figs (*fig.*) is, as Kevin Cathcart notes, one of only three instances in the Targum in which a command to perform a symbolic act is transformed into a command to prophesy.[102] In Zech. 11.4, 15 Yhwh's command to 'become a shepherd' is translated as a command to prophesy to the leaders of the 'flock'; while in Hos. 3.1 the targumist saves the prophet from yet another disastrous liaison, by transforming the command to 'love' an adulterous woman into a command to preach to Israel using a metaphor of 'betrayal'.[103] In extreme cases the targumists invert Yhwh's command, in order to save the prophet from humiliation: thus Yhwh in the

---

101. K.J. Cathcart and R.P. Gordon, *The Aramaic Bible*. XIV. *The Targum of the Minor Prophets* (Edinburgh: T. & T. Clark, 1989). Cathcart provides an interesting commentary on the translation of symbolic acts into commands to prophesy in 'Targum Jonathan to Hos. 1–3', *IBS* 10 (1988), pp. 37-43.

102. Cathcart, 'Targum Jonathan' (see previous footnote).

103. The Targum of Hos. 3.1 reads as follows: 'The Lord said to me again, "Go and speak a prophecy concerning the house of Israel, who are like a woman loved by her husband, but she betrays him. And just as he loves her and does not wish to send her away, so does the Lord love the people of Israel, although they turn away after the idols of the nations. However, if they repent, they will be forgiven, and they shall be like a man who made a mistake and said something while intoxicated with wine".' As Cathcart and Gordon explain, by adjusting the Hebrew עֲנָבִים to the Aramaic *bhmryh* (lit. 'in his wine') the targumist compares Israel to a drunkard rather than a prostitute (*The Aramaic Bible*. XIV. *The Targum of the Minor Prophets*, p. 35, n. 1). The adjustment is similar to the transformation of *diblayim* to fig leaves, and enables the translator to dilute Israel's offence (cf. 'The Miscreant Schoolboy' and 'The Lethargic Queen' in §2.1 above on Midrash Rabbah).

Targums emphatically asserts, 'do not become a shepherd', 'do not take a woman of harlotry'. As Cathcart observes, such inversions of the text are extremely ironic when read in the light of Rabbi Judah's injunction, 'He who translates a Biblical verse literally is a liar; but he who elaborates on it is a blasphemer'.[104]

2.3. *The Babylonian Talmud: Hosea the Clown*

The Babylonian Talmud is, on the surface, far less coy than the Midrash and the Targum in its response to Hosea's marriage. The 'wife of harlotry' remains uncensored; the only adjustment is that the marriage is reduced from symbolism on a grand scale to the prophet's private re-education programme. Other commentators 'solve' the text by dissolving the link between prophet and prostitute, but the Talmud attempts to loosen the link between signifier and signified. Although Hosea marries a promiscuous woman, the marriage has no larger significance: the prophet is not a symbol of Yhwh, nor is Gomer a representative of wayward Israel.

In the talmudic version of Hos. 1.2, Hosea is an amateur prophet who has not yet mastered the genre. When the Holy One complains, 'My children have sinned', the text contrasts the correct response, 'These are Thy children..extend Thy mercy to them', with Hosea's inept reply: 'The whole world is Thine; exchange them for a different nation.'[105] The bathos of the contrast establishes Hosea as the creature of comedy, the prophetic clown, who has not learnt his lines properly and must be taught a lesson. Even the patience of the divinity is tested beyond its limits: in exasperation, the Holy One adopts a tone of contempt and asks, 'What shall I do with this *old man*?'[106]

Like Polonius in *Hamlet*, Hosea is a bumbling old man whose eyes ooze with plum tree gum and who displays a 'plentiful lack of wit'. As a lesson in divine compassion the Holy One orders him to marry a harlot, and waits until she has borne him three children before asking him to leave her, just as Moses left his wife in response to the divine calling. Attached to his wife, despite her faults, Hosea protests that he can

---

104. *T. Meg.* 4.41; *b. Qid.* 49a.

105. *Pes.* 87a-b. Unless otherwise specified, all translations are from H. Freedman, *The Babylonian Talmud: Seder Mo'ed* (London: Soncino Press, 1938).

106. *Pes.* 87a (my italics).

'neither expel nor divorce her',[107] and so provides the cue for the moral of the narrative. As the Holy One steps in and explains, if Hosea 'can feel like that even though [his] wife is a whore and [he] cannot be sure that the children are [his]', how can God be expected 'to exchange the Israelites...the descendants of [his] proved servant Abraham, Isaac and Jacob'?[108]

The primary concern of the Talmud is to restore the relationship between Israel and Yhwh, using Hosea as a sacrifice of atonement. In this reading the prophet is not the suffering victim or illustrator of Yhwh's displeasure with Israel: rather, he is the source of that displeasure and the three curses uttered by Yhwh against the nation are uttered solely because of him.[109] All vacillations in Yhwh's perception of Israel are removed and the text stresses, above all, Yhwh's constancy. Like the writers of the Talmud, Israel is a faithful 'Jew', who already knows and can recite the right answers, and the only focus for exhortation and repentance is the figure of the prophet himself.[110]

Whereas the MT suggests that Yhwh's relationship with Israel is as tenuous as the relationship between a prophet and a prostitute, the

---

107. *Pes.* 87b.

108. *Pes.* 87b (trans. H.L. Ginsberg, 'Hosea, Book of', in G. Roth and C. Wigoder [eds.], *Encyclopaedia Judaica* [Jerusalem: Macmillan, 1971], XVIII, cols. 1010-25, [1011]).

109. *Pes.* 87b.

110. The Talmud is virtually alone in condemning Hosea for his marriage to a promiscuous woman. The only other commentator, to my knowledge, who allows for the possibility that the prophet might be at fault is Peter Damian, the eleventh-century reformer. Like the Talmud, Damian sets the prophet up as an example of a man who misunderstood God's intention and was punished. Because their father delighted in Gomer's 'wickedly soothing caresses' (p. 398), Hosea's children displeased God and therefore received negative names such as 'Jezreel' and 'Not-Loved'. As the Talmud casts Hosea as a bad prophet, Damian casts him as the unworthy church leader. Because he chooses his family inappropriately, he brings disaster upon himself, and is held up as a warning to the bishops Damian addresses. Just as the contributors to the Talmud made Hos. 1.2 fit into a wider theological agenda and affirm Yhwh's constant love for Israel, so Damian's manipulation of this passage fits into a wider agenda for the instruction of clergy. Damian also wrote a *Liber Gomorrhianus* against clerical marriage, and so seized on the relationship between Hosea and Gomer as an example of a disastrous partnership (P. Damian, 'Letter 59', in *The Fathers of the Church*. II. *Peter Damian, Letters 31-60* [trans. O.J. Blum; Washington DC: Catholic University of America Press, 1990], pp. 394-403).

Talmud presents a far more palatable picture in which God and the people of God are partners in wisdom. The attraction of the revised version is that accusation is deflected away from the nation, and by implication from the reader: conventional roles are reversed and the people share a superior vantage point with the deity and laugh and wonder at the prophet's incomprehension. By detaching the religious macrocosm from the domestic microcosm, the marriage is transformed from a prophetic visual aid into an entertaining spectacle. The liaison is innocuous rather than dangerous, comic rather than tragic, because it is not an issue of national pride but merely the prophet's own *affair*.

As a result of talmudic revision the marriage of Hosea and Gomer is not only comic and inoffensive, but also strangely appropriate. If the marriage of prostitute and prophet appears awkward and imbalanced, it can be corrected by improving Gomer's image or, as in this case, by denigrating Hosea. The assumption of the text is that marriage to a prostitute constitutes dishonour for a true man of God, but that the imbalance is alleviated when that man is also a fool. Both Hosea and Gomer are subjects of scorn and mockery, and the offensive verse is rewritten as a marriage of a whore to a clown.

Like her husband (the bad Jew) Gomer-bat-Diblayim (the bad woman) is the object of rabbinic contempt. Her name is passed around and punned on with easy familiarity:

> *Gomer*. Rab said, [That intimates] that all satisfied their lust [*gomerim*] on her; *the daughter of Diblayim*: [a woman of] ill fame [*dibbah*] and the daughter of a woman of ill fame [*dibbah*]. Samuel said: [It means she was as sweet in everyone's mouth as a cake of figs [*debelah*]. While R. Johanan interpreted: [It means] they all trod upon her as a cake of figs [is trodden].[111]

Like a passage of Mishnah, 'Gomer' provokes her own gemara, and the prostitute becomes, effectively, the plaything of wordplay. The name of the prostitute is dangerous and provocative: according to rabbinic legend, 'Rahab' cannot be mentioned without men spilling their seed, and 'Gomer', similarly, is a springboard for contempt *and* sexual fantasy. Manhandling the prostitute's name and character produces images of sexual excess: she satisfies the lust of 'all' men; she is sweet in 'everyone's' mouth; and 'all' men, in an overt sexual innuendo, are said to 'tread' on her. Free association on the name Diblayim illustrates the

111. *Pes.* 87a-b.

double-sidedness of the reaction: links with 'ill-fame' and 'fig-like succulence' reveal more about the rabbis' ambiguous feelings towards the promiscuous woman than about the possible etymology of her name.[112]

2.4. *Abraham Ibn Ezra and Maimonides: Confining the Woman to Dream*

Early Jewish commentary, like the Midrash, struggled with the image of Gomer-bat-Diblayim and her unholy relations with the prophet, and Rashi went to considerable lengths to restore proper relations between them. Conflating the words לְךָ קַח ('go take') to לְקַח as in לֶקַח טוֹב, ('good instruction', cf. Prov. 4.2), he cunningly rescripted the divine command as a command to teach, rather than marry, the woman of harlotry. An ingenious pun, which allows him to restore the prophet to a proper pedagogic relationship with the woman, does not look out of place in the slippery semantics of Rashi's commentary, but imaginative inventions look distinctly odd in the meticulously 'literal' studies of Abraham Ibn Ezra. Because Ibn Ezra's reaction to the promiscuous woman is so out of character, it is a good indication of commentators' determination to exclude the subversive female from the text and to retrieve the text's morality, even at the expense of cherished methodologies.

The figure of the prostitute exerts a powerful force over the exegete, and embarrassed efforts to avert his gaze force him into a methodological impasse. Ironically Abraham Ibn Ezra, a 'great champion of plain

---

112. Modern commentators continue the tradition of proposing various fantastic interpretations of Gomer's name and, like their rabbinic predecessors, betray as much about themselves as about 'the text'. *Gomer* has been variously related to the Arabic *gemratun*, burning coal, and to fullness or plenitude (see Wolff, *Hosea*, pp. 16-17), while *diblayim* has been taken as a reference to the woman's breasts, her cheapness and religious preferences. Charles Hauret is certain that the name masks 'a sexual allusion' and is unsure only of which possibility is correct. *Diblayim* may be a way of characterizing her as an adherent of the Baal cult, in which cakes of figs were offered alongside raisin cakes; it may be a proverbial expression, characterizing her as a 'common woman, ready to sell herself for a ridiculous salary of two fig cakes'; or it may, as the dual form suggests, be an allusion to her breasts, and a lascivious and mocking description of her as 'the woman with two cakes of figs' (C. Hauret, *Amos et Osée: Un livret de famille originale* [Paris: Beauchesne, 1970], pp. 141-42).

sense'[113] and staunch opponent of 'allegorisis', avoids confrontation
with the immoral woman by recourse to the realm of allegory, or
dream. As a determined advocate of *peshat*, that is 'simple' or 'literal'
interpretation, he vituperously condemns the 'method of uncircumcised
scholars who claim that the whole Pentateuch consists of parables and
allegories', and dismisses their fabrications as 'useless words driven by
vapour'.[114] He then proceeds to vaporize Hosea's unfortunate domestic
situation into the realm of dream, which, like allegory, is a kind of symbolic stratosphere in which events have no tangible reality and, presumably, no detrimental moral effect. In the medium of the dream vision,
symbols can mix and strange liaisons are permissible: dreams are by
definition 'other' and 'strange', and nothing therefore constitutes an
offence. A prophet and prostitute can meet and mix as abstract concepts, since oxymorons and paradoxes are expected in dreams, but the
mixing of symbols does not constitute sexual intercourse, nor does it
have the same procreative force: the marriage is merely an effect of the
dream, and the offspring are the offspring of the imagination.

Ibn Ezra advocates הדרך הישרה, the 'straight way', of direct and unin-
ventive interpretation,[115] but his analysis of Hos. 1.2 suggests that it is
easier to lay a straight path than to keep within its confines. In the
special case of Gomer, his rejection of literal interpretation is just as
vehement as his condemnation of allegory, and is presented as an
authorial (and hence authoritative) pronouncement: 'Thus says Abraham
[Ibn Ezra] the author: It is inconceivable that God should command one
to take a harlot and conceive children of harlotry'.[116] Like the Targum,
Ibn Ezra pronounces conception inconceivable. Trapped between a
rejection of allegory (according to the exegete's own standards) and a
rejection of a literal reading (in order to preserve what are thought to be
Yhwh's standards) he is forced to commit the exegetical sin of allegory,
albeit thinly disguised in the form of a 'vision of prophecy [or]...a
dream of the night'.[117] The dream-mode allows the exegete to relegate
events to the realm of *quasi*-reality: the effect is like Nikos Kazantzakis's

113. D. Boyarin, *Intertextuality and the Reading of Midrash* (Bloomington and
Indianapolis: Indiana University Press, 1990), p. 50.

114. A. Lipshitz, *The Commentary of Rabbi Abraham Ibn Ezra on Hosea* (New
York: Sepher-Hermon Press, 1988), p. 7.

115. Lipshitz, *Ibn Ezra on Hosea*, p. 4.

116. Lipshitz, *Ibn Ezra on Hosea*, p. 20.

117. Lipshitz, *Ibn Ezra on Hosea*, p. 20.

The Last Temptation of Christ, in which a scandalous love affair between Christ and Mary Magdalene is consigned to Christ's tortured hallucinations on the cross.[118]

Ibn Ezra is determined to contain the awkward figure of the prostitute and references to marriage, conception and birth, within the safe parenthesis of 'dream' or reality at one remove. Whenever Gomer or intercourse are mentioned, he reacts with an instant reiteration of the dream framework. References to the 'wife of harlotry' are kept to a minimum and she is gestured to obliquely as 'the woman previously mentioned' and 'the woman mentioned above', as if one specific reference to her were quite enough.[119] Yet despite attempts to contain immorality in another realm, it is debatable, as in *The Last Temptation*, whether this effect is actually achieved or whether, as Bishop Horsley maintained, 'the signification of the emblem, whether the act were done in reality or vision, [is] the same.'[120]

From Ibn Ezra's perspective, the dream serves the dual purpose of retaining the prophet's integrity (he did not lie, the events are not false), but of denying the literal truth of the account. Yet despite his attempts to delineate between allegory and dream, the difference between Ibn Ezra's 'dream vision' and allegory, or a 'description of a subject under the guise of some other subject' (*OED*) seems purely one of definition. In exactly the same way as the uncircumcised allegorists, he points to a series of one-to-one correspondences: the phrase *and she bore a son* 'is to be understood as the generation following Jeroboam, the son of Joash'; the conception of the daughter, Lo-Ruhamah, refers to the following generation; and the reference to the birth of Lo-Ammi means that the 'exiled tribes begot children in Israel'.[121] The dream sequence is merely a gentle ushering into an allegorical interpretation in which the text is viewed primarily as a puzzle to be decoded.

The motives behind the transformation from reality to dream which are concealed by Ibn Ezra become more explicit in Maimonides' *Guide*

118. Kazantzakis's novel and Martin Scorsese's film adaptation (Cineplex Odeon, 1988) proved highly controversial, because Christian viewers found the extremely long dream/hallucination sequence as 'real' as the rest of the film.

119. Lipshitz, *Ibn Ezra on Hosea*, p. 21.

120. This statement is attributed to Horsley by J. Calvin, *Commentaries on the Twelve Minor Prophets*. I. *Hosea* (trans. J. Owen; Edinburgh: Edinburgh Printing Company, 1846), p. 43. As Calvin supplies no reference, I have been unable to trace the original source.

121. Lipshitz, *Ibn Ezra on Hosea*, pp. 21-22.

of the Perplexed. Hosea's marriage is presented as one element in a long catalogue of indignities suffered by the prophets, and the figure of Hosea, with a harlot on his arm, comes at the end of a carnivalesque parade of Old Testament *nevi'im*, assuming undignified postures, sporting absurd visual aids, and dressed (or not) in peculiar clothing. The purpose of the dream is clearly to relieve the embarrassment of the prophets and, unlike the Talmud, to prevent too much blurring between the roles of prophet and clown. The dream is a vehicle for salvaging prophetic dignity: as Maimonides protests, 'God is too exalted that he should turn his prophets into a laughing stock and a mockery for fools by ordering them to carry out crazy actions'.[122]

2.5. *Fathering an Orthodoxy: Augustine and Jerome*

Maimonides' *Guide* is revealing because he not only provides a potential solution to Hosea's marital problems, but confesses the outrage that necessitated it. Similarly, the writings of the Church Fathers are of particular interest, not only for the emphatic answers they give to the question of Hosea's marriage, but the way in which those answers betray the virulent questions of their opponents. St Augustine famously found the book both 'difficult', and 'profound',[123] and J.F. Burroughs, a seventeenth-century commentator, gives the background to the book's difficulty. According to Burroughs, Augustine was challenged by 'one Faustus, a Manichee', who used Hosea's marital difficulties as a proof-text for the Bible's immorality: 'That Old Testament of yours, Moses and the Prophets, is that of God? Do you not find there a command to take a wife of whoredoms, and can this be from God?'[124] Augustine's reply—that perhaps she was called a prostitute because of her past misdeeds but had reformed by the time of her marriage—evaded the charge on a chronological technicality and set up an escape route that

122. M. Maimonides, *The Guide of the Perplexed* 98b (trans. S. Pines; Chicago: University of Chicago Press, 1963), p. 405. Compare the Deist Matthew Tindal's much later protest: 'How many commands did God give to his prophets, which if taken according to the letter, seem unworthy of God, as making them act like mad men, or idiots?' (*Christianity as Old as the Creation* [London, 1730], p. 255).

123. Augustine, *City of God*, XVIII.28 (cited by A. la Bonnardière, 'Saint Augustine et le prophète Osée', *VSpir* 143 [1989], pp. 623-32 [623]).

124. Augustine cited by J. Burroughs, *An Exposition of the Prophecy of Hosea* (Edinburgh: James Nichol, 1643), p. 7. I have used Burroughs as my source for Augustine's dispute with Faustus as I have been unable to trace the original debate. Burroughs supplies no reference.

has been used by commentators throughout the centuries. In the course of its evolution, the story of Gomer's regrettable past has lost its tentative nature and become fully assimilated in the critical canon as one of the most popular views.

Like Augustine's defensive apologetic, Jerome's account of Hosea's marriage bears the traces of virulent opposition. Embarrassed by the lewd private and public life of the prophet and the questions that arose from it, Jerome constructs an emphatic, yet bizarre, case for the defence. His argument, that 'There is no shame in the commands of God' and that 'what God initiates is always honest,'[125] suggests a context in which God and Hosea were accused of destroying their credibility by jeopardizing their moral integrity. Jerome's retort is emphatic—'Sed respondebis...et nos dicemus' ('You will reply...and we shall repeat')— implying that the text requires not only apologetic but a double barricade of defence.

In his case for the defence[126] Jerome constructs a fantastic oxymoron, the chaste harlot. The marriage, he maintains, involved a transfer of qualities in one direction only: thus, 'The prophet did not lose his chastity because he was joined to a harlot, but the harlot gained a chastity she did not have previously; especially because Hosea did what he did not for the sake of excess, not because of lust or his own will, but because he obeyed the will of God'.[127] Like all good figures of grace, Hosea was able to influence without being influenced: Gomer did not merely abandon prostitution before her marriage, as in Augustine's account, but was redeemed through her relationship with the prophet. Jerome effectively inverts the arguments of his opponents: the basis of the protest is that Gomer's immorality is transferred by association, but the basis of the answer is that Hosea's morality remakes his errant wife.

125. 'In typo, quia si fiat, turpissimum est. Sed respondebis: Deo iubente, nihil turpe est; et nos dicemus: nihil Deus praecipit nisis quod honestum est, nec iubendo turpia, facit honesta quae turpia sunt' (Jerome, *Commentaria in Osee prophetam*, in J.P. Migne [ed.], *Divinae Bibliotheca Pars Prima: Hieronymi Opera*, 9 [Patrologia: Series Latina, XXV; Paris: Vrayet de Surcy, 1845], col. 823, cited by Bitter, *Die Ehe*, p. 29).

126. Stephan Bitter aptly calls Jerome's theology *ein Plädoyer* ('a summation'; *Die Ehe*, p. 29).

127. *Commentaria in Osee prophetam* (Patrologia: Series Latina, XXV, col. 823), cited by M. Luther, *Lectures on the Minor Prophets* (trans. H.C. Oswald; St Louis: Concordia, 1975), p. 3.

2.6. *Luther and Calvin: Textual Reformation*

The actor who is given the part of Iago need not himself be a bad man.[128]

In the image of the chaste harlot, Jerome reads Hos. 1.2 as 'Paradise/ Innocence Regained'. Luther reads it as 'Paradise Never Lost'. 'People stir up big questions', he complains, 'on account of Gomer's harlotry'.[129] To avoid these big questions, he re-presents the text as a stylized drama in the manner of a medieval morality play. 'Wife of harlotry', he argues, is merely an extension of the naming-games in the rest of the chapter: like Jezreel, Lo-Ruhamah, and Lo-Ammi, the prophet's wife assumes a role and becomes a visual aid in her husband's didactic drama. In Luther's version, as in *Everyman*, characters stalk the stage heavy-handedly presenting their didactic moral; the *Wife of Harlotry,* like *Good Deeds*, is an actor with a pedagogic purpose, who is by no means implicated by her role.

Like Ibn Ezra, Augustine and Jerome, Luther constructs strict guidelines by which the text is to be correctly interpreted:

> *Do not take this to mean*, then, that harlotry is charged to the wife, but *understand* that the wife has *allowed* herself, her sons, and her husband to be so named because of the people and against the people, as if she were saying: 'I am called a harlot and my husband is called a whoremonger because you are harlots and whoremongers.' Oh, how great a cross they suffered with those insulting names for the sake of the Word of God![130]

The wife of harlotry is redeemed from whore to suffering servant of God, and the stage is effectively the means of her redemption. Calvin, similarly, reforms the text by separating the prophet's private life from his role as mime artist, but whereas Luther allows Gomer to remain on the condition that she undergoes conversion, Calvin erases her altogether, reducing her, as the Targum does, to a pile of figs. In Calvin's version of the play, Hosea stands before his audience with only one prop, a putrefying pile of figs, which he then 'names for his wife'.[131] The effect of such a performance is extremely bizarre and not entirely dissimilar to the surreal and minimalist theatre of Samuel Beckett.

Calvin's stage functions, like Ibn Ezra's dream vision, as a way of

---

128. H.H. Rowley, 'The Marriage of Hosea', in *Men of God: Studies in Old Testament History and Prophecy* (London: Nelson & Sons, 1963), pp. 66-97 (75).

129. Luther, *Lectures on the Minor Prophets*, p. 3.

130. Luther, *Lectures on the Minor Prophets*, pp. 3-4 (my italics).

131. Calvin, *Hosea*, p. 48.

disposing of the undesirable woman. Anxious to consign harlotry to the realm of the imagination, he constantly reiterates that his peculiar drama bears no resemblance to any persons, living or dead. Concerned that even the substitution of a woman by figs may not be enough to under-score the unreality of the events, he constantly reminds his audience that this is 'a parable (so to speak)', a presentation 'as in a living portraiture'.[132] To make it absolutely clear, Hosea begins by announcing, 'The Lord places me here as on a stage', and constantly stresses his role as an 'exhibit' who has 'assumed a character'.[133]

As in Ibn Ezra's account, it is at the moments of conception and birth that assurances that this is only a staged analogy come thick and fast. When Hosea begins to speak about taking a wife of harlotry, Calvin instantly interposes with a parenthetical 'let the reader understand': of course 'the whole people knew he had done no such thing'.[134] As soon as the wife conceives, she is instantly relegated to the realms of the imaginary: 'It now follows, the wife conceived', Calvin writes, hurriedly adding, '—the imaginary one, the wife as represented and exhibited'.[135] The X-rated presentation is censored and edited, and a potentially dangerous text is explained and reformed. Hosea himself, Calvin assures the weak-hearted, 'had ever lived virtuously and temperately', and 'they all knew that his household was exempt from every reproach'.[136]

3. *Modern Mythmakers, or Twentieth-Century Darshanim*

Modern critical commentary conceives of itself as having advanced beyond a naive, pre-critical phase of interpretation in which elaborate allegories of figs and intricate dramas were considered appropriate scholarly responses to texts. With the rise of historical criticism the main critical concern became the 'objective' investigation of the historical circumstances of the text, yet investigation of the book of Hosea has always involved a secret subversion of the rules. One of the consequences of historical criticism was that the question of the text's validity became inextricably entangled with the proof of the text's historical authenticity: as Hans Frei points out, preserving a text meant

132. Calvin, *Hosea*, p. 45.
133. Calvin, *Hosea*, p. 45.
134. Calvin, *Hosea*, p. 45.
135. Calvin, *Hosea*, p. 48.
136. Calvin, *Hosea,* p. 45.

establishing its historical validity.[137] Proving the validity of Hos. 1.2 has, paradoxically, always depended on affirming its non-historicity, and on altering the text to read, in some subtle fashion, 'The Lord did *not* say to Hosea, "Go take a wife of harlotry"'.

In this section I want to look how the 'modern myth-makers',[138] as H.L. Ginsberg calls them, or twentieth-century *darshanim*, have compiled their own creative *gemara*, a cluster of colourful stories around the edges of the text. The means of expression may be more sophisticated, but the strategies of control are strikingly similar, I suggest, to those adopted by pre-critical scholars. I want to focus, in particular, on critical attempts to rewrite the marriage as a tragic love story, to protest the woman's innocence, to see the woman's role as a mask or an act, to consign her to the realm of the unreal, or to erase her completely. The five studies represent the most prominent approaches to the text and are examined under the headings 'Romance, or Gomer the Beloved', 'Hagiography, or Gomer the Saint', 'Masks and Visions', 'Escape by Metaphor', and 'Redaction Criticism: From Moral to Textual Corruption'.

3.1. *Romance, or Gomer the Beloved*
My first example of twentieth-century *aggada* is a poignant tale of star-crossed lovers, a testimony to the eternal principle, *amor vincit omnia*. As medieval illuminators decorated their texts with aesthetic flourishes, so scholarly sentiment at the turn of the century constructed a florid romance around the borders of the text. T.K. Cheyne, in the Cambridge Bible Commentary of 1887, tells a harrowing and tragic love story which is rather like an upmarket, scholarly, station-bookshop romance. To give some indication of the imaginative excesses involved, I tell this 'sad story' as a story, using the storyteller's words wherever possible.[139]

As a northern prophet, Cheyne's Hosea was affected 'by the genial moods of nature in the north' and had an 'expansive, childlike

---

137. H. Frei, *The Eclipse of Biblical Narrative* (London: Yale University Press, 1980).

138. Ginsberg, 'Hosea', *EncJud* VIII, col. 1012.

139. Metacommentating on a commentary by T.K. Cheyne is to some extent an ironic activity, for Cheyne himself questioned the 'objectivity' of the commentator and observed that 'it is not unimportant to notice how the intellectual phases and material surroundings of a writer have affected his criticism' (*Founders of Old Testament Criticism: Biographical, Descriptive, Critical Studies* [London: Methuen, 1893], p. 7).

character.'[140] The exquisite love poem which we know as 'The Song of Songs' affected him deeply, and in it he read of the 'rustic beauties of northern Israel', beautiful not only in their 'external attractions' but also in their 'gentle and noble womanly virtues'.[141] He fell in love, and in Gomer-bat-Diblayim he thought he had found a 'bride like the Shulamite of his favourite poem'.[142] He married her, but she proved tragically unworthy: to his unutterable grief he found that instead of a 'lily of the valley' he had inadvertently enfolded in his arms a 'lily torn and trampled in the mire'.[143]

Hosea's pursuit of his beloved, despite her betrayal, is attributed by Cheyne to 'heart-logic'[144]—a compulsion which the critic, and his many successors, seem to share. Carried away on a tide of romanticism, critics suspend all critical judgment, and the figure of the prostitute seems to make a fool of them. Like babbling fools in front of a beautiful woman, they compete in descriptions of just how beautiful she was and how much Hosea loved her. O.R. Sellers, writing in 1924, takes up the story with musical accompaniment: Hosea loved Gomer, he maintains, despite her sullied reputation, and if we doubt that it is possible to love such a woman, he appeals to a contemporary song lyric for evidence. In the words of the twentieth-century song 'I've found my sweetheart Sally' Sellers encapsulates the depths of an ancient Israelite prophet's love. The concept of Hosea the romantic is pushed to its most extreme limits as the prophet 'sings': 'What she has been, what she has done, I never care to know, because to me she'll always be as pure as driven snow'.[145]

Supported by such eminent figures as Wellhausen, W.R. Harper and W. Robertson Smith, the 'tragic story of Hosea's sin-blasted home life'[146] was assimilated as a critical commonplace. S.L. Brown, in his introduction to his commentary (1932), finds no reason to explain, or

140. T.K. Cheyne, *Hosea: With Notes and Introduction* (Cambridge Bible Commentary; Cambridge: Cambridge University Press, 1887), p. 10.

141. Cheyne, *Hosea*, pp. 14-15. Cheyne combines fantasy and censure when he describes Gomer as a 'rustic beauty' who betrays her husband. A. van Selms, similarly, is wry, but perhaps ironically approving, when he notes that Hosea's wife was 'something of an expert in the erotic arts' (A. van Selms, 'Hosea and Canticles', *Die Oud Testament Werkgemeenskap in Suid-Afrika* 7–8 [1964–65], pp. 85-90 [88]).

142. Cheyne, *Hosea*, p. 20.

143. Cheyne, *Hosea*, p. 20.

144. Cheyne, *Hosea*, p. 19.

145. O.R. Sellers, 'Hosea's Motives', *AJSL* 41 (1924–25), pp. 243-47 (244).

146. W.E. Crane, 'The Prophecy of Hosea', *BSac* 89 (1932), pp. 480-94 (481).

question, the now canonized story, and gives a simple, unproblematic summary. 'These chapters', he explains, 'describe how his marriage to a woman whom he greatly loved and the breaking up of his home through his wife's adultery led the prophet to understand more fully than before the heinousness of Israel's apostasy and the depth of Yhwh's love for his people'.[147] In an article by George Farr, which appeared in 1958, the canonical status of this story is made even more explicit. In an essay entitled 'The Concept of Grace in the Book of Hosea', Grace is given a capital letter, and Farr opens with a credal statement, '*We believe that* there was only one woman in Hosea's life; she was truly his wife and the marriage was originally for love'.[148] As the Nicene creed moulds the life of Christ into an orthodoxy, so critics extract tenets of belief from, or impose them on, the book of Hosea. As the creed was normalized, it became increasingly difficult to argue against. In the early days of this myth's evolution the love story had its opponents; C.H. Toy, writing in 1913, parodied the extravagant trend and protested: 'The romantic history of a man wounded in his deepest feelings through an ill-fated marriage that saddened his life and coloured his thought seems to me to have no foundation in the text.'[149] Yet as the myth became dominant the questions subsided. Hosea's 'emotional solidarity'[150] with Yhwh is now a critical commonplace: thus Hosea gives us 'the most moving image of divine love';[151] no biblical prophet exceeds 'his creativeness regarding divine passion';[152] and the story of Hosea is 'God's Love Story'[153] since the prophet's call turns his life 'into a sanctuary where God's holy love was to be known'.[154]

The theological gains from the love story are immense. Despite the

147. S.L. Brown, *The Book of Hosea with Introduction and Notes* (Westminster Commentaries; London: Methuen, 1932), p. 1.

148. G. Farr, 'The Concept of Grace in the Book of Hosea', *ZAW* 70 (1958), pp. 98-107 (100 n. 3); my italics.

149. C.H. Toy, 'Note on Hosea 1–3', *JBL* 32 (1913), p. 75-79 (77).

150. M. McGuire, 'Sympathy and Prophetic Consciousness in Hosea', *Review for Religious* 39 (1985), pp. 884-93 (884).

151. G. Koonthanam, 'Divine Love in the Prophet Hosea', *Jeedvahara* 13 (1983), pp. 130-39 (130).

152. Koonthanam, 'Divine Love', p. 130.

153. G.W. Anderson, 'Hosea and Yahweh: God's Love Story', *RevExp* 72 (1975), pp. 425-36.

154. D.A. Hubbard, *Hosea: An Introduction and Commentary* (TOTC; Leicester: Inter-Varsity Press, 1989), p. 19.

great violence of ch. 2 and his frequent prophecies of doom, Hosea passes into the critical institution as a prophet of grace and a forerunner of Christ. The NEB endorses this perspective, translating אֵשֶׁת זְנוּנִים as 'unworthy woman' and so demonstrating that modern translation is no more immune to ideological influence than the Targums. Male critics cannot find words enough to express their solidarity with the suffering of Hosea the victim, and G.A.F. Knight strains the sentence, as well as the facts, in writing of 'poor dejected, spurned and broken-hearted Hosea'.[155] The nineteenth-century commentator G.W. Ewald let the critical imagination run riot: personifying the text, or textualizing the man, he regarded 'Hosea', the person and book, as a single entity, and regarded textual rupture as evidence for the agony of the prophet's 'painfully agitated heart'.[156] According to Ewald, Hosea's pain was such that he could not speak in calm and measured sentences: thus the 'whole discourse often breaks itself up into sobs'.[157] George Farr has to resort to hyperbole to convey his sympathy and writes of a Hosea who 'suffered far more poignantly than Job'.[158] Jumping from Hebrew חֶסֶד to Christian grace, H.H. Rowley describes Hosea by borrowing from the theology of the Epistle to the Hebrews:

> Like Another, he learned obedience by the things that he suffered, and because he was not broken by an experience that has broken many others, but triumphed over it and in triumphing perhaps won back his wife, he received through the vehicle of his very pain an enduring message for Israel and the world.[159]

The next story, in which the image of the prostitute is sanctified and generally cleaned-up, may take its precedent from the same Epistle, for was it not the writer to the Hebrews who restyled the image of the Old Testament prostitute Rahab to feature as an exemplary figure in a catalogue of faith?

155. G.A.F. Knight, *Hosea: Introduction and Commentary* (London: SCM Press, 1960), p. 60.

156. G.W. Ewald, *Commentary on the Prophets of the Old Testament. I. Joel, Amos, Hosea and Zechariah* (trans. J.F. Smith; London: Williams & Norgate, 1875), p. 218.

157. Ewald, *Commentary on the Prophets*, p. 218.

158. Farr, 'The Concept of Grace', p. 103.

159. Rowley, 'The Marriage of Hosea', p. 97.

3.2. *Hagiography, or Gomer the Saint*

In the love story, Hosea's affection triumphs over Gomer's vice: as Sellers puts it, to *him* she will always be 'as pure as driven snow'. In the second story Gomer's innocence is visible for all to see: critical consensus triumphs over Gomer's reputation, and the prostitute is given a posthumous pardon. The first story is that of the forgiven and chastened harlot; the second is paradoxically that of the *chaste* harlot. Critics who are disinclined to 'perpetuate the slander against Gomer's wifely virtue'[160] write redemptively in the tradition of Jerome.

Like their predecessors, modern critics are often forced into a critical impasse by their determination to redeem the 'wife of harlotry'. In a presidential address to the (then) Society of Biblical Literature and Exegesis in 1928, L.W. Batten attempted to make Gomer into the centrepiece of Christian hagiography. In a world in which secular writers are intent on 'strip[ping] the saints of their halo', the Christian exegete, according to Batten, can follow an 'opposite and more kindly course'.[161] The magnanimous exegete is committed to the reinstatement of fallen angels, and so does not merely follow Christ's example, but fulfils Christ's role, erasing sins and restoring people to a right relation with morality and with God. Batten describes his work on Gomer's character in specifically redemptive terms, as 'put[ting] a bit of a long overdue halo about the head of one heretofore adjudged worthy of stoning for her sins'.[162] The critic assumes a God- or specifically Christ-like authority by showing indulgence to the woman of harlotry and restraining the stones of her critics.

Arguing that Gomer should be considered innocent until proven guilty, Batten styles his argument on the model of the courtroom. In the absence of evidence (Gomer left no diaries and there were no eyewitnesses), Batten adopts a strange posture of authority, constantly using phrases such as 'naturally', 'I think we would all agree',[163] and 'beyond reasonable doubt'.[164] Like a professional lawyer on a losing case the author uses rhetoric to conceal a paucity of evidence, and his text is full

---

160. R.H. Pfeiffer, *Introduction to the Old Testament* (New York: Harper & Row, 1941), p. 568.

161. L.W. Batten, 'Hosea's Marriage and Message', *JBL* 48 (1929), pp. 257-73 (257).

162. Batten, 'Hosea's Message', p. 257.

163. Batten, 'Hosea's Message', p. 262.

164. Batten, 'Hosea's Message', p. 272.

of emotive appeals to the ladies and gentlemen of the jury. The extraneous appeals to reason which are affixed to the argument seem to be an attempt to compensate for the lack of reason in its internal construction.

Batten claims that his interpretation is self-evident precisely because it (self-evidently) is not. When the article is stripped of its legal polemic, the vindication of Gomer is found to rest on such flimsy claims as: 'The comparison of wicked Israel to the adulterous wife shows that Hosea had a high conception of the duty of marital fidelity, and his idea of faithfulness would *naturally* have come from what he had seen in his helpmeet'.[165] Interpreting the use of the third person, as opposed to the first person, as personal shyness on Hosea's part, Batten argues that someone so reticent about his personal life would hardly be likely to break his silence to reveal the 'deepest pain of his life'.[166] Should a preacher be judged by his sermon illustration? 'I think we would all agree that were a preacher today to compare backsliders to the faithless in marriage, we should not dream of inferring that his figure was due to domestic troubles of his own.'[167] Having dismissed most of critical history and the evidence of ancient manuscripts as scandalmongering, Batten himself plays the part of the defending attorney, the judge and the jury; the case for the prosecution is not presented, and has obviously been dismissed out of court. By presenting only one side of the story, Batten exaggerates the critical tendency to produce a univocal reading, which represses all possible contradictions. His criticism seems to be as much against what Milton termed 'this whore pluralitie' as against the whore herself. As a caricature of the omnipotent reader, Batten's 'hearing' ends with a declaration of the reader's despotic power, and the judge's hammer comes down with absolute certainty. 'The court is all-powerful', Batten pronounces, 'and finds a verdict easy: the charge against Gomer is dismissed. Next case.'[168]

Batten's article is a particularly extreme example of the imposition of the critical will on the text. The female is shaped by the male, the Hebrew text is Christianized and moralized, the text is coerced by the powerful reader, and ambiguity bows to the critical demand for univocality. In each case the weaker capitulates to the stronger and the

---

165. Batten, 'Hosea's Message', p. 262.
166. Batten, 'Hosea's Message', p. 262.
167. Batten, 'Hosea's Message', p. 262.
168. Batten, 'Hosea's Message', p. 275.

dominant ideology triumphs. Not all readings are so obvious in their ideological biases, and many are more convincing in their scholarship. The careful commentator H.W. Wolff, for example, does not completely erase Gomer's promiscuity, but instead seeks to provide mitigating circumstances. Arguing for Canaanite bridal initiation rites in which the young bride-to-be would have sex with a stranger, he claims that Gomer was not 'an especially wicked exception', merely an 'average, modern Israelite woman'.[169] His theory of Gomer as a 'thoroughly modern miss' is revealing, because, untypically, he goes to great lengths to uphold a disputed cultic practice.[170] The concerned critic presides over the text and, consciously or unconsciously, acts sacrificially to redeem it. As Ibn Ezra sacrifices his commitment to literal interpretation, Wolff briefly relinquishes his concern for historical precision and transgresses his own standards, in effect, so that Yhwh and Hosea will not be found transgressing theirs.

3.3. *Masks and Visions: Hosea on the Psychiatrist's Couch*
Though they re-emerge in a more sophisticated and subtle form, the ancient escape routes of 'dream' and 'stage' still feature prominently in twentieth-century commentary. Critics are preoccupied with the status of the marriage and its precise relation to reality. Commentators separate into three camps: those who see the marriage as 'dream'; those who explain it as 'allegory'; and those (notably few) who see the events as 'real'.[171] The question of the relationship between the book and 'real life' has dominated scholarship and has set the parameters of criticism within very narrow confines. New commentators on the book of Hosea tend not only to focus exclusively on the marriage, but to add their own endorsement to one of the three positions: metacommentary, in contrast, questions the assumptions of the question, with the aim of broadening the critical agenda.

In modern as in ancient commentary, one of the primary escape

---

169. Wolff, *Hosea*, p. 15.

170. Brevard Childs comments that, compared with Wolff's generally careful approach to texts, this thesis seems 'especially bold' (*Introduction to the Old Testament as Scripture* [London: SCM Press, 1979], p. 376).

171. A survey of the three positions and their exponents is given by R. Gordis, 'Hosea's Marriage and Message', *HUCA* 25 (1954), pp. 9-35. Interestingly, Gordis lists Ibn Ezra as an advocate of 'allegory' rather than 'dream', and illustrates the tenuous nature of the distinction.

routes is to displace offensive events from the external world to Hosea's private imagination: 'No other course is left to us', wrote C.F. Keil in 1880, 'than to picture to ourselves Hosea's marriage as *internal events*'.[172] Whereas the ancient commentators were limited to the vocabulary of 'dream' and 'visions', twentieth-century commentators have a range of psychological terms at their disposal—such as the 'repressed unconscious', or 'prophetic ecstasy'—to describe the special circumstances under which these strange events took place. A. Allwohn adapts the dream to the twentieth century when he places Hosea on the psychoanalyst's couch and provides his 'diagnosis' (*Feststellung*): that the prophet suffers from 'a nervous restlessness'[173] as indicated by the turbulent prose of the narrative.

Allwohn's Hosea does not dream, but suffers emotional excess that unbalances him and makes him super- and sub-normal, a 'superman' and a 'monster' (*ein Übermensch und ein Unmensch*).[174] In a state of ecstatic intoxication, he transcends and transgresses existing moral frameworks, and abandons himself to his unconscious sensual drives.[175] Hosea's railings against whoredom are the 'conscious' and 'transformed' expression of his unconscious 'dark desires'[176] and though Gomer is a real woman, she begins as a fantasy in the prophet's imagination. Allwohn, like the Talmud, sees Hosea as a culpable and weak figure, and in blaming the prophet he exonerates the divinity, since Hosea uses the command of God as an excuse for following his own sensual imagination.[177]

Allwohn's clinical transposition of the 'dream' is exceptional in that it works on the prophet's character and virtually ignores Gomer's. Stage imagery, in contrast, tends to reiterate old techniques: Yehezkel Kaufmann's position, surprisingly, coincides with Luther's when he asserts that 'Gomer must play the role of a harlot, going about with the appearance of a harlot to symbolise the apostasy of Israel'.[178] According

172. C.F. Keil, 'The Minor Prophets', in C.F. Keil and F. Delitzsch, *Biblical Commentary on the Old Testament* (trans. J. Martin; Edinburgh: 1880), p. 35 (my italics).

173. A. Allwohn, *Die Ehe des Propheten Hosea in psychoanalytischer Beleuchtung* (BZAW, 44 ; Berlin: de Gruyter, 1926), p. 53.

174. Allwohn, *Die Ehe*, p. 46.

175. Allwohn, *Die Ehe*, p. 53.

176. Allwohn, *Die Ehe*, p. 63.

177. Allwohn, *Die Ehe*, p. 54.

178. Y. Kaufmann, *The Religion of Israel: From its Beginnings to the Babylonian*

to Kaufmann, Hos. 1.2 is a 'prophetic theatrical act'[179] and harlotry is merely Gomer's costume. On the basis of Hos. 2.4, which implores her to 'remove her harlotries from her face, and her adulteries from between her breasts', he concludes that Gomer's harlotries are 'some cosmetic or face covering'[180] like stage make-up or the mime artist's mask, which can be removed as soon as the play is over. In his imagery of masks and theatrical cosmetics, Kaufmann invites us to peep at Gomer in her dressing room after the show, slipping out of the role of harlot just as easily as she takes off her costume. In the next examples Gomer slips out of the role of 'harlotry' even more subtly and discretely, as the reality of her offence is softened until it becomes 'just a metaphor'.

3.4. *Escape by Metaphor*

Like the stage and the dream, ecstasy or the unconscious, metaphor is another realm of unreality to which the offensive woman can be confined. Because truth is conventionally associated with the literal, metaphor is taken to be a dilute or distorted form of truth, and the force of words and phrases can be made less innocuous by dismissing them as 'only a metaphor'. As W.V.O. Quine observes, 'When explication banishes a problem it does so by showing it to be in an important sense unreal; viz., in the sense of proceeding only from needless usages'.[181] One way of banishing the אֵשֶׁת זְנוּנִים, and of preventing needless worry over the text's immorality, is to show that Gomer is a wife of idolatry rather than a wife of harlotry, and that harlotry is 'only a metaphor' for religious zeal. Leroy Waterman not only banishes the problem of the promiscuous woman, but transforms her harlotry into virtue by insisting that she was 'not a woman who meant to be bad, or was conscious of being bad', but was 'a brave woman, a devoted woman, yes and a true-hearted woman too'.[182] The basis of the transformation is the transformation of the metaphor: for him Gomer is a woman of impressive

Exile (trans. M. Greenberg; London: George Allen & Unwin, 1961), pp. 370-71.

179. Kaufmann, *The Religion of Israel*, p. 371.

180. Kaufmann, *The Religion of Israel*, p. 370. Like all solutions of Hosea's marital problems this solution provides problems of its own. If Gomer's harlotries are merely a theatrical mask for use in a play commissioned by Yhwh, why is Hosea suddenly so emphatic that she remove them?

181. W.V.O. Quine, *Word and Object* (Cambridge, MA: MIT Press, 1960), p. 260.

182. Waterman, 'The Marriage of Hosea', p. 201.

religious commitment, and her only mistake is to direct it towards a religion that is unworthy of her.

In the MT 'harlotry' is a signifier of 'idolatry', but many critics maintain that the signifier is completely absorbed by the signified. J. Coppens, for example, insists that Gomer is 'neither a fornicator nor an adulteress' but a 'child of the Israelite nation', and is only a prostitute in the 'religious, metonymic sense of the word'.[183] Later in his paper, however, he betrays himself and shows that his conclusion was preordained by his ideological expectations. Having considered a literal reading he rejects its irreligiosity: his paper changes direction with the tell-tale phrase 'On the other hand, for those of us who are of the opinion that *Gomer's reputation must be improved*'[184]—which leads into an exploration of the metaphorical alternative. The metaphorical option acts as a safety net for those who cannot read the text literally: Coppens writes emphatically, 'Il faut blanchir Gomer' ('We *must* whiten Gomer').[185] Coppens's whitening is effectively textual white-washing: he foregrounds what many critics conceal, and highlights the influence of his own preferences as reader on his description of the text.

There are two ways of using metaphor to redeem Gomer. The first is to reduce harlotry to an image of idolatry; the second is to stress Gomer's role as a substitute for the nation. Because Gomer 'is' Israel, and Israel is also portrayed as a child with his parent (Hos. 11.1-3), some critics deduce that Gomer must be child-like and innocent, and must therefore be a virgin at the point of her marriage. Since Gomer and the child describe the same tenor, Israel, the assumption is that they will share the same qualities; however, although the nation is also described as a 'stubborn heifer', 'half-baked bread', and a 'crooked merchant', no attempt is made to harmonize these images. My suspicion is that altering Gomer to fit the tenor Israel is a foil for altering her to fit the moral requirements of a biblical text; adjusting the text on a figurative level adjusts it on a moral level, and I.H. Eybers rejoices to find how, with a little metaphorical remanoeuvring, all 'ethical objection' 'disappears entirely'.[186] A.B. Davidson, in the first edition of *A Dictionary of the*

183. J. Coppens, 'L'histoire matrimoniale d'Osée' (BBB, 1; Bonn: Peter Hanstein, 1950), pp. 38-45 (39-40).

184. Coppens, 'L'histoire', p. 43.

185. Coppens, 'L'histoire', p. 43.

186. I.H. Eybers, 'The Matrimonial Life of Hosea', OTWSA 7–8 (1964–65), pp. 11-34 (20).

Bible, argues that Gomer cannot already be a 'sinner' because this 'does not suit the symbolism' and is a sense which 'the words cannot bear'[187]—for 'words' and 'symbolism' substitute 'commentator'; perhaps it is a sense that does not suit the commentator, and that he cannot bear. The woman in the text is a moral misfit, and critics need a woman to fit; Norman Snaith makes this need explicit when he writes: 'If the allegory is to be complete, *we need a Gomer who* is at first faithful and later becomes unfaithful'.[188] The tell-tale phrase 'we need a Gomer who' implies that there are potentially many versions of Gomer, and that they are selected, like models from a catalogue, to serve a particular textual look.

3.5. *Redaction Criticism: From Moral to Textual Corruption*

If the task of the metacommentator is to locate 'the glance that designates, in the process of *avoiding* the object forbidden',[189] commentaries that gloss over Hos. 1.2 are particularly revealing. The technique may be more discrete, but G.A.F. Knight, like Midrash Rabbah, attempts to circumnavigate the אֵשֶׁת זְנוּנִים by making much of the phrase 'so he went' and praising Hosea's obedience, without confronting the dilemma of what Hosea went to do.[190] Walter Vogels obscures the moral dilemma with praise and applauds the prophet for conforming 'sa vie à sa foi et à sa prédication' ('his life to his faith and his preaching') and for living out his own sermon illustration.[191] As Vogels deflects attention from the actual marriage to the marriage of life and faith, Charles Hauret forgets the imperfection of a potentially 'scandalous' marriage and focuses on the perfect conjunction of idolatry and harlotry, which he sees as Yhwh's symbolic trump card, and celebrates it as a 'comparison parfaite' ('perfect comparison').[192]

---

187. A.B. Davidson, 'Hosea', in J. Hastings (ed.), *A Dictionary of the Bible* (Edinburgh: T. & T. Clark, 1st edn, 1904), p. 421. The second edition rectified this evasion by deliberately confronting the 'sordid, solid facts' (J. Paterson, 'Hosea', in F.C. Grant and H.H. Rowley [eds.], *A Dictionary of the Bible* [Edinburgh: T. & T. Clark, 2nd edn, 1963], p. 398).

188. N.H. Snaith, *Amos, Hosea, and Micah* (London: Epworth Press, 1959), p. 53 (my italics).

189. Jameson, 'Metacommentary', p. 16 (my italics).

190. Knight, *Hosea*, pp. 41-42.

191. W. Vogels, '"Osée–Gomer": *car* et *comme* "Yahweh–Israël", Os 1–3', *La nouvelle revue théologique* 103 (1981), pp. 711-27 (722-23).

192. Hauret, *Amos et Osée*, p. 139.

Redaction criticism, while it has had some important suggestions to make concerning Judaean editing of the text,[193] has sanctioned the tendency to gloss over the difficult woman with the support of an 'objective' methodology. Using the theory of a deuteronomistic redactor, critics such as Harper, Batten, Birkeland, Heerman and North[194] have elided the phrase 'of whoredoms', as, in Batten's words, a 'clumsy gloss'.[195] The elision, which is often based on spurious reasoning,[196] allows the critic to achieve what F. North terms a 'Solution of Hosea's Marital Problems by Critical Analysis', simply by ascribing the seeming *moral* corruption of the text to *textual* corruption. Rather like those who protest that Gomer *became* harlotrous, the redaction critic preserves the wife in her original pure form without the 'harlotries' which, he claims, were added later.

The problem with redaction criticism is that it can look suspiciously like the scholar's own editing.[197] The critic can effectively place in the

193. For a detailed study of Judaean influence on Hosea see G.I. Emmerson, *Hosea: An Israelite Prophet in Judaean Perspective* (JSOTSup, 28; Sheffield: JSOT Press, 1984).

194. W.R. Harper, *A Critical and Exegetical Commentary on Amos and Hosea* (ICC; Edinburgh: T. & T. Clark, 1905); A. Heerman, 'Ehe und Kinder des Propheten Hosea', *ZAW* 40 (1922), pp. 287-312; Batten, 'Message'; H. Birkeland, *Zum hebräischen Traditionswesen: Die Komposition der prophetischen Bücher des Altes Testaments* (Oslo: Jacob Dybwad, 1938); F. North, 'Solution of Hosea's Marital Problems by Critical Analysis', *JNES* 16 (1957), pp. 128-30.

195. Batten, 'Message', p. 265.

196. North, for example, argues tortuously: 'The superscription of the book ends with the Hebrew words "the Lord" and "Hosea", so it is superfluous to repeat these names immediately, when all that is needed is "he said to him". The fact that such pleonasm is common in the Hebrew language *is no proof that it is not regularly a sign of a change of hand*. Therefore [Hos. 1.2] is probably secondary material' ('Solution', p. 129; my italics). North argues defensively, and against the evidence, that the verse is secondary because writers do not repeat themselves. Excision based on this kind of argument, or merely on a sense that a phrase has a 'superfluous feel to it' (W.D. Whitt, 'The Divorce of Yahweh and Asherah in Hos. 2.4-7; 12ff', *SJOT* 6 [1992], pp. 31-67 [60]) points to a deeper ideological motive behind the redaction critical façade.

197. A former biblical scholar, now an editor, draws an analogy between the two activities when he writes: 'All Bible scholars, to the extent that they are preoccupied with redaction, must become editors' (J.R. Miles, 'Radical Editing: *Redaktionsgeschichte* and the Aesthetic of Willed Confusion', in R.E. Friedman [ed.], *The Creation of Sacred Literature: Composition and Redaction of the Biblical Text* [Berkeley: University of California Press, 1981], pp. 85-98 [85]).

hands of redactors 1, 2 and 3 the editorial changes that *he* would like to make. The redactionist's scissors are potentially all-powerful and he can cut and paste the text until its ideology is a reprint of his own. The danger of the theoretical Ur-text is that it can become a repository for all the critic's ideals, and anything which does not fit this ideal vision can be described as a 'later addition'. Some critics might more accurately be termed reactionist rather than redactionist since, as H.H. Rowley complained, they tend to 'get rid of the difficulty of Hos. 1.2 by the familiar expedient of surgery, and delete the inconvenient words'.[198] As Melville Scott protested, in an early critique of W.R. Harper: 'All the passages which have been...excised have the same fault in the eyes of the modern radical critic, viz. that they contradict his cherished theories. This is their crime and excision is their punishment'.[199] As the approach that most vividly illustrates the critic's inability to tolerate the MT, redaction criticism acts as a symbol for the relationship between Hos. 1.2 and its interpreters. The problems that the redactor locates *within* the text result from the redactor's tense relationship *with* the text: on one level the problematic relationship is that between prophet and prostitute, but on another it is the relationship between the critic and the text. Hosea 1.2 elicits creative reader-response not only because it is 'fraught with background', but because the few events it foregrounds are offensive to biblical scholars. The disjuncture that commentators locate within Hosea's marriage is also the difference between their expectations and a recalcitrantly immoral text, and the 'gaps' they fill are not only the gaps within the text, but the distance between the text and their own sense of a biblical narrative.

4. Art and Commentary: Blurring the Boundaries

In his analysis, 'Inconstancy in the Book of Hosea', Karl Plank describes Hosea as a 'scroll of agony which records the screams of a betrayed lover'.[200] As the emotive title 'The Scarred Countenance' might suggest, he produces a highly emotive reading, and blurs the boundaries between commentary and art by drawing imaginative analogies between Hosea 1–3 and Arthur Miller's *After the Fall*. Conversely, Mieke Bal

198. Rowley, 'The Marriage of Hosea', p. 75.
199. M. Scott, *The Message of Hosea* (New York: Macmillan, 1921), p. 22.
200. K.A. Plank, 'The Scarred Countenance: Inconstancy in the Book of Hosea', *Judaism* 32 (1983), pp. 343-54 (343).

problematizes the concept of boundary between (objective) commentary and (subjective) art from, as it were, the other side of the divide, when she describes the work of biblical 'artists' such as Rembrandt or Thomas Mann in a phrase that could very easily be used of the commentators above. Rembrandt and Mann, she suggests, 'transfer their own pre-occupations onto the screen provided by the bare biblical sentence'[201]— a statement that could just as easily be applied to interpreters such as Cheyne, Batten, Allwohn, Eybers, Harper and Kaufmann.

Bal's description, I suggest, does not distinguish between artists and commentators, but unites them. In the next stage of this study I want to explore further the vulnerability of the distinction between art and inter-pretation, fact and fiction, by examining five self-consciously artistic productions of Hosea's marriage. In a study of a range of artistic inter-pretations from the thirteenth-century Conradin manuscript to four twentieth-century readings—Izachak's *A Passion Play in Three Acts* (1929); Simon Ginzburg's 'Ahavat Hoshea' (1935); Isaac Bashevis Singer's 'Gimpel the Fool'; and Norman Nicholson's *A Match for the Devil* (1953)—I want to ask how they differ from, or overlap with, the 'solutions' described above. Do the artistic productions indulge in a greater degree of poetic licence than more sober scholarly approaches or does the difference lie not in content but in the style of presentation?

4.1. *Picturing the Harlot: The Conradin Manuscript*
The illumination to the thirteenth-century Conradin manuscript (see Fig. 1.1) occupies a liminal position between commentary and art. As an artist's impression it is, like the other works of fiction in this section, self-consciously artistic, but on another level it claims, like the commentaries above, to come directly 'from' the text (to which it is connected by a banner, or tendril of decoration).[202] One way of reading this is as a

201. M. Bal, *Reading 'Rembrandt': Beyond the Word–Image Opposition* (Cambridge: Cambridge University Press, 1991), p. 115.

202. As part of the process of preparing this manuscript for publication, I applied to the Walters Art Gallery, Baltimore for an enlarged photograph of the original. It then became clear that the couple were not connected to the text by a 'banner' or 'tendril of decoration' as I first supposed, but that the banner, which emerged from Gomer's side of the picture, was in fact a snake. Seeing the magnified picture altered my reading, for the 'banner' was no longer merely a link connecting the picture to the text, but a serpent, linking Gomer to Eve and her dubious biblical heritage. As well as being a statement about the connection between word and image, the sinister serpent graphically underscores the moral divisions in the picture, between

visual illustration of the critical illusion: the interpretation seems to come from the text, it derives its authority from its seeming dependence on the text, and it sets the parameters in which acceptable readings may operate. As the Conradin text is framed by an illustration, so the text of Hos. 1.2 has, throughout the centuries, been framed by a particular version of Hosea's marriage: the dominant reading, like the picture positioned in the right hand corner of the manuscript, catches the eye and controls the interpretation.

Like the sexual reveries of Midrash Rabbah or T.K. Cheyne's dream of a 'rustic beauty', the illumination of the marriage suggests a mixed response to the figure of the prostitute. At first glance it presents a tableau of grace in which the prophet inclines his head to bless his prodigal wife; man stoops to redeem and to master, and Hosea's stance is paternal and tender, while Gomer functions as the ideal wife. However, Gomer's posture of repentance is also a posture of provocation, and the direction of Hosea's gaze defines Gomer as an object of desire. Guided by the prophet's gaze, the viewer's eyes are fixed on the woman, who averts her eyes in a gesture that may be submissive, but may also be coy and demure.

Dressed in lighter tones, Gomer is the woman in white, like Batten's redeemed angel. Paradoxically, however, the curves of her leg, thigh and stomach are clearly visible beneath the lines of her dress. The figure of the prophet is swathed in folds, but the figure of the woman is clearly visible. Even as the artist situates her in a posture of repentance, he delineates, and seems to admire, her dangerous sexuality.

The Conradin manuscript illustrates the critical tension in commentaries that seek to erase, and also to contemplate, the figure of the prostitute. Although Gomer's head is bent in seeming submission, her lower arm is extended to touch the prophet's cloak. The gesture is loving, sexual, provocative, almost teasing—her lower hand is extended just below the belt. Hosea grasps her arms (undecidedly to restrain her/to hold her) and, like Gomer is clearly smiling. The tableau of forgiveness is also a picture of two lovers, and the woman who takes the initiative provokes censure and a smile. The message is mixed: harlotry is and is not desirable; the woman bows her head and reaches out, submits and refuses to submit.

benevolent prophet and fallen woman, daughter of Eve and forerunner of Christ.

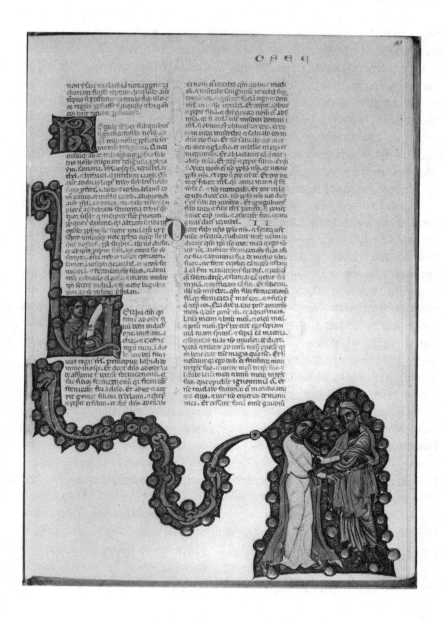

Fig. 1.1. From the *Conradin Bible*, Ms. W 152, fol. 10
(Baltimore, Walters Art Gallery), reprinted from
H.L. Ginsberg, 'Hosea, Book of', *EncJud*, VIII, cols. 1010-25 (1013).

4.2. *Izachak: 'The Marriage of Hosea: A Passion Play in Three Acts*[203]
In the preface to his outrageous 'Passion Play', the pseudonymous
playwright 'Izachak' tries to draw a distinction between his own enterprise and the critical tradition. In an argument not dissimilar to Sontag's
he dismisses the 'pious impiety' and 'sacred sacrilegiousness'[204] of biblical exegesis and insists that drama is a more appropriate medium of
interpretation. He rejects the 'narrow morality'[205] that has been imposed
on the text, but then goes on to promote, like his exegetical predecessors, the 'moral strength' of the text and Hosea's 'moral greatness'.[206]
Even as he dismisses critical solutions to this 'strange anomaly in the
ethics of Hebrew antiquity', he proposes his own 'dramatic solution of
the strange marital life of the prophet'.[207]

To read Hosea correctly, Izachak insists, ironically, the reader must
come with an '*unadulterated* mind'.[208] His own reading, however, is
coloured by the critical consensus, and even the strangest excesses of his
interpretation have their roots in critical tradition. The basis of his distinction between drama and exegesis—that the dramatist uses the imagination to supply 'lacking lights and shadows'[209]—is ironically also the
basis of similarity. Izachak's idealization of Hosea as 'a man who had
come in the floating purple robes of a king and had departed in the
blood-drenched garment of a suffering Christ',[210] is both distinct from,
and very close to, critical anthems to Yhwh's 'suffering servant',[211]
while his characterization of Gomer as the 'fig-cake eater' is only a mild
extension of critical naming-games.

As Izachak's play is based on caricatures, so the play itself is a caricature of the critical tendency to portray the woman as 'other'.
Developing the critical protest, that, as Burroughs puts it, 'If "the
woman is the glory of the man" (1 Cor. 11.7), what [...] glory would
Hosea have had in such a match as this!',[212] Izachak transfers the

203. Izachak, *The Marriage of Hosea: A Passion Play in Three Acts* (New York:
Halcyon, 1929).
 204. Izachak, *A Passion Play*, p. 6.
 205. Izachak, *A Passion Play*, p. 6.
 206. Izachak, *A Passion Play*, p. 5.
 207. Izachak, *A Passion Play*, p. 5.
 208. Izachak, *A Passion Play*, p. 6 (my italics).
 209. Izachak, *A Passion Play*, p. 6.
 210. Izachak, *A Passion Play*, p. 6.
 211. Rowley, *The Marriage of Hosea*, p. 97.
 212. Burroughs, *The Prophecy of Hosea*, p. 8.

revulsion of the critic/playwright to the prophet himself, so that Hosea 'shudders' at the sight of his wife[213] and cannot overcome his 'disgust' for her.[214] Marriage to Gomer is for him a 'slow, torturing death'[215] and the humiliation of the marriage is attributed to his wife's physical, rather than moral ugliness. The imbalance is illustrated in extreme physical contrast: Hosea is beautiful and 'women stare at him in a frenzy of delight',[216] while Gomer is 'not a woman' but a 'monster'.[217]

Izachak's description of Gomer draws on every possible category of the subhuman. She is an animal, a 'wild ape',[218] whose 'hands hang below her knees'[219]; she is unnaturalness personified, whose eyes 'trickle...green and yellow pus'[220] and whose body is a 'monstrous mass'[221]; and she is associated with other-worldly power, as a distorted woman, or 'witch'.[222] Like the most extreme 'other', Caliban in *The Tempest*, she is a creature of abject servility,[223] a deformed slave linked with the dark and supernatural[224] and with the dangerous forces of non-civilization. One of the symptoms of her uncivilized condition is her inability to speak: as Caliban knows only how to curse, so Gomer speaks in ungrammatical, infantile tones, and her proud boast 'I have bought me lovers'[225] suggests that her mind, like her body, is malformed. As Caliban represents the colonizer's fear of the other, so Izachak's Gomer represents the monstrosity of the untamed woman. Both inspire fear and contempt, by defying colonial/patriarchal definitions.

By making the wife of harlotry, a critical eye-sore, into the epitome of

213. Izachak, *A Passion Play*, p. 60.
214. Izachak, *A Passion Play*, p. 109.
215. Izachak, *A Passion Play*, p. 80.
216. Izachak, *A Passion Play*, p. 99.
217. Izachak, *A Passion Play*, p. 103.
218. Izachak, *A Passion Play*, p. 13.
219. Izachak, *A Passion Play*, p. 14.
220. Izachak, *A Passion Play*, p. 14.
221. Izachak, *A Passion Play*, p. 33.
222. Izachak, *A Passion Play*, p. 13.
223. As Caliban pleads, 'Let me lick thy shoe' (*The Tempest*, III.ii.16), so Gomer waits, and is even prepared to pay, for a man that can 'use her' in the cultic rituals (*A Passion Play*, p. 28).
224. Izachak's Gomer is a 'witch',and associates herself with the dark powers of Moloch; Caliban is born of the witch Sycorax and worships the god of the island, Setebos.
225. Izachak, *A Passion Play*, p. 106.

ugliness, Izachak dramatizes the shame of the union and underlines Hosea's heroism. Yet even as he sets up the prophet's magnanimous act, his sense of propriety cannot permit it: Hosea sacrifices his dignity by marrying Gomer in public, but retains his private integrity, for the text insists that he never overcame his disgust for her and never had sexual intercourse. Like Luther's 'dramatic' interpretation of the narrative, Izachak's drama struggles to insist that Hosea is a suffering martyr for allying himself with such a woman, but also that the sexual alliance did not really take place. As Luther insists that the fact that the family was only play-acting only enhanced the prophet's suffering obedience, so Izachak claims that Hosea did, and did not, 'take' a 'wife of harlotry'.

4.3. *Simon Ginzburg: 'Ahavat Hoshea'*

In her analysis of Ginzburg's poem *Ahavat Hoshea*, Janine Strauss argues that although the 160-page epic appears highly inventive, it is in fact based on details from the biblical text and its 'traditional interpretation'.[226] In the space of her article she does not discuss the allusions in detail, but tracing critical themes throughout the poem I suggest that the poet has drawn on diverse and even conflicting critical traditions. The initial meeting of the prophet and his beloved reverberates with echoes of the 'love story' tradition: as in Cheyne's account, Hosea loves his wife at first sight, and loves her 'tenderly and trustingly'.[227] Ginzburg follows the tradition in so far as Gomer betrays Hosea and Hosea is devastated, but he also departs from it to insist that the prophet is not the only victim. In a provocative combination of the love story tradition and critical attempts to redeem the 'wife of harlotry', Ginzburg maintains that Gomer inflicts suffering on Hosea *and* that she is 'fundamentally innocent'.[228] As H.W. Wolff deflects blame from the woman to society, so Ginzburg locates the fault in the parental home and in the symbolism of the text: Gomer is conditioned to act in a certain way because her mother is vain and immoral, but also because she is

---

226. J. Strauss, 'Hosea's Love: A Modern Interpretation', *Judaism* 19 (1970), pp. 226-33 (229). I have been unable to trace the original poem by Ginzburg, or indeed to find any other collections by this poet, as Strauss does not give details of the source from which she is working. My only access to the poem has been through the often extensive sections translated by Strauss, and through Strauss's own analysis.

227. Strauss, 'Hosea's Love', p. 227.

228. Strauss, 'Hosea's Love', p. 227.

constrained by her symbolic function as an אֵשֶׁת זְנוּנִים.[229]

By combining the love story tradition, which vilifies Gomer, and the redemptive tradition, which excuses her, Ginzburg creates a relationship that is psychologically complex, and that develops, rather than dissipates, the tensions implicit in the marriage of a prophet with a promiscuous woman. Like Charles Hauret, however, he also provides relief from the lack of marital harmony in the perfect pairing between signifier and signified, and intricately interweaves the religious apostasy of Israel and Hosea's private agony. The timing of the poem reinforces the aptness of the metaphor: having watched 'a night of festive fires' to Baal—which he interprets as 'prostitution' and 'shame',[230]—Hosea then discovers that Gomer (his betrothed) has soiled her purity when she was very young. In his ensuing dialogue with the deity the two infidelities intersect, as in a 'whisper/Like a heart beat' God asks, 'Is your pain deeper/ Than the pain in God's heart?'[231]

As the rabbis and the targumists adjusted and diluted Gomer's character, so Ginzburg dilutes the force of Yhwh's 'command'. His God does not issue crude commands but speaks in the soft accents of dawning revelation, and defends his purpose with a detailed and sensitive explanation. Critical justifications of Hos. 1.2 are put into the mouth of the deity, and because Yhwh speaks in the tone of his twentieth-century readers and critics, fear is alleviated of the stark arbitrariness of his command. The impropriety of the command is diluted by Yhwh's rationality and Hosea's enthusiasm:

> A flash of lightening seemed to lighten his dark path:
> It was the work of him who is perfect in knowledge!
> Gomer was a sign for the land,
> She would be a symbol, a model for the people![232]

Ahavat Hoshea is full of intertextual references and critical motifs, developed almost beyond the point of recognition. The motif of 'empathy' between God and Hosea is developed into lengthy rebuke of the prophet by the deity:

> When a rot settled in Ephraim's tree,
> Did you try to cure it?

229. As Strauss points out, 'She does not betray Hosea because she loves another man, but because she is destined by God to betray him' ('Hosea's Love', p. 228).
230. Ginzburg, *Ahavat Hoshea*, III.655.
231. Ginzburg, *Ahavat Hoshea*, III.633-34.
232. Ginzburg, *Ahavat Hoshea*, III.658-62.

> But as soon as the harm starts reaching you,
> Your soul can no longer
> Contain its grief.[233]

Even Ginzburg's most idiosyncratic inventions, such as *Hidlai*, the Machiavellian lover, whose black eyes smoulder like embers, can be traced back to critical 'mythology'. Reading between the lines, *Hidlai*, from the root חדל, is the perfect partner for Gomer (from the root גמר): 'end' meets 'completion', in a powerful extension of Rabbi Judah's interpretation that 'Gomer' signifies the termination of Israel's power.[234]

4.4. *Isaac Bashevis Singer: 'Gimpel the Fool'*[235]

As the title implies, Singer's 'Gimpel the Fool' draws on the talmudic tradition of the foolish prophet. Gimpel's confession to the reader that he is known as 'imbecile, donkey and fool', but that 'the last' name has 'stuck',[236] is the first clue that he has another alias, the prophet Hosea.[237] Credulous and docile, 'Gimpel' is duped into marriage with the notorious 'Elka' (whom he believes to be a 'virgin pure')[238] but is puzzled to find a crib among their wedding presents. Though she 'swears at [him] and curses, [he] cannot get enough of her',[239] and even when he discovers her in bed with another man, he 'does not have it in [him] to be really angry'.[240]

In his analysis of 'Gimpel the Fool and the Book of Hosea' Thomas Hennings claims that the symbolism of Singer's narrative is the same as that of the biblical text, and thus that Gimpel is 'godlike',[241] but to assume that Singer is simply retelling the original story is to underestimate the sophistication of the narrative. *Gimpel* is in fact a double displacement—Singer's retelling of a story retold in the Talmud—and the

---

233. Ginzburg, *Ahavat Hoshea*, III.645-50.

234. *Pes.* 87a.

235. I.B. Singer, 'Gimpel the Fool', in *Gimpel the Fool and Other Tales* (Harmondsworth: Penguin, 1981), pp. 9-24.

236. Singer, 'Gimpel', p. 9.

237. Another clue is that Gimpel is a baker—an allusion to theories that Hosea was a baker, due to 'numerous references to ovens and baking' in his book (Paterson, 'Hosea', p. 398).

238. Singer, 'Gimpel', p. 11.

239. Singer, 'Gimpel', p. 15.

240. Singer, 'Gimpel', p. 17.

241. T. Hennings, 'Singer's "Gimpel the Fool" and the Book of Hosea', *JNT* 13 (1983), pp. 11-19 (12).

author both extends and interrogates features of his rabbinic source. By casting Gimpel as the narrator, he provides some supremely comic moments[242] and makes 'the prophet', as the Talmud does, into an object of fun. Yet the focalization of events through the eyes of the fool not only enhances the comedy of the situation, but questions it, by introducing an element of pathos and empathy into the reader's relationship with the narrator. Since Gimpel's point of view is the only perspective that the reader is familiar with, she tends to see things his way and can never feel entirely alienated from him. The sense of superior knowledge and distance, so essential to comedy, is both enhanced and questioned, as the reader is allowed to listen to Gimpel's secret thoughts and enter into the mind of the 'fool'.

Using Gimpel as narrator enables Singer to incorporate another strand of the critical tradition, the dream–reality debate. Critics have variously interpreted Gimpel's strange observations that 'Whatever doesn't really happen is dreamed at night'[243] and that 'the world is an entirely imaginary world...only once removed from the real world'[244] as an attack on Cartesian philosophy, or an argument for ethical relativism, but in my opinion it is more likely that the author is subtly incorporating ideas from Maimonides. The narrator's uncertainty illustrates the credulity of the 'fool' but it also snatches away the reader's certainty about the status of events. Maimonides' argument frames the text and creates a general sense of disorientation, for if the narrator himself is unsure of where the boundaries between dream/fiction lie, how can the reader be sure about the 'reality' of the events he narrates? Gimpel provides a clue to reading this riddling text when he sets himself up as the ultimate unreliable narrator and admits that he often 'spin[s] yarns—improbable things that could never have happened—about devils, magicians wind-mills and the like'.[245] If Gimpel tells stories and is prone to 'hallucinations',[246] how are we to read the story of his marriage to Elka, and how does this reflect on the reality of the 'original' narrative?

Singer's text is full of cryptic allusions and references to Jewish

---

242. Gimpel's comic obsession with the violent Elka is enhanced by the use of the first person: 'I adored her every word. She gave me bloody wounds though' (Singer, 'Gimpel', p. 15).

243. Singer, 'Gimpel', p. 23.

244. Singer, 'Gimpel', p. 24.

245. Singer, 'Gimpel', p. 23.

246. Singer, 'Gimpel', p. 17.

tradition. When he tries to retract his petition for divorce, Gimpel discovers the sheer volume of debate on the question of remarriage to a harlot. As the rabbis dispute his case for months, he confides to the reader that he 'hadn't realised that there could be so much erudition about a matter like this'[247] and so comments on the critical obsession with the morality of Hos. 1.2 and Hos. 3.1. Finally Gimpel is saved by the Yanover rabbi who finds an 'obscure reference'[248] in Maimonides that favours him. The Yanover rabbi can use Maimonides in such a way as to endorse Gimpel's return to Elka; the irony, however, is that Maimonides himself would only countenance such a liaison in a dream.

4.5. *Norman Nicholson: 'A Match for the Devil'*[249]
Although Gimpel is a fool, Elka is by no means a heroine but a comic character in her own right. Her mouth is 'on a hinge',[250] she eats excessively and is prone to violence—to redeem her, Gimpel, like L.W. Batten, must clutch at straws, and the only excuse he can suggest is that 'women are long on hair and short on sense'.[251] Norman Nicholson's[252] Hosea, like Gimpel, is also a 'fusspot and a fool',[253] a 'lame donkey'[254] and a 'weak' character,[255] but in his play *A Match for the Devil*, which was first performed at the Edinburgh Festival in 1953, Nicholson takes the task of improving Gomer's character much more seriously. As in Izachak's 'Passion Play', the tension of the relationship is expressed in the characterization and physical appearance of husband

---

247. Singer, 'Gimpel', p. 17.

248. Singer, 'Gimpel', p. 18.

249. N. Nicholson, *A Match for the Devil* (London: Faber & Faber, 1953).

250. Singer, 'Gimpel', p. 13.

251. Singer, 'Gimpel', p. 17.

252. Norman Nicholson (1914–87) was described in a rather patronizing obituary in *The Times* as 'the most gifted English Christian provincial poet of his century'. Despite the two rather limiting qualifiers ('Christian' and 'provincial'), Nicholson was, in fact, quite well known, having published six collections of poetry (*Five Rivers* [1944], *Rock Face* [1948], *The Pot Geranium* [1954], *No Star on the Way Back* [1967], *A Local Habitation* [1972], and *Sea to the West* [1981]). His poetry focused on the small Cumberland industrial town in which he grew up; he also wrote a critical biography of William Cowper. *A Match For the Devil* is, to my knowledge, the only play he ever wrote. It was first performed at the Edinburgh Festival in 1953.

253. Nicholson, *A Match*, p. 48.

254. Nicholson, *A Match*, p. 51.

255. Nicholson, *A Match*, p. 55.

and wife, but in this case the bias is reversed and the weight of hyperbole is in Gomer's favour.

The characterization in Nicholson's play is an inversion of Izachak's: Hosea is a 'scraggy old cockerel'[256] and a 'muddle-minded old badger',[257] while Gomer 'swill[s] the very flagstones with a bucketful of light'.[258] Though he appeals to the tradition of empathy between the prophet and the deity, Nicholson also appears to parody it, and Hosea's claim that he has 'felt the anguish in God's heart, the *divine angina*'[259] seems to follow, and comically deflate, critical ideas that the prophet entered into the divine heart. Ultimately it is Gomer, not Hosea, who occupies the moral high ground and who has to teach her 'lanky, shanky, comical, cranky, blind-eyed blockhead of a husband'[260] the true meaning of forgiveness. Radically, she finds Hosea's (and by implication Yhwh's) concept of forgiveness inadequate, and Nicholson begins to move outside the parameters set by the critical tradition in a critique of the ideology of the text, and particularly of the role given to the אֵשֶׁת זְנוּנִים.[261]

5. *Concluding Comments*

A close reading of the texts in sections 2, 3 and 4 suggests that the divisions between the three sections are largely artificial. The same stories and solutions are repeated throughout, and the only variation is in the style and register in which the stories are told. The tale of the 'bad woman', for example, is told with different emphases that reflect the readers' contrasting contexts: the rabbis mock the 'cheap' woman who can be purchased for two cakes of figs; Cheyne laments this 'lily torn and trampled in the mire', and Izachak depicts Gomer as an extreme caricature, a misshapen monster or repulsive witch. The rabbinic reading reflects a tradition in which words 'echo and re-echo', and in which the 'underlying, offbeat',[262] punning meaning is valued; Cheyne's reading

256. Nicholson, *A Match*, p. 34.

257. Nicholson, *A Match*, p. 40.

258. Nicholson, *A Match*, p. 32.

259. Nicholson, *A Match*, p. 58 (my italics).

260. Nicholson, *A Match*, p. 75.

261. For a more detailed analysis of how Nicholson moves outside the theological tradition, see Chapter 4, 'Gomer's Marriage', §2.5.

262. This description of the workings of Talmud is taken from W.G. Braude, 'Open Thou My Eyes', in A. Corre (ed.), *Understanding the Talmud* (New York:

evokes the sentimentalism and melodrama that was in vogue in the mid to late nineteenth century, while Izachak poses an alternative to 'scholarly' interpretation and deliberately strains poetic licence to its very limits.

A simple comparison of interpretations demonstrates Fish's claim that the reader, like a sentence, is 'never not in a context'.[263] The fact that the reader's context and theological orientation can often be discerned from his reading is particularly threatening to nineteenth- and twentieth-century commentary because, unlike fictional and pre-critical readings, it bases its authority on claims to objectivity and even historicity. This study has shown that critical interpretation clearly blurs with the fictional and pre-critical interpretations against which it endeavours to define itself. There is obvious continuity, for example, between Batten's attempt to restore Gomer to 'angelic' status and Nicholson's description of a woman who 'swill[s] the very flagstones with a bucketful of light':[264] both swathe the figure of the prostitute in an other-worldly aura, and the only difference is that Batten dilutes his story of redemption with rationalistic phrases such as 'naturally' and 'I think we would all agree'.

As the difference between scholarly discourse and storytelling is sustained at the level of lexis, so the distinction between critical and pre-critical scholarship is largely an effect of vocabulary and convention. When he claims that Gomer is essentially virtuous but has been led astray by cultic practices, Wolff is effectively repeating Luther's argument, but his erudite notes on the historical 'Canaanite cult', and the moderate and measured tone of the language, provide a striking contrast to Luther's polemic. Whereas Luther overtly expresses his aversion to the idea that a prophet's wife might be harlotrous, Wolff does not foreground his disagreement with the text at this point, and his response is far less reactionary, and far more convincing. Critical language, as opposed to Reformation polemic, is language in which one hides oneself, but whether the commentator openly declares that he does not want Gomer to be harlotrous, or constructs a complex quasi-historical excuse for her, the response, I suggest, is essentially the same.

With the exception of the Talmud, Peter Damian (and possibly Allwohn's psychological and Cheyne's tragical readings), all of the

Ktav Publishing House, 1975), pp. 55-61 (56).
263. Fish, 'Normal circumstances', p. 637.
264. Nicholson, *A Match*, p. 32.

responses in sections 2 and 3 attempt to dilute, rather than exploit, the mismatch of the marriage. The whole impetus of criticism appears to be to tame the טְמֵאָה until she becomes a creature befitting a biblical text: as Cheyne beautifies her physically as a 'rustic beauty of Northern Israel', so most commentators beautify her morally and give her a new religiously marketable image. The self-consciously literary approaches, in contrast, tend to emphasize the promiscuity of the 'wife of harlotry': Singer's Elka is notorious and deceitful; Izachak's Gomer *begs* to play a part in the fertility ritual; and Nicholson's Gomer is a defiant cult prostitute who audaciously questions the whole ideological basis of the biblical text. Even when they are written by an openly Christian poet like Nicholson, the fictional responses seem far less concerned with redeeming Gomer's reputation than their critical counterparts, and my own reading, outlined below, is a continuation of this more marginal, but to my mind more provocative, response to 'Hosea's Marriage'.

5.1. *Rereading Hosea 1.2: Yhwh's 'irreverent wit'*

Is the covenant a tether, or a chain, or *living intercourse?*[265]

In order to sanctify the text, many critics claim that the marriage is 'only a metaphor' (or a 'dream' or 'allegory'). Another way of reading the marriage is, however, as a combination that is *like* a metaphor, or more extremely, like a metaphysical conceit. Metaphor is the conjunction of elements that are, and are not, appropriate partners, but in the metaphysical conceit the inappropriateness of the union is foregrounded. As Samuel Johnson famously complained, in metaphysical poetry 'two heterogeneous elements' are 'yoked by violence together': the pairing is disjunctive, awkward and highly precarious, and represents for the poet a 'triumph of wit'.

John Donne is perhaps the most audacious of the group of poets whose images consist of 'paired antagonists locked together'.[266] In 'The Flea' he draws an elaborate analogy between sex and flea bites (and by analogy between the strained copula of his metaphor and the unlikelihood of copulation), while in 'A Valediction: Forbidding Mourning' he relentlessly pursues a perverse analogy between lovers and a pair of compasses. His imagery offends not only because it is logically audacious

---

265. Heschel, *The Prophets*, p. 50.
266. J. Carey, *John Donne: Life, Mind and Art* (London: Faber & Faber, 1981), p. 264.

but because it is bawdy, sexual, and manifestly 'un-poetic'. Most extremely, he makes uneasy bedfellows of sex and religion by, for example, canonizing his lovers[267] and entreating God to 'ravish' him.[268]

Because of his bold disrespect for the sanctity of logic and religion, Donne is accused of 'irreverent wit'.[269] A similar accusation could be levelled at Yhwh, who in Hos. 1.2 arranges an audacious coupling between a prophet and a 'woman of harlotry'. The marriage, which is literally a 'marriage made in heaven', not only subverts idealistic notions of harmony and apropriateness, but brings the most extreme opposites into conjunction. Hosea's only defining feature is that he receives words from Yhwh; Gomer's only defining feature is that she has relationships with other men. One is the voice of orthodox religion, the other the personification of sexual immorality; the stark and minimal characterization means that their marriage is a simple and resonant clash between two polarized symbols and mutually exclusive world views.

Like the awkward conjunction of the wolf and the lamb in Isa. 11.6 and 65.25, the marriage is an outrageous mismatch with dangerous implications. The lying down of the lion with the lamb is dangerous only for the lamb; the lying down of the prophet with the promiscuous woman poses a threat to the entire edifice of Old Testament morality. The Yhwh in Hosea 1–3 seems disturbingly and radically different from the Yhwh who, in Leviticus, enforces a rigid and eternal separation 'between holiness and the common, between the unclean and the clean' (Lev. 10.9-10).[270] The Hebrew Bible, which endeavours to preserve distinct categories and enforce sexual morality, problematically embraces a text which disturbs those standards and produces the most extreme metaphor or 'category mistake'.

267. Donne, 'The Canonization' (1633), in C.A. Patrides (ed.), *The Complete English Poems of John Donne* (London: Dent, 1985), p. 57.

268. Donne, Sonnet 14, 'The Holy Sonnets' (1633), in Patrides (ed.), *The Complete English Poems of John Donne*, p. 443.

269. J.L. Winny, *A Preface to Donne* (London: Longman, 1981), p. 132.

270. Although the Pentateuch offers no specific injunction against marriage to a prostitute, it appears that Yhwh in Hosea and Yhwh in the Pentateuch work on a radically different basis. The conflict becomes more acute in Hos. 3.1, where Yhwh commands Hosea to love an adulterous woman again, in direct contravention of the Law of the Sotah in Num. 5. According to Numbers, the woman suspected of adultery must submit to the test of the bitter waters, and if found guilty must die. Hos. 3.1, in contrast, refers to a proven adulteress, but commands the prophet to love, rather than to stone her.

The sense that Yhwh is transgressing his own standards of purity and separation is a mute, rather than a moot, point in Hosea criticism. Few critics discuss their anxieties about this text in detail, but reveal the basis of those anxieties by reworking the text in a particular way. The preceding analysis suggests that commentary attempts to reinstate 'platonic' standards—in both senses of the word. The assumption behind most critical revisions of the marriage is that the text should uphold logical categories and preserve a proper distance between antitheses, and that it should ensure that the only relationship between a man of God and such a woman is a platonic (asexual) one.

The idea that Yhwh, like a metaphysical poet, forges bizarre and dangerous liaisons, foregrounds two aspects of the marriage metaphor that have traditionally been repressed. Critics have insisted on logical and sexual propriety: as Batten and Hengstenberg insist, a prophet must be considered 'reasonably consistent',[271] and Yhwh himself cannot act 'arbitrarily',[272] while Lippl declares that 'the marriage between Yhwh and Israel could not be regarded as a sexual relationship, but...only as a legal relationship without any sensual traits'. To regard the marriage as a legal covenant, he adds, mitigates the image's 'dangerous character'.[273]

The image of the metaphysical conceit recaptures the audacity of the marriage metaphor, not only by foregrounding the transgression of categories and the threat of sexuality, but by highlighting the precariousness of the prophet–prostitute, and by analogy divine–human, relationship. Much has been written on the analogy between 'marriage' and 'covenant', but commentators tend to focus on marriage as an abstract ideal, a love relationship, rather than as the strained coupling presented in this text. Even critics like Walter Brueggemann,[274] who emphasize the

271. Batten, 'Hosea's Message', p. 261.

272. E.W. Hengstenberg, *Christology of the Old Testament* (trans. T. Mayer; Edinburgh: 1954), I, p. 180.

273. J. Lippl, 'Der Prophet Osee übersetzt und erklärt', in F. Feldman and H. Herkeene (eds.), *Die heilige Schrift des Alten Testaments, übersetzt und erklärt in Verbindung mit Fachgelehrten* (Bonn: Peter Hanstein, 1937), pp. 7-84 (39, 'Geschlechtsbeziehung, sondern analog dem Bundesverhältnis, nur als Rechtverhältnis gefasst und nicht mit sinnlichen Zügen belastet werden. Damit hatte die Vorstellung ihre gefährlichen Charakter eingebüsst').

274. Brueggemann writes, 'By the time of the eighth-century prophets, it was apparent to those who really understood the covenant that the essential dimension of the contemporary Yhwh–Israel covenant was its brokenness' (*Tradition For Crisis: A Study in Hosea* [Richmond: John Knox Press, 1968], p. 89).

brokenness of the covenant/marriage relationship, resist the possibility that on one level this text might be saying that Yhwh's relationship to Israel is as tenuous, and as liable to disintegration, as the relationship between a prophet and a promiscuous woman. In the oxymoron 'wife of harlotry', the inevitability of disintegration is foregrounded: Yhwh, like Donne, not only 'strains relationships to the point where they seem about to crack',[275] but foregrounds their vulnerability.

275. Winny, *A Preface*, p. 95.

Chapter 2

'SIGN LANGUAGE': A SEMIOTIC ANALYSIS OF HOSEA 1–3

> Criticism is the pursuit of signs, in that critics, whatever their persuasion,
> are incited by the prospect of grasping, comprehending, capturing in their
> prose, evasive signifying structures.[1]

Yhwh's command לֵךְ קַח-לְךָ אֵשֶׁת זְנוּנִים is, as the previous chapter demonstrated, generally interpreted in terms of 'love', 'romance', 'morality' and 'immorality', but this interpretative focus has eclipsed and marginalized another angle of approach. In 1913 C.H. Toy claimed that 'In Hosea 2–9, the wife seems to be introduced simply for the purpose of accounting for the children; symbolical names for the children were desired, and the natural preliminary was marriage'.[2] The MT, significantly, has nothing to say about Hosea's love or the question of morality, and gives only one rationale for taking a 'wife of harlotry': 'for the land commits great harlotry by forsaking the Lord'. The only motivation given for the marriage is starkly pragmatic: Hosea must be a husband so that he can be a father, and Gomer is conscripted as a signifier of 'idolatry' and as a source of future signs.

The action of taking a wife of harlotry is not overtly ethical or romantic, but it is overtly semiotic: that is, it focuses on the generation of meaning and the production of signs. Hosea 1.2 is one of a series of overtly semiotic actions, which include the conception and the naming of the three children in ch. 1, and the purchase and subsequent confinement of the adulteress in ch. 3. In this analysis I want to examine the way the text creates and uses signs, and to look in detail at the strange and distinctive sign-language that is produced. My analysis of the prophetic signs is based on theories from the diverse and even disparate field of semiotics, which I shall also be examining in detail in this chapter.

1. J. Culler, *The Pursuit of Signs: Semiotics, Literature, Deconstruction* (London: Routledge & Kegan Paul, 1981), p. vii.
2. C.H. Toy, 'Note on Hosea 1–3', *JBL* 32 (1913), pp. 75-79 (76).

This analysis is divided into four sections. In the first I briefly distinguish between the type of approach I am adopting and conventional perspectives on Hosea 1–3 using Roland Barthes's distinction between 'readerly' and 'writerly' responses to texts. In the second section I provide a summary of 'semiotics': I give a brief account of the history of the field and suggest some potential points of intersection between semiotics and biblical studies, and then go on to sketch some essential principles by outlining the key ideas of five major contributors. To represent the breadth of the discipline, I look at the work of Ferdinand de Saussure and Charles Sanders Peirce (the so-called founders of semiotics), the 'Prague School' of theatrical semiotics (in which semiotics and structuralism intersect) and Roland Barthes and Julia Kristeva (who could be classed as poststructuralist semioticians). In the third section I propose a semiotic analysis of Hosea 1–3 and consider various aspects of the prophetic sign-language, and in the fourth and final section I draw these different strands of analysis together.

1. *Readerly and Writerly Texts*

In *S/Z* Roland Barthes distinguishes between two types of texts: the 'readerly' (*lisible*) and the 'writerly' (*scriptible*). The readerly text is a classic text: it does not disturb the reader but reinforces her expectations and gratifies the desire for a unified meaning and narrative closure. The writerly text, in contrast, is so-called because it enlists the reader 'no longer [as] a consumer' but as a 'producer', or co-writer, of the text.[3] The readerly text 'tightly controls the play of signification by subordinating everything to transcendental meaning',[4] but the writerly text incorporates 'multiple voices' and 'different wavelengths' that are liable to 'dissolve' into one another, and 'shifts from one point of view to another, without warning'.[5]

Although Barthes defines 'readerly' and 'writerly' as innate qualities of the text, he suggests that, in practice, these qualities are also an effect of the reader's approach. *S/Z* is a very writerly reading not of an audaciously plural, postmodern text, but of a readerly classic, Balzac's

---

3. R. Barthes, *S/Z* (trans. R. Miller; Oxford: Basil Blackwell, 1990), p. 4.
4. K. Silverman, *The Subject of Semiotics* (Oxford: Oxford University Press, 1983), p. 243.
5. Barthes, *S/Z*, p. 174.

Sarrasine.[6] Barthes implies that a readerly text results from the assumption that 'the *author* goes from signified to signifier, from content to form, from idea to text, from passion to expression; and [that] in contrast, the *critic* goes in the other direction [and] works back from signifiers to signified'.[7] The process is described in metaphors of delivery and discernment of the divine voice: the readerly text is 'like a pregnant female, replete with signifieds which criticism cannot fail to deliver',[8] or the 'author is a god (his place of origin is the signified)' and the critic is 'the priest whose task it is to decipher the writing of the god'.[9]

Critical approaches to the book of Hosea, and to the Hebrew Bible in general, have, according to Barthes' definition, been 'readerly'. As Peter Miscall observes, images have usually been treated as subordinate to meaning and as the container for contents, and this reflects a 'powerful Western tradition that privileges mind over body, intellect over imagination, concept over form' (and signified over signifier).[10] Studies of Hosea have focused on what the text means rather than how it means, yet even as they present a unified message for the text (that Yhwh tells Israel to abandon her apostasy), some critics betray discomfort with the signifying structure and suggest that it obfuscates as much as it expounds. H.W. Wolff laments the lack of coherent allegory;[11] J.L. Mays terms Jezreel a sign of 'tantalizing opaqueness',[12] and Renaud notes the 'va-et-vient constant du signifiant au signifié' ('the constant to-ing and fro-ing of the signifier [Gomer] and signified [Israel]')[13] in ch. 2. Andersen and Freedman and McKeating note how the focus shifts

6. Barbara Johnson explores the tension between Barthes's choice of text and his distinction between 'classic' and 'readerly' texts in 'The Critical Difference', *Diacritics* 8 (1978), pp. 2-9 (4).

7. Barthes, *S/Z*, p. 174.

8. Barthes, *S/Z*, p. 201.

9. Barthes, *S/Z*, p. 174.

10. P.D. Miscall, 'Isaiah: The Labyrinth of Images', in S.D. Moore and D. Jobling (eds.), *Poststructuralism as Exegesis* (Semeia 54; Atlanta: Scholars Press, 1991), pp. 103-21 (103).

11. H.W. Wolff, *A Commentary on the Book of Hosea* (trans. G. Stansell; Herm; Philadelphia: Fortress Press, 1974), p. 33.

12. J.L. Mays, *Hosea: A Commentary* (OTL; London: SCM Press, 1969), p. 27.

13. B. Renaud, 'Osée 1–3: 'Analyse diachronique et lecture synchronique: problèmes de méthode', *RevScRel* 57 (1983), pp. 249-60 (256).

uncomfortably between the divine and the human levels, sometimes blurring the link so that it is impossible to tell whether Yhwh or Hosea is speaking,[14] sometimes stretching the link to the extent that 'the allegory breaks down'.[15]

Critical asides suggest that it is difficult to read Hosea 1–3 simply as an allegory to be decoded. The text begins with the promise of a read-erly text and suggests that just as the דְּבַר יְהוָה has been communicated to Hosea, so it will be transferred to the reader: the noun is singular, sug-gesting a unified word which will be revealed to the audience by the prophet. In order to impart this message the prophet is instructed to marry a 'wife of harlotry' who gives birth to three infant signifiers. The text at this point becomes literally a 'pregnant woman' replete with meanings and the promise of delivery, but the child-signs, rather than being a clear communication of a divine message, are complex signs, with various levels of symbolism. Jezreel, for example, has at least four meanings: it is a geographical location, a moment in history, an invoca-tion 'May El sow!', and a pun on the name of Israel (יִזְרְעֶאל/יִשְׂרָאֵל). Lo-Ruhamah and Lo-Ammi are potentially more transparent—until the names are inverted in Hos. 2.3. Is Jezreel a promise of fertility, or a threat of punishment; is Israel loved, and a people, or is she not loved, and disowned? The inversion of the names suggests that Hosea 1–3 can be read as a writerly text that, according to Barthes's definition, 'shifts from one point of view to another, without warning'.[16]

Although the critical tradition testifies that it is possible to read this text as a tightly controlled process of signification, directed towards a single, transcendent meaning, comments that the text is fragmentary and the sign-language disjointed suggest that it is possible to see in Hosea 1–3 the symptoms of a writerly, as well as a readerly, text. A writerly text involves multiple voices and makes it difficult to discern who is speak-ing: critics confess that particularly in ch. 2 they find it hard to dis-

---

14. Andersen and Freedman observe that 'some of the ideas [in chapter 2] apply mainly to Hosea and Gomer; some apply best to Yhwh and Israel; many make good sense in both sets', while McKeating argues that 'the prophet is thinking simultane-ously of his unfaithful wife and the unfaithful Israel, and his language is appropriate sometimes to the one, sometimes to the other' (F.I. Andersen and D.N. Freedman, *Hosea: A New Translation with Introduction and Commentary* [AB; New York: Doubleday, 1980], p. 220; H. McKeating, *The Books of Amos, Hosea and Micah* [Cambridge: Cambridge University Press, 1971], p. 83).

15. Andersen and Freedman, *Hosea*, p. 242.

16. Barthes, *S/Z*, p. 174.

entangle the voice of Yhwh from the voice of Hosea and to separate the realm of the signifier from the realm of the signified. The writerly text foregrounds heterogeneity: Hosea 1 not only pairs a prophet and a prostitute but creates an uneasy link between a domestic microcosm and a national macrocosm, God and man, and infant signifiers and giant concepts. The writerly text foregrounds the process of meaning manufacture and demonstrates *how* the text signifies: Hosea 1 focuses on the taking of the woman and the conception of signs, so staging the elaborate process by which the meanings in this text are made.

In analyses of biblical texts, the role of the critic as priest, deciphering the writing of the god, takes on a particular significance. Theologically orientated readings of this text often overlook the level of the signifier in the rush to get to the real meaning, prophetic revelation, but in this literary reading I shall be adopting a different kind of critical project, which seeks, as Culler suggests, to capture evasive signifying structures. My approach is an inversion of the critical tradition in that it privileges signifier over signified, and focuses on how, rather than what, the text means. The theory behind this strategy is the theory of semiotics, which I explain in detail below.

2. Theories of Semiotics

2.1. Semiotics: The Evolution of a 'Discipline'

At the end of Locke's *Essay concerning Human Understanding*, space was left, proleptically, for '*Semeiotike*, the doctrine of signs', which, alongside *Physike* (natural philosophy) and *Praktike* (ethics), would comprise the third branch of the sciences. The 'business' of *Semeiotike* would be 'to consider the nature of signs the mind makes use of for the understanding of things, or conveying its knowledge to others',[17] but it was not until the turn of the twentieth century that this 'business' truly got under way. The space in Locke's essay was filled by the work of Charles Sanders Peirce (1829–1914) and Ferdinand de Saussure (1857–1913), which took place virtually simultaneously on opposite sides of the Atlantic, and was largely published posthumously in the early twentieth century. The manifestos for *la sémiologie* and 'semiotics' are widely known:

17. J. Locke, *An Essay Concerning Human Understanding* (London: J.M. Dent & Sons, 1947), IV, Chapter xxi, §§2–4, p. 354.

A science that studies the life of signs in society is conceivable; it would be a part of social psychology and consequently of general psychology; I shall call it *semiology* (from the Greek *semeion,* 'sign'). Semiology would show what constitutes signs, what laws govern them. Since the science does not yet exist, no-one can say what it would be; but it has a right to existence, a place staked out in advance.[18]

Logic, in its general sense, is, as I believe I have shown, only another name for the *semiotic*, the 'quasi-necessary' or formal doctrine of signs. By describing the doctrine as 'quasi-necessary,' or formal, I mean that we observe the characters of such signs as we know, and from such an observation, by a process which I will not object to naming Abstraction, we are led to statements, eminently fallible, and therefore in one sense by no means necessary, as to what *must* be the characters of all signs used by a 'scientific' intelligence, that is to say by an intelligence capable of learning by experience.[19]

On one level Saussure and Peirce created Locke's anticipated project, but on another level they, like Locke, anticipated a discipline whose existence was yet to be realized. Ironically, their descriptions of semiotics as a study awaiting its ultimate realization coincide with the current state of the discipline in the 1990s, in which semiotics is receding into obscurity, and, in the field of literary theory, now exerts only a limited and minor influence.

The history of semiotics is a fluctuating one: the discipline thrived in the 1940s (in the work of the Prague Circle) and in the 1970s (which saw the first Congress of the Association of Semiotic Studies and the launch of new journals such as *Semiotica*), but it faded into relative obscurity in the 1980s and 1990s. The discipline suffered because of internal inconsistencies and anomalies in its reception, and, more than any other branch of literary theory, was marginalized by being affiliated to, and absorbed by, other theories. Since it is based, like structuralism, on Saussure's distinction between the signifier and the signified, semiotics has habitually been seen as a subsidiary of structuralism rather than a discipline in its own right. With the advent of deconstruction it has also

18. F. de Saussure, *Course in General Linguistics* (ed. C. Bally and A. Sechehaye; trans. W. Baskin; Glasgow: Collins, 1974), p. 16. Unless otherwise specified this is the edition that I shall be referring to in discussions of Saussure's *Course*.

19. C.S. Peirce, *The Writings of Charles Sanders Peirce*. II. *Collected Papers* (ed. C. Hartshorne, P. Weiss and A.W. Burks; 8 vols.; Cambridge, MA: Harvard University Press, 1931–58), p. 227.

been reduced to a preface to poststructuralism, and has been seen reductively, merely as the basis for Derrida's 'grammatology'.

Semiotics is not only the victim of critical fashions and misconceptions but has also suffered from its own internal flaws. As it has paradoxically been absorbed into structuralism *and* poststructuralism, semiotics has also been too ambitious, and too trivial, in its scope. On one hand it has declared a kind of cultural imperialism, claiming 'everything' as its object of study; on the other, it has, as Barthes observes, been extraordinarily preoccupied with 'codes of no more than slight interest, such as the Highway Code'.[20] As Umberto Eco wryly observes, 'A discipline...[that] declares itself as concerned with the entire universe (and nothing else) is playing a risky game'[21]—but ironically, critics like Eco, who recognise the dangers of claims to omnidisciplinarity, are capable of making the opposite mistake. Eco, for example, devotes a whole book to the semiotic study of canal lock mechanisms,[22] a subject which is of little interest to readers and critics, and is more adequately explored by mechanical engineers.

Eco's preoccupation with an analysis of electronic impulses in the 'Watergate Model' betrays another weakness of semiotics: as a discipline it has aspired to be over-disciplined and to achieve quasi-scientific status. Critics have, revealingly, attempted to encapsulate signification using mathematical formulae, but, rather than producing a single formula, they have produced various definitions that range from Saussure's definition of the relationship between signifier and signified (Sr/sd) to Hjelmslev's description of the relationship (R) between the expression plane (E) and the content plane (C): (ERC). Any mathematical representation of the ambiguous sign seems condemned, as Barthes observes, to a certain kind of 'clumsiness',[23] and also reveals what formulaic expression attempts to obscure. The sheer diversity of formulae foregrounds the fact that the relationship between the signifier and the signified is arbitrary (since the signified 'sign' can apparently be represented by any number of formulaic signifiers). It also reveals the inevitable operation of connotative meanings, even as semioticians try to screen these meanings out by confining the sign to a denotative definition. The use of

20. R. Barthes, *Elements of Semiology* (trans. A. Lavers and C. Smith; New York: Hill & Wang, 1968), pp. 9-10.

21. U. Eco, *A Theory of Semiotics* (London: Macmillan, 1977), p. 7.

22. Eco, *A Theory of Semiotics*.

23. Barthes, *Elements of Semiology*, p. 48.

mathematical formula does not have a purely denotative function, and, as semioticians are probably quite aware, it is also an attempt to equate semiotic study and science, and to elevate the study of signs by implying that it is empirical. Formulaic definitions of the sign are not an erasure of connotative meanings but an expression of them: ERC, for example, means denotatively 'the relationship between the expression plane E and the content plane C', but it also means, connotatively, 'semiotics is a science'.

Verbal definitions of signification, like their mathematical counterparts, also foreground the plurality that many semioticians seek to deny. The fact that a signifier can gesture to many different signifieds (and vice versa) is demonstrated in conflicting interpretations of the terms *sign* and *symbol*. In the writings of C.S. Peirce the symbol is specifically non-analogical, while in popular concepts of symbol, and the definition given by Hegel, its analogical status is essential. In the semiotic theory of Julia Kristeva the word 'sign' signals a non-transcendental entity (as opposed to the 'symbol', which is the mediation of the unknown by the known), while in Saussurean linguistics the word 'sign' specifically refers to a particular coalition of signifier and signified. The fact that any comprehensive survey of semiotics must use distinguishing possessives such as 'Kristeva's sign' or 'Peirce's symbol' demonstrates that the relationship between signifier and signified is, in most forms of discourse, not automatic but arbitrary. Definitions are signs, and definitions are malleable: the sheer variety of definitions for 'sign' suggests that flexibility and arbitrariness are inevitable features of signification.

Semiotics has only partly brought Saussure's anticipated project into existence because it has screened out the ambiguities of the *Course in General Linguistics*. In the *Course* Saussure describes two main features of linguistic signs: their arbitrariness, and their tendency to consolidate into a system, through convention. As a sign-system language is a special case, because it 'eludes the individual or social will';[24] but once semiotics moves outside the linguistic system it will, Saussure predicts, have to take into account social and individual choices. The study of the sign at large, outside the realm of linguistics, will, Saussure claims, be a highly complex procedure that can only be realized as 'a part of social psychology'.[25]

In the light of the ambiguities of Saussure's *Course*, it is ironic that the

24. Saussure, *Course*, p. 17.
25. Saussure, *Course*, p. 16.

development of semiotics throughout the twentieth century has generally repressed arbitrariness and pursued systematicity. In extending the
boundaries of analysis, semioticians have looked for sign-systems that
replicate the systematicity of language, and have been attracted to
systems like the Highway Code or binary mathematical systems because
such systems eliminate human choice. The debate over whether the term
'semiotics' should include the study of language, or should be restricted
to the 'study of non-linguistic sign-systems',[26] is ironic, for in seeking to
move outside language, semioticians have searched for signs that are as
much like language as possible. Roland Barthes's argument that language is a part of semiotics because 'every semiological system has its
linguistic admixture'[27] could be ironically extended: the study of semiotics is language-dependent because most objects of study are modelled
on language.

2.2. *Semiotics and Biblical Studies*
In a century in which semioticians have sought scientific objects of
study, and in which religion and science have been cast as mutually
antipathetic, it is not surprising that signs in biblical texts have not been
the focus of semiotic analysis. Douglas Greenlee, a commentator on
C.S. Peirce, encapsulates the attitude of most semioticians when he
allows religious signs just one sentence in his analysis and condemns
such signs as a semiotic aberration. 'Objects can and do become signs
for the most *uncritical* and *uncontrolled* thought', he writes, 'as when
pious individuals take calamities as signs of the displeasure of
Providence'.[28] The interpretation of physical phenomena as signifiers for
a divine signified has not been accommodated within the realm of
semiotic study—presumably as the association is non-automatic,
extremely arbitrary, and subject to individual and social psychology.

Julia Kristeva picks up on the perceived dichotomy between semiotics
and religion in her analysis, 'The System and the Speaking Subject'.
Semioticians, she argues, are trapped by the boundaries of their own
definitions, and 'their own metalanguage can apprehend only that part
of the signifying process belonging to the domain of the general

26. P. Guiraud, *Semiology* (trans. G. Gross; London: Routledge & Kegan Paul,
1975), p. 1.

27. Barthes, *Elements of Semiology*, p. 10.

28. D. Greenlee, *Peirce's Concept of Sign* (The Hague: Mouton, 1973), p. 17
(my italics).

metalanguage to which their own efforts are tributary'.[29] The only elements of signification that they can perceive are those which they themselves have defined: 'the vast remainder has, historically, to find a home in religion'.[30] Religion is defined as the realm of the surplus, of signs that do not fit into the quasi-scientific metalanguage, and yet, paradoxically, it is also the realm which has been 'notoriously, if more or less marginally, associated with semiotic reflection since the Stoics'.[31]

To alienate religion from semiotic study is to deny the deep history of the pursuit of signs. Some of the most acute early definitions of signification originate in theology: Augustine's definition, for example, that 'A sign is something which, in addition to the substance absorbed by the senses, calls to mind of itself some other thing' is still quoted by Roland Barthes in *Elements of Semiology*.[32] From this philosophically adept definition it is a definite regression to the loose definitions in current biblical dictionaries, in which the sign is described as being based on 'the basic idea of pointing to something'[33] or is merely classified according to types. As semiotics has suffered from the exclusion of religious signs and its limiting concentration on logically watertight models, so biblical studies, on the other side of the chasm, has suffered from a recent lack of semiotic reflection.

The silence between semiotics and biblical studies has been mutually observed, largely because biblical scholars have misunderstood semiotics to be a subsidiary of, and even a synonym for, structuralism. Greimas's actantial grid, also called the semiotic square, has contributed to the view that semiotics *is* structuralism; the proceedings of a conference on Semiology and Exegesis, for example, have been published under the subheading 'An Exploration of the Possibilities Offered by Structuralism for Exegesis'.[34] Mark Stibbe seems alone in offering a corrective when he argues that, though emerging from the same roots in Saussure's

29. J. Kristeva, 'The System and the Speaking Subject', *TLS*, 12 October 1973, pp. 1249-50 (1250).

30. Kristeva, 'The System and the Speaking Subject', p. 1250.

31. Kristeva, 'The System and the Speaking Subject', p. 1250.

32. Augustine, cited by Barthes, *Elements of Semiology*, p. 100.

33. V.R. Gordon, 'Sign', in G.W. Bromiley (ed.), *International Standard Bible Encyclopaedia* (Grand Rapids: Eerdmans, rev. edn, 1988), IV, p. 505.

34. D. Patte (ed.), *Semiology and Parables: An Exploration of the Possibilities Offered by Structuralism for Exegesis* (from a conference entitled 'Semiology and Exegesis', Vanderbilt University, Nashville, 15-17 May 1975; Pittsburgh: The Pickwick Press, 1976).

Course, 'semiotics should be seen as a distinct though related discipline' because it is primarily concerned not with so-called 'deep structures' but with *signs*.[35] The only other use of the terms *signifier* and *signified* in biblical studies (to my knowledge) is Susan Wittig's discussion of a 'Theory of Multiple Meanings',[36] in which the terms are defined on the largest possible scale, and the text as signifier is depicted as being variously interpreted by readers to produce a plurality of textual signifieds.

The Hebrew Bible, and particularly the prophetic texts, are rich in signs, and semiotics, despite its flaws, is rich in insights about signs. In this analysis I want to bring together a prophetic text and semiotic theory, but first it is necessary to examine that theory in more detail by looking at the contributions of five prominent semioticians.

2.3. *Ferdinand de Saussure: The Arbitrary Sign and the Meaning of Difference*

Ferdinand de Saussure, the so-called father of modern linguistics, has, by extension, a paternal stake in the associated fields of structuralism and semiotics. His linguistic vocabulary has been adapted throughout faculties of arts, and the distinction between synchronic and diachronic,[37] and between the syntagmatic and the paradigmatic,[38] are widely known. The

---

35. M.W.G. Stibbe, 'Semiotics', in R.J. Coggins and J.L. Houlden (eds.), *A Dictionary of Biblical Interpretation* (London: SCM Press, 1990), p. 618.

36. S. Wittig, 'A Theory of Multiple Meanings', in J.D. Crossan (ed.), *Polyvalent Narration* (Semeia, 9; Atlanta: Scholars Press, 1977), pp. 75-103.

37. A synchronic approach separates language, or any system, from its state of historical flux and contingency, and examines it as a hermetically sealed and self-sufficient system, a *Gestaltenheit*, which exists at any given moment in time. A diachronic approach, conversely, situates the object of study within the chronological flux, in which a self-contained system is inconceivable. It is erroneous to assume that a synchronic approach is simply ahistorical and a diachronic approach historical: a synchronic approach could be applied, for example, in a study of language in 1757. The distinction between synchronic and diachronic enables the theorist to distil a particular linguistic moment from the historical continuum—as Fredric Jameson writes: 'Saussure's originality was to have insisted on the fact that language as a total system is complete at every moment, no matter what happens to have been altered in it a moment before' (F. Jameson, *The Prison House of Language: A Critical Account of Structuralism and Russian Formalism* [Princeton: Princeton University Press, 1972], pp. 5-6).

38. Paradigmatic relations are the vertical relations between a given word in a sentence and any word that could replace it (in the sentence pattern *subject predicate object adjunct*, the predicate X is in paradigmatic relation to any other predicate);

difference between phonemics (differences in sound that affect meaning) and phonetics (sound differences that are extraneous to meaning) has been abbreviated and generally assimilated in the categories 'emic' and 'etic'.[39] In this brief analysis I want to focus on three aspects of Saussure's *Course in General Linguistics*: the relationship between the signifier and the signified; the proposed arbitrariness of the sign; and the difference between words, through which meaning is constituted.

The problem with studying the popular edition of Saussure's *Course* is that it is not a transcript of his lectures but the course as perceived by two of his colleagues, Charles Bally and Albert Sechehaye. As Jonathan Culler argues, the students' notes (published in 1967 by Rudolf Engler) would seem to suggest an alternative prioritizing of concepts, with the arbitrary sign at the pinnacle of Saussure's system.[40] The hyperbole is Saussure's own: 'The hierarchical place of this truth', one student quotes him as saying, 'is at the very summit. It is only little by little that one recognizes how many different facts are but ramifications, hidden consequences of this truth.'[41] Following Culler, I intend to take arbitrariness as the pivotal concept and examine Saussure's theories of the sign from this starting point.

The 'sign' in Saussurean linguistics is the specific, technical term which describes the union of a signifier (or sound-image) with a

syntagmatic relations are the horizontal, combinatory relationships (between *subject* and *predicate*, *predicate* and *object*).

39. These terms, derived from social science, have been introduced to the field of biblical studies by M.G. Brett (see 'Four or Five Things To Do with Texts: A Taxonomy of Interpretative Interests', in D.J.A. Clines, S.E. Fowl and S.E. Porter [eds.], *The Bible in Three Dimensions: Essays in Celebration of Forty Years of Biblical Studies in the University of Sheffield* [JSOTSup, 87; Sheffield: JSOT Press, 1990], pp. 357-77).

40. The *Course in General Linguistics* is in fact a conflation of three different courses, taught by Saussure at the University of Geneva (1907; 1908–1909; 1910–1911). Since Saussure died in 1913 before transferring his lectures to manuscript, the course was compiled by Bally and Sechehaye from students' notes, as they had not themselves attended the lectures. The publication of the students' own notes in 1967 suggests errors in three respects: the popular edition of the *Course* is Bally's and Sechehayes's creation in terms of its order (which differs significantly from Saussure's own); its minimal discussion of the arbitrariness of the sign; and its discussion of the sound plane of language, which is far less terminologically scrupulous than Saussure's. (See J. Culler, *Saussure* [Glasgow: Collins, 1976], p. 17.)

41. Saussure, *Cours de linguistique générale* (ed. R. Engler; Wiesbaden: Otto Harrassowitz, 1967–74), p. 153.

conceptual signified. The *Course* states that there is 'no natural connection' and 'no fixed bond' between signified and signifier,[42] and describes language as subverting logical patterns of kinship. Unlike other human institutions, such as law or custom, language subverts the principle of the 'natural relations of things' since 'The arbitrariness of...signs theoretically entails the freedom of establishing just any relationship between signifier and signified'.[43] This is only true of the inaugural sign, however, and once it passes into common usage (as it must, to form a language) freedom changes into fixity, fluidity is made static, and the arbitrary sign becomes completely *motivated*. When a sign becomes a convention, writes Saussure, 'We say to language "Choose!" but we add "It must be, this sign and no other".'[44]

Though freedom and fixity are antithetical aspects of the sign, one is the natural consequence of the other. Whereas systems that are based on reason are subject to discussion and revision, language, which is created outside rational constraints, is upheld purely by convention. The connection between the concept 'book' and the associated sound-image is a relationship beyond negotiation. Thus the freedom with which the signifier and signified are associated leads to permanence, and Saussure can speak of the interrelated, as well as the contradictory, 'immutability and mutability' of the sign.[45]

Although the concept of arbitrariness is central to Saussure's work, it is not, as he himself implies, a universal principle without any exception. Possible challenges to the concept come from onomatopoeic words, symbols, and ironically, from words like *la sémiologie*; but the *Course* only deals with the first two categories. Though he concedes that German, Italian, French and English dogs may be mutually comprehensible (*wau-wau, bau-bau, oua-oua, bow-wow*), Saussure points out that genuinely mimetic sound is rare (the French interjection *aie*, for example, is phonetically distinct from the English *ouch*). The symbol, however, poses a far greater challenge because, as Saussure acknowledges:

> One characteristic of the symbol is that it is never wholly arbitrary; it is not empty, for there is the rudiment of a natural bond between the signifier

42. Saussure, *Course*, p. 69.
43. Saussure, *Course*, p. 75.
44. Saussure, *Course*, p. 71.
45. Saussure, *Course*, p. 71.

and the signified. The symbol of justice, a pair of scales, could not be replaced by any other symbol, such as a chariot.[46]

Though Saussure argues that the significant semiotic fact here is the *conventionalization* of the relation between two terms and not their similarity, he also acknowledges that the second of these relations tends to obscure the first. Symbols are thus dismissed from semiotic investigation on the rather vague grounds that they are not 'wholly arbitrary': as Saussure argues, 'Signs that are wholly arbitrary realise better than the others the ideal of the semiological process'.[47] The third challenge arises somewhat ironically from the coincidence between his choice of term for the science of signs, *la sémiologie*, and Peirce's 'semiotics', which betray linguistic motivation because they were conceived independently, on opposite sides of the Atlantic. This is not a serious challenge however, because semiotics/*la sémiologie* is a motivated, secondary term, derived from the arbitrary relation between the Greek *semeion* and the concept 'sign' (and from the academic convention that equates scientific terms with classical languages).

The lack of correlation between signifier and signified is, as Jonathan Culler points out, a 'rather obvious fact about language',[48] and hardly represents a major linguistic innovation. However, although critics have often interpreted the notion reductively, arbitrariness involves the signifier *and* the signified, and both are described as reciprocally dependent. Though Saussurean linguistics has been heralded as a 'modern Adamic enterprise',[49] Saussure vigorously opposes the model of language as nomenclature suggested in Gen. 2.19, for in a Saussurean model of language concepts do not and cannot exist independently of their sound-images. This theory is demonstrated in a brief comparison of languages: there are no 'pets' and no 'wickedness' in French, the verb *aimer* makes no distinction between liking and loving, and the English verb 'to know' makes no distinction between *connaître* and *savoir*. For an English speaker, light at the wavelength 650-640 nanometres changes from 'red' to 'orange', but in Hindi 'red' and 'orange' are one and the same cultural unit; conversely, the Russian primary colours *goloboj* and *sinij* are subsections of the inclusive category 'blue', rendered 'light

46. Saussure, *Course*, p. 68.
47. Saussure, *Course*, p. 68.
48. Culler, *Saussure*, p. 21.
49. V.B. Leitch, *Deconstructive Criticism: An Advanced Introduction* (New York: Columbia University Press, 1983), p. 7.

blue' and 'dark blue' in English. There is no such thing as 'blueness'—
the phenomenon, like the phonetic sound pattern, is arbitrary. As
spectrums of 'loving' and 'knowing' are compartmentalized differently
(thus arbitrarily) in English and French, so even such a fundamental
structure as the colour system, which so thoroughly codes our perceptions, is described not as a pre-existent phenomenon that language has
named, but a linguistic phenomenon which language has made.

In Saussurean linguistics the signified is not the 'thing' but its mental
image; it has no greater claim to substance or actuality than the signifier.
The signified is not the concrete, nor even the *a priori* part of the equation: it cannot exist separately from the signifier because it can only be
defined by it, that is 'within the signifying process, in a quasi-tautological
way'.[50] Neither signifier nor signified exists independently of the signifying equation: the signifier refers to something which can only be
expressed through it, and the terms exist in mutual dependence. This
interlocking of signifier and signified so that the two cannot be dissoci-
ated is called *isology*, and the signifier and signified are termed the two
relata of the sign.

As the word *relata* implies, reciprocal relations are of vital importance
in Saussurean linguistics. The signifier and signified exist only as they
are relative to one another, but this is only one dimension of a
Saussurean theory of linguistic relations. Signs depend on an internal
relation between signifier and signified (which Saussure calls
signification) and an external relation with other signs (which gives signs
their *value*). To describe the two dimensions of relationship, Saussure
uses the analogy of a piece of paper: if three shapes are cut out (A, B
and C), the pieces have a comparative value in relation to one another
and also have two sides (A-A′, B-B′, C-C′) which are a model of
signification. The theory of value means that any meaning is properly a
meaning of difference: the word *sign*, for example, does not mean
autonomously but only in so far as it is phonemically distinguishable
from 'sin', 'fine', 'seen', and so on, and semantically distinguishable
from associated terms (symbol, icon, index). The meaning of difference
is demonstrated most famously in Saussure's example of a set of chess
pieces:

> Take a knight, for instance. By itself is it an element in the game?
> Certainly not, for by its material make-up—outside its square and the
> other conditions of the game—it means nothing to the player; it becomes a

50. Barthes, *Elements of Semiology*, p. 43.

real, concrete element only when endowed with value and wedded to it.
Suppose that piece happens to be destroyed or lost during a game. Can it
be replaced by an equivalent piece? Certainly. Not only another knight but
even a figure shorn of any resemblance to a knight can be identical provided the same value is attributed to it. We see then that in semiological
systems like language, where elements hold each other in equilibrium in
accordance with fixed rules, the notion of identity blends with that of
value and vice versa.[51]

Saussure's conclusion, famously, is that 'in language there are only differences without positive terms'.[52] Difference, which is usually perceived
as the space between positive terms, is the universal feature of language:
the concept of identity is absorbed into that of value, and the sign *is*
nothing—except what the other signs are not.

In an essay entitled 'Saussure, the Sign, Democracy', Roland Barthes
describes the phenomenon of value in a monetary metaphor. There is,
he observes, 'fudiciary anxiety' in the idea of the sign: since the relationship between signifier and signified is arbitrary, like the 'connection of
paper to gold', it is 'mobile, precarious, nothing certifies it'.[53] If
language were merely signification, it would be unstable, but what
stabilizes the system is convention and, ultimately, the relative value
among signifiers. In the absence of any actual signified, words, like cur-
rencies, are guaranteed by relative exchange rates. Between words there
are permanent and unchanging meanings of difference, a kind of
linguistic ERM.

2.4. *Charles Sanders Peirce: The Interpretant, Unlimited Semiosis, and the Icon, Index and Symbol*

The writings of Charles Sanders Peirce, in eight volumes,[54] are an
attempt to arrive at a definitive notion of the sign. In the final analysis,
the sign is more quantified than qualified: Peirce's work yields a possible
59,049 categories of sign, and yet still flounders to produce the ultimate

51. Saussure, *Course*, p. 110 (my italics).

52. Saussure, *Course*, p. 120.

53. R. Barthes, 'Saussure, the Sign, Democracy', in *The Semiotic Challenge* (trans. R. Howard; Oxford: Basil Blackwell, 1988), pp. 151-59 (154).

54. *The Writings of Charles Sanders Peirce*. II. *Collected Papers* (ed. C. Hartshorne, P. Weiss and A.W. Burks; 8 vols.; Cambridge, MA: Harvard University Press, 1931–58), is the text to which I shall be referring in this section. A fifteen-volume edition, edited by M.H. Fisch and E.C. Moore, is currently in prepa-
ration.

definition. A sign, or *representamen*, is 'something which stands to somebody for something in some respect or capacity' (2.228); it is 'anything which determines something else (its *interpretant*) to refer to an object to which it itself refers (its *object*)' (2.303). Douglas Greenlee recommends that 'the student of Peirce does best to give up the project of reconciling everything Peirce has to say about signs, especially when utilizing his categorial framework, and admit that contradictions exist in the Peircian texts';[55] a common and useful vocabulary, however, can be extracted.

In this brief analysis I want to consider the 'interpretant' and 'unlimited semiosis', as well as Peirce's most well-known terms, the 'icon', the 'index' and the 'symbol'.

2.4.1. *The Interpretant and 'Unlimited Semiosis'*

The fundamental principle of Peirce's definition of semiotics is that a sign 'stands for' something (its *object*); it can be interpreted by another sign (its *interpretant*) and it stands for something in some respect (its *ground*). This definition corrects that of Terence Hawkes, followed by Mark Stibbe, who both make the common mistake of identifying interpretant and interpreter.[56] An interpretant is not 'somebody' but 'any sign which interprets another sign, whether that interpreting sign be a thought in somebody's mind, a written translation, a sentence spoken, or anything else that is interpretative'.[57] As Peirce writes in private correspondence to Lady Welby:

> I define a sign as anything which is so determined by something else, called its object, and so determines an effect upon a person, which *effect* I call its interpretant, that the latter is thereby mediated directly by the former.[58]

The proper definition of the interpretant is vital, because it is the key to the related concept of *semiosis*. For Peirce, 'semiosis' is a 'co-operation of three subjects such as a sign, its object and its interpretant, the trirelative influence not being in any way resolvable into actions between pairs' (5.484). Semiosis occurs only when interpretation is necessary,

---

55. Greenlee, *Peirce's Concept of Sign*, p. 5.
56. T. Hawkes, *Structuralism and Semiotics* (New Accents; London: Routledge, 1989), p. 127; Stibbe, 'Semiotics', p. 618.
57. Greenlee, *Peirce's Concept of Sign*, p. 26.
58. *Charles Sanders Peirce's Letters to Lady Welby* (ed. I.C. Leib; New Haven: Whitlock's, 1963), p. 29 (my italics).

and it is interesting that Peirce, in contrast to later semioticians such as Umberto Eco, does not regard automatic reflexes and mechanical oper- ations as signs. In contrast to a Saussurean semiotic, which dwells on dichotomies and reciprocal relations, Peirce's theory is triadic, and the presence of the awkward third term seems to make his theory less neat and lucid than Saussure's.

Peirce's awkward third term is the *interpretant*, which transforms simple dyadic causality into triadic semiosis. The insertion of the inter- pretant is not only the essential feature of semiosis, but is also the reason why semiosis is never finite, but multiple. The consequences of the interpretant go on, in Peirce's words, 'ad infinitum' (2.492), because the interpretant can be established only by means of another sign, which in turn has its interpretant, and so on. For Peirce as for Saussure, 'the identity of the sign depends upon relational properties',[59] but in Peircian semiotics one relationship relentlessly gives birth to another. The image of 'an endless series of representations, each representing the one behind it' is a recurring one:

> Now the Sign and the Explanation together make up another Sign, and since the explanation will be a Sign, it will probably require an additional explanation, which taken together with the already enlarged Sign will make up a still larger Sign... (2.230; cf. 4.536; 5.473-92);

and ultimately it finds expression in the provocative image of a semiotic striptease:

> The meaning of a representation can be nothing but a representation. In fact it is nothing but the representation itself conceived as stripped of irrel- evant clothing. But this clothing can never be stripped off; it is only changed for something more diaphanous. So there is an infinite regression here. Finally, the interpretant is nothing but another representation to which the torch of truth is handed along, and as representation, it has its interpretant again. Lo, another infinite series (1.339).

In a proleptically post-modern passage, Peirce describes the infinite deferral of meaning, in which the bare truth is ultimately unattainable.

2.4.2. *Icon, Index and Symbol*
Peirce's self-confessed 'triadomany' (1.568) leads to another famous threesome, the icon, index and symbol, which is Peirce's 'most fun- damental division of signs' (2.275), and also the most accessible and

---

59. Greenlee, *Peirce's Concept of Sign*, p. 32.

well-used aspect of his theory. This distinction acts as a supplement to Saussure, since it investigates the sign in its referential dimension; whereas Saussure is only concerned with the intrinsic relationship between the sound configuration 'ochs' and the idea 'ox', Peirce extends his study to the relationship between 'ox' as concept and 'ox' as creature and referent. The three categories can be roughly defined as follows:

The Icon. The icon 'stands for something merely because it resembles it' (3.362); the icon and its object have 'community in some quality'.[60] Icons are not simply like their object but *exhibit* that likeness: the iconic sign seems *fit,* justified by a high degree of obvious correlation between sign and external referent. Common examples of icons are paintings, photographs, maps and statues.

The Index. An index means as dark clouds mean rain, smoke means fire, or sobbing means sorrow. Indexical signs include pointing fingers, portents, a knock at the door, barometers, weathercocks and symptoms of disease. An index indicates it has a causal or sequential relationship with its referent. There is literally no smoke without fire, no symptom without disease; as Peirce puts it, 'An index is a sign which would, at once, lose the character which makes it a sign if its object were removed' (2.304). Indices are further subdivided by Peirce into *designations*, such as 'personal, demonstrative and relative pronouns (and) proper names' which 'act to force attention to the thing intended' (8.368), and *reagents* (for example pink litmus, which points to the presence of an acid). Both designations and reagents 'cannot denote unless the interpreting mind is already acquainted with the thing it denotes', and work by means of a shared code (8.368).

The Symbol. A tree is represented iconically by a painting, indexically by a pointing finger, and symbolically by the word 'tree' (*arbre, Baum, arbor*). In Peirce's words, 'a Symbol is a sign which refers to the Object that it denotes by virtue of a law, usually an association of general ideas, which operates to cause the Symbol to be reinterpreted as referring to that object' (2.249). Peirce's 'symbol' is analogous to Saussure's 'sign': the relationship between the *signifier/ signans* and *signified/signatum* is 'arbitrary' (Saussure) or 'imputed' (Peirce).

60. Peirce, cited by Hawkes, *Structuralism and Semiotics,* p. 128.

The three categories overlap: it may be argued, for example, that all icons are also symbolic, since in order to designate an object by likeness, a sign must have been appointed to serve as a representative by *convention*. Keir Elam cautions against applying the terms with 'naive absolutism',[61] while Roman Jakobson argues that a single sign need not be confined to one category only, and may incorporate all three. According to Jakobson, there are many potential permutations, such as 'symbolic icons', 'iconic symbols', 'indexical symbols', and the dominant mode depends ultimately on the context of the sign.[62]

2.5. *The Sign in Performance: The Semiotics of Theatre*

Semiotics has been particularly influential in analyses of performance, and the elementary principles of theatrical semiosis suggest several analogies with prophetic texts. In this section, I want to outline three features of theatrical semiotics: *semiotization, transformability*, and the Brechtian *Verfremdungsaffekt* ('alienation effect').

Semiotization and transformability are fundamental features of theatrical semiotics defined by the so-called 'Prague Circle' in the 1930s and 1940s. Semiotization is the process whereby 'the stage radically transforms all objects and bodies defined within it, bestowing upon them an overriding signifying power which they lack'.[63] On stage, objects are semiotized as they begin to 'play a part', and 'acquire special features, qualities and attributes they do not have in real life'.[64] As the Austrian playwright Peter Handke observes, although a chair on stage may be identical to those the audience are sitting on, once staged it becomes 'a theatrical chair'[65] a representative of a whole class of objects—'Chair'.[66]

61. K. Elam, *The Semiotics of Theatre and Drama* (London: Routledge, 1991), p. 22.

62. See R. Jakobson, *Coup de l'oeil sur le développement de la sémiotique* (Bloomington: Indiana University Press, 1975), and 'Language in Relation to Other Communication Systems', in Jakobson (ed.), *Selected Writings* (The Hague: Mouton, 1971), III, pp. 697-708.

63. Elam, *The Semiotics of Theatre*, p. 7.

64. P. Bogatyrev, 'Semiotics in the Folk Theatre', in L. Matjeka and I.R. Titunik (eds.), *Semiotics of Art: Prague School Contributions* (Cambridge, MA: MIT Press, 1976), pp. 33-49 (35).

65. P. Handke, 'Nauseated by Language (Interview with Arthur Joseph)', *The Drama Review* 15 (1971), pp. 56-61 (57).

66. Elam, *The Semiotics of Theatre*, p. 8.

'*All* that is on stage is a sign',[67] writes Jiri Veltrusky. Drama, like poetry, is a genre that creates expectations of universal significance, in which all components are expected to have a hidden meaning. The reader/spectator instinctively finds signifieds for the objects and actions on stage and 'understands even (the) non-purposive components of the actor's performance as signs'.[68]

If drama is a type of discourse in which every feature is automatically interpreted as a signifier, these signifiers are in flux and can be attached to various signifieds. The theory of transformability suggests that the signifier, like the actor, can assume multiple roles: thus a sword handle, a symbol of war, can become a cross of reconciliation by a simple change in position, and an adjustment to the audience's visual and hence moral perspective. The principle of transformability is effectively acted out in a metadramatic interlude in Shakespeare's *The Two Gentlemen of Verona* in which Launce, the clown, has difficulty in matching signifiers to their appropriate signifieds:

> Nay, I'll show you the manner of it. This shoe is my father; no, this left shoe is my father: no, no, this left shoe is my mother; nay, that cannot be so neither—yes, it is so; it is so; it has the worser sole. This shoe, with the hole in, is my mother, and this my father. A vengeance on't! there 'tis: now, sir, this staff is my sister; for, look you, she is as white as a lily and as small as a wand: this hat is Nan, our maid: I am the dog; no the dog is himself, and I am the dog—O! the dog is me and I am myself; ay, so, so.[69]

Comically, Launce enacts what the Prague theorists term the 'generative capacity' of the signifier (thus the left shoe, differently interpreted, can signify father and mother) and discovers how signifieds can be 'transformed in the most rapid and varied fashion'.[70] Faced with a paucity of signifiers he has to improvise and use his own footwear: thus he enacts another dimension of theatrical semiotics, the 'problem of semiotic economy',[71] or the difficulty of cajoling complex meaning from a limited range of props.

---

67. J. Veltrusky, 'Man and Object in the Theatre', in P.L. Garvin (ed.), *A Prague School Reader on Aesthetics: Literary Structure and Style* (Washington: Georgetown University Press, 1964), pp. 83-91 (84).

68. Veltrusky, 'Man and Object', p. 85.

69. Shakespeare, *The Two Gentlemen of Verona*, II.iii, ll. 15ff.

70. P. Bogatyrev, 'Les signes du théatre', *Poétique* 8 (1971), pp. 517-30 (519).

71. Elam, *The Semiotics of Theatre*, p. 14.

The principle of transformability suggests that in theatrical representation, as in Saussurean linguistics, the relationship between signifier and signified is arbitrary. This is most apparent in Launce's monologue, or in modernist, minimalist plays such as *Waiting for Godot*, which contravene the conventions of realism and foreground the artificiality of the performance. As Saussure intervenes in linguistic structures to argue that the seeming naturalness of language is a product of convention, so Shakespeare and Beckett intervene in dramatic structures to suggest that representations are not given but produced. Since dramatic signs are produced by arbitrary conventions, there is no reason why a shoe cannot be equated with a parent, or why parents should not appear on stage, as in *Endgame*, in dustbins.

To use the language of the Russian formalist Victor Schlovsky, performances like Launce's monologue or Beckett's plays *defamiliarize* the process of signification by *laying bare the device*.[72] Since perception is habitualized, automatic, Schlovsky argues, it is the task of the artist to make objects strange to the reader, and most extremely, to defamiliarize the medium of communication. 'Laying bare the device' is the most extreme form of defamiliarization (*ostranenie*), because the very medium of communication (or sign production) foregrounds its artificiality and counters the reader's expectations. As examples Schlovsky cites the disjunctive narrative of Laurence Sterne's *Tristram Shandy*, comprising blank and marbled pages and a preface in the middle of the book, and Tolstoy's *Kholstomer*, in which the narrative is spoken by a horse.

The theories of 'defamiliarization' and 'laying bare the device' are most clearly enacted in Brechtian theatre. As defamiliarization is a response to unseeing viewing, in which objects are habitually seen 'as if enveloped in a sack',[73] so Brechtian theatre is directed at audiences who

---

72. V. Schlovsky, 'Art as Technique' and 'Sterne's Tristram Shandy: Stylistic Commentary', in T. Lemon and J. Reis (eds.), *Russian Formalist Criticism: Four Essays* (Lincoln, NB: University of Nebraska Press, 1965), pp. 3-57. Though borrowed from the context of Russian Formalism, Schlovsky's theory of defamiliarization is important to the field of semiotics because it is a reaction against a simplistic view of representation advanced by Potebnya. Potebnya argues that the function of an image (that is a signifier) is to clarify a signified, but Scholvsky argues that the motive of sign-production is not illumination, but defamiliarization.

73. Schlovsky, 'Art as Technique', p. 11.

are conventionally 'in torpor',[74] a 'credulous hypnotized mass'[75] who 'stare rather than see, and listen rather than hear'.[76] Brecht creates a *Verfremdungsaffekt* (also known as an 'alienation', or 'A-effect') by staging the play in such a way that it seems to *quote* gestures and attitudes rather than imitate them. Actors are directed to speak their lines as if 'playing from memory',[77] and to foreground, rather than conceal, the play's artificiality. As Laurence Sterne defamiliarizes actions by placing them in slow motion,[78] so in Brecht's theatre 'the general gesture of showing accompanies each of the particular gestures shown'.[79] As Sterne's text is habitually interrupted by a voice that foregrounds the text's textuality,[80] so in Brechtian theatre 'a narrative voice interposes itself between the audience and the events enacted on stage'[81] to remind them that what they are watching is merely 'a handful of cardboard, a little miming, a bit of text'.[82] However, Brechtian theatre is defamiliarizing not only because it is 'fragmentary and episodic'[83] like *Tristram Shandy*, but because it is 'direct and didactic',[84] and converts emotion into stylized gestures. 'Epic' as opposed to 'dramatic' theatre is an 'object of instruction'[85] rather than a form of entertainment: 'Instead

74. J. Willett, *The Theatre of Bertolt Brecht: A Study From Eight Aspects* (London: Eyre Methuen, 1977), p. 172.

75. Brecht, 'Kleines Organon für das Theater' (Potsdam, 1949); J. Willett, in *Brecht on Theatre* (trans. and ed. J. Willett; London: Eyre Methuen, 1974), p. 188.

76. Willett, *The Theatre*, p. 166.

77. Willett, *The Theatre*, p. 168.

78. So, for example, Tristram's father 'take[s] his wig from off his head with his *right* hand, and with his left pull[s] a striped *India* handkerchief from his right coat pocket' (L. Sterne, *The Life and Opinions of Tristram Shandy* [Harmondsworth: Penguin, 1987], p. 172).

79. Brecht, in E. Hauptmann (ed.), *Gesammelte Werke*, XVI (Frankfurt: Suhrkamp, 1967), p. 697 (my translation).

80. Sterne constantly foregrounds the writing process, in comments such as 'What I have to inform you, comes, I own, a little out of its due course—for it should have been told a hundred and fifty pages ago, but that I foresaw that 'twould come in pat hereafter, and be of more advantage here than elsewhere' (*Tristram Shandy*, p. 159).

81. R. Speirs, *Bertholt Brecht* (London: Macmillan, 1987), p. 49.

82. Brecht, 'Kleines Organon', trans. Willett, *The Theatre*, p. 166.

83. Willett, *The Theatre*, p. 173.

84. Willett, *The Theatre*, p. 170.

85. Brecht, cited by Willett, *The Theatre*, p. 170 (no reference is given, and I have been unable to trace the original).

of sharing an experience', Brecht wrote, 'the spectator must come to grips with things'.[86]

For Schlovsky, defamiliarization is an aesthetic device; for Brecht, it is a political tool. Both strategies have implications for semiotic study because they intervene in, and foreground, the mechanics of representation, but, as Elizabeth Wright points out, Brechtian theatre sets up a series of specifically *'social, political* and *ideological* interruptions' to 'remind us that representations are not given but produced'.[87] Like Saussurian linguistics, the A-effect shows that 'no representation is fixed and final',[88] that signs are arbitrary, and that dominant social signs, like language, are not natural, but a result of (ideological) convention. The audience is not the passive recipient of a signification but is involved in its construction: the spectator's position is radically reconstructed so that she is 'never only at the receiving end of a representation, but included in it'.[89]

2.6. *Roland Barthes: Mythologies*

Theatrical semiotics is a particularly useful prologue to a study of prophetic signs because it extends semiotics from the level of word and associated concept to the realm of representation (or metaphor). Roland Barthes similarly pushes semiotics from the level of the signifier and the signified to what he calls 'second-order signifying systems', but unlike the semioticians of the Prague Circle, he sees representation as an extension of the work of Saussure, which he takes as 'methodologically exemplary'.[90] As Barthes demonstrates that one signifier and signified together may form another signifier, which has its own signified, and so on, he takes Saussurean concepts outside the realm of linguistics, but also describes a process that is not unlike Peirce's theory of semiosis, or signifying chains. Barthes's work on myth represents an intersection between the three approaches explored above: it is the point at which Peirce's concept of unlimited semiosis, a Saussurean definition of the

---

86. Brecht, cited by Willett, *Brecht on Theatre*, p. 168 (no reference is given, and I have been unable to trace the original).

87. E. Wright, *Postmodern Brecht: A Re-Presentation* (London: Routledge, 1989), p. 19.

88. Wright, *Postmodern Brecht*, p. 19.

89. Wright, *Postmodern Brecht*, p. 19.

90. R. Barthes, 'Myth Today', in *Mythologies* (trans. A. Lavers; London: Jonathan Cape, 1972), pp. 109-59 (113).

structure of the sign, and the study of the sign in its representative dimension, meet.

Though Barthes's work on semiotics is extensive, I shall here be confining myself to the volume *Mythologies*, which examines the way in which culture assigns to various inanimate objects a second dimension of meaning. In 'Myth Today' Barthes picks up, by way of example, a black pebble, which he 'can make...signify in several ways'. On one level it is a 'mere signifier', but if it is 'weigh[ed]...with a definite signified (a death sentence, for instance, in an anonymous vote) it will become a sign'.[91] A pebble on its own is 'just' a pebble, but a pebble used as a casting vote is outweighed by its own significance. A mythical object or sign is never 'just' that object, it is the object plus a surplus of significance, an object that is picked up by society and *used*. In Barthesian terms the pebble simply as pebble is an 'empty signifier' (a vacant space, with no specific signified), but as a signal for impending death it is 'full' (its meaning is attached). An object becomes a sign when it is given an additional weight or burden of significance, a 'social usage' over and above its 'physical matter'.[92]

A black pebble connoting a death sentence evokes a sense of past- and other-ness, and suggests that myth belongs to the domain of primitive anthropology. Barthes debunks this assumption by demonstrating the Western predilection for attaching weighty *connotative* meanings to simple *denotative* signs: in European society, for example, a bunch of roses exists in two dimensions, as a horticultural entity and as a signifier of love/passion. The signifier 'roses' is in a different category from the signified 'love', and the relation between signifier and signified is therefore 'not one of equality but one of equivalence'.[93] As in Saussurean linguistics, the sign is the associative total of signifier and signified, and is effectively 'roses "passionified"'.[94] The sign can be decomposed into its signifier and signified theoretically but not experientially, because, observing a bunch of red roses, the mind registers the object and the message simultaneously rather than sequentially. Effectively there is no signifier and signified but only the conglomerate sign. The association of roses and love is a meaning produced by a particular society, and these habitual signs together form a gigantic societal myth, a network through

91. Barthes, 'Myth Today', p. 113 (my parentheses).
92. Barthes, 'Myth Today', p. 109.
93. Barthes, 'Myth Today', p. 112.
94. Barthes, 'Myth Today', p. 113.

which the world is ordered and meaning assigned to otherwise meaningless objects.

As Jean-François Lyotard points out, it is easy to perceive the founding myths of other cultures, but it is relatively difficult to see the myths of one's own.[95] Barthes's redefinition of 'myth' has post-modern implications, for he confounds the illusion of a post-mythical society by demonstrating how all culture, including, perhaps particularly, his own, is a product of signs. Barthesian 'myth' is not defined by content but by form: it is a 'mode of signification'.[96] Twentieth-century French society is no less mythical, no less structured by signs, than a medieval legend or an Old Testament prophetic text, for myth occurs every time an object 'pass(es) from a closed, silent existence to an oral state, open to appropriation by society'.[97] A tree is 'just' a tree, but the Green Movement, no less than the writer of Genesis 3, utilizes it for a specific signifying function. Barthes effectively redefines myth from a 'fictitious story' to a meaning that is made every time an object/event is given a deeper significance.

For Barthes 'myth' is the semiotic expression of an ideology, or as Kaja Silverman puts it, 'the deployment of signifiers for the purpose of expressing and surreptitiously justifying the dominant values of a given historical period'.[98] The signs appropriated need not be momentous, nor must the connotations given to those signs be profound: any object, Barthes argues, can potentially become the 'prey of mythical speech for a while',[99] and he demonstrates this in *Elements of Semiology* where he explores the myths of a consumer society, and the semiology of cars, fashion, food and perfume. For Barthes twentieth-century Western society is not so much post-mythical as supra-mythical. His most famous example of myth is set, appropriately, not on Greek Olympian heights but in the 1950s, in a barber's shop:

> I am at the barber's, and a copy of *Paris-Match* is offered to me. On the cover, a young Negro in a French uniform is saluting, with his eyes uplifted, probably fixed on a fold of the tricolour. All this is the *meaning* of the picture. But, whether naively or not, I see very well what it

95. J. Lyotard, *The Postmodern Condition: A Report on Knowledge* (trans. G. Bennington and B. Massumi; Manchester: Manchester University Press, 1984).
96. Barthes, 'Myth Today', p. 109.
97. Barthes, 'Myth Today', p. 109.
98. K. Silverman, *The Subject of Semiotics*, p. 27.
99. Barthes, 'Myth Today', p. 110.

signifies to me: that France is a great Empire, that all her sons, without colour discrimination, faithfully serve under her flag, and that there is no better answer to the detractors of an alleged colonialism than the zeal shown by this Negro in serving his so-called oppressors. I am therefore again faced with a greater semiological system: there is a signifier, itself already formed with a previous system (*a black soldier is giving the French salute*); there is a signified (it is here a purposeful mixture of Frenchness and militariness); finally there is the presence of the signified through the signifier.[100]

The photograph comprises several signs, a negro, a soldier, a uniform, a salute, and so forth, which function on the first-order of signification (the realm of denotation) and produce what Barthes terms the 'meaning of the picture'. On this level of signification the photographic image of the soldier and flag is the denotative signifier, and the concept, 'a black soldier is saluting the French flag' is the signified. The photograph and concept together form the first-order sign, and this sign is in turn a signifier in the second-order (or connotative) realm. At this level the sign in its entirety becomes a signifier for the ideological (mythical) signifieds, 'nationalism' and 'militarism'.

The domain of 'myth' is constructed like that of language, but on a larger scale: Barthes extends Saussure's linguistic theory from the denotative to the connotative realm.[101] In considering pebbles and roses, Saussure would only concern himself with the relationship between the sound-image (pebble/rose) and the concept of roses and pebbles, but Barthes makes an important 'lateral shift' and 'shift(s) the formal signification of the first system sideways.'[102] This leads to the following model:[103]

---

100. Barthes, 'Myth Today', p. 116.

101. Barthes is not the first to explore the realm of connotation in semiotic analysis, and the model described in *Mythologies* bears the imprint of the work of the Danish linguist Louis Hjelmslev. Much earlier than Barthes, Hjelmslev wrote, '[I]t seems appropriate to view the connotators as content for which the denotative semiotics are expression, and to designate this content and this expression as a semiotic, namely a *connotative semiotic*. In other words, after the analysis of the denotative semiotic is completed, the connotative semiotic must be subjected to an analysis according to just the same procedure' (*Prologemena to a Theory of Language* [trans. F.J. Whitfield; Madison, WI: University of Wisconsin Press, 1969], p. 119).

102. Barthes, 'Myth Today', p. 115.

103. Barthes, 'Myth Today', p. 115.

1. Denotative Signifier	2. Denotative Signified	
3. Denotative Sign * I CONNOTATIVE SIGNIFIER	II CONNOTATIVE SIGNIFIED	
III CONNOTATIVE SIGN		

1st Order — row 1 and 3. 2nd ORDER — connotative rows.

An important point emerges from this model, which Barthes implies but does not develop. Second-order signification can be so powerful, and so dominant, that the first-order sign may be eclipsed and lost in the larger meaning. Paul Valéry gives an example of a small boy in a French lycée reading *quia ego nominor leo* in his Latin grammar. The primary statement, 'because my name is lion', is, Valéry argues, almost lost in the contextual meaning, 'I am a grammatical example meant to illustrate the rule about the agreement of the predicate'.[104] The statement's pedagogic context provides a more fundamental and pertinent signification which 'imposes'[105] itself over and above any other. Another example might be the classic illustration of Saussurean linguistics, comprising a signifier *arbor*, and a signified, a picture of a tree. The signifier (*arbor*) and signified (the picture) form a first-order sign, but this sign is itself a signifier for a large-scale signified, 'Saussurean linguistics' or 'semiotics'. The picture, like the Latin sentence, becomes a cipher for a pedagogic model and declares, above its more obvious meaning, 'I am a model of the workings of the signifier and signified'.

Valéry argues, in his example of the Latin sentence, that the primary meaning becomes 'virtually irrelevant'; similarly, Barthes argues that the first-order signs become 'almost transparent',[106] as windows for a larger ideological meaning. As the words 'almost' and 'virtually' imply, however, the first-order meaning cannot be simply erased, and this generates a tension between first- and second-order signification. Barthes hints at this when he writes:

> [The negro] is not a symbol of the French Empire: he has too much presence, he appears as a rich, fully experienced, indisputable image. But at the same time the presence is tamed, put at a distance, made almost transparent; it recedes a little, it becomes the accomplice of a concept

104. P. Valéry, *Tel Quel* 2 (1960), p. 191, cited by Barthes, 'Myth Today', p. 116.
105. Barthes, 'Myth Today', p. 116.
106. Barthes, 'Myth Today', p. 118.

which comes to it fully armed, French imperiality: once made use of, it becomes artificial.[107]

The negro is both a living entity in his own right and a signifier in a larger scheme of meaning. He exists autonomously and at the same time is subordinated to a larger signifying cause. The tension is that the second-order, or mythical signifier is also a self-contained sign in its own right. *Quia ego nominor leo* will always on some level mean simply that.

Myth is 'defined', argues Barthes, by 'a game of hide and seek between the meaning and the form'.[108] Though the terms 'form' and 'meaning' are riddled with problems, and the terms 'second-order signifier' and 'second-order signified' would have been more precise, the hide and seek analogy hints at an alternating obscurity, changing roles and changing emphases, between the two dimensions of the sign. The negro, the pebble, the rose and the Latin sentence are all caught up in the conflict between the primary and the secondary: the second-order meaning (empire, death, passion, grammar) vies with the first-order form (negro, pebble, rose, sentence). The site of tension is marked with an asterisk on the diagram above; it is not merely a point of transition, but a point of potential struggle.

2.7. *Julia Kristeva: Semiotics and the Ideologeme*

Julia Kristeva, like Roland Barthes, contributes to 'la sémiologie de "deuxième génération"'.[109] Sixty years after the appearance of the term she can justifiably speak of 'classical' semiotics[110] which she seeks both to appropriate and transcend, like a sober revolutionary. On one hand she speaks of a 'phase of semiology which is now over: that which runs from Saussure and Peirce to the Prague School and structuralism'; on the other she refuses to offer a critique of its ideological bias 'without recognizing the truth it has contributed by revealing and characterizing the immanent causality and/or the presence of a social-systematic constraint in each social functioning'.[111] Kristeva's position is a post-structuralist one with all the ambiguities that that involves, for there can

107. Barthes, 'Myth Today', p. 118.
108. Barthes, 'Myth Today', p. 118.
109. E. Benveniste, 'Sémiologie de la langue', *Semiotica* 1 (1969), pp. 127-35 (135).
110. J. Kristeva, 'Semiotics: A Critical Science and/or a Critique of Science', in T. Moi (ed.), *The Kristeva Reader* (Oxford: Basil Blackwell, 1986), pp. 75-87 (81).
111. Kristeva, 'The System and the Speaking Subject', p. 1249.

be no anti-system without a system, and if poststructuralism divorces itself from founding systems in claims of 'post-ness', it still retains past 'structures' in its title, and is inextricably connected to, and dependent on, the systems it seeks to transcend.

The linchpin of Kristeva's argument is Peirce's statement that a symbol 'refers to an object it denotes by virtue of a law'.[112] Kristeva retains the principle of 'law' but with all the negative connotations that it has accrued in a postmodern context. In one of her early manifestos for a revised semiotic, 'The System and the Speaking Subject',[113] she describes semiotics as a 'socially subservient system' which myopically focuses only on the 'systematic, systematizing, or informational aspect of signifying practices'.[114] Semiotics is systematic and systematising because it studies a system, and it *is* a system and so does not merely study but imitate. Kristeva's challenge is to look for a more radical concept of signs that does not affirm the system by its own habitual systematisation, and which, while acknowledging the system as fact, does not endorse it by mimicry.

The tendency of classical semiotics is to analyse all signs using 'logico-mathematical tools'[115] and to study only signs that correspond to the terms set out in semiotic theory; but Kristeva, in contrast, is interested in signs that break, rather than affirm, the social contract. Although her early work might itself be described as logico-mathematical, Kristeva's semiotic, as it develops, focuses increasingly on the ideological motivation of signs, and the type of signifying structures that are usually outside the boundaries of classical semiotic theory. Kristeva, like Barthes, explores the idea of the sign as part of a wider social and ideological context, and focuses increasingly on signs that function asystematically, or even anti-systematically, in order to transgress and to shock. In this brief analysis I want to examine these key strands of her semiotic theory by outlining the evolution of her definitions of the term 'semiotic' and her theory of the sign as *ideologeme*.

It is inevitably confusing that, having used the word 'semiotic' to describe a past system which she criticizes, Kristeva appropriates the term for a new critical venture which she inaugurates. In 'The System

112. Kristeva, 'From Symbol to Sign', in Moi (ed.), *The Kristeva Reader*, pp. 62-73 (64).
113. Kristeva, 'The System and the Speaking Subject', pp. 1249-50.
114. Kristeva, 'The System and the Speaking Subject', p. 1249.
115. Kristeva, 'The System and the Speaking Subject', p. 1249.

and the Speaking Subject' the word 'semiotic' is used in its classical sense; in *La revolution du langue poétique*, published only a year later, the term is resurrected with a completely different sense (and no footnote to explain the transition). Kristeva's treatment of the term 'semiotic' is typical of her treatment of literary keywords: she appropriates it into her own scheme of thought, and regenerates it in an idiosyncratic, anarchic fashion. Deviation is not, however, an accident of meaning, rather it *is* her meaning; in a colloquium on psychoanalysis and politics Kristeva expresses her attitude towards literary and political conventions: 'I never intended to follow a correct Marxist line, and I hope I am not correctly following any line whatsoever'.[116]

Between 1973 and 1974 Kristeva's definition of 'semiotic' did not undergo subtle shifts in nuance, but was reversed from 'the system' to the 'anti-system'. In the pivotal essay, 'The Ethics of Linguistics' (March 1974) she uses the word 'semantic' as a cipher for organized signification, and 'semiotic' for the disruptive semiotic rhythm that irrupts within it. 'Semiotic' develops from a definition into a metaphor for that which counters and disturbs the system. To use Barthes's terms, Kristeva takes the first-order sign, 'semiotic', and shifts the signification sideways, so that 'semiotic' connotatively comes to mean that which is connotative, muted, and repressed within the text.

One of the ways in which the contrast between semantic and semiotic is expressed is in the distinction between 'language' and 'poetry'. Language is the realm of semantics, of dictionary definitions, and semiotics is the force of 'upheaval, dissolution, and transformation'[117] that disturbs accepted signifying structures and introduces a disturbing counter-rhythm. Analysing the poetry of the Soviet poets Mayakovsky and Khlebnikov against the Formalist backdrop of the Soviet state, Kristeva builds up two opposing paradigms: the poet–the mother–the other–the force–the rhythm (the semiotic); the word–paternal law–repetitive sonority–the limiting structure–the master (the semantic). The two are perceived as vying, struggling, and yet paradoxically mutually interdependent: the transgressor needs the system, and 'Only by vying

116. Kristeva's statement from the Milan conference, 'Psychoanalysis and Politics' (December 1973), is taken from A. Verdiglione (ed.), *Psychoanalyse et politique* (Paris: du Seuil, 1974), p. 73.

117. Kristeva, 'The Ethics of Linguistics', in *Desire in Language: A Semiotic Approach to Literature and Art* (ed. L.S. Roudiez; Oxford: Basil Blackwell, 1980), pp. 23-35 (25).

with the agency of limiting and structuring language' does the semiotic become 'a contestant—formulating and transforming'.[118]

Kristeva's theories are themselves a kind of poem, in which 'semiotic' and 'semantic' do not take on a fixed meaning, or even a field of meaning, but are applied to fields as diverse as Soviet poetry and gender. Her analysis of Soviet poetry, for example, grows beyond a reading of Mayakovsky and Khlebnikov to a statement about the 'masculine' and 'feminine', and as her two paradigms suggest, she assigns to 'semiotic' and 'semantic' a female and male gender. In a development that is only grammatically (and academically) possible in French, Kristeva makes much of the feminine gender of *la sémiologie* and argues that the radical, the semiotic, is synonymous with the feminine. In a blurring of boundaries, the semiotic project intersects with a feminist agenda: 'It was perhaps also necessary to be a woman', Kristeva suggests, 'to attempt to take up the exorbitant wager of carrying the rational project to the outer borders of the signifying venture of men'.[119]

Kristeva's redefinition of 'semiotic' as the 'subversive' countertext, opened up across the closed symbolic order of a society or text, is evocative not only of feminist discourse but of deconstruction. As Kristeva describes the sign as *ideologeme*, another dimension of literary study is brought into play. The ideologeme is the point at which semiotic theory and Kristeva's theories of intertextuality intertextually interact: the sign is no longer seen as an isolated element, but rather the sign and the text are placed 'within the general text [culture] of which they are a part and which is in turn part of them'.[120] The sign becomes part of its context—a 'mosaic of quotations', a 'place' in which 'various textual surfaces of past and present cultures cross',[121]—but it need not merely repeat those structures, but can also radically transform them. Some ideologemes merely affirm the dominant ideology: they borrow from the text of society and culture, but leave the macro-text untouched. Other signs, however, handle the dominant ideology far less reverentially, and both borrow and distort recognizable motifs. The faithful ideologeme does not disturb the social and historical text, and appears so natural that it is hard to discern its ideological bias. The radical sign, in

118. Kristeva, 'The Ethics of Linguistics', p. 29.
119. Kristeva, *Desire in Language*, p. x.
120. Kristeva, 'The Bounded Text', in *Desire in Language*, pp. 36-63 (36).
121. Kristeva, 'The Bounded Text', p. 36.

contrast, has the potential to shock and disturb: it 'redistributes' emphases and ideas and so re-shapes the boundaries and conventions of the social/historical macrotext.

In this section, I have established a diverse semiotic vocabulary, and explained the theoretical basis behind terms such as 'first-' and 'second-order signifiers', 'semiosis', 'laying bare the device', and the 'ideologeme'. In the next section, I shall be using these terms, and the theories associated with them, in an analysis of the sign-language of Hosea 1–3. The sign language will be considered under seven headings: 'Hosea 1 as Theatrical Performance'; 'Hosea 1 as a Process of Defamilialization'; 'The Elusive Referent'; 'The Manipulation of Signs in Hosea 1 and 3'; 'The Semiotics of Hosea 2'; 'The Battle Between First- and Second-Order Signification'; and *'La Sémiologie*: A Counter-Perspective'. In the fourth and concluding section of this chapter I shall draw my observations together.

3. *Sign Language in Hosea 1–3*

3.1. *A 'Curious, Ritualized Dumb-Show': Hosea 1 as Theatrical Performance*

In semiotic terms, Hosea 1–3 begins with a crisis of semiotic economy, that is, with a word to communicate and no signifiers or props. As Launce improvises and uses his own footwear, so the prophets of the Hebrew Bible fashion meaning from everyday objects, such as clay (Jer. 18.1-10), tiles (Ezek. 4.1-3), baskets of summer fruit (Amos 8.1-3), and even, like Launce, from their own items of clothing.[122] Hosea, like Isaiah,[123] represents the extreme of this resourcefulness and literally produces the signs he will use. The metaphor of 'conceiving meaning' is acted out in this eighth-century text: Hosea makes (fathers) the signifiers and crafts significance from members of his own family. Hosea 'takes' (has sexual intercourse with) Gomer-bat-Diblayim, and she gives birth to three children, who are then appropriated as a kind of text.

---

122. Jeremiah uses a loincloth as a symbol of the fate of Judah and Jerusalem (Jer. 13.1-11); Ezekiel represents the fate of Jerusalem with portions of his own hair (Ezek. 5).

123. The naming of Isaiah's sons שאר ישוב (Isa. 7.3) and מהר שלל חש בז (Isa. 8.3), and particularly the birth and naming sequence in Isa. 8.3-4, is strikingly similar to the process of 'conceiving' (of) the three child signs in Hos. 1.

Reproduction and production merge: the process of conceiving children runs parallel to the process of conceiving (of) meaning: by causing the woman to reproduce, Hosea produces a meaning, and he does so under Yhwh's direction.

'Production' and 'direction' are theatrical terms, and Hosea 1 is in many respects analogous to a theatrical performance. Gabriel Josipovici describes the text as a 'curious, ritualized dumb-show';[124] although he does not describe details in the text that contribute to this response, one factor, I suggest, is the curious and ritualistic way in which the text lays bare the conditions of its staging. The text describes in (literally) laborious detail the devices it proposes to use for signification: Yhwh commands Hosea to take a 'wife of harlotry' (Hos. 1.2); Hosea takes Gomer-bat-Diblayim (Hos. 1.3); and the remainder of the chapter is a reiterated pattern of conception, birth and naming. Gomer conceives and bears a son, and Hosea names him Jezreel (Hos. 1.4); she conceives and bears a daughter, and Hosea calls her Not-Pitied (Hos. 1.6); she conceives and bears another son, and Hosea calls him Not-My-People (Hos. 1.9).

The sign-language of Hosea 1 is laboured over: the audience sees not a complete play but a production in process, in which the signifiers are made, and attached to their signifieds. The text takes the reader behind the scenes, as it were, of the signifying process: as Schlovsky defamiliarises actions, by placing them in slow motion so Hosea 1 foregrounds the mechanics of representation. Like a play by Bertolt Brecht or Samuel Beckett, the text debunks all illusions of realism and lays bare the process of sign formation. By foregrounding the contrivance involved in the creation of meaning, the text defamiliarizes the apparent naturalness of sign-systems, and suggests covertly what Saussure argues overtly: that signs are not given, but made.

Hosea 1 is like Brechtian theatre in that it constantly draws attention to its artificiality. Brechtian theatre sums up in a 'mimetic and gestural expression' the 'social relationships prevailing between people';[125] Hosea 1 expresses in stark, clipped acts of naming the perceived relationship between Yhwh and the nation. As Brecht occasionally incorporates stage directions spoken out loud,[126] so Hosea 1 includes the

124. G. Josipovici, *The Book of God: A Response to the Bible* (New Haven: Yale University Press, 1988), p. 180.
125. Willett, *Brecht on Theatre*, p. 139.
126. Willett, *Brecht on Theatre*, p. 138.

director (Yhwh's) voice (Hos. 1.2, 4, 6) explaining the strategy behind the signification. What is 'shown' is not only 'accompanied' but virtually eclipsed, by a long description of the process of showing,[127] so that in a sense, this text is as much about the process of signification as about the apostasy of a nation.

3.2. *Making Strange(rs): Hosea 1 as a Process of Defamilialization*

> When the actor appears on stage, besides what he is actually doing he will at all points discover, specify, imply what he is not doing; that is to say he will act in such a way that the alternative emerges as clearly as possible, that his acting allows the other possibilities to be inferred and only represents one of the possible variants. He will say, for instance, 'You'll pay for that' and not say 'I forgive you'. He detests his children; it is not the case that he loves them. He moves down stage left and not up stage right. Whatever he doesn't do must be contained in what he does... The technical term for this procedure is fixing the 'not...but' (Bertolt Brecht, 'A Short Description of a New Technique of Acting which Produces an Alienation Effect').

The foregrounding of the process of signification in Hosea 1 creates a Brechtian *Verfremdungsaffekt*. This effect is enforced by two other features of the chapter: the appropriation of children as signs, and the naming of the children with negative names. The use of living signifiers makes the text extremely 'strange' to the modern reader, but even more disturbing is the process by which the prophet makes strangers of his children. As the text lays bare the process of signification, so it defamiliarizes family bonds: the woman who might be expected to be alienated from the prophet—the 'woman of harlotry'—becomes his wife, while conversely, the offspring from that marriage are alienated.

The A-effect is, as Brecht put it, 'the exact opposite of that which aims at empathy'.[128] The Brechtian actor is detached, and the play is openly didactic and unemotional (*sachlich*);[129] as Raman Selden observes, the style is 'diagrammatic' in the sense that the performance 'indicates' rather than 'reveals' a meaning.[130] Hosea 1 similarly puts all emotion in abeyance, and subverts one of the most natural affinities, the

---

127. Willett, *Brecht on Theatre*, p. 136.

128. Willett, *Brecht on Theatre*, p. 136.

129. Willett, *Brecht on Theatre*, p. 168.

130. R. Selden, *A Reader's Guide to Contemporary Literary Theory* (Brighton: Harvester Press, 1985), p. 32.

affinity between father and child. The startling union of Hos. 1.2 is paralleled in an equally startling act of distanciation, in which the prophet's children are labelled 'Jezreel', 'Lo-Ruhamah' and 'Lo-Ammi'. The names Lo-Ruhamah and Lo-Ammi, in particular, exploit the subversion, by foregrounding the natural affections that the names negate. Like Brecht, the author fixes the 'not...but' and foregrounds the natural alternative even as it is repudiated: the children are not loved but detested, and rather than saying 'I forgive you', their father says 'You'll pay for that'.

The defamiliarization of an object, writes Schlovsky, involves a 'game of non-recognition' in which the 'object is not called by its proper name'.[131] Hosea 1 doubly alienates the modern reader by using children as signs, human figures as figures of speech, and by then giving them the most violent and condemnatory and overtly improper names. The 'game of non-recognition' is taken to extremes in a text which practises, effectively, *defamilialization*, by defamiliarizing natural ties and giving children names of rejection and banishment. The children are not only defamiliarized by impeding recognition between the audience and the strangely named child-sign, but are defamilialized in the sense that the negative names imply a lack of recognition between the children and their own father.

'Signs that are wholly arbitrary', writes Saussure, 'realise better than others the ideal of the semiological process'.[132] A sign-system that has passed into convention, like language, preserves the illusion that there is a natural, motivated connection between signifier and signified; similarly second-order signs, such as the link between roses and passion, appear natural when considered within the context of a particular social myth. As Terence Hawkes suggests, while we might allow that auditory signs are arbitrary, we expect visual signs to exhibit at least a degree of iconicity;[133] however, the mythology of Hosea 1, which links newborn infants to the violent history of Israel, bloodshed (Hos. 1.5) and national stigma, seems, in contrast, not only aniconic, but the complete antithesis of the expected iconic relation. The coupling of children and non-love is striking and perverse, and it is reasonable to suggest that it would have appeared so in any society and any historical context. The text is like a dramatization of Schlovsky's theory: if improper naming makes an

131. Schlovsky, 'Art as Technique', p. 21.
132. Saussure, *Course*, p. 68.
133. Hawkes, *Structuralism and Semiotics*, p. 136.

object more noticeable, then these children are certainly designed to command the audience's attention. The conjunction of children and terms of banishment is in its own way as disturbing as the conjunction of prostitute and prophet, and contributes to the text's capacity to disturb the reader, and its reputation as a notoriously 'problematic' text.

The naming of the child-signs in Hosea 1 not only demonstrates the dissolution of the bond between father and child, Yhwh and Israel, but also demonstrates the lack of what Saussure terms a 'natural connection' and a 'fixed bond'[134] in the connection between signifier and signified. The arbitrariness and fragility of the link is made manifest in Hos. 2.1-3, when the same signifiers are used to represent completely antithetical signifieds. The children who once meant 'Not-Loved' and 'Not-My-People' now mean 'Loved' and 'My People'; like Launce's shoes, they exhibit the principle of transformability. In the most extreme form of the Brechtian 'not...but', the text not only suggests alternative gestures but *pursues* two mutually exclusive gestures: thus Hosea hates his children and does not love them; he loves them and does not hate.

Hosea 1–3 acts out at the level of second-order signification principles that Saussure applied to first-order signification: that is, the level of language. Normally the arbitrariness of mythological or symbolic systems is concealed by conventionality, which suggests 'a natural bond between signifier and signified',[135] but in this strange sign system, which is set up precisely by breaking natural links, the arbitrariness of second-order signs is foregrounded. The link between children and non-love is a deliberate subversion of natural connections, and when the same children are used as signifiers of an opposite signified, the text suggests that, as far as second-order systems are concerned, everything depends on the whim of the sign-maker. The illusion that there is always a rationale between second-order signifiers and signifieds is disturbed by the manifestly irrational action of Yhwh, who appears to be more motivated by passion than reason, and who causes signifiers to lurch precariously from one meaning to another.

The idea of a divinely ordained or natural meaning is defamiliarized in a text in which God himself creates bizarre and opposite meanings. For in the strange sign-language designed by Yhwh there is no connection that cannot be made, and no connection that cannot be broken. The text flamboyantly acts out some of the fundamental principles of semiotics

134. Saussure, *Course*, p. 69.
135. Saussure, *Course*, p. 68.

by using a sign-language that it is manifestly man- (or God)-made, arbitrary and subject to alteration. There is nothing natural, dependable or stable about the meanings created; rather, the sign-language is a kind of game with the audience, in which meaning itself is defamiliarized and expectations are inverted.

3.3. *The Elusive Referent*

The word that comes to Hosea is, on closer examination, strangely self-reflexive. כִּי-זָנֹה תִזְנֶה הָאָרֶץ מֵאַחֲרֵי יְהוָה, Yhwh commands לֵךְ קַח-לְךָ אֵשֶׁת זְנוּנִים. The כִּי clause, which might be expected to relate the signifier (the 'wife of harlotry') to the signified (the land), merely reiterates the terms of the signifier and repeats the verb זנה. Lands are not promiscuous but women are; the concept 'the promiscuous land' is dependent on, and created by, the signifier, the אֵשֶׁת זְנוּנִים.

A 'readerly' approach to texts assumes that the author goes from 'signified to signifier, from content to form, from idea to text', and that it is the task of the critic to 'work back from signifier to signified'.[136] Saussure, in contrast, argues that the signified does not precede the signifier and cannot be detached from it, but rather that it is defined 'within the signifying process, in a quasi-tautological way'.[137] The same principle, Barthes suggests, applies to second-order signs: there is no signifier or signified, but only the conglomerate sign, roses passionified[138]—or, in this case, the harlotrous land. Rereading the prophetic text in the context of Barthes and Saussure's semiotic theories suggests that the book of Hosea establishes a new sign-system, or mythology, in which the land is inextricably linked to harlotry and faithlessness.

Most commentators assume that the 'great harlotry of the land' is the pre-condition that inspires the text, and that the 'wife of harlotry' and 'children of harlotry' are gathered to illustrate this already established point. Hosea 1.2 subverts this readerly assumption by presenting a signified that is tautologically dependant on its signifier, and by giving the wife of harlotry sequential priority in the command. As the instruction to 'take a wife of harlotry' precedes the accusation 'for the land commits great harlotry', so the signified is dependent on, and constructed in terms of, the signifier. It does not exist on its own terms, but

---

136. Barthes, *S/Z*, p. 174.
137. Barthes, *Elements of Semiology*, p. 43.
138. Barthes, 'Myth Today', p. 113.

rather borrows the verb זנה, suggesting that the 'harlotrous land' is the creation, rather than the *a priori* condition, of the text.

Semiotic theory enforces a vital distinction between the *signified* and the *referent* of the signifier. In Hos. 1.2 the signifier is the אֵשֶׁת זְנוּנִים, the signified is the concept, 'the harlotrous land', and the referent is the real historical condition of the nation of Israel. In Peirce's terms, the land is the object that inspires the sign, the sign is the 'wife of harlotry', and the interpretant is 'the harlotrous land'. The interpretant is not the same as the object but is an interpretation of the sign, and this in turn gives rise to several related interpretants in critical analysis of the text. Critics write, for example, of a land permeated by the 'smog of apostasy', in which the 'airdex had become lethal',[139] but this is merely an extrapolation from the prophetic rhetoric, a continuation of the sign, rather than a description of its original object (or referent). The referent is, as it were, beyond the margins of the text, and criticism does not solve, but rather continues, the process of semiosis.

The three child-signs, Jezreel, Lo-Ruhamah and Lo-Ammi, demonstrate most clearly the dependence of the signified on the signifier, and the impossibility of inferring an original referent (or 'object') from this text. The naming of the children, like the taking of the wife of harlotry, is explained by a tautological כִּי clause, which reiterates the terms of the name and recoils back upon itself. Jezreel is so called because God will punish the house of Jehu for the 'blood of Jezreel', and break 'the bow of Israel' in the valley of Jezreel; Not-Loved is so called because Yhwh will no more have pity on the house of Israel; and the 'explanation' for the name 'Not-my-people' is that Israel is not Yhwh's people and he is not their God.

As Andersen and Freedman observe, Hosea 1 is obstinately elliptical about the land (or nation) which is the ostensible focus and audience of the address. Unlike the parallel text of Amos, which complements its strange sign-language of plumb-lines (Amos 7.7-9) and summer fruits (Amos 8.1-3) with descriptions of its social and economic context, Hosea 1 determinedly avoids reference to the social milieu in which it is situated.

Remarks about the state of society to which the oracle is addressed are lacking. Yhwh does not say clearly what the house of Jehu has done that requires judgement. He does not say what Israel and Judah have done to

139. J.F. Craghan, 'The Book of Hosea: A Survey of Recent Literature on the First of the Minor Prophets', *BTB* 1 (1971), pp. 81-170 (84).

extinguish his love. He does not say what act of covenant violation required the decision to make them 'Not my people'.[140]

Andersen and Freedman's comment is a provocative starting point, but requires clarification and adjustment. No text, even a text which constantly depicts its social context, can provide unmediated access to the real historical referent: all texts are interpretations and are ideologically motivated. But whereas most texts present the *illusion* of an accessible referent by means of description, Hosea 1 debunks that illusion: the only historical information that is given is the chronology of Hos. 1.1. In the strange sign-language that follows, not only is the referent, the land, invisible, but even the statements about the land (the signifieds) are inextricably bound to the rhetoric of the signifier. The text demonstrates the difficulty of producing statements about the land in terms that are independent of the child signifiers; the only statements that can be deduced from this text are that Israel is not loved, that the nation is not Yhwh's people, and that the house of Jehu will be punished for the blood of Jezreel. This inescapable tautology is repeated at the level of 'text' and 'referent': there is no referent that is detachable from the terms of the text and that is free from the ideological interpretation that the text puts upon it.

The statements 'Israel is not loved' and 'Israel is not Yhwh's people' are interpretants of signs that are themselves ideological interpretations of the state of the nation. The names 'Lo-Ruhamah' and 'Lo-Ammi' foreground the fact that the signs are not descriptive but interpretative, because they are relational names that point not only to the interpreted object (the nation) but to the interpreter. The names raise the question, not-loved and not accepted by whom?, and point to the Yahwistic perspective which conceives them. Israel is not loved by Yhwh and not Yhwh's people, and the text foregrounds its own status as a semiotic interpretation from a distinct ideological perspective.

The manipulation of the term 'Jezreel' in Hos. 1–3 seems to illustate and enforce Peirce's statement that a sign can only yield an interpretant and cannot provide access to the original historical referent. Although, as Andersen and Freedman note, the connection is not clearly elucidated, a specific link is established between Jezreel, the child-sign, and punishment for the 'blood of Jezreel' that occurred during the time of Jehu. The sign is a sign in the classical sense of 'portent', and is a statement

---

140. Andersen and Freedman, *Hosea*, p. 199.

that the bloodshed of Jezreel will be avenged. In 2 Kings 9–10, however, Jezreel is interpreted not as bloodshed to be avenged, but the vengeance of bloodshed and a way of 'aveng[ing] on Jezebel the blood of Yhwh's servants the prophets and the blood of all the servants of the Lord' (2 Kgs 9.7). In 2 Kings Yhwh, as represented by Elisha, proleptically describes Jezreel as a positive act of vengeance; in Hosea 1, as represented by Hosea, he describes the same event analeptically as a moral outrage to be avenged. Hosea's sign 'Jezreel' does not mimic history but recreates history by radical reinterpretation: after passing through Hos. 1.4, Israel's 'history' will never be the same again.

Critical treatment of the sign 'Jezreel' tries to rationalise the conflicting verdicts of 2 Kings 9–10 and Hos. 1.4. D.A. Hubbard argues that it was 'always obvious that Jehu and his descendants had overplayed their hand' and in their 'ambition' had 'outstripped any sense of divine commission',[141] while Andersen and Freedman suggest that 'Hosea viewed the behaviour of Jehu in a dual light: in the very act of carrying out the divine judgement against the house of Ahab, he overstepped the bounds of his mandate and showed that arrogance and self-righteousness that was the undoing of the previous dynasty'.[142] The assumption is that the sign Jezreel must agree with the interpretation given in 2 Kings because it is a direct mediation of the same historical event. As the co-existence of two mutually antipathetic accounts suggests, however, histories are not given but made, and the sign Jezreel is a semiotic interpretation, an ideological emblem of an event, rather than a reconstruction.

In Julia Kristeva's terms, Jezreel and his brother and sister signs are *ideologemes*. They are 'places' in which 'various textual surfaces and networks...of past and present cultures cross', a 'mosaic of quotations', the 'ground upon which the epistemological, social and political reworkings of an entire era are put into play'.[143] Jezreel reworks the politics of an entire era: in this sign a popular perception of the violent overthrow of the Omri dynasty is itself violently overthrown. As Jezreel subverts the canon of history, so Lo-Ruhamah and Lo-Ammi threaten the foundations of epistemology and religion by reworking traditional perceptions of God and national identity. Lo-Ruhamah subverts the

141. D.A. Hubbard, *Hosea: An Introduction and Commentary* (TOTC; Leicester: Inter-Varsity Press, 1989), p. 62.

142. Andersen and Freedman, *Hosea*, p. 180.

143. Kristeva, 'The Bounded Text', in *Desire in Language*, p. 36.

equation between God and love and mercy that occurs frequently in the Hebrew Bible (cf. Exod. 34.6; Deut. 4.31; Joel 2.13; Jon. 4.2; Pss. 86.15; 103.8; 111.4; 145.8; Neh. 9.17, 31; 2 Chron. 30.9) and reworks and ironically echoes the use of the verb רחם in Yhwh's encounter with Moses at Horeb. The name expresses the corollary to Yhwh's promise, 'And I will favour those I favour, and I will pity those I pity (אֲרַחֵם)' (Exod. 33.19). Ironically, and yet perhaps appropriately, a text which accuses Israel of reading the images and idols of Canaanite religion in a distorted manner plays with and distorts images from Israel's past. The sign Lo-Ammi, most radically, plays on and negates the covenant state-ment in Lev. 26.12 in which Yhwh pledges, 'I will walk among you, and will be your God and you will be my people' (וְאַתֶּם תִּהְיוּ לִי לְעָם).

While it is impossible to extrapolate from the wife of harlotry and her children to a real historical referent, it is equally impossible not to read these signs as part of the wider *text* of Israel. Hosea 1 is a mosaic of quo-tations, a patchwork of other texts, that at the same time radically inverts the motifs and assumptions that it borrows. The text does not bring us closer to Israel's real history, but helps to construct or decon-struct perceptions of that history by vying with some of the nation's other versions of itself. Against Walter Brueggemann I suggest that this text represents not *Tradition for Crisis*,[144] but tradition *in* crisis, as the signs jeopardize and subvert the nation's most fundamental assumptions.

3.4. *Semiotic Strategies: The Manipulation of Signs in Hosea 1 and 3*

'Representation hardly ever depended on the representation's likeness to the thing portrayed'.[145]

Hosea 1–3 moves suddenly between iconic and starkly aniconic signs. The 'wife of harlotry' is clearly an icon for idolatry,[146] and the pursuit of other lovers is an explicit analogy for the pursuit of other gods. The sign poses no problem in itself since 'women' and 'harlotry' are naturally

144. W. Brueggemann, *Tradition for Crisis: A Study in Hosea* (Richmond: John Knox Press, 1968). Brueggemann argues that Hosea 'handle[s] old traditions faith-fully but creatively' (p. 14), but in my opinion the inversion of divine promises and the reinterpretation of the events at Jezreel constitute a manipulation of religious tradition that is more 'creative' than 'faithful'.

145. Bertolt Brecht, cited in Willett, *Brecht on Theatre*, p. 182.

146. The sign 'idolatry is harlotry' is a popular motif in the prophetic literature, and is therefore also a symbol because it signifies by convention (cf. Isa. 1.21; Jer. 2.20; 3.1, 3; Ezek. 16.15, 30, 31, 33).

linked (within a patriarchal ideology); it only becomes problematic when placed in conjunction with a man of God. The only oxymoron is between the sign and its context; the associated phrase 'children of harlotry' is, in contrast, *internally* oxymoronic, awkward and abrasive.

Whereas the association between 'wife' and 'harlotry' has required no explanation in itself,[147] the association of children and harlotry, innocence and sexual promiscuity, has jarred with commentators and resulted in a range of explanations. Critics have suggested that the name, unlike their mother's, 'casts no slur' upon their characters,[148] and conversely, that the sins of the mother are visited upon the children.[149] The 'children of harlotry' have been qualified as offspring resulting from their mother's prostitution, as 'offspring from [a] womb resulting from the cult of Baal, and therefore *religiously* the offspring of harlotry',[150] and as personifications of original sin, that is, children tainted by the desire to consort with other lovers/gods from the moment of their birth. What matters to this analysis is not the relative merits of the arguments but the fact of their existence, which, like the sheer volume of commentary on Hos. 1.2, suggests that there is a problem in the text, or between the text and reader, that demands resolution.

Although they are introduced in the same clause as a kind of signifying package,[151] the children of harlotry are not like the 'wife of harlotry' because they are not clearly iconic. The tensions in the collective sign יַלְדֵי זְנוּנִים anticipate the strain in the individual signs, in which the innocence of the signifier (the child) exists in stark contrast to the guilt of the signified (the Northern Kingdom). As commentators compensate for the strained relationship between Hosea and Gomer by deflecting attention to the perfect comparison between idolatry and prostitution, so commentators attempt to produce some kind of signifying rationale for these ostensibly arbitrary and morally problematic signs. H.D. Beeby, for

147. Although the phrase אֵשֶׁת זְנוּנִים has aroused much scholarly interest, most studies have focused on the etymology and semantic field of the dual form זְנוּנִים.

148. J.M. Powis Smith, 'The Marriage of Hosea', *BW* 42, pp. 94-101 (100).

149. Charles Hauret suggests that 'la perversion de la mère rejaillira sur ses enfants' ('the mother's perversion will redound on her children'; *Amos et Osée: Un livret de famille originale* [Paris: Beauchesne, 1970], p. 139).

150. Mays, *Hosea*, p. 26 (my italics).

151. The RSV separates the wife of harlotry and the children of harlotry, by translating Yhwh's command as 'Go take a wife of harlotry and have children of harlotry'. The MT in contrast, presents the wife and children as joint objects of the verb 'to take': לק קח-לך אשת זנונים וילדי זנונים.

example, underplays the negativity of the name, emphasizes that Lo-Ruhamah, linked to רֶחֶם (womb), is an appropriate name for a female child, and tries to reinforce the link between signifier and signified by suggesting that 'the handicap of...a mere daughter' symbolizes the 'frailty and dependence of Israel'.[152]

Despite attempts to produce harmonious relationships between signifier and signified, the child-signs are manifestly aniconic and signify indexically. The transition between the 'wife of harlotry' and the 'children of harlotry', from icon to indices, allows the author to manipulate the sign-language towards a distinct ideological agenda. Gomer-bat-Diblayim is the crux of the signifying structure—she plays the part of the 'wife of harlotry' and functions as an icon for the accusation of idolatry. At the same time, she is an image that, as Yeats might put it, 'begets fresh images', and is the key figure in a process of semiosis. The first generation sign gives birth to second generation signs, which, as the term 'children of harlotry' implies, are connected through her to the related ideas of harlotry and idolatry. The child-signs have no natural connection to these terms but are connected to them through their mother. The birth is a false link in the chain of semiosis, which connects the child-signs to the idea of harlotry not by a natural semantic/semiotic relationship, but by a different kind of relationship. The idea of 'giving birth to' is a natural relationship that functions as a substitute for a natural, or recognizable relationship between children and harlotry: it is a subtle point of transition that allows the text to equate idolatry with the terms of punishment expressed in Jezreel, Lo-Ruhamah and Lo-Ammi.

According to Peirce, a semiotic chain occurs when a sign leads to its interpretation, which in turn constitutes another sign, and so on. Although the ultimate meaning is never reached, the chain at least creates the illusion of a semiotic striptease in which the meaning of the first sign will eventually be revealed. Hosea 1 involves a far more riddling process of semiosis: the signs that follow the 'wife of harlotry' do not explain her—indeed they are not semiotically connected to her at all—and the only link between them is not one of meaning but of birth. The sexual life that is on one level an icon for idolatry is on another level the literal cause of the three children who develop an entirely independent semiotic function of their own. The children 'mean' as dark clouds mean rain: they function as indexical 'pointing fingers' in the prophetic

---

152. H.D. Beeby, *Grace Abounding: A Commentary on the Book of Hosea* (Grand Rapids: Eerdmans, 1989), p. 16.

text. The signifieds of these bizarre signifiers are forms of national punishment, and they point to the spectre of divine rejection.

The linchpin of the signifying chain in Hosea 1 is sexual intercourse. Intercourse is an icon of idolatry but on a literal level it leads to children; the implication is that as surely as sex leads to conception and birth, so idolatry leads to the wrath of Yhwh. The chain is not a natural semiotic extension of the motif 'idolatry is harlotry', nor is it an attempt to elucidate the initial sign; rather, it uses a different kind of 'natural' connection to craft the meaning 'idolatry means punishment'. The human relationship between the signifiers, mother and children, creates an artificial link between the signifieds of the two generations of signs. As mother is related to child, so idolatry, the signified of the wife of harlotry, is cunningly *related* to curses, and harlotry, quite literally, gives birth to punishment.[153]

Many critics describe Hosea 1 and Hosea 3 as parallel texts, but at the same time find it difficult to ascertain the precise nature of the relationship. Hosea 3.1, in which Yhwh instructs Hosea to 'love a woman who is beloved of a paramour and is an adulteress' (מְנָאָפֶת), imitates, albeit with a different tone and emphasis, Hos. 1.2, but at this point the two narratives diverge, and the מְנָאָפֶת fulfils a different signifying function to the אֵשֶׁת זְנוּנִים. The analogies that exist between the two texts are complex and ambiguous, and cannot be reduced to the verdict that they are two versions of the same events told in the third and then the first person, or even that they are two ways of expressing a similar meaning. If the meaning of the symbolism is not the same, however, the method for crafting meaning is strikingly similar, and one way in which the texts overlap is in their manipulation of signs to distinct ideological ends.

The link between the מְנָאָפֶת of Hos. 3.1 and the apostasy of the nation is, like the link between the 'wife of harlotry' and idolatry, manifestly iconic. The connection between signifier and signified is developed to almost allegorical proportions in the accompanying commentary:

> And the Lord said to me, 'Go again, love a woman who is beloved of a
> paramour and is an adulteress; *even as the Lord loves the people of Israel,*

153. A New Testament analogy is Jas 1.15, in which birth (this time as a metaphor) is used to forge links between 'desire', 'sin' and 'death'. The idea of a natural link between generations is used to connect otherwise unrelated concepts and to craft a new theological equation. 'Desire', 'sin' and 'death' are effectively portrayed as three generations of women in the statement 'Then desire when it has conceived gives birth to sin, and sin when it is full grown brings forth death'.

> *though they turn to other gods and love cakes of raisins'* (Hos. 3.1; my
> italics).

As in ch. 1, however, the clear iconicity of the opening verses develops
into a far more cryptic and aniconic sign-language, as, in a process that
is almost as elaborate as the catalogues of conception, birth and naming
in ch. 1, the prophet insists that the woman must 'dwell as [his] for
many days' (3.3) to demonstrate that 'Israel shall dwell many days
without king or leader, without sacrifice or pillar, without ephod or
teraphim' (3.4).[154] The lengthy terms given to the adulteress, that 'she
shall not play the harlot or belong to another man' (3.3), foreground the
problems in establishing an appropriate signifier, just as Hosea 1 foregrounds the laborious process of producing signs for a prophetic text.

The אֵשֶׁת זְנוּנִים has a primary signifying function as an icon of idolatry,
and a second, indexical function, in that she causes, or gives birth to,
signs of punishment. In the adulteress the two functions are conflated in
the same figure: in Hos. 3.1 she is used to signify the land's desertion of
Yhwh for other gods and raisin cakes; and in Hos. 3.3-4 she is confined,
and adapted to become a signifier for the sons of Israel's loss of leader-
ship and of religion. She fulfils the function of the אֵשֶׁת זְנוּנִים as a signifier
of idolatry, and the function of the child-signs, as a portent of punishment, but, as in ch. 1, the primary signifying function is far more neat,
more iconic, than its extension. To a lesser degree than the signifiers
Jezreel, Lo-Ruhamah and Lo-Ammi, the 'confined adulteress' co-exists
uneasily with her signified, and the signified is defamiliarizing because it
is the inverse of what might be expected.

The problem with the child-signs is that the innocent signifier is used
as a signifier for the guilty land, resulting in a resonant clash of values.
The problem with the 'confined adulteress' is that the loss of illegitimate
contact with other lovers is used as a signifier for the loss of seemingly
legitimate political and religious institutions.[155] As the expected names

---

154. I have translated שַׂר as 'leader' rather than 'prince' (RSV) because in English
'prince' suggests membership of the royal family. In the Hebrew Bible, שַׂר means
'master', 'chief', 'commander', as well as 'noble': it is a term applied to men with an
important administrative or military function.

155. Though the phrase וְגַם אֲנִי אֵלַיִךְ is elliptical, and thus ambiguous, the denial of
illegitimate sex is the overriding sense of Hos. 3.3. The role of the woman as an
adulteress is stressed, and the particle לֹא is prefixed to the actions of harlotry (תִזְנִי
לֹא) and of belonging to other men (וְלֹא תִהְיִי לְאִישׁ). The positioning of the athnach
under לְאִישׁ separates the relation with the prophet from the relation with other men,

for the child-signs are names of acceptance and belonging, so the expected signified for the woman denied other lovers is a land denied access to other gods. Surprisingly, Hos. 3.4 presents the reader with a catalogue which is dominated not by symbols of the Baal cult, but by terms which are inextricably entwined with Israel's own political and religious life.

In Hos. 3.1 the signified of adultery is harlotry, consorting with gods who love raisin cakes; in Hos. 3.3-4 the signified for the denial of access to other lovers is the loss of king and leader, sacrifice and pillar and ephod and teraphim. The two-fold denial at the level of the signifier, לֹא תִזְנִי וְלֹא תִהְיִי לְאִישׁ results in a sixfold denial at the level of the signified, and the taboo spheres of activity, the signified of 'illicit sex', are presented in three symbolic pairs. The pairs are symbols in Peirce's sense: they symbolize by convention and refer to social and religious conventions in the life of Israel. The prophet is not merely erasing a selected catalogue of six items but the national identity that is associated with them; as Andersen and Freedman observe, 'the list in total stands for national existence and their disappearance signals the end of the state'.[156]

Rather than presenting the reader with a list of items that are distinctively Canaanite, such as Baalim and raisin cakes, Hos. 3.4 confronts the reader with a list of items that are by no means foreign to the texts and history of Israel. 'King and leader' symbolize government, the political and administrative life of the nation; 'sacrifice and pillar' symbolize the sacrificial rituals of the Israelite cult, and the sanctuaries and pillars associated with those rituals—such as those at Bethel (Gen. 28.18, 22; 35.14)

and implies, as Andersen and Freedman point out, that 'the relation with the husband is defined by other words, and is to follow a different course' (*Hosea*, p. 303). To extend the negative to the final clause, so that the woman is denied access to the prophet as well as to other lovers, it is necessary to considerably amplify the passage: thus the REB renders Hos. 3.3: 'You will live in my house for a long time and you will not lead an immoral life. You must have relations with no-one else, indeed not even with me'. While this sense cannot be completely ruled out, it is also true that translators have to go to considerable lengths to achieve it (cf. n. 45). The simplest and most obvious sense is to assume that the verb הִיה is implied, so that the sense is, as the RSV suggests, 'so will I also be to you' (cf. 'you shall not belong [i.e. 'be to'] another man'). The meaning is therefore one of mutual contract—as the prophet enforces exclusive commitment to him, so he, in a parallel clause, promises exclusive commitment to the adulteress.

156. Andersen and Freedman, *Hosea*, p. 305.

and Shechem (Gen. 33.20; Josh. 24.36)—while 'ephod and teraphim'
evoke a tradition of divination of the divine will that ranges from the
Levitical priesthood (symbolized by the ephod)[157] to the use of household gods, or images (teraphim).[158] Of these only teraphim are associated primarily with foreign gods: in Genesis 31 Rachel steals the household teraphim, which Laban calls his 'gods' (Gen. 31.30); and in
Gen. 35.2 Jacob admonishes his household to rid themselves of the
foreign gods (אֱלֹהֵי הַנֵּכָר) which they have brought back with them.
Banned by Josiah's reforms (2 Kgs 23.24) and condemned by Samuel
(1 Sam. 15.23), teraphim are the only objects on the list that have never
had a firm place in Israelite tradition, and in this catalogue of foundational religious and political institutions תְּרָפִים is effectively the odd word
out.

In Alexander Pope's 'The Rape of the Lock', Belinda's dressing-table
is adorned with 'Puffs, powders, patches, Bibles, billet-doux'.[159] 'Bibles'
is a lexical misfit, the odd word out in a category of trivia, and it jars
because it is unexpected. In Hos. 3.4 the opposite is true: the lexical
misfit is תְּרָפִים because it *is* expected. Only teraphim suggest the 'other
gods' or idols that are the expected signifieds for the acts of committing
harlotry and belonging to other men. 'Pillar' (מַצֵּבָה), to a lesser extent,
might also be included in this category not because the term is incompatible with Israelite tradition (indeed, pillars play an important role in
the religion of the patriarchs) but because pillars can be confused with
symbols of foreign gods. Unlike teraphim, pillars have a legitimate function in Israel's religious tradition, but in Deuteronomy the writer asserts
that this is undermined by their ambiguous appearance: in

---

157. The ephod, an 'item of priestly apparel' or a 'sacred vestment', is usually
mentioned only in conjunction with a priest (see, for example, Judg. 17.5; 18.4, 17,
18, 20; 1 Sam. 21.9; 22.18; 23.16; 30.7). Hos. 3.4 is the only instance in which it
occurs independently (C. Meyers, 'Ephod', in D.N. Freedman [ed.], *The Anchor
Bible Dictionary* [New York: Doubleday, 1992], II, p. 550).

158. R.K. Harrison defines teraphim as 'a type of idol or image, often associated
with divination...similar to the *penates* of the Romans...the exact appearance and
function [of which] are unknown' ('Teraphim', in G.W. Bromiley [ed.], *The
International Standard Bible Encyclopaedia* [Grand Rapids: Eerdmans, 1988], IV,
p. 793).

159. A. Pope, 'The Rape of the Lock', Canto I, l. 138, in R. Sowerby (ed.),
Alexander Pope: Selected Poetry and Prose (London: Routledge & Kegan Paul,
1988).

Deut. 16.21-22, 'pillars' are described as hated by God because they resemble trees planted as an Asherah.

The signified of the 'confined adulteress', like the signifieds of the child-signs, is unfamiliar, defamiliarizing, and the inverse of what might be expected. 'Other gods', the anticipated signified, is in the background rather than the foreground, but the text mitigates the shock by smoothing the transition between Hos. 3.3 and 3.4. Through repetition of the phrase יָמִים רַבִּים and the verb יָשׁב and by echoing the reiterated negative לֹא (3.3) in the reiterated particle אֵין (3.4), the text enforces the link between the two verses and creates the illusion that Hos. 3.4 is the natural extension of Hos. 3.3. The grammatical and lexical mirroring fulfils a similar function to the births in ch. 1, by easing the reader across an awkward transition in the absence of any expected or natural, semantic/semiotic connection.

Critical treatment of Hosea 3, like commentaries on Hosea 1, suggests that critics have been aware of, and sought to remedy, disjuncture and seeming inappropriateness in the text.[160] As Charles Hauret celebrates Hos. 1.2 as a 'perfect comparison', and H.D. Beeby emphasizes the appropriateness of the gender of the second child, so Hubbard implies that the sign in Hos. 3.3 and 3.4 possesses perfect internal symmetry:

> Gomer is to be deprived of intercourse: Israel of *king, prince, sacrifice* and *pillar, teraphim* and *ephod*. The deprivation is suitable and thorough.[161]

Like the MT, Hubbard stresses the common motif of deprivation, but does not attempt to describe how king and leader, sacrifice and pillar, ephod and teraphim correspond to an adulteress's liaisons with her lovers. The connection can only be made through the process of denial rather than the activities that will be denied, but denial/deprivation is only one way of describing the prophet's symbolic actions in Hos. 3.3. Common assessments of Hos. 3.3 proposed by commentators are that the wife is being purified, placed in 'quarantine',[162] or that she who lacks restraint is being subjected to a period of control. A period of

160. The most obvious example of this is redaction criticism, which has traditionally assigned the chapter to at least two authors (see, for example, L. Ruppert, 'Erwägungen zur Kompositions- und Redaktionsgeschichte von Osea 1–3', *BZ* 26 [1982], pp. 208-23).

161. Hubbard, *Hosea*, p. 93.

162. A.D. Tushingham, 'A Reconsideration of Hosea Chapters 1–3', *JNES* 12 (1953), pp. 150-58 (155).

purification provides an awkward contrast to the removal of some of the
key features of Israelite religion, while Hos. 3.4 seems to suggest not the
imposition, but the disintegration of order, through the withdrawal of
fundamental political and religious structures.

Unlike Hubbard, H.W. Wolff highlights the disparity between the two
verses but seeks to resolve that disparity by redaction. He explains the
peculiarity that in Hos. 3.4 'legitimate as well as illegitimate contact is
prevented'[163] by trying to establish a similar heterogeneity at the level of
the signifier. וְגַם אֲנִי אֵלַיִךְ should, he claims, be read as a statement that
Hosea will also deny himself to Gomer, and to support this sense Wolff
proposes either that לֹא אֵלַךְ has been lost as a homoeoteleuton, or that
אֵלַיִךְ should be read as עָלַיִךְ (that is, 'I will also be against you').[164] As
evidence for this emendation he cites critical tradition,[165] the need to
balance the parallelism between the two clauses in vv. 3, and, most
revealingly, the fact that negative meaning is 'presupposed by the words
of interpretation in verse 4'.[166] His third statement betrays his own presupposition and suggests that he is responding to a semiotic, rather than
a textual problem; like Eybers and Snaith on the relationship between
'Gomer' and 'Israel', Wolff is trying to achieve a perfect pairing
between signifier and signified.

Despite attempts to transform the statement into a denial of legitimate
and illegitimate contact, most commentators, including Wolff,
instinctively interpret Hos. 3.3 as a way of shielding the woman from

---

163. Wolff, *Hosea*, p. 62.

164. Wolff, *Hosea*, p. 56.

165. The conversion of Hos. 3.3 to a denial of legitimate as well as illegitimate
sexual contact has a long history in the critical tradition. The earliest emendation was
made by Kimchi and Ibn Ezra, who inserted לֹא אָבוֹא; the most recent emendation is
Andersen's suggestion that תֵּשְׁבִי should be read as 'you will wait' rather than 'you
will dwell' so that the last clause is the promise of a fully restored relationship—'then
indeed I will be yours' (Andersen and Freedman, *Hosea*, p. 291). Unlike Wolff I am
sceptical about the assumption that the popularity of a particular interpretation in the
critical tradition is evidence for its correctness; older interpretations do not naturally
possess more authority, and Ibn Ezra and Kimchi, writing in the twelfth century, had
no more access to 'the authentic text' than the modern commentator. On closer examination it becomes apparent that although critics have been united in their desire to
alter the text, they have done so in different ways, suggesting that what they object to
is the awkward sense and peculiar semiosis, rather than a particular word or phrase
that betrays evidence of a redactor.

166. Wolff, *Hosea*, p. 56.

temptation and from her own weaknesses. 'The woman who could no longer resist temptation', writes Wolff, 'was saved from it',[167] but the problem then becomes, how does this relate to the signified—are 'king and leader, sacrifice and pillar, ephod and teraphim', by extension, temptations to evil? Many commentators conclude that the negativity of the signifier transfers to the signified, and that Hosea was opposed to the monarchy and to Israelite as well as Canaanite cultic practices. J.L. Mays, for example, argues that Hosea, 'like Amos, rejects Israel's sacrifices', and denounces ephod and teraphim 'as a ritual for getting a divine revelation apart from tradition or the prophetic message'. He concludes that Hos. 3.4 concentrates on 'the removal of all that stood between Israel and the ancient and true relation to Yhwh'.[168]

Whether or not commentators choose to interpret Hos. 3.4, in the light of Hos. 3.3, as a catalogue of 'seductive influences',[169] the close conjunction of the illegitimate with the legitimate, like the close conjunction of the prophet and prostitute, or guilt and innocence in the child-signs, results in an interpretative crisis. Signifier and signified are mutually influenced by their co-existence, and if the signifier is 'the denial of illegitimate sex', this certainly implies something about the catalogue of symbols in v. 4. King, leader, sacrifice, pillar and ephod are, like Jezreel, ideologemes that extend into Israel's history and interact with other texts of that history, and, like Jezreel, they have in other texts a generally positive sense.[170] As Jezreel is given negative connotations, the

167. Wolff, *Hosea*, p. 62.

168. Mays, *Hosea*, p. 59. As Hosea is seen as a book that proleptically anticipates Christian salvation, so Hos. 3.4 is seen as the removal of cultic accessories that hampered a true relation with God. From a twentieth-century Protestant perspective, it is easy to see the removal of ritual as a positive act, but this overlooks the fact that for an Israelite audience in the eighth century, cult practices and the worship of Yhwh were not detachable concepts.

169. Tushingham, 'A Reconsideration', p. 155.

170. This is not to say that the institutions cannot be abused (many kings, for example, are not given a particularly good press in Kings and Chronicles) but rather that the institutions themselves are generally accepted as part of the fabric of society. In a particularly relevant perversion of Israelite institutions, Judg. 8.24-28 describes how Gideon made an 'ephod' and Israel 'played the harlot' after it; but unlike the descriptions of teraphim, this is not a critique of the convention as such, but the use to which it had been put. There is an important difference between institutions that are part of the Israel's identity but which are occasionally misused, and objects such as teraphim, which are persistently regarded with suspicion throughout the Hebrew Bible. Though they are occasionally presented as a pair (Judg. 17.5; 18.14, 17, 20)

precise nature of which is unclear, so king and leader, sacrifice and pillar, ephod and teraphim are interrogated and exposed to suspicion by means of their repositioning as signifieds of adultery.

Hosea 1 and 3 are parallel texts in the sense that they are semiotically parallel. Both begin with a promiscuous woman who is used as a signifier of the apostasy of the nation, but both move beyond a simple harlotry/adultery–idolatry equation, to use the women's sexuality in new and creative ways. In Hosea 1 the woman's sexuality is unrestrained, and results in three new child-signs. In Hosea 3 the restraint of the woman's sexuality becomes a sign in itself. From the expected analogy 'idolatry is harlotry', both texts develop a strange semiotic chain that ends in bizarre and defamiliarizing meanings: Hosea 1 'produces' a reversal of traditional understandings of Yhwh's relation to Israel, and Hosea 3 ends by equating adultery not with idolatry, but with elements from Israel's own religion.

Although Hosea 1 and 3 follow similar semiotic paths and pass from the familiar to the cryptic and defamiliarizing, there is a marked difference in terms of Yhwh's involvement with the proceedings. In Hosea 1 he directs the process of semiosis: he instructs Hosea on the naming of each child and manipulates the chain of signs towards his ultimate meaning: idolatry means (or leads to) alienation from the deity. In Hosea 3, in contrast, the process of semiosis has its own momentum, and, as Wolff perceptively observes, 'More is accomplished than the command [Hos. 3.1] indicates, and the interpretation [Hos. 3.3] goes beyond the previous symbolic action'.[171] The only meaning that Yhwh commands is a simple allegorical tableau of forgiving love (Hos. 3.1), and the text moves beyond the divine initiative when it creates from the מְנָאֶפֶת new and increasingly shocking signifieds.

3.5. *The Semiotics of Hosea 2: The Blurring of Signifier and Signified*
In Hosea 1 and Hosea 3 a firm division is established between signifier and signified. The sign-language is patterned and formulaic, and each symbolic person or action (each signifier) is explained in an interpretative gloss. The components of the sign are clearly demarcated: Hos. 3.3 specifically describes the signifier, and Hos. 3.4 the signified; and simi-

---

there is a radical difference between descriptions of the ephod and of teraphim: the prophet Samuel, for example, wears an ephod (1 Sam. 2.18, 28) and yet condemns the use of teraphim (1 Sam. 15.23).

171. Wolff, *Hosea*, p. 58.

larly the four signs in ch. 1 are split into signifiers (the wife of harlotry, Jezreel, Lo-Ruhamah and Lo-Ammi) and signifieds (for the land commits great harlotry; for I will punish the house of Jehu; I will no more have pity on the house of Israel; you are not my people and I am not your God). Hosea 2, in contrast, respects no neat boundaries, and the text creates, as Walter Vogels puts it, *un entrecroisement constant* ('a constant intersection')[172] between Hosea–Gomer and Yhwh–Israel.

Hosea 1 and 3 neatly compartmentalize sexual and family terms associated with the signifier (harlot, adulteress, children and lovers) and the terms defining the national macrocosm (the land, the house of Jehu, the house of Israel, king and leader, sacrifice and pillar, ephod and teraphim). Hosea 2, in contrast, mixes the two levels of lexis, so that it is impossible to perceive where the signifier ends and the signified begins. Although many commentators attempt to mark transition points in the text where the focus unequivocally shifts from Hosea–Gomer to Yhwh–Israel, such distinctions are extremely difficult to sustain[173] because language from the physical level of the signifier (breasts [2.4], nakedness [2.5, 11, 12], thirst [2.5], lovers [2.7] and children [2.3-4]) co-exists in the same phrase, or clause, with terms evocative of the national and religious life of Israel (wilderness [2.5], feasts, new moons, sabbaths [2.13] and Baals [2.10, 18, 19]). The only exceptions are the two cosmic promises that frame the text, 2.1-2 and 2.18-25, in which the dominant terms of the lexis are Judah, Israel, the land (2.2), Baal (2.18-19), covenant (2.20) and heaven and earth (2.23). These two statements, which enclose the text, step free from the semiotic entanglements of the

172. W. Vogels, '"Osée–Gomer": *car* et *comme* "Yahweh–Israël", Os 1–3', *NRT* 103 (1981), pp. 711-27 (719).

173. Although he remarks on the constant interweaving of signifier and signified in this chapter, Vogels still attempts to separate the divine from the human by confining each to different verses. Basing his argument on the fact that in 2.3-5 the children are addressed in the second person but in 2.5b-6 they are addressed in the third person, he argues that the human speaker is replaced by the divine, since Hosea would automatically address his children directly ('Osée–Gomer', p. 715). In my opinion a text that describes Hosea's experiences in the third person in ch. 1 and in the first person in ch. 3 allows no such easy divisions; the text shifts from one mode of address to another, but this is not firm evidence for a transition between signifier and signified. Although Hosea 1 is in the third person, it is no more or less concerned than ch. 3 with the human level of the text; in Hosea 2, similarly, the shift in the narrator's perspective does not directly correspond to transitions between the 'domestic' and the 'cosmic' levels.

intervening chapter; the passages are comfortably unambiguous, because the domestic signifier recedes into the background and the emphasis is placed firmly on the universal signified.

The focus of Hos. 2.3-17 is a woman who is at once a mother, wife and harlot—an extension of the role of Gomer-bat-Diblayim—and an embodiment of a wider signifying function, as a signifier of the nation. In Hos. 2.10, almost imperceptibly, 'she' becomes 'they' as the male speaker protests:

> And she did not know that it was I who gave her (אָנֹכִי נָתַתִּי לָהּ) the grain,
> the wine and the oil, and who lavished upon her (הִרְבֵּיתִי לָהּ) the silver and
> gold which they used for Baal (עָשׂוּ לַבָּעַל).

The statement functions doubly as an aggrieved husband's threat to withdraw provision from his wife, and as Yhwh's protest against idols offered to Baal. As 'she' merges into 'they', staple provisions that a husband might be expected to provide for his wife develop into silver and gold, precious metals used to craft idols. In Hos. 2.16-17, similarly, the lexis of the signifier fades into the signified: the woman is to be seduced, the speaker will speak tenderly to her and she will answer as in the days of her youth 'at the time when she came out of the land of Egypt'. The sexual language of seduction coexists with historical references to the Valley of Achor and the Exodus: as provisions in 2.10 develop into silver and gold, so the wilderness develops from a location for seduction at the level of the signifier to a symbol of Israel's past and a component of the signified.

In Hosea 2 there is no stark distinction between signifier and signified, but rather an amalgam, 'the harlotrous woman/harlotrous land'. Renaud offers a cinematic analogy:

> In cinematic language, one would refer to 'fade in/fade out'; the woman
> represents Gomer and Israel at one and the same time.[174]

In Hosea 1 and 3 Yhwh–Israel and Gomer–Hosea are like separate frames of a film compiled in a montage, but in Hosea 2 the signifier and signified fade into one another, as when one frame is superimposed on the next in a cinematic mix or dissolve. The 'va-et-vient constant du signifiant au signifié'[175] or, as Vogels puts it, the 'glissements'

---

174. 'En langage cinématique, on parlerait de fondu-enchaîné: la femme represénte à la fois Gomer et Israël' (Renaud, 'Osée 1–3', p. 255).

175. Renaud, 'Osée 1–3', p. 256.

('slippages')[176] between the two levels of the text are subtle, and, as it were, blurred at the edges, so that it is impossible to discern where one frame ends and the next begins.

Hosea 2.3-17, like Hosea 1 and 3, is based on the sign 'the land is like a harlotrous woman', but its expression is less explicit and it pervades the text, as Renaud suggests, 'en creux' ('in the background').[177] In Hosea 1 and 3 the text moves from signifier to signified so that the reader is in no doubt where the ultimate emphasis lies; but in Hos. 2.3-17 it is more difficult to discern which level of the sign, the human or the national, receives ultimate emphasis. In Hos. 1.2 'the wife of harlotry' is clearly subordinated to, and used as a signifier of, the harlotrous land; but in Hos. 2.5 the same motifs, the woman and land, co-exist in a far more complex and ambiguous relationship. The male threat,

> Lest I strip her naked
> and make her as the day she was born,
> and make her like a wilderness,
> and set her like a parched land
> and slay her with thirst,

combines starkly physical terms such as 'nakedness', 'birth', 'thirst' with 'wilderness' and 'parched land', but no longer subordinates the woman to the land in a clearly demarcated signifying relationship. This is more than a mere anthropomorphism: the woman does not simply embody the land, but dominates this passage. *She* will be like a parched land and *she* is the focus of the sentence; if any element in this passage is subordinate, it is the 'wilderness' and 'parched land', which are virtually used as signifiers of *her*.

In Hosea 2.3-17 the woman outgrows her role as mere signifier, and is graphically described in a way that threatens to eclipse and marginalize the signified. The signifier is described in details that far exceed its semiotic function: thus in Hos. 2.8-9, the speaker does not merely say that he will prevent his wife from pursuing her lovers, but goes as far as to describe the means of entrapment he will use (thornbushes and walls),

176. Vogels, 'Osée–Gomer', p. 718.
177. Renaud, 'Osée 1–3', p. 256.

which can have no possible equivalent at the level of the signified. Similarly, in Hos. 2.12-13 the threat that the woman will be stripped before her lovers and trapped in her jealous husband's hand makes the corresponding threat, that Yhwh will terminate Israel's festivals, rather timid by comparison.

Like the equation between children and curses in Hosea 1, the conjunction of signifier and signified in Hos. 2.3-17 is awkward; but this is not because the signified outweighs the signifier, but because the signifier is described in far more detail than the signified. At the level of the signifier the text presents a compelling drama of pursuit (2.9), seeking (2.9), slaying (2.5), trapping (2.8), and seduction (2.16) that threatens to dwarf by contrast the religious life of Israel. The level of the signifier is not only intensely dramatic, but overtly sexual. The signifier has the lure of pornography, and in a sequence for which it is hard to find any direct analogy at the level of the signified, the woman is stripped three times, her breasts and genitalia exposed (2.5, 11, 12).

In his analysis of Hosea 2, Renaud describes the blurring of human signifiers and national signifieds as a *double entendre*, but I would argue that to express idolatry in terms of harlotry/adultery is to create a euphemism *in reverse*. The spiritual is described in terms of the physical, and an abstract concept is literally embodied: in an inversion of the innuendo, the sexually explicit subject matter is also semiotically explicit, while the more decorous meaning is implicit in the text. Even the most dominant and coherent sign in Hosea 1–3, 'idolatry is harlotry', encompasses a sense of strain, because issues of religious commitment are expressed in images of sexual intercourse and are personified in promiscuity. The strain permeates the text, but becomes more explicit in ch. 2, in which the sexual imagery reaches, as it were, its climax.

Hosea 2 does not merely embody 'idolatry' as 'harlotry', but highlights and exploits the analogy by focusing relentlessly on the woman's body. The stark physicality of the signifier is foregrounded, and human life is reduced to its very essence—nakedness, sex, thirst and passion. The predominance of the human drama, the use of titillating sexual imagery, ensures, on one level, the attention of the audience. The danger is that the signifiers sex and seduction may themselves exhibit a seductive power, and lure the reader's attention away from the 'real' meaning of the text.

3.6. *Proper and Improper Names: The Battle Between First- and Second-Order Signification*

'What's the *use* of a child without a meaning?' (The Red Queen, *Alice in Wonderland*)

In Nathaniel Hawthorne's *The Scarlet Letter*, Hester Prynne, a 'woman of adultery', is marked by the Puritan community with a scarlet letter 'A'. Her daughter Pearl, the offspring of her sexual liaison, becomes, similarly, a 'living hieroglyphic',[178] a 'scarlet letter endowed with life'.[179] Hosea 1 introduces a similarly 'significant family':[180] a mother marked by 'harlotry' and children who, as Powis-Smith and Beeby observe, function as 'walking sermons',[181] 'living pulpits, walking placards'.[182] Like the chair placed on stage, the prophet's family are semiotized: they are the 'objects' used to represent an entire category, the people who come to stand for 'a people'.

The majority of commentators tend to ignore or repress this living dimension of the text. The emphasis, to use J.L. Mays's distinction, is on 'divine word' rather than 'human life',[183] and despite the laborious lengths to which the text goes to produce a play with living participants, the appropriation of woman and children as signs is repressed in secondary texts. E. Jacob, for example, maintains that 'Les enfants ne sont que les figurants' ('The children are only images'),[184] and his commentary, like many others, could equally describe a text in which Yhwh states directly, 'Call the land Jezreel/Lo-Ruhamah/Lo-Ammi'. If the majority of commentators ignore the incorporation of the prophet's family into the process of semiosis, what is the function of these bizarre signifiers: are they superfluous to the text's meaning, or does their presence actually alter the impact and message of the text?

In a brief aside H.W. Wolff suggests that living signifiers have a drastic impact on the signifying process. The appropriation of children as signs does not, he confesses, elucidate a meaning so much as split the reader's

178. N. Hawthorne, *The Scarlet Letter* (New York: Norton, 1978), p. 148.

179. Hawthorne, *The Scarlet Letter*, p. 76.

180. Hubbard, *Hosea*, p. 58.

181. J.M. Powis-Smith, 'The Marriage of Hosea', p. 100.

182. Beeby, *Grace Abounding*, p. 15.

183. Mays, *Hosea*, p. 23.

184. E. Jacob, 'Osée', in *Osée, Joël, Abdias, Jonas, Amos* (CAT; Neuchâtel: Delachaux et Niestlé, 1965), p. 21.

response. In his commentary on Hosea 1 he pauses at the naming of Lo-Ruhamah and asks:

> But who is the subject of this sentence, i.e. who is not to receive Yhwh's mercy? In analogy to other related symbolical names, this is not to be found in the child herself, even though this confusingly suggests itself in this very case.[185]

Wolff points to an interpretative ambiguity in which two signifieds, the child and the land, compete for one signifier, Lo-Ruhamah. He describes a tangled and disturbing semiotic but attempts to compensate for this with a far less compelling solution. His assertion that the name is simply not to be applied to the child herself is unexplained and unconvincing, and suggests that although he is aware of a dual signified, he finds one of these impossible to accept. Retaining Wolff's description without the easy resolution, I suggest that this fundamental ambiguity pervades the sign-language, and that a dual signified 'confusingly suggests itself' in *every* act of name-giving.

According to Peirce, proper names are indices, and more specifically 'designations'. Like a pointing finger, they 'act to force attention to the thing intended',[186] that is, to the person named. In Hosea 1 commentators claim that new rules are made: the name is meant to point *away* from the person. To redirect one's gaze in this way is a difficult manoeuvre with any name, but particularly with names that seem to be fundamentally descriptive. In the Hebrew Bible names often have an iconic function that complements and reinforces the indexical link between signifier and signified. Names describe the circumstances of the child's birth, or act as a proleptic summary of a character's function. As Mieke Bal observes, 'Far from being sheerly deictic, like names in today's Western culture, [biblical names often] have a specific meaning that integrates the character into its life, and can also imprison it there'.[187] In the book of Ruth, for example, the principle 'nomen atque omen'[188] is emphatically enforced. The endings of the narrative are implicit at the beginning: Mahlon ('Sick-One') and Chilion ('Perishing One') die, all that is seen of Orpah ('Back of the Neck') is the back of

185. Wolff, *Hosea*, p. 20.

186. Hartshorne, Weiss and Burks (eds.), *The Writings of Charles Sanders Peirce*, VIII, p. 368.

187. M. Bal, *Lethal Love: Feminist Literary Readings of Biblical Love Stories* (Bloomington and Indianapolis: Indiana University Press, 1987), p. 73.

188. Plautus, *The Persian*.

her neck, and if Naomi ('Pleasant One') thinks she's been misnamed, that's because she does not know the end of the story. Names are all-knowing and can, as in the case of Naomi, know more about the people than the people themselves: they are all-powerful, and the name propels the individual to her inevitable end.

Biblical characters, Mieke Bal writes, are frequently 'subjected to [their] name, determined by it'.[189] A name such as 'Not-Loved', for example, might reasonably be expected to set the parameters of the child's life, but, although they are accustomed to the special uses of names in biblical narratives, scholars seem to suspend these expectations in the special case of Hosea. Andersen and Freedman actually begin their analysis of the name Lo-Ruhamah with an admission:

> Since names can be ominous, it is possible that this one does not describe an accomplished fact, but announces a destiny—'Let her not be pitied'.[190]

But they then go on to separate this destiny from the child and transpose it to the nation with no other rationale for their decision than an honestly confessed 'preference':

> We prefer to take the name to be a statement of the fact of a complete change in Yhwh's relationship with Israel. He has ceased to feel compassion toward them.[191]

By a subtle transition from 'her' to 'them' Andersen and Freedmen focus on the level of the signified, the land, to the exclusion of the child-signifiers. The disturbing erasure of paternal feeling in Hosea 1 is itself erased in a reversal of the text's own emphases. Hosea 1 focuses on the taking of a wife of harlotry and the production of child-signs, and the level of the signifier receives at least as much attention as the level of the signified. Commentators, in contrast, concentrate almost exclusively on 'Yhwh' and the 'land', and lose sight of the domestic microcosm in their attempts to describe the larger picture. On one level the movement from signifier to signified expresses a readerly desire to move from the clues to the hidden meaning of the text, but on another level analyses of Hos. 1.3-8, like analyses of Hos. 1.2, suggest an aversion to the text's transgression of reason and morality. Like the marriage between a prophet and a wife of harlotry, the misnaming of the children constitutes a morally distasteful scene, and emphasis on the signified is a way of

189. Bal, *Lethal Love*, p. 74.
190. Andersen and Freedman, *Hosea*, p. 188.
191. Andersen and Freedman, *Hosea*, p. 188.

saving the child, and the text, from the threat of paternal anger.

The appropriation of people as signifiers creates a sense of discomfort that few commentators are prepared to confront. The tension described and then dismissed by Wolff is effectively the tension between a first- and second-order signified, the first-order signified being the combination of the child and the name, and the second-order signified the condition of the land in relation to Yhwh. As a black pebble can be appropriated as a signifier of death, so Gomer and her children become signifiers of punishment and national curses. They assume mythical proportions as, like the pebble, they are 'over-determin[ed] by multiple meanings which [they do] not carry in ordinary usage', and are 'weigh[ed] with a definite signified'[192] which threatens to dwarf and eclipse their individual existence. Like the pebble which cannot be separated from the concept death and the roses which are always roses passionified, Gomer and her children are attached to portentous secondary meaning as automatically as a person is associated with their name. The figures' identities are defined in terms of their mythical signified: thus Gomer is known as the 'wife of harlotry'; Lo-Ruhamah is inseparable from a negation of pity; and Lo-Ammi is identified by lack of identity as a non-people. In Barthesian terms, there is no detachable signifier and signified but merely the conglomerate sign. As an object selected for social usage becomes inseparable from its second-order signified, so Gomer and her children, once appropriated for a divine agenda, become inextricably entangled with a negative abstract universe of promiscuity and non-love, rebuke and ostracization.

All mythologies involve a conflict between first- and second-order signifieds, but in Hosea 1–3 the difference in scale between the domestic microcosm and the national macrocosm makes those tensions more abrasive and acute. The 'wife of harlotry' is not merely a signifier of harlotry but of 'great harlotry', an infinitive absolute (1.2), and the use of newborn infants as signifiers for national curses highlights the distortion of scale. The contrast between the tiny signifiers and the gigantic signifieds is on one level ludicrous; like Chaucer's *Nun's Priest's Tale*, the text sets up a bathetic contrast between the domestic world and the grander spheres of philosophy and religion. Chauntecleer's erudite discussions provide a ludicrous contrast with his role as farmyard chicken; similarly, although Gomer's infidelity is, on one level, like the infidelity of Israel, it is, on another level, not like it at all.

192. Barthes, 'Myth Today', p. 113.

The disproportion between human signifiers and cosmic signifieds can also be interpreted in terms of (in)justice, since, when human signs are 'weighed' and 'overdetermined' by an unrelentingly negative signified, this process looks disturbingly like scapegoating. Yhwh's curses may be ultimately directed at the people of Israel, but the only people visible in this text are Gomer and her children; they are the only figures to whom these curses are specifically attached, and the only figures who cannot escape from them, because by them their identity is constituted. As inferior members of a patriarchal society, Gomer and the children are named by Hosea/Yhwh and appropriated into their symbolic structure; they are the 'actors' in this strange semiotic charade, but they are also in a sense its victims. As J.L. Mays notes (revealing a certain degree of discomfort), 'There is a *severe concentration* on the divine word through the prophet's family life';[193] severity is a notable feature since, effectively, all the sins of Israel are focused upon the figures in Hosea's family, and all the resulting punishment is heaped upon their heads.

The tension between first- and second-order signification in this text is exacerbated not only by a sense of disproportion and a conflict between the domestic microcosm and the national macrocosm, but also by the humanity of the signifiers. All first-order signs, as Barthes suggests, possess an autonomy that undercuts their appropriation in social (or prophetic) myth, but when the signifier is a human in his/her own right, the independent life of the signifier is strangely highlighted. The Negro soldier in *Paris-Match* is not fully appropriated as a signifier of French imperialism: he 'recedes a little' and becomes 'the accomplice of a concept',[194] but still exerts a presence in his own right. In Hosea 1 the appropriation of Gomer and her children is less subtle and more complete: almost nothing is revealed about the human characters that is not absolutely vital to the sign-language, but even here there are hints of characterization that extends beyond a reductive signifying function. The text only requires a stereotype, a 'wife of harlotry', for its signifying purposes, and yet it also points to a specific woman, Gomer-bat-Diblayim, whose name hints at a history, and a family, which extends beyond her reductive role in the text. The dual name 'wife of harlotry' and Gomer-bat-Diblayim sets up a tension between the single feature to which the woman is reduced and an acknowledged potential for characterization beyond the boundaries of the text. From a twentieth-century

193. Mays, *Hosea*, p. 23 (my italics).
194. Barthes, 'Myth Today', p. 118.

perspective, the appropriation of people as signifiers or 'walking placards'[195] seems both reductive and unjustified, but it is possible to read Hosea 1 as a text in dissonance with itself. As Hawthorne protests against the appropriation of a person as a text, and the reduction of Hester Prynne to a 'general symbol at which the preacher and the moralist might point',[196] so Hosea 1 hints that Gomer exceeds her role as a scarlet letter in the sign-language of the text.

The function of signs in Hosea 1 can be described using Barthes's model of myth (§2.6), but with a few important qualifications. Taking Lo-Ruhamah as an example, the signification can be basically represented as follows:

	1. 'Not-Loved' (the name)	2. The Child	
1st Order	3. The Child is Not-Loved *		
	I THE CHILD NOT-LOVED	II THE LAND	
2nd ORDER			
	III THE LAND IS NOT LOVED BY YHWH		

On a primary level the sign is the combination of the name and the child and the primary signified is that 'the child is Not-Loved'. The child and the concept together form the first-order sign, and this becomes in turn a signifier for the second-order realm, as Yhwh's drama imposes a 'lateral shift' and 'shift(s) the formal signification of this first system sideways.'[197] The name Not-Loved that is applied to the land is not simply a name, but a name that has already been used of someone else and that comes, as it were, with a person attached. Like Valéry's Latin sentence that has a dual meaning ('My name is lion' and 'I am a grammatical example') the child has an identity, 'I am Lo-Ruhamah', and a pedagogic purpose, 'I am a function of my father's sign-system'.

In Barthes's model of myth, the first-order sign is denotative, and its secondary extension covert or connotative, but in Hosea 1 both levels of signification are made equally explicit. The name of the child is applied to the land not by inference but by an overt connection—'for yet a little while I will punish the house of Jehu for the blood of Jezreel..for I will no more have pity on the house of Israel...for you are not my people and I am not your God' (Hos. 1.4, 6, 9). The second-order sign is not

195. Beeby, *Hosea*, p. 15.
196. Hawthorne, *The Scarlet Letter*, p. 60.
197. Barthes, 'Myth Today', p. 115.

subtly mediated through the first-order association of child and curse, but rather the link between the land and the curse exists autonomously and is explained in its own right. The child-signs are not necessary, because the message can be, and is, clearly stated independently of them; their function, I suggest, is not to clarify but rather to disturb the equation between statements of rejection and the land.

Although, as Andersen and Freedman point out, the reader is never told the precise nature of Israel's crimes against Yhwh, the metaphor of harlotry suggests a crime of infidelity that lends a sense of justice and appropriateness to the verdict 'The nation is Not Loved/the nation is Not My People'. The purpose of the child-signs is not to further illuminate the message, for it requires no clarification, but rather to introduce a sense of outrage and inappropriateness to the act of naming that affects the reader's understanding of the naming of the land. The child-signs do not signify with the main signifying line of the text but against it: the outrage implied in a father misnaming his children affects the reader's perception of the second-order sign. On its own the second-order sign appears perfectly reasonable and justified, but when coupled with the first-order equation between children and rejection, it becomes by implication unnatural and outrageous.

In Barthes's reading of the photograph in *Paris-Match*, it is the secondary signified ('That France is a great empire, that all her sons, whatever their colour, faithfully serve under her flag')[198] that makes the reader uneasy, but in Hosea 1 it is the primary signified ('the child is Not-Loved') that creates the strongest sense of discomfort. The sheer perversity of a father naming his children with curses comments on, and potentially subverts, the associated verdict that the land is not loved. Hosea 1.4-9 is not, therefore, simply a familiar prophetic diatribe against the nation, but a diatribe that is defamiliarized by the parallel act of a father rejecting his (apparently innocent) children. Even as Yhwh severs relations with Israel, he uses signs to foreground the unnaturalness of that severance; in a more subtle version of the conflict in Hos. 11.7-9,[199] Yhwh states, and undercuts, his statement, proclaims and recoils from the proclamation.

198. Barthes, 'Myth Today', p. 116.
199. In Hos. 11.8-9, in the midst of a negative oracle, 'Yhwh's' heart is 'overturned', or as the RSV puts it, 'recoils within [him]' (נהפך עלי לבי).

3.7. *La Sémiologie: A Counter-Perspective*

> Beloved
> you are my sister
> you are my daughter
> You are my face; you are me
> I have found you again; you have come back to me
> You are my Beloved
> You are mine
> You are mine
> You are mine
>
> I have your milk
> I have your smile
> I will take care of you[200]

In the previous section I suggested that the name Gomer-bat-Diblayim gestures to a character and a history that exceeds her stereotypical signifying function; in this section, using Kristeva's definition of *la sémiologie*, I want to argue that intimations about the lives of mother and children not only transcend, but also potentially transgress, the text's signifying structure. It is possible that Gomer and her children are by no means completely subservient to their signifying function, but on the contrary, open up a transgressive semiotic which militates against the correct signifying line of the text.

Within the didactic paternal drama, directed and produced by Yhwh and Hosea, there is evidence of a countertext, *la sémiologie*, the female voice, which pushes signification beyond the boundaries of the 'signifying ventures of men'.[201] As soon as Gomer gives birth to the children, her right to name them is denied and she is silenced, but although it is given no voice, the maternal force within the text is not eradicated, but continues to exert a strong and silent force. Hosea (under the instruction of Yhwh) names the second child Not-Loved; Gomer, in a silent and rebellious dumb-show of love, is depicted weaning her. Weaning implies a prior act of suckling, a gesture of love, that counters the father's harsh decree. The text's attention to fine detail at this point is uncharacteristic and seems to subvert, rather than enforce, the prophetic master-text. Coinciding with the name Not-Loved is an image of the mother weaning her child that subverts the text by softening it, as if to add a parenthetical 'not really'.

200. T. Morrison, *Beloved* (London: Picador, 1988), p. 216.
201. Kristeva, *Desire in Language*, p. x.

As in Kristeva's analysis of Soviet poetry, transgressive maternal power denies the signifying line of the limiting structure, the paternal law. The mention of weaning is a question mark in the margins of divine and prophetic authority: it shows that Yhwh/Hosea's verdict is not universal but individual (and even idiosyncratic). The absolutism of male signification is subjected to scrutiny, for Not Loved, quite manifestly, *Is Loved*, and this raises the question Not Loved by whom? The gesture of weaning challenges the reductive names given not only to the children but to Gomer herself: as Not Loved, from another perspective, manifestly is loved, so the negatively depicted harlot is also a suckling and nurturing mother.

Gomer-bat-Diblayim does not speak but makes a silent dissident gesture which reasserts the voice of normality and reason. The final ironic twist is that the main paternal text is radical and deviant, and it is the *transgressive* semiotic, the sign of love given by the mother, which quietly reasserts the voice of reason by reacting to the newborn child in the expected manner. Hosea and Yhwh have the power to create the dominant signifying structure, but Gomer's action seems more appropriate, and the mother, the *other*, poses a real counter-challenge for the sympathy of the reader. In the next chapter I want to explore other conflicts between the main argument of the text and subversive countervoices in a deconstructive reading of Hosea 1–3.

4. *Concluding Comments*

The function of signs in prophetic texts is, as Phyllis Bird argues, to 'shock', to 'intimate' a meaning and to 'confound' the reader.[202] Criticism of Hosea 1–3 has, I suggest, created a false sense of intimacy between the ancient text and modern reader, and has concentrated on what signs intimate rather than other potentially more puzzling semiotic effects. The text has been viewed, as Schlovsky might put it, 'habitually', and has been seen as a 'silhouette', an outline, 'as if in a sack'.[203] By looking in detail at the mechanisms and paradoxes of signification, I

---

202. P.A. Bird, 'The Harlot as Heroine: Narrative Art and Social Presupposition in Three Old Testament Texts', in M. Amihai, G.W. Coats and A.M. Solomon (eds.), *Narrative Research on the Hebrew Bible* (Semeia 46; Atlanta: Scholars Press, 1989), pp. 119-39 (121).

203. Schlovsky, 'Art as Technique', p. 11.

have tried to impede the 'automatism of perception'[204] that characterizes critical response, and to recreate a sense of the semiotic impact of
this text.

As critics tend to explain or dilute the tensions between the prophet
and the wife of harlotry, so they soften the shock-value of the text when
they focus exclusively on what, rather than how, the text means. Seen
merely as a series of statements, Hosea 1–3 appears to be a fairly standard prophetic text, in which Yhwh announces his displeasure with the
people, threatens them with the consequences of their apostasy, and
offers them the possibility of reunion. The meaning of the text, however,
is not merely a series of statements, for these statements are interpretations, signifieds of various signifiers. As the tensions in the marriage
cannot simply be reduced to the meaning 'Israel is apostate', so the
tensions within the sign cannot be reduced to simplistic statements such
as 'Yhwh is angry at Israel's apostasy' and 'Yhwh threatens Israel with
being a non-people'.

Hosea 1–3 comprises a strange and strained sign language in which
semiotic tensions are an integral part of the text's meaning. The most
striking semiotic feature of this text (which is most evident in chs. 1 and
3) is the strong sense of dissonance between signifiers and signifieds
expressed, for example, in the bizarre linkages between children and
curses, or between abstinence from harlotry and abstinence from Israel's
religious traditions. Even the pairings that possess an obvious rationale,
such as the conjunction between harlotry and idolatry, are underscored
by a sense of disjuncture and inappropriateness. The motif 'Israel is a
prostitute', for example, is graphically developed to the point where the
signifier outgrows and eclipses its signified: if 'harlotry' is a reasonable
signifier for 'idolatry', the act of stripping a woman and exposing her to
her lovers constitutes an increasingly bizarre symbol for the call to
religious reform.

A reading that stresses the capacity of the sign-language to shock and
confound is, I suggest, an appropriate response to this defamiliarizing
text. As I have attempted to detach Hosea 1–3 from its all too familiar
critical context, so the text detaches itself from, and subverts, some of
the fundamental assumptions of the people to whom it is addressed. The
ideologemes Jezreel, Lo-Ruhamah and Lo-Ammi are calculated to confound and to shock, as they deliberately invert the nation's most fundamental perceptions of itself. The capacity to shock is not incidental to the

---

204. Schlovsky, 'Art as Technique', p. 13.

text's meaning but is a crucial part of that meaning; indeed the only feature that unites the signs in this text is their tendency to bring in the unexpected.

Hosea 1–3 begins with, and is dominated by, the strained conjunction between prophet and prostitute, and this sense of strain is mirrored in the awkward pairings in the textual sign-language. As Hosea's partner is not only unexpected but the complete inversion of expectation, so child-signifiers are used to mean 'alienation', and adultery is equated with, among other things, Israelite religious practice. The mismatch between human and semiotic partners contributes to the overall impression that Hosea 1–3 is a strange looking-glass text, rather like a bizarre world designed by Lewis Carroll. It is a world in which children are given a meaning, and where expectations are turned on their heads, and in which the sign-language that begins in a 'curious' semiotic charade tends not to resolve itself, but to get curiouser and curiouser.

Chapter 3

DERRIDA AMONG THE PROPHETS:
A DECONSTRUCTIVE READING OF HOSEA 1–3

> Their books are also different. Works of fiction contain a single plot with all its imaginative permutations. Those of a philosophical nature invariably include both the thesis and the antithesis, the rigorous *pro* and *con* of a doctrine. A book which does not contain its counterbook is considered incomplete (Jorge Louis Borges, 'Tlön, Uqbar, Orbis Tertius').

At the end of the previous chapter I suggested that the weaning of Not-Loved is a moment of conflict in which the prophetic rhetoric vies with, and is potentially subverted by, an almost imperceptible countervoice. In this chapter I argue that this countervoice is not limited to an isolated moment in the text, but that it pervades it: the book contains its 'counterbook' and debates with, critiques, and undercuts itself. In Borges's terms Hosea 1–3 is not a work of fiction with a single plot, but is like a philosophical text that includes a thesis and an antithesis. The juxtaposition of opposites and the coincidence of affirmation and denial is a defining feature of the text: thus, for example, 'Not-Loved' is also called 'Loved', and in ch. 2 the accepted deity (Yhwh) is described in terms associated with the rejected deity (Baal).

To explore the interpretative aporiae[1] of Hosea 1–3, I shall be drawing largely on the work of a writer who, unlike Borges, deliberately problematizes the border between literature and philosophy. Jacques Derrida's 'manifesto' is that all texts, including works of fiction and philosophy, inevitably incorporate self-subverting features, because all texts contain forces, or give rise to interpretations, that cannot be tamed into conformity with the author's, or text's intention. Logic and

---

1. I shall be using the term 'aporia' to mean a site of conflict, an intersection between affirmation and denial. As George Puttenham writes in his *English Poesie* (1589), 'Aporia, or the Doubtfull' is 'so called…because oftentimes we will seem to cast perills, and make doubt of things when by a plaine manner of speech we might affirme or deny them' ('Aporia', *OED*).

language are limited, and all texts 'make the limits of their language tremble' and inadvertently reveal how their own logical premises are 'divisible and questionable'.[2] In this study I want to show how these ideas work in connection with Hosea 1–3, but before embarking on a study of deconstruction and a deconstructive reading of the text, I want to outline briefly my approach to Jacques Derrida.

I find it ironic that reactions to a strategy for deconstructing binary opposition have fallen firmly into two camps, and that deconstruction has been denounced as a 'terrorist weapon'[3] or dangerous nihilism, or has been applauded as liberation from orthodoxy. In a recent dispute over whether Derrida should be granted an honorary degree from the University of Cambridge, Derrida was extremely and oppositely celebrated as an 'exhilarating sceptic' and condemned for his 'semi-intelligible attacks' on the values of reason and scholarship.[4] Intriguingly, both sides used the same argument—that Derrida was anti-orthodox—and saw this as a good or bad thing according to their predilection towards revolutionaries. While the protest petition claimed that the effect of Derrida's work 'has been to deny and to dissolve those standards of evidence and argument on which all academic disciplines are based',[5] supporters such as George Steiner and Germaine Greer maintained that they were not 'frightened' or 'afraid' of nihilism: 'Academics *should* be frightened', Greer claimed, 'regularly'.[6]

The so-called war among Cambridge academics is a good example of the way in which deconstruction provokes a starkly polarized response. The debate as presented in *The Sunday Times* is rather aptly accompanied by a photograph of Derrida looking singularly enigmatic and flanked by smiling supporters on the right hand side and sombre opponents on the left (see Fig. 3.1). Strangely, a group of texts that question the structure of antithesis and the very possibility of choice is presented as something which the reader must choose either to endorse or reject. I suggest that Derrida's texts demand a different kind of

2.   J. Derrida, 'Deconstruction and the Other', in R. Kearney (ed.), *Dialogues with Contemporary Continental Thinkers* (Manchester: Manchester University Press, 1984), pp. 107-25 (112).

3.   P. de Man, cited in C. Norris, *Deconstruction: Theory and Practice* (New Accents; London: Routledge, 1982, rev. edn 1991), p. xi.

4.   'Cambridge Dons Declare War Over Philosopher's Honorary Degree', *The Sunday Times*, 10 May 1992.

5.   'From Professor Barry Smith and others', letter in *The Times*, 9 May 1992.

6.   G. Greer and G. Steiner, *The Sunday Times*, 10 May 1992, p. 5.

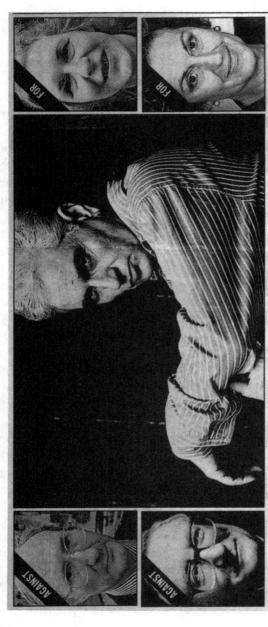

Cambridge dons declare war over philosopher's honorary degree

Pros and cons the row over Jacques Derrida, above, has split Cambridge. Supporters Gillian Beer, top right, and Germaine Greer are ranged against Howard Erskine-Hill, top left, and Derek Brewer

Fig. 3.1. *The Sunday Times*, 10 May 1992, p. 5

approach which is neither one of reverential awe nor of complete dismissal: it is not neutral, nor non-committal, but rather approaches 'Derrida' as he reads other texts.

In a strategy that I shall examine in more detail later, Derrida reads the texts of Plato and Rousseau by seizing on words that can be oppositely interpreted, and pursues the interpretation in both directions. One interpretation is conservative—it is that which has been traditionally upheld by the academy—while the other is subversive, unexpected, undermining, deconstructive. 'Derrida', similarly, has become a hinged word in the culture of criticism, and simultaneously evokes a reaction of affirmation and denial. As Derrida reads *pharmakon* as 'medicine' and 'poison', and *supplément* as 'completion' and 'lack', so I want to read 'Derrida' as a revolutionary and a threat, and deconstruction as a process that is replete with insights but that is also constituted by a sense of limitation and lack. According to Derrida, texts comprise a main argument and a dissonant counterargument which is comparatively muted and implicit in the text's own structure. In this text, this description of Derrida's approach to other texts, there is a main argument which promotes Derrida, but also a subversive countervoice (expressed in footnotes and asides) that discusses deconstruction's own limits and myopiae.

Although I shall be basing my description of deconstruction on Derrida's texts, I also want to suggest that deconstruction is a kind of Frankenstein's monster that outgrows the terms of the project outlined by its 'inventor'. This point, however, is not alien to Derrida's texts, and Derrida himself suggests that deconstruction precedes, and in a sense escapes him, and that it works inevitably in all texts including his own.[7] Critics such as Lionel Abel, who seek to invalidate deconstruction by triumphantly showing how Derrida's texts are vulnerable to deconstruction,[8] are engaging in a rather ironic critical act. By exposing the double logic at work in Derrida's texts, they are affirming with him the

7.   Derrida frequently hints at the vulnerability of his own argument: in the preface to *Of Grammatology,* for example, he writes: 'I have attempted to produce, often embarrassing myself in the process, the problems of critical reading' (*Of Grammatology* [trans. G. Chakravorty Spivak; Baltimore and London: Johns Hopkins University Press, 1976], p. lxxxix).

8.   Lionel Abel triumphantly shows how Derrida questions 'truth' and 'logic' and yet uses logic to demonstrate the truth of his own arguments, the assumption being that if Derrida can be shown to be using logic then deconstruction in its entirety is 'disproved' (L. Abel, 'Jacques Derrida: His "Difference" with Metaphysics', *Salmagundi* 25 [Winter 1974] pp. 3-21).

universality of deconstruction; they are also displaying a fundamental misunderstanding of deconstruction by suggesting that deconstruction is synonymous with the debunking of the text. To deconstruct, according to Derrida's definition, is not to score a point over a text but to show how the text's observations and assumptions encounter their own limitations. Only the completely self-conscious text that assumes nothing is immune to deconstruction, and in this chapter I want to hint at how deconstruction might work in Derrida's own texts, as well as considering in detail the possibilities for deconstruction in Hosea 1–3.

Although a binary opposition between theory and practice is somewhat ironic in a study of deconstruction,[9] I shall be retaining this division in the structure of this chapter. In the first half (§§1–3) I consider various aspects of the theory of deconstruction, and in the second half (§§4 and 5) I explore the effects of deconstruction in Hosea 1–3.

My analysis of theory is divided into three sections. In the first section, 'An Introduction to Deconstruction', I outline the transition from semiology to grammatology and describe the stylistic audacity and transgression of genre that characterizes Derrida's texts. I also consider the problems, and the necessity, of translating Derrida's texts into descriptive language, and give my own description of deconstruction 'in other words'.

In the second section, 'Deconstructive Strategies', I look in increasing detail at the outworking of deconstruction in Derrida's own texts. I begin by describing the 'double gesture' and look at the components of that gesture, reversal and displacement; I then consider two versions of displacement, palaeonomy and the undecideable. Narrowing the focus even further, I go on to look more closely at the logic of the undecideable and to consider how Derrida reads the terms *pharmakon,* the *supplément* and the *parergon* in the texts of Plato, Rousseau and Kant.

In the third and final part of the theory section I look at how deconstruction has been received by biblical scholars and suggest that, ironically, a general rejection of deconstruction has coincided with a new, quasi-deconstructive description of biblical texts. I consider Derrida as a prophet among the prophets, and as a rabbi among the rabbis, and end with a sample of Derrida's own distinctive biblical exegesis, his discussion of the tower of Babel.

---

9.   Derrida would deconstruct the hierarchy theory–method (in which practice is seen as the expression of self-contained 'theory') as he deconstructs fundamental hierarchies such as speech–writing.

1. *An Introduction to Deconstruction*

1.1. *From Semiology to Grammatology: Writing and Difference*

> Languages, as we know, are diacritical realities; each element within them
> is in itself less important than the gap that distinguishes it from other
> elements.[10]

Deconstruction, as Derrida acknowledges, begins in semiology.
Typically, he takes elements and motifs from the theories I described in
the previous chapter and pushes them to their limits: thus Peirce's
description of infinite semiosis, which goes on *ad infinitum*, is transformed by Derrida into his own idiom in which the deconstruction of
the transcendental signified gives rise to the limitlessness of play.[11] In
this section I want to trace the development from semiology to
'grammatology', and to show how Derrida's ideas relate to foundational
concepts in semiotics. In particular, I shall be looking at Derrida's
extensive use of Saussure and the way in which he incorporates and
resists certain elements in the *Course in General Linguistics*.

In *Of Grammatology* Derrida situates himself firmly in the tradition of
Saussure by announcing his own project, grammatology, using exactly
the same words that Saussure used to introduce semiology: 'I shall call it
[grammatology]...Since the science does not yet exist, no one can say
what it would be; but it has a right to existence, a place staked out in
advance.'[12] Later, in an interview with Julia Kristeva, he explained that
Saussure is essential because he 'contributed greatly to turning against
the metaphysical tradition the concept of the sign that he borrowed from
it'. Saussure's radical contribution was his definition of signifier and
signified as the two faces of one and the same production, and the
related argument that signifieds, like signifiers, are arbitrary. Derrida
pushed these statements to their logical conclusion and argued that there
can be no transcendental signified, or pure referent, which begins the
process of representation, since there can be no pure starting point,
truth, or reality that is not already an effect of language.

10. Derrida, *Dissemination* (trans. B. Johnson; Chicago: University of Chicago
Press, 1982), p. 250.

11. Derrida, *Of Grammatology*, pp. 49-50.

12. Derrida, *Of Grammatology*, p. 51. Borrowing words and situating his
writing in other texts is a deliberate ploy on Derrida's part, and a way of insisting that
deconstruction is not the new, ultimate method to replace all previous methods.

For the structuralists, the most important feature of Saussure's thought is binary opposition (between signifier and signified). For Derrida, the most important feature is the idea that language is made up of 'differences without positive terms'. Unlike the structuralists, he is intrigued by the image of language as a differential network of meaning and he develops this in his own motifs of *différance* and 'the trace'.

Différance is the 'systematic play of differences, of traces of differences, of the spacing [*éspacement*] by which elements relate to each other.'[13] In French *différance* combines the alternative senses of 'differing' and 'deferral', and like 'spacing' in English it is at once a noun and a verb, and so also refers to movement and to state. Derrida uses a word with different and unsynthesizable meanings to represent the idea of an interval that structures oppositions but cannot itself be reduced to either element of an opposition. Since in a text 'no element can function as a sign without relating it to another sign',[14] texts are structures of infinite referral in which meaning is always borrowed and derived and anticipates another meaning (which is also borrowed and derived). As Derrida puts it, 'the play of differences involves syntheses and referrals that prevent there from being at any moment or in any way a simple element that is present in and of itself and refers only to itself.'[15] Each element is 'constituted with reference to the trace in it of the other elements in the sequence or system' and so 'there are only, everywhere differences and traces of traces'.[16]

The idea of texts being 'woven'[17] from *différances* is essential to Derrida's reading strategy, or 'deconstruction', in which he pursues the play of *différance* and the 'occulted...movement of the trace'[18]—that is, the often perverse signifying logic by which one element is linked to another. However, although Saussure inspires the revolutionary idea of *différance* and turns against the metaphysical tradition, he also paradoxically endorses it. Derrida's 'concept'[19] of *différance* is obtained

13. Derrida, 'Semiology and Grammatology', in Derrida, *Positions* (trans. A. Bass; Chicago: University of Chicago Press, 1981), pp. 17-36 (27).

14. Derrida, 'Semiology and Grammatology', p. 26.

15. Derrida, 'Semiology and Grammatology', p. 26.

16. Derrida, 'Semiology and Grammatology', p. 26.

17. Derrida, 'Semiology and Grammatology', p. 26.

18. Derrida, *Of Grammatology*, p. 47.

19. 'Concept' is placed in inverted commas because Derrida is quite specific that *différance* is 'neither a word nor a concept' (Derrida, 'Positions', *Diacritics* 2 [1972], pp. 35-43 [35]). *Différance* cannot be proffered as the new starting point for a new

by pursuing ideas in the *Course*, but his 'concept' of 'writing' is defined over and against them. If Saussure is described as a proto-deconstructionist, he is also described in less flattering terms as endorsing logocentric assumptions 'in the accents of the moralist or preacher'.[20]

In his image of 'the preacher', Derrida reacts against what he regards as a Calvinist strain in Saussure's writing which reinforces hierarchical oppositions (like that between soul and body). In Saussure's *Course*, the hierarchy maintained is that between speech and writing, and Derrida calls this the Saussurean limitation.[21] Having shown that both signifier and signified are arbitrary and that neither precedes the other, Saussure relapses into conventional perceptions when he argues that writing is a signifier of the ultimate signified, speech, and claims that 'Writing exists for the sole purpose of representing [speech]'.[22] Having shaken the idea that language is made up of presences, he still regards writing as *vicieuse* (defective)[23] because it stands for absence and distance between sender and receiver. Derrida argues that Saussure's claim that writing is exterior and 'unrelated to the inner system of language'[24] is symptomatic of a fear of the 'erasure' of 'presence'[25] which the *Course* ironically anticipates. His reaction against this element in Saussure is not a critique and correction; rather, he shows how binary structures and hierarchies (speech–writing, presence–absence) are absolutely necessary to our way of thought, even though they are self-subverting: 'It is not a question of rejecting these notions;' he writes, 'they are necessary and, at least at present, nothing is conceivable for us without them'.[26]

In contrast to Saussure's semiology, which ultimately resists its own argument, Derrida inaugurates grammatology. The name is a self-conscious attempt to use writing rather than speech as the model for all discourse, and to acknowledge and pursue, more relentlessly than

---

analysis of language, because *différance* is itself a product of a conflict between two entities.

20. Derrida, *Of Grammatology*, p. 34.
21. Derrida, *Of Grammatology*, p. 34.
22. F. de Saussure, *Course in General Linguistics* (ed. C. Bally and A. Sechehaye; trans W. Baskin; New York: Philosophical Library, 1959), p. 45, cited in Derrida, *Of Grammatology*, p. 30.
23. Saussure, *Course*, p. 31, cited in Derrida, *Of Grammatology*, p. 38.
24. Saussure, *Course*, p. 44, cited in Derrida, *Of Grammatology*, p. 33.
25. Derrida, *Of Grammatology*, p. 139.
26. Derrida, *Of Grammatology*, p. 13.

Saussure, the idea that all language is based on absence and deferral, qualities usually associated with writing and dismissed as an unfortunate side-effect of indirect communication. Derrida does not use 'writing' in the conventional sense of 'marks on a page', however, but fixes ('grafts') a 'new concept' to 'the old name'.[27] 'Writing' in Derrida's texts is a cipher for 'that which exceeds—and which has the power to dismantle—the whole traditional edifice of Western attitudes to thought and language';[28] it is typically debased and outlawed because it is at once 'the source of cultural activity, *and* the dangerous knowledge of its own constitution which culture must always repress.'[29]

1.2. *Philosophy as a Kind of Writing: Audacious Style*

> He might... perplex textuality... by teasing out the tantalising echoes and overlapping senses... he might disappear down a deep intertextual crevasse between Hegel and Nietzsche, only to reappear on the far-out side of a passage from Husserl.[30]

27. Derrida, 'Signature, Event, Context', *Glyph* 1 (1977), pp. 172-97 (195).

28. Norris, *Deconstruction: Theory and Practice,* p. 29. Derrida frequently plays with the idea of writing and, as Herbert N. Schneidau puts it, 'destroys our neat scheme of assigning the invention of writing to Sumer, 3100 BCE'. He mixes references to the conventional history of writing (such as markings on cave walls and the discovery of the Tartaria tablets) with discreet allusions to DNA and other 'programs' involved in all living substance (H.N. Schneidau, 'The Word against the Word: Derrida on Textuality', in R. Detweiler (ed.), *Derrida and Biblical Studies. Semeia* 23 [1982], pp. 5-28 [10]).

29. Norris, *Deconstruction: Theory and Practice*, p. 32 (my italics). Misunderstandings on this point have led to some peculiar critiques of the science of writing, or grammatology. John M. Ellis tries to dismantle Derrida's whole argument simply by arguing that 'speech quite clearly existed long before the invention of writing', because 'there still exist in the world languages that are spoken but not written' (J.M. Ellis, *Against Deconstruction* [Princeton: Princeton University Press, 1989], p. 21). Ironically, Ellis believes that Derrida's commentators have been blinded by erudition, and speculates that these objections have probably not been raised because 'the argument would drop below the required level of complexity if it dealt with them' (p. 22). As Christopher Norris points out: 'When Ellis deplores what he sees in Derrida—and in French intellectuals at large—as highbrow "contempt for a stationary target of simple-mindedness", his phrase not only misses the mark but comes back like a boomerang' (C. Norris, 'Limited Think: How not to Read Derrida', in *What's Wrong with Postmodernism: Critical Theory and the Ends of Philosophy* [Hemel Hempstead: Harvester Wheatsheaf, 1990], pp. 134-63 [148]).

30. H. Felperin, *Beyond Deconstruction: The Uses and Abuses of Literary Theory* (Oxford: Clarendon Press, 1985), p. 120.

3. *Derrida among the Prophets*   159

As an exploration of writing as a transgressive force, *Of Grammatology* begins with the cataclysmic title, 'The End of the Book and the Beginning of Writing',[31] and represents the transition from the conventions of closure, epitomized by the 'book', to a way of writing that is eternally open, audacious, and unlike any other text. *Dissemination* begins, 'This (therefore) will not have been a book';[32] the conventions of causal logic, 'therefore', are placed in parentheses, and this transgression is paralleled in a deliberate subversion of the conventions of scholarly discourse. Derrida's texts are less like manuals than poems: the language is overtly metaphorical and intertextual, and he works parasitically within the texts of, for example, Rousseau, Hegel, Husserl, Freud, Saussure and Mallarmé. Resisting the style of deductive, causal reasoning, which he would maintain is merely an effect of style, he proceeds by the most transgressive 'reasoning' possible, often using puns, the most extreme 'sin against reason..in which an accidental or external relationship between signifiers is treated as a conceptual relationship'.[33] In *Glas*, 'Ca' becomes a cipher for *ça*, 'that', and for *savoir absolu, s.a.*, which in turn is a cipher for Hegelian philosophy. In a complex essay on Plato's cave, he intertwines a Platonic theory of mimesis and Mallarmé's *Mimique*, and contrasts the *antre*, or 'cave', which sets up rigid distinctions between darkness and light, real and apparent, with the transgressive *entre*, or 'betweenness', of Mallarmé's texts.[34] As Richard Rorty observes, it can almost sound 'as if [Derrida] really thought that the fact that, for example, the French pronunciation of "Hegel" sounds like the French for "eagle" was supposed to be relevant for comprehending Hegel'.[35] But Derrida's work is not about understanding or mastering a text, but setting language to work in texts about language.

31. Derrida, *Of Grammatology*, p. 6.

32. Derrida, *Dissemination*, p. 3.

33. J. Culler, *On Deconstruction: Theory and Criticism after Structuralism* (London: Routledge, 1993), pp. 91-92.

34. These signifiers do not achieve permanent status but are transformed punningly into *ancre* (anchor) and *encre* (ink), the anchor being a cipher for permanence and immutability, and the ink for fluid writing, in which images are constantly transformed and in which 'opposites mix'. (Derrida, *Dissemination*, p. 152).

35. R. Rorty, 'Philosophy as a Kind of Writing: An Essay on Derrida', *NLH* 10 (1978), pp. 141-60 (147).

In an essay entitled 'Philosophy as a Kind of Writing', Richard Rorty suggests that we think of Derrida as answering the question 'Given that philosophy is a kind of writing, why does this suggestion meet with such resistance?'[36] Derrida's forays into philosophy are an attempt to discover how philosophers perceive writing, and why 'they should find the suggestion that this is what they are doing so offensive'.[37] The central violent hierarchy that Derrida deconstructs is the distinction between philosophy and language, and his audacious style is a way of exploding the pretensions of certain philosophers who, in an attempt to produce a 'philosophy of language', imply that philosophy transcends language. He does this by taking to their extremes words, metaphors and associations that he finds hidden in philosophy's texts: he does not invent new images but develops existing ones and makes philosophy 'even more impure—more unprofessional, funnier, more allusive, sexier, and above all, more "written"'.[38]

In Derrida's writing, as Stephen D. Moore puts it, the 'propositional diction of traditional philosophical discourse' is 'dropped altogether' to be replaced by a 'dense interlace of allegory and etymology, pun and allusion'.[39] In the essay 'White Mythology,[40] for example, he sets metaphors to work in the texts of philosophy and deconstructs the distinction between 'proper, philosophical' language, and 'playful, literary' language, using vivid images of knife-grinders, flowers, the sun and precious stones. A commentary on this text might (rightly) say that Derrida is breaking down the distinction between metaphor and reason, and 'arguing' that all language is metaphorical, but in fact he is not arguing at all, because he transgresses rational structures as determinedly as he defies a traditional understanding of reason. 'Arguing' that 'concept' itself is just a metaphor,[41] Derrida steals the phrase 'White Mythology' from Anatole France's *Garden of Epicurus* and uses it to describe the way in which metaphor and writteness are repressed in philosophical texts. 'White Mythology' grows into a motif for metaphors

36. Rorty, 'Philosophy as a Kind of Writing,' p. 144.

37. Rorty, 'Philosophy as a Kind of Writing', p. 144.

38. Rorty, 'Philosophy as a Kind of Writing', p. 144.

39. S.D. Moore, *Literary Criticism and the Gospels: The Theoretical Challenge* (New Haven: Yale University Press, 1989), pp. 146-47.

40. Derrida, 'White Mythology: Metaphor in the Text of Philosophy', *NLH* 6 (1974), pp. 7-74.

41. Derrida, 'White Mythology', p. 23.

that are repressed, but that 'yet remain, active and stirring, inscribed in white ink, an invisible drawing covered over in the palimpsest'.[42]

It is interesting that many critics have responded to Derrida by accusing him of regression into irrationality. Howard Felperin describes deconstruction as 'apocalyptic irrationalism',[43] while Jürgen Habermas attacks him for refusing to honour the proper genre distinctions that govern the 'philosophical discourse of modernity'.[44] Both critics attempt to redraw firm boundaries between metaphor and philosophy, rationalism and irrationality, and revealingly, both assume that a discourse that is overtly metaphorical must be irrational or non-serious.[45] In doing so, both place themselves in the position of the philosophers who believe that they can transcend language, a belief rigorously contended by Derrida.

Felperin's and Habermas's arguments do not reply to deconstruction but rather respond with a reiteration of belief, and reassert the hierarchy between literature and philosophy which, for Derrida, characterizes Western metaphysics. Their ardent defence of the distinction between literature and philosophy merely confirms, from Derrida's perspective, the pervasiveness of the hierarchy and the deep-rootedness of the instinct to try and separate philosophy from language. Habermas's description of a quest for enlightenment (which, because it is 'unfinished', presumably has hope of attaining its final goal), and of deconstruction as a regression, follows, as surely as Rousseau's *Confessions*, the structure of the fall, and asserts a distinction between the origin and the deviation, the proper and the regression. By describing grammatology as an aberration, Felperin and Habermas confirm Derrida's perception of the prejudices of Western metaphysics and set themselves up in juxtaposition, rather than in response, to Derrida.

One of the ironies of Habermas's and Felperin's denunciations of deconstruction is that they find themselves making statements that are

---

42. Derrida, 'White Mythology', p. 11.

43. Felperin, *Beyond Deconstruction*, p. 112.

44. J. Habermas, *The Philosophical Discourse of Modernity: Twelve Lectures* (trans. F. Lawrence; Cambridge: Polity Press, 1987).

45. Derrida would argue that there is a significant difference between undoing (or deconstructing) the discourse of rationalism, and regressing into irrationality, since one act displaces (or deconstructs) the hierarchy between reason and non-reason (or philosophy and metaphor), while the other keeps it firmly in place.

not so radically different from those made by Derrida. Both regard grammatology as an aberration, and the instinctive way in which they use the word 'irrationalism' to describe what Derrida does with language shows the indefatigability of binary opposition and the deep-rootedness of fundamental dichotomies of pureness and contamination. Derrida also argues that Western metaphysics is ultimately ineradicable and that it is the nature of all discourse to resist the implications of language. Yet he would also argue that his writing expresses the fundamental nature of discourse, and that the whole history of philo-sophical discourse is riddled with parables, images and counterarguments which his style merely emphasizes and condenses.

As academics at Cambridge differ not in their descriptions of decon-struction but in their attitudes towards revolution, so Derrida and Habermas/Felperin differ not in their descriptions of Western meta-physics but in their attitudes towards the system. For Derrida it is a flawed but insurmountable tradition; for Habermas and Felperin it is the true expression of rationalism which must be preserved at all costs.[46] Though, from Derrida's perspective, Habermas and Felperin miss the point when they describe grammatology as irrationalism, there are also coincidences in their respective descriptions of deconstruction. Felperin's equation between deconstruction and 'liminal phenomena' such as 'ghosts, guerrillas, or viruses',[47] is used as part of his denunciation of Derrida, but it is not difficult to imagine Derrida using a similar phrase as an apposite description of his approach to texts.

1.3. *Negotiating between the Ludic and the Lucid: Deconstruction—in Other Words*

> It is my hope that this book will be understandable and thought-provok-ing. Yet the very comprehensibility of this book must be, paradoxically, its most serious limitation.[48]

A text that deliberately aims to subvert conventions of communication and structures of Western thought will inevitably be perceived by some

---

46. Given that Derrida himself asserts the ineradicability of Western metaphysics, it is ironic that Habermas and Felperin argue for its preservation. Derrida does not portray deconstruction as a contender that threatens to overthrow the system, but rather as a subversive countervoice that works within it.

47. Felperin, *Beyond Deconstruction*, p. 110.

48. G. Aichele, *Limits of Story* (Atlanta: Scholars Press, 1985), p. 139.

readers as 'obscurantism designed to exclude all but an elite'.[49] Indeed, there is one school of thought that maintains that deconstruction should be preserved as an elitist pursuit: in June 1981 *Newsweek* praised the original 'professorial practitioners of deconstruction' as 'formidable men of letters who have bent deconstruction to their own individual and practical purposes', but warned graduate students not to commit 'the pedagogic error of allowing one theory of language to determine their response to great literature'.[50] The adjective 'formidable' is revealing; another more critical way of seeing Derrida and the so-called Yale deconstructionists is as 'the chiefs of a hermeneutic Mafia or the high priests of a new mystery cult'.[51] The incomprehensibility of a book can also be its most serious limitation, and for many readers the promotion of idiosyncrasy over communication renders the 'classic' texts of deconstruction almost perversely inaccessible and ensures that they receive only limited circulation.[52]

I find it strange that, when legislating about a group of texts that deconstruct the hierarchy between the original and the derivative, critics are often so keen to enforce a distinction between pure (Derridean) and derivative deconstruction (as practised by graduate students). The implication—that deconstruction is only proper when uncontaminated by translation or mediation—is strikingly similar to Rousseau's distinction between pure nature and adulterated culture that Derrida so vigorously deconstructs. Derrida's deconstruction of origins and his work on the process of translation can be turned back on itself and applied to his own texts. In this section I give a 'derivative' definition of the deconstructive process and attempt to describe deconstruction *in other words*.

One of the most difficult features of Derrida's writing is that it is frequently punctuated with seemingly perverse disclaimers such as 'deconstruction is not a method and cannot be transformed into one',[53]

49. Felperin, *Beyond Deconstruction*, p. 112.

50. *Newsweek*, 22 June 1981, p. 83.

51. Felperin, *Beyond Deconstruction*, p. 112.

52. The restriction as well as the preservation of deconstruction is implied in the *Newsweek* article. The author seems anxious to confine deconstruction to an elite not only to avoid the contamination of pure deconstruction, but also to keep it from having a widespread effect on responses to 'great literature'.

53. Derrida, 'Letter to a Japanese Friend', in P. Kamuf (ed.), *A Derrida Reader: Between the Blinds* (Hemel Hempstead: Harvester Wheatsheaf, 1991), pp. 270-76 (273). This statement can be interpreted in mutually subverting (or undecideable) directions, as a statement of hubris and humility, deference and self-promotion.

or *différance* is 'neither...a word nor a concept'.[54] Most extremely, Derrida seems to avoid all possibility of definition by declaring that 'All sentences of the type "deconstruction is X" or "deconstruction is not X" *a priori*...miss the point'. The assertion is not, in fact, a statement about the impossibility of definition, but rather a reminder that 'one of the principal things at stake in what is called in my text "deconstruction" is precisely the limiting of ontology and above all of the third person present indicative: S *is* P'.[55] The point still remains, however: if deconstruction is an interrogation of being and an attempt to deconstruct the fundamental binary opposition between what is and what is not, this makes it extremely difficult to define deconstruction in the standard language of affirmation and denial.

The conflict between 'the philosophical limiting of ontology' and the

Advocates of deconstruction, such as Geoffrey Hartman, interpret the statement as 'methodological pathos', a humble acknowledgment of 'the self-invalidating nature of all methodologies' (G.H. Hartman, 'The State of the Art of Criticism', in R. Cohen [ed.], *The Future of Literary Theory* [London: Routledge, 1989], pp. 86-101 [100]). Derrida allows the formation of no master-theory outside of the text and so demonstrates, as Stephen Moore puts it, the experience of being 'unable to dominate a text', which is also the experience of 'being mortal' (*Literary Criticism and The Gospels*, p. 131). From a sympathetic perspective, Derrida's statement can be read as a denunciation of authority, a declaration that he does not want to become (as he has in some quarters become) the new literary guru. The desired effect on the reader is perhaps the same as Kierkegaard's pseudonymous author, Johannes Climacus's, reaction to Lessing: 'Even if I strove... to become Lessing's disciple, I could not, for Lessing has prevented it. Just as he himself is free, so I imagine that he desires to make everyone else free in relation to himself' (S. Kierkegaard, *Concluding Unscientific Postscript* [Princeton: Princeton University Press, 1941], p. 67).

A more cynical way of reading the disclaimer that 'deconstruction is not a method' is as a means of establishing deconstruction as an 'ahistorical master-strategy' (M. Poovey, 'Feminism and Deconstruction', *FS* 14 [1988], pp. 51-65 [61]) and a deliberately hard act to follow. Like the New Criticism, which effectively took over the concept of 'newness' and made it difficult for New-er criticisms to follow it, deconstruction takes over the concept of method not by monopolizing it but by invalidating it. The subversion of method implies that all further methods will fall back into the metaphysical fallacy and so represent a relapse rather than a progression. Even as he denies the myth of a transcendent 'ultimate criticism', Derrida creates the conditions for deconstruction to become it, and Derrida's work has, not surprisingly, been followed by a pregnant critical pause.

54. Derrida, 'Positions', p. 35.
55. Derrida, 'Letter to a Japanese Friend', p. 275.

need to define what deconstruction *is*, is already present in Derrida's texts. He demonstrates his own assertion that Western Metaphysics is vulnerable to deconstruction, and yet is also insurmountable, when he resorts to the language of ontology to claim that 'deconstruction is not a method'. Furthermore, he proposes retrospectively what deconstruction is:

> [I have] tried to work out what was in no way meant to be a system but rather a sort of strategic device, opening into its own abyss, an unclosed, unencloseable, not wholly formalizable ensemble of rules for reading, interpretation and writing.[56]

Although he defines deconstruction in terms of the non-system and emphasizes that it cannot exist independently of the texts in which it operates, Derrida cannot avoid the implication that deconstruction is an entity. Even as he maintains that it 'borrows from a heritage the resources necessary for the deconstruction of that heritage itself',[57] he virtually personifies deconstruction as a borrower or thief and implies that it is a distinct entity which is therefore accessible to definition.

The process of translating Derrida's 'strategy' into a method, or his poetic paranomasia into the discourse of rationalism, is a process which begins in Derrida's own texts and is continued by critics such as Barbara Johnson, Christopher Norris, Gayatari Spivak and Jonathan Culler. Christopher Norris unequivocally re-establishes binary opposition in the discussion in his book *Deconstruction: Theory and Practice*, and against Derrida's claims that 'by no means does [deconstruction] constitute a lexicon',[58] Sharon Crowley provides a glossary of terms.[59] The process of deriving a method from Derrida's text began, Derrida claims, with the term deconstruction, which Derrida calls an 'ugly and difficult

56. Derrida, 'The Time of a Thesis: Punctuations', in A. Montefiore (ed.), *Philosophy in France Today* (Cambridge: Cambridge University Press, 1983), pp. 34-50 (40).

57. Derrida, 'Structure, Sign and Play in the Discourse of the Human Sciences', in *Writing and Difference* (trans. A. Bass; London: Routledge, 1990), pp. 278-93 (282).

58. Derrida, 'Positions', p. 35. Compare a similar comment in *Dissemination*: 'A...reading...should no longer be carried out as a simple table of concepts or words, as a static or statistical sort of punctuation. One must reconstitute a chain in motion, the effects of a network and the play of a syntax' (*Dissemination*, p. 194).

59. S. Crowley, *A Teacher's Introduction to Deconstruction* (Illinois: National Council of Teachers of English, 1989), p. 55.

word'[60] and which he had only written 'once or twice' before 'all of a
sudden [it] jumped out of the text and was seized by others'.[61] In a
literary context dominated by structuralism it was inevitable that when
someone said 'destructure', 'destructuring' or 'deconstruction', the
word would acquire an extraordinary pertinence: thus his counter-
philosophy came to be known as 'deconstruction', even though, for
Derrida, it 'was not at all the first or the last word, and certainly not a
password or slogan for everything that was to follow'.[62]

Although it begins as a motif in Derrida's texts, 'deconstruction', and
the strategies associated with it have grown beyond Derrida's texts into
a term and a method. This is not simply, as Rudolph Gasché protests, a
lamentable 'toning down' of Derrida's work to create 'a few sturdy
devices for the critic's use',[63] but rather the end of a process that had, as
it were, 'always already' begun in Derrida's own writing. Since we have
no words for 'terms' that are neither words nor concepts, it is inevitable
that words like *différance* should become, as Richard Rorty puts it, 'new
subject *matter*'.[64] The only way of describing deconstruction is to create
a sense of a new and alternative system, or as Barbara Johnson puts it,
Derrida's 'other logic'.[65] As Gayatari Spivak explains in her commentary on deconstruction, 'a certain view of the world, of consciousness,
and of language has been accepted as the correct one, and if the minute
particulars of that view are examined, a rather different picture
emerges'.[66] In the following definitions, which unashamedly make use of
the phrase 'deconstruction is/is not', I attempt to sketch some aspects of
this alternative picture.

1.3.1. *Deconstruction is not destructive*
Derrida is reluctant to inaugurate deconstruction as a master-concept,
because it implies destructuring: a negative act of retaliation that is the

60. Derrida, 'Interview with Alan Montefiore', in D. Jones and R. Stoneman
(eds.), *Talking Liberties* (London: Channel 4 Television, 1992), pp. 6-9 (7).

61. Derrida, *The Ear of the Other: Otobiography, Transference, Translation*
(ed. C.V. McDonald; trans. P. Kamuf and A. Ronell; New York: Schocken Books,
1985), p. 86.

62. Derrida, *The Ear of the Other*, p. 87.

63. R. Gasché, 'Deconstruction as Criticism', *Glyph* 6 (1979), pp. 177-215
(183).

64. Rorty, 'Philosophy as a Kind of Writing', p. 151 (my italics).

65. B. Johnson, 'Translator's Introduction', in Derrida, *Dissemination*, p. xvi.

66. G.C. Spivak, 'Translator's Preface', in Derrida, *Of Grammatology*, p. xiii.

inverse of all constructive approaches. To counteract the undertones of destruction and the caricature of the deconstructionist as destroyer, Derrida offers an alternative picture of his relation to his texts: 'I love very much everything that I deconstruct in my own manner; the texts I want to read from a deconstructive point of view are texts I love, with that impulse of identification which is indispensable for reading. They are texts whose future, I think, will not be exhausted for a long time..my relation to these texts is characterised by loving jealousy and not at all by nihilistic fury (one can't read anything in the latter condition).'[67]

1.3.2. *'Deconstruction is...the active accomplice of a repressed but already articulate language*[68]

Deconstruction exposes the ghostly underside of any text not by imposing a different logic, but by 'driv[ing]' the text's own logic to its 'ultimate conclusions'.[69] In an act of critical mutiny, deconstruction gets inside the text and turns the text against itself—the choice of the word 'drives' is an apt one, since it implies pushing a philosophy over the edge and past the brink of madness or the limits of control.

1.3.3. *Deconstruction is not an attempt to expose the 'flaws or weaknesses or stupidities of an author*[70]

Deconstruction does not expose a particular author's stupidity but the inevitable contradictions and flaws in a universal system of thought (described in the all-encompassing term 'Western metaphysics'). By pushing the textual logic to the point where it begins to flounder, deconstruction exposes a cultural rather than an individual myopia, and demonstrates how 'what [the author] sees is systematically related to what he [*sic*] does not see'.[71] As Derrida puts it, 'The [deconstructive] reading must always aim at a certain relationship, unperceived by the writer, between what he [*sic*] commands and what he does not command of the patterns of the language that he uses'.[72]

67. Derrida, *The Ear of the Other*, p. 87.
68. Norris, *Deconstruction: Theory and Practice*, p. 41.
69. Norris, *Deconstruction: Theory and Practice*, p. 30.
70. Johnson, 'Translator's Introduction', p. xv.
71. Johnson, 'Translator's Introduction', p. xv.
72. Derrida, *Dissemination*, p. 158.

1.3.4. *Deconstruction is not a version of 'misreading'.*

Although it has often been mistaken as another postmodern adventure in misreading,[73] deconstruction is not based on the idea of the reader but on the more conventional concepts of 'author', 'intention' and 'text'. The distinction between what the author does and does not command of the language that he or she uses invokes the concepts of author and intentionality: the implication is that deconstruction is the discovery of the textual countervoice that defiantly and inevitably transgresses a definable authorial agenda. The constant use of the motif of writing suggests an emphasis not only on writing over speech, but writing over reading—the focus is on the aporiae that are 'always already' inscribed. Deconstruction is a phenomenon that theoretically takes place independently of any reader: the reader does not creatively produce a textual countermeaning but rather 'discovers' the contradictions that have already been produced within the language of the text.

In one of his many riddling disclaimers Derrida asserts that deconstruction is neither analysis nor critique. It is not analysis because analysis implies reducing the text to a 'simple element' or an 'indissoluble origin', and these values 'are themselves philosophemes subject to deconstruction'; and it is not a critique because '*krinein*, or...*krisis* (decision, choice, judgement, discernment)' implies a transcendental point of view, from which the critique is made.[74] Because deconstruction

> cannot legitimately transgress the text toward something other than it, toward a referent (a reality that is metaphysical, historical, psycho-biographical, etc.) or toward a signified outside the text whose content could take place, could have taken place, outside of language,[75]

the reader cannot replace the text as the new centre of meaning. Derrida significantly refers not to an individual reader but a universal read*ing*: 'Our reading must be intrinsic and remain within the text'.[76]

---

73. Ellis, for example, describes Derrida in terms more appropriate to Harold Bloom in a chapter entitled, 'What Does it Mean to Say that All Interpretation is Misinterpretation?' (*Against Deconstruction*, pp. 97-112).

74. Derrida, 'Letter to a Japanese Friend', p. 273.

75. Derrida, *Of Grammatology*, p. 158.

76. Derrida, *Of Grammatology*, p. 159. Another way of seeing deconstruction and reader-response is as ways of accounting for the same phenomenon that produce radically different conclusions. Both approaches attempt to describe why different and even mutually exclusive interpretations can be produced from the same text, but while reader-response describes 'difference' as the space between differing readers

Deconstruction and reader-response are both poststructuralist because they are both responses to, and displacements of, structuralism; but whereas reader-response criticism is a reply to structuralism's focus on text, deconstruction retains structuralism's text-based emphasis.[77] The deconstructive manifesto, that 'what the author sees is systematically related to what he [*sic*] does not see',[78] can be applied to all authors, including Derrida, for even as he challenges the subordination of writing to speech and absence to presence, he fails to react to one of the foundational hierarchies of structuralism: the exclusion of the reader in the concentration on the text. The repression of the role of the individual reader jars abrasively with the manifest idiosyncrasy of Derrida's writing, and constitutes one of the main aporiae in Derrida's own texts. Derrida's work is so distinctive, and so obviously conditioned by resonances from his own philosophical training, that it is hard to imagine that any reader could produce the same erudite chains of linkage, or tease out the same, allegedly 'given' text within the text.

1.3.5. *Deconstruction is text-based, but redefines the concept of text*

Although deconstruction is orientated towards the concept of text rather than reader, Derrida does not merely repeat the structuralist/New Critical concept of the text as entity. Deconstruction, like reader-response, is poststructuralist and therefore problematizes the structuralist definition of text; but whereas reader-response theorists alter the idea of text by bringing in a new figure, the reader, Derrida problematizes the concept of textual borders and argues that everything is text, or famously, that *il n'y a pas de hors-texte* ('there is nothing outside [or that cannot be described as] text').[79] As Kevin Hart points out, 'the doctrine that there is nothing outside the text is neither esoteric nor difficult: it is merely that there is no knowledge of which we can speak which is unmediated'.[80] Derrida is not promoting a formalist doctrine of

and reading communities, deconstruction describes *différance* as an insurmountable feature of language, located firmly within the text.

77. This is not surprising considering that deconstruction was conceived entirely independently of reader-response theories, and that Derrida's first 'deconstructive' paper, 'Structure Sign and Play in the Discourse of the Human Sciences', was presented at a conference as early as 1966 ('The Languages of Criticism and the Sciences of Man', Johns Hopkins University, Baltimore).

78. Johnson, 'Translator's Introduction', p. xv.

79. Derrida, *Of Grammatology*, p. 158.

80. K. Hart, *The Trespass of the Sign: Deconstruction, Theology and*

text which outlaws social or political concerns or autobiographies of the author's life and context, but is rather redefining all these fields as further networks, or texts, rather than points of reference which transcend the text and provide privileged points of access into it.

Derrida's statement that 'our reading must be intrinsic and remain within the text' must be read, therefore, within the context of his redefinition of text. This is not a statement about rigid textual borders, but is rather a statement about the impossibility of transcending or solving the text. The statement *il n'y a pas de hors-texte* is expressed in a kind of immanent critique which relentlessly quotes from the text in question and adopts its vocabulary, but then pursues the ramifications of those ideas beyond the boundaries of what might be traditionally considered 'the text'. This type of approach, which does not transcend but extends the text, is contrasted with readings which seem cavalierly to dismiss the text in question, and that do not seem to need the text at all but rather 'that take place in nonreading, with no work on what was thus being demonstrated'.[81]

1.3.6. *Deconstruction is not a joyous affirmation of word-play*

In 'Structure, Sign and Play in the Discourse of the Human Sciences',[82] Derrida sets up tension between two interpretations of interpretation: the 'Rousseauistic' and the 'Nietzschean'. One is 'saddened, negative, nostalgic, guilty' and 'dreams of deciphering a truth or an origin which

Philosophy (Cambridge: Cambridge University Press, 1989), p. 26.

81. Derrida, 'Living On: *Border Lines*', in H. Bloom (ed.), *Deconstruction and Criticism* (New York: Seabury Press, 1979), pp. 75-176 (84). An example of this type of approach is John Searle's 'Reiterating the Differences: A Reply to Derrida' (*Glyph* 1 [1977], pp. 198-208), which replies to Derrida without ever quoting from his texts. Searle appeals to truth as a transcendental point of reference by arguing that Derrida shows a 'distressing penchant for saying things that are obviously false', (p. 203) about J.L. Austin's *How to Do Things with Words* (London: Oxford University Press, 1963), but in doing so retreats into the kind of illusion of transcendence, or reductive summary of a text, that Derrida's detailed readings deliberately counteract. Searle argues that Derrida is a semantic game player, and accuses him of trivializing an important text, but Derrida argues in retaliation that his reading is serious while Searle trivializes. A serious reading of a text, he contends, must work within the terms of the text; a non-serious reading, in contrast, dismisses the text and escapes from it in reductive, transcendent concepts 'about' it. (For Derrida's pointed reply to Searle, in which he relentlessly quotes from Searle's text, see Derrida, 'Limited Inc.', *Glyph* 2 [1977], pp. 162-254.)

82. Derrida, 'Structure, Sign and Play', pp. 278-93.

escapes play and the order of the sign'; the other is no longer turned toward 'the lost or impossible presence of the absent origin', and joyously affirms the play of a 'world of signs' which is no longer bound to concepts such as origin, fault and truth.[83] Most commentators assume that Derrida renounces the first to take up the second: thus Wayne Booth depicts Derrida as practising an 'endless, treacherous and terrifying' dissemination of texts that leads the reader to an *'errance joyeuse'*,[84] James Hans unequivocally associates Derrida with 'freeplay',[85] and Denis Donoghue argues that because Derrida favours the second mode of interpretation he trivialises human discourse.[86] Mark C. Taylor labels the two definitions as 'logocentrism's interpretation of interpretation' and 'deconstruction's interpretation of interpretation',[87] thus aligning Derrida firmly and unequivocally with Nietzsche.

As Kevin Hart and Stephen Moore point out, Derrida's own commentary on these two interpretations of interpretation debunks the possibility of simply 'exit[ing] from the first system to pass cavalierly to the second'.[88] The distinction between the two modes is followed not by a choice but by a subversion of the whole concept of choice: thus Derrida argues that 'although these two interpretations must acknowledge and accentuate their difference and define their irreducibility, I do not believe today that there is any question of *choosing*'.[89] Hart provides an excellent commentary on this seemingly bizarre statement. There are, he suggests, three interpretations of interpretation in this text, the Rousseauistic, which assumes a ground, the Nietzschean, which celebrates groundlessness, and Derrida's own, which explores the relationship between them. Derrida does not decide between two different concepts but rather probes the very possibility of conceptuality: as Hart concludes, 'It would seem that Derrida's claim is not that we should support one sort of interpretation over another, but that the condition

83. Derrida, 'Structure, Sign and Play', p. 292.

84. W. Booth, *Critical Understanding* (Chicago: University of Chicago Press, 1979), p. 216, cited in Hart, *The Trespass of the Sign*, p. 118.

85. J.S. Hans, 'Derrida and Freeplay', *MLN* 94 (1979), pp. 809-10.

86. D. Donoghue, *Ferocious Alphabets* (London: Faber & Faber, 1981), pp. 165-66, cited in Hart, *The Trespass of the Sign*, p. 119.

87. M.C. Taylor, 'Deconstruction: What's the Difference?', *Soundings: An Interdisciplinary Journal* 66 (1983), pp. 387-403 (396), cited in Hart, *The Trespass of the Sign*, p. 119.

88. Moore, *Literary Criticism and the Gospels*, p. 138.

89. Derrida, 'Structure, Sign and Play', p. 293 (my italics).

of possibility of the Rousseauistic interpretation also enables the Nietzschean interpretation'.[90]

References to play in Derrida's text have led to caricatures of deconstruction as 'a kind of free-for-all hermeneutic romp',[91] 'wordspinning nonsense',[92] or a game of 'relativist abandon',[93] but a closer reading of Derrida's texts disturbs the simplistic equation between deconstruction and hermeneutic anarchy. Just as a careful reading of 'Structure, Sign and Play' suggests that Derrida does not simply add his own affirmation to Nietzsche's joyous affirmation of word-play, so his descriptions of the play involved in deconstruction undercuts impressions of anarchy with terms evocative of constraint. In a volume of interviews with modern

90. Hart, *The Trespass of the Sign*, p. 122. Although Hart's argument is complex, I want to trace the main outline of it here, as it provides a vital counter to the idea that Derrida is simply dismissing one mode of interpretation in favour of another. What preoccupies Derrida, argues Hart, is the way in which the proper (Rousseauistic) reading provides the basis for the improper (Nietzschean) reading: one is made necessary by the other, and to debunk one is therefore to debunk the other. In a complete inversion of most commentators' understandings of this text, Derrida is not arguing that the Rousseauistic reading should be dropped in favour of the Nietzschean, but that the existence of the two is inextricably connected. This is due to a fundamental paradox at the heart of interpretation in which, as Foucault puts it, to interpret or comment 'is to admit by definition an excess of the signified over the signifier; a necessary, unformulated remainder of thought that language has left in the shade... but to comment also presupposes that this unspoken element slumbers within speech, and that by a superabundance proper to the signifier, one may, in questioning it, give voice to a content that was not explicitly signified' (M. Foucault, *The Birth of the Clinic* [trans. A.M. Sheridan Smith; New York: Vintage Books, 1975], p. xvi).

If the text is the signified, and interpretation the signifier, proper interpretation promotes the signified (the origin) over the signifier (S/s) and improper interpretation does the reverse (s/S). Improper interpretation is not alien to the proper tradition, but is its inevitable corollary: it is merely a reversal, a possibility 'always already' contained within a Rousseauistic definition of the interpretative quest. Because it is merely the inversion of a proper approach to interpretation, a Nietzschean approach still remains within the metaphysical tradition: it is implicit within it and does not therefore constitute its deconstruction. As I shall discuss later, deconstruction inverts and displaces the system—it is a twofold act—and because Nietzsche merely inverts the metaphysical tradition, Derrida must be doing something rather more in 'Structure, Sign and Play' than simply aligning himself with him.

91. Norris, 'Limited Think', p. 137.

92. Norris, 'Limited Think', p. 147.

93. Norris, 'Limited Think', p. 146.

critics Derrida describes the so-called freeplay of deconstruction as a way of showing 'that the structure of the machine, or the springs, are not so tight, so that you can just try to dislocate [*sic*]'.[94] Deconstruction, by definition, works within the interstices of a structure: as Kevin Hart suggests, 'freeplay is neither completely free nor all that playful', and 'like "free verse" it has constraints of its own'.[95]

2. *Deconstructive Strategies*

2.1. *Positions: The 'Double Science'*

'Take a repressed and subjugated theme, pursue textual ramifications and show how these subvert the very order that strives to hold them in check.' Recipes for deconstruction (this one is by Christopher Norris) give a good idea of the practice of deconstruction, but in this section I want to look in more detail at the strategies employed by Derrida and the subtleties involved in his manipulation of texts.

'Positions', an interview with Jean-Louis Houdebine and Guy Scarpetta,[96] is one of the rare instances in which Derrida defines a 'general strategy of deconstruction' independently of the intricacies of a particular text. As the title 'Positions' implies, deconstruction is not a single unified strategy but a 'double gesture': the deconstructionist takes a double position with respect to a textual hierarchy and engages in what Derrida terms '*split* writing' or a '*double* science'. The double science involves two elements, *reversal* and *displacement*, but it is not correct to describe these elements, as J.P. Leavey does, as 'two steps'.[97] Reversal and displacement (reinscription) are inextricably connected and occur simultaneously: put simply, reversal inverts the hierarchy so that the subordinate term becomes dominant, and displacement functions as

94. Interview with Derrida, in I. Salusinszky, *Criticism in Society: Interviews with Jacques Derrida, Northrop Frye, Harold Bloom, Geoffrey Hartman, Frank Kermode, Edward Said, Barbara Johnson, Frank Lentricchia and J. Hillis Miller* (London: Methuen, 1987), pp. 8-26 (20).

95. Hart, *The Trespass of the Sign*, pp. 120-21.

96. Derrida, 'Positions', *Diacritics* 2 (1972), pp. 35-43 (35); a revised version appears in the volume of the same name, *Positions* (trans. A. Bass; Chicago: University of Chicago Press, 1981), pp. 37-96, but I refer to the earlier version throughout unless otherwise specified.

97. J.P. Leavey, 'Four Protocols: Derrida, his Deconstruction', in R. Detweiler (ed.), *Derrida and Biblical Studies* (Semeia, 23; Atlanta: Scholars Press, 1982), pp. 43-57 (50).

a strategic device that prevents a new hierarchy forming, or an old one reforming, as the new absolute paradigm or truth.

The task of the deconstructionist, as defined by Derrida, is to locate the hierarchies that the text is consciously promoting or unconsciously taking for granted and, by working within them, to make the text 'insecure in its most assured evidences'.[98] The act of reversal is described in almost revolutionary terms and is necessary because to 'take an attitude of neutralising indifference with respect to the classical oppositions would be to give free reign to the existing forces that have historically dominated the field'.[99] The term 'violent hierarchy'[100] is used as shorthand for an opposition in which two terms do not peacefully co-exist but in which one term is vigorously and relentlessly demoted (examples include the privileging of speech over writing, or absence over presence). Reversal resurrects the demoted term and makes it an active player in discourse: thus 'writing' and 'absence' become key motifs in Derrida's texts.

The function of displacement is to work alongside reversal so that 'writing' and 'absence' do not become the new dominant terms. Deconstruction is not a way of usurping one set of values with another, or of establishing a new order; rather, its purpose is to open a 'snag in writing that cannot be mended'.[101] The old hierarchy (e.g. speech–writing) and the new (writing–speech) must be kept in tension, so that each is perpetually subverted by a sense of the alternative. The possibility of either, or neither, term being dominant or subordinate is achieved by using what Derrida terms 'bifocal'[102] or split writing, which is a way of suspending the text between two mutually incompatible possibilities.

If reversal is a way of questioning assumptions, displacement is a way of keeping those questions open. 'Split writing' defers the sense of an answer by trying to write the 'both/and', or more specifically, the 'either/or' that is also 'neither/nor'.[103] Because split writing supports both terms, it also, by implication, denies them. In Derrida's texts it takes two main forms: *palaeonymy*, or the science of old names, and the *undecideable*.

98. Derrida, *Of Grammatology*, p. 73.
99. Derrida, *Dissemination*, p. 6.
100. Derrida, 'Positions', p. 36.
101. Derrida, *Dissemination*, p. 26.
102. Derrida, 'Positions', p. 36.
103. Derrida, 'Positions', *Diacritics* 2 (1972), p. 36.

2.2. *Strategies of Displacement*

2.2.1. *Palaeonymy: The Science of Old Names*

> Why should an old name, for an indeterminate time, be retained? Why should the effects of a new meaning, concept or object be damped by memory?[104]

In his 'Letter to a Japanese Friend',[105] Derrida asserts that deconstruction cannot 'be' something. What he means is that the statement 'deconstruction is...' cannot be used without the verb 'to be' being suspended and interrogated. The statement of definition 'deconstruction is...' is so fundamental to our thinking (and our grammar) that it cannot be replaced. But at the same time Derrida wants to question the metaphysics of presence that is inescapably bound up with this simple verb, and to place its philosophical implications, its history and its presuppositions under extreme suspicion.

To keep the gap open between the classical logical system and the subversion/interrogation of that system, Derrida uses *palaeonymics* or *palaeonymy*, the so-called science of old names. The verb 'to be' is retained, for it is logically insurmountable, but it is written *sous rature* (under erasure) to displace a sense of unquestioning familiarity. In the act of thinking a word 'under erasure' and displacing the ontology of the 'is', the reader comes closer to the strategy of deconstruction. Although deconstruction cannot be simply defined, it is intimated in the crisis of its own definition: it cannot 'exist' except in a questioning of its whole existence.

Writing a word *sous rature* is rather like placing it in exaggerated inverted commas—it is the most extreme act of philosophical defamiliarization. Inverted commas enable the writer to distance herself from the implications of the word: they imply that someone else said it, that she distances herself from it, and that she is writing, as it were, with raised eyebrows. To use a word in inverted commas is to use it and yet not entirely agree with it. To use a word *sous rature* is to question the entire philosophical and ontological framework in which it participates.

The idea of palaeonymy is at least partly derived from Martin Heidegger. As the similarity between the names implies, 'deconstruction' borrows from and adapts Heidegger's *Destruktion* or *Abbau*: the

104. Derrida, *Dissemination*, p. 3.
105. Derrida, 'Letter to a Japanese Friend', in Kamuf (ed.), *A Derrida Reader*, pp. 270-76.

idea that in defining, the philosopher must always confront the problem of definition. In *Zur Seinsfrage* Heidegger considers the definition of nihilism and non-being, and concludes that

> no information can be given about nothingness and Being and nihilism, about their essence and about the (verbal) essence (it *is*) of the (nominal) essence (*it* is) which can be presented tangibly in the form of assertions (it is).[106]

To convey the fact that 'being' is an inaccurate word *and* a word that language must use because it has no other, he adopts 'the sign of crossing through, which both retains, and dispenses with the word—being'.[107]

Derrida also adopts the sign of crossing through (to̶ ̶b̶e̶) but for him it has a more radical meaning. He uses Heidegger as writing *sous rature* uses words: that is, he repeats his words and strategies but suspends belief in the philosophical tradition from which they came. Although Heidegger, like Nietzsche, is proleptically deconstructive and 'brackets the logical assumptions that inhabit the very grammar and predicative structure of Western thought',[108] he ultimately subscribes to a belief in Being as the ground of existence prior to all knowledge. Heidegger regards Being as a transcendental, theological signified, which is inarticulable (a kind of negative theology); Derrida sees 'Being' as another case of the metaphysical pursuit of truth and origin, a desire for something that precedes and exceeds the play of signification.

2.2.2. *Undecideables*

The *undecideable* is a term *sous rature*: Derrida is careful to specify that it is not an entity and is only so called 'by analogy'.[109] According to his definition, the undecideable is any term or motif that 'escapes from inclusion in the philosophical (binary) opposition and which nonetheless inhabit[s] it, resist[s] it and disorganise[s] it but without ever constituting a third term, without ever occasioning a solution'.[110]

Undecideables are elusive motifs that span two mutually incompatible possibilities and suspend the reader between opposite choices. The

106. M. Heidegger, *The Question of Being* (trans. W. Klauback and J.T. Wilde; New York:, 1958), pp. 80-81.

107. Heidegger, *The Question of Being*, p. 81.

108. Norris, *Deconstruction: Theory and Practice*, p. 69.

109. Derrida, 'Positions', p. 36.

110. Derrida, 'Positions', p. 36.

undecideable 'produces an effect of indefinite fluctuation between two possibilities', although, as Derrida stresses, both 'poles of reading' are not 'equally obvious'.[111] Undecideables condense in one motif what Paul de Man calls the dilemma of 'unreadability'. They act as a focal point for the way in which a text 'leads to a set of assertions that radically exclude each other' and 'compel[s] us to choose while destroying the foundations of any choice'.[112]

Undecideables are 'points of indefinite pointing: they mark the spots of what can never be mediated, mastered, sublated or dialecticized'.[113] Derrida is careful to differentiate between the function of the undecideable and the resolution involved in the Hegelian concepts of 'dialectic' or 'sublation'. In *Dissemination* he writes:

> It is not a question of repeating... what Hegel does with German words such as Aufhebung, Urteil, Meinen, Beispiel, etc., marvelling at the happy accident that steeps a natural language in the element of dialectic. What counts here is not the lexical richness, semantic openness of a word or concept, its depth or breadth, or the sedimentation in it of two contradictory significations (continuity and discontinuity, inside and outside, identity and difference, etc.). What counts here is the formal and syntactic activity (*practique*) that composes and decomposes it.[114]

Undecideables are not important in themselves, nor are they the only points on which a clever deconstructionist can pin her argument. Rather, undecideables are symptoms and focal points of a deeper logic at work in texts, and of the necessity by which texts will always work against themselves.

The important feature of undecideables is not an overdetermination or plurality of meaning, but a hinged, double and opposite meaning, which allows (indeed invites) the reader to read the text against the grain of its main argument. Peggy Kamuf describes the double action of the undecideable brilliantly: 'It enters the dialectic from both sides at once

111. Derrida, *Dissemination*, p. 225. As David Clines points out, 'If a discourse should undermine itself in the same manner and with the same degree of explicitness that it asserted it we should be merely confused or else amused at its incompetence as a discourse, and pronounce it as simply incoherent' (D.J.A. Clines, 'Deconstructing the Book of Job', in *What Does Eve Do to Help and Other Readerly Questions to the Old Testament* [JSOTSup, 94; Sheffield: JSOT Press, 1990], pp. 106-23 [107]).

112. P. de Man, *Allegories of Reading: Figural Language in Rousseau, Nietzsche, Rilke and Proust* (New Haven: Yale University Press, 1979), p. 245.

113. Derrida, *Dissemination*, p. 221.

114. Derrida, *Dissemination*, p. 220.

(remedy–poison, good–bad, positive–negative) and threatens the philosophical process from within'.[115] The essay 'Positions' provides a long list of the undecideables used by Derrida,[116] and each is associated with a particular text (the *pharmakon* with Plato's *Phaedrus*, the *supplément* with Rousseau's *Confessions*, the *hymen* with Mallarmé's *Mimique*, and so on). The following sections consider three undecideables: the *pharmakon* (the undecideability of translation), the *supplément* (the undecideability of beginnings), and the *parergon* (the undecideability of boundaries).

The Pharmakon and the Undecideability of Translation

> The pharmakon is neither the cure nor the poison, neither good nor evil, neither the inside nor the outside, neither speech nor writing...[117]

Socrates	Since Beauty and Ugliness are opposites, they are two.
Glaucon	Of course.
Socrates	And as they are two, each of them is single.
Glaucon	That is so.
Socrates	The same is true of justice and injustice, good and evil, and all qualities...[118]

> Plato would like to isolate the good from the bad, the true from the false. He leans over further: they repeat each other.[119]

Derrida's deconstruction of Plato's *Phaedrus* in 'Plato's Pharmacy' is a focal point for dismantling the distinction between literary and philosophical language. It is an extension of Nietzsche's argument in *Im Fall des Socrates*, in which he famously collapses the distinction between the reason of the philo-sophs and the rhetoric of the sophists. It is no accident that Nietzsche's claim that truths are a 'mobile marching army of metaphors, metonymies and anthropomorphisms...illusions which one has forgotten that they are illusions'[120] is quoted in many prefaces to Derrida since Derrida's work extrapolates from Nietzsche's critique of Platonic philosophy. The background to 'Plato's Pharmacy' is the Nietzschean idea that, as Robert Pirsig puts it, 'The halo round the

115. Kamuf, in Kamuf (ed.), *A Derrida Reader*, p. 113.

116. Derrida, 'Positions', p. 36.

117. Derrida, 'Positions', p. 36.

118. Plato, *The Republic* (trans. D. Lee; Harmondsworth: Penguin, 1987), 475c-476a.

119. Derrida, *Dissemination*, p. 169.

120. F. Nietzsche, 'On Truth and Falsity in their Ultramoral Sense', in O. Levey (ed.), *The Complete Works of Friedrich Nietzsche*, II (New York, 1964), p. 180.

heads of Plato and Socrates is now gone [because] they are consistently doing what they accuse the Sophists of doing—using emotionally persuasive language for the ulterior purpose of making the weaker argument, the case for dialectic, appear stronger'.[121]

'The sound of these arguments rings so loudly in my head', writes Derrida, 'that I cannot hear the other side'.[122] Working within a text by Plato, Derrida confronts the legacy of Platonic opposition at its core and shows how the promotion of, for example, dialectic over rhetoric, consistently represses another set of values. The Platonic texts are self-assured and manipulating: Socrates declares 'Follow my lead'[123] not only to characters like Glaucon and Phaedrus but effectively to Western civilization.[124] Derrida does not oppose Platonic logic, because to do so would ironically be to oppose antithetical thinking by setting up a new antithesis and hierarchy: Plato—Derrida. Rather, he attempts to find a way of engaging with a text that 'avoid(s) frontal and symmetrical protest, opposition in all forms of *anti*',[125] and he does this by pursuing the inexorable logic of the undecideables *pharmakon* and *pharmakeus*.

In the *Phaedrus* writing is described as a *pharmakon,* which means both 'cure' and 'poison'. Although its original inventor offered it as a remedy (for weakness of memory), Socrates describes it as a dangerous drug. Whether it is cure or poison, the *pharmakon*, writing, is an artificial addition *added* to pure thought or philosophy. But Plato deconstructs his own argument when he describes philosophy itself as sorcery, *pharmakon*. His interlocutors suggest that Socrates, who works by indirection and enchantment, would be arrested on arrival in a new town as a *pharmakeus* (variously 'magician', 'sorcerer', 'poisoner'), and in the *Critias* sorcery and philosophy are equated in a prayer that the gods may 'grant us that most effective medicine (*pharmakon teleôtaton*), that most effective of medicines (*ariston pharmakon*), knowledge

---

121. R. Pirsig, *Zen and the Art of Motorcycle Maintenance* (London: Bodley Head, 1974), p. 378.

122. Derrida, *Dissemination*, p. 169.

123. Plato, *The Republic*, 474c.

124. The twentieth-century Israeli poet Yehuda Amichai makes the link when he describes himself, like Glaucon, as 'one of Socrates disciples': 'Walking by his side/ hearing his opinions and histories/ It remains for me to say/Yes. Yes it is like that/ You are right again/ Indeed your words are true' (*Selected Poems* [trans. A. Gutmann; London: Cape Goliard, 1967], unnumbered).

125. Derrida, *Margins of Philosophy* (trans. A. Bass; Chicago: University of Chicago Press, 1982), p. xv.

(*epistemen*)'.[126] Philosophy, which is presented as a remedy to rhetoric and writing, is itself a derivative of writing and another version of the *pharmakon*. As Derrida puts it, the text presents 'the philosophical, epistemic order of the logos as antidote, as a force inscribed within the general, alogical economy of the *pharmakon*'.[127]

The *Phaedrus* has traditionally been classed as a fragmented and flawed text, and critics and translators have tried to control its ambiguities, translating *pharmakon* as remedy *or* poison. Translators, Derrida observes, 'have turned *pharmakon* on its strange and invisible pivot, presenting it from a single one, the *most reassuring of its poles*'.[128] The 'imprudence and empiricism of the translators' has patched over 'the redoubtable, irreducible, difficulty of translation' and 'obliterated' the 'strange logic' that links the signifier to the signified.[129] Derrida, in contrast, uses the undecideability of the *pharmakon* to demonstrate how the text is ordered by the 'graphic' of *différance* (rather than the logic of reversal) that Plato can only partially control.

By drawing attention to the undecideability of the *pharmakon*, Derrida reopens the text that has been sealed by univocal translation and shows how the link between signifier and signified is 'malleable'[130] and marked by *différance*. The *pharmakon* highlights the 'irreducible difficulty of translation', not only of Greek to another language but of Greek, the language of philosophy, to itself, and demonstrates the 'violent difficulty of transference of a nonphilosopheme [that is, a written word] into a philosopheme [a philosophical term removed from the equivocality of writing]'.[131] Pursuing the chain of metaphor in a defiantly anti-rhetorical text, Derrida at once defies the text *and* subordinates himself, more than most commentators, to the minutiae of its logic and the details of its words. The logical parameters that the text sets for itself cause words to rebound and contradict themselves: 'The walled-in voice strikes against the rafters, the words come apart, bits and

---

126. This description of the working of the *pharmakon* is based on Culler's account in *On Deconstruction*, pp. 142-43 (142).

127. Derrida, *Dissemination*, p. 124.

128. Derrida, *Dissemination*, p. 97 (my italics).

129. Derrida, *Dissemination*, pp. 71-72.

130. Derrida, *Dissemination*, p. 72.

131. Derrida, *Dissemination*, p. 72 (the explanations in square brackets are the translator's).

pieces of sentences are separated, disarticulated parts begin to circulate through the corridors, become fixed for a round or two, translate each other, become rejoined, bounce off each other, become rejoined, bounce off each other, come back like answers'.[132] Ironically, Derrida's description of words ricocheting against the limits (walls) of Plato's texts sounds very like criticisms of his own essays as 'autistic echo chambers',[133] but this is precisely the effect he hopes to achieve. Derrida's texts are confusing and self-subverting because he intends to make explicit what is implicit in all texts: that is, the disorientating and eternal play of *différance* 'to which there is no answer and from which there is no escape'.[134]

Within the conventions of dialectic, described by Derrida as 'an operation of mastery',[135] opposites threaten to collide and deconstruct the main discourse. Even in *The Republic*—a text that depends on separating light from shadows, reality from mimesis, and what *is* from what *is not*—Glaucon tells a children's riddle about a man who was not a man (a eunuch) who threw a stone that was not a stone (a pumice stone) at a bird that was not a bird (a bat) sitting on a twig that was not a twig (a reed).[136] The comic extract is meant to supplement the text's argument and is presented as a neatly ordered rhetorical device—a paradox—but potentially it suggests the possibility of aporiae, and draws attention to the deconstructive capacity of language and its tendency to transgress binary opposition. Within a text about the segregation of the *is* and the *is not*, there is a confrontation, as Derrida would put it, between the *et* of conjunction and opposition and the *est* of equality, showing, as J. Hillis Miller somewhat ironically observes, that 'The so-called deconstruction of metaphysics has always been a part of metaphysics, a shadow within its light'.[137]

132. Derrida, *Dissemination*, p. 169.

133. V.B. Leitch, *Deconstructive Criticism: An Advanced Introduction* (New York: Columbia University Press, 1983), p. 47.

134. Derrida, *Dissemination*, p. 216.

135. Derrida, *Dissemination*, p. 5.

136. Plato, *The Republic*, 479c.

137. J. Hillis Miller, 'The Still Heart: Poetic Form in Wordsworth', *NLH* 2 (1971), pp. 297-310 (298). I find the observation ironic because Hillis Miller describes the deconstruction of Plato using a Platonic metaphor.

The 'Dangerous Supplement':[138] *Jean Jacques Rousseau and the Problem of Beginning*

> The supplement is neither a plus nor a minus, neither an outside nor the complement of an inside, neither an accident nor an essence.[139]

One of Derrida's most logically audacious claims is that there is no such thing as the 'virginity of a story of beginnings'.[140] The deconstruction of the concept of 'origin' is worked out most specifically in his treatment of Rousseau's *Confessions* and *Essay on the Origin of Languages* in *Of Grammatology*,[141] but is often referred to obliquely in the (in)famous phrase 'always already'. Derrida's point is that the pure is always already impure, good is always already evil, and that in all violent hierarchies the superior term is always already dependent on, and contaminated by, its inferior. The prelapsarian is impossible to conceptualize, and even in Milton's ambitious attempt in *Paradise Lost,* paradise is always already lost and Eve is coy and wanton before the serpent's entrance.[142]

Milton himself sounds like a disciple of Saussure when he writes in *Areopagitica* that 'that which purifies us is trial, and trial is by what is

138. Derrida, *Of Grammatology,* p. 141.

139. Derrida, 'Positions', p. 36.

140. Derrida, 'White Mythology', p. 29.

141. Another deconstruction of the concept of origin is 'The Time Before First', in *Dissemination.* The theme, that 'all oppositions based on the distinction between the original and the derived, the simple and the repeated, the first and the second etc., lose their pertinence' (*Dissemination,* p. 330) is essentially the same, but the argument is harder to follow. In a complex argument hinging on tenses, Derrida claims that 'any statements about the fiction of the origin, about the indeterminacy of the seminal imperfect into which the pluperfect of some event without a date, of some immemorial birth is inserted ('something had begun...') cannot themselves escape the rules they set forth' (*Dissemination,* p. 335). Since tenses make it possible to graft onto beginnings as well as endings, it is always possible to inscribe another beginning before the beginning. Derrida implies that the concept of origin is deconstructed by language's own rules, and the idea of 'first' becomes meaningless because, grammatically, it is always possible to insert another 'time before first'.

Derrida's deconstruction of 'origin' also has much in common with Nietzsche's critique of causality in *Will To Power*, in which he argues that 'cause' is actually an effect created by *chronologische Umdrehung* ('chronological reversal'). On feeling pain, and spying a pin, we label the pin as 'cause' and the pain as 'effect', but in fact the pin is the 'effect' and the pain the 'cause' that led us to look for it (F. Nietzsche, *Will To Power*, cited in Culler, *On Deconstruction*, p. 86).

142. In Book V, for example, Eve is narcissistic and falls in love with her own image. Impossibly, her weakness must precede the fall, and yet she must be perfect.

contrary',[143] because he seems to imply that virtue can emerge only as a consequence of struggle with evil. If meaning is an effect of difference, and good is defined by its differential relation to evil, then it follows logically that there can be no single starting point that is not dependent on another term for definition. Terms like *différance* or the *trace*, which Derrida uses to describe the space between words, cannot be originary terms either, because they are the product, not the starting point, of the interaction between two words. Extending the logic of Saussure's meaning of difference leads to the aporia of nonoriginary origins and the conclusion that all 'immediacy is derived'[144]—ideas that are totally unacceptable within the parameters of classical logic.

Rousseau 'occupies a privileged place...in the history of logocentrism'[145] because his writing is a perfect example of the idealization and moral judgment implicit in violent hierarchies. His texts are manifestos against debasement, of nature into culture, speech into writing, and melody into harmony, and are absolutely dependent on the concept of a pure origin. His writing is a clear demonstration of the tendency of all metaphysicians, 'from Plato to Rousseau, from Descartes to Husserl', to place 'good before evil, the positive before the negative'[146] and to structure their logic on the model of the fall. For Derrida this is not merely 'one metaphysical gesture among others', but 'the most constant, profound, and potent procedure' of 'returning "strategically" in idealization, to an origin or to a "priority" seen as simple, intact, normal, pure, standard, self-identical, in order then to conceive of (*pour penser ensuite*) derivation, complication, deterioration, accident, etc.'[147]

Derrida argues that Rousseau works against himself because his argument 'twists about in a sort of oblique effort to act as if degeneration were not prescribed in the genesis and as if evil supervened upon a good origin'.[148] He works within the *Confessions* as he works within *Phaedrus*: that is, not by imposing external terms on the text, but by using hinged words within it. In the *Confessions* and the *Essay on the Origin of Languages* the linchpin of the texts' undoing is the seemingly

---

143. Milton, *Areopagitica*, cited in R. Selden, *A Reader's Guide to Contemporary Literary Theory* (Brighton: Harvester Press, 1985), p. 87.
144. Derrida, *Of Grammatology*, p. 157.
145. Derrida, *Of Grammatology*, p. 97.
146. Derrida, 'Limited Inc.', p. 236.
147. Derrida, 'Limited Inc.', p. 236.
148. Derrida, *Of Grammatology*, p. 199.

harmless word *supplément*, which 'harbours within itself two significations whose cohabitation is as strange as it is necessary'.[149] A 'supplement', according to Webster's dictionary, is 'something that completes or makes an addition', and Derrida explores the consequences of this double logic within Rousseau's texts.

The perverse logic of the supplement at work in Rousseau's argument is most clearly demonstrated in a close reading of the relationship between speech and writing. Rousseau, like Shakespeare, demotes writing as 'the quill' that 'comes too short':[150] he argues that 'languages are made to be spoken' and that 'writing serves only as a supplement to speech'.[151] Speech and writing are clearly delineated by Rousseau to the extent that 'The art of writing does not depend at all on that of speaking'.[152] Speech is associated with presence and immediacy, and writing is used as a kind of scapegoat for all the less palatable aspects of language such as distance, ambiguity and misunderstanding; as Newton Garver puts it, Rousseau regards writing as 'an exteriority', because 'it is based on some convention that lies outside the matter being expressed [such as] an ideography, or syllabary, or an alphabet'.[153]

The central polemic of Rousseau's texts regards writing as an unnecessary extra that is added on to speech, and which, unlike speech, is not in direct contact with presence. But occasionally he hints at another relationship between speech and writing when, for example, he confesses,

> I would love society as others do if I were not sure of showing myself not just at a disadvantage but as completely different from what I am. The decision I have taken to write and hide myself is precisely the one that suits me. If I were present people would never have known what I was worth.[154]

Rousseau describes how he replaced speech with writing, and thus suggests an affinity between the two (since to function as a substitute, writing must in some way resemble what it replaces). The closeness of

149. Derrida, *Of Grammatology*, p. 144.

150. Shakespeare, *Sonnets*, 83.7.

151. Rousseau, cited in Derrida, *Of Grammatology*, p. 144.

152. Rousseau, *Essai sur l'origine des langues* (Bordeaux: Ducrois, 1968), p. 23.

153. N. Garver, 'Derrida on Rousseau on Writing', *Journal of Philosophy* 74 (1977), pp. 663-73 (669).

154. Rousseau, *Confessions*, cited in Derrida, *Of Grammatology*, p. 142 (as Derrida gives no refererence I have been unable to trace the original statement).

speech to writing is not only suggested by the logic of substitution but is explicitly stated by Rousseau, for far from directly mediating presence, speech fails to show the author as he truly is.

In this extract from the *Confessions*, Derrida argues, Rousseau confesses more than he intends. The main argument, which subordinates writing to speech, is deconstructed by a rhetorical aside in which Rousseau slips into the traditional argument of the writer and 'says'[155] that what he is doing is restoring through the absence of writing a presence that has been missing from speech. The same narrator maintains that writing is an unnecessary supplement (i.e. addition) to speech, that writing replaces (i.e. acts as a substitute for) speech, and that writing fills up the lacks in (i.e. completes) speech. Each of these functions could be described in the phrase 'writing is a supplement', but each statement describes a radically different relationship between speech and writing. The first statement suggests that speech is complete, the third that it is lacking; the first statement underlines the difference between writing and speech, and the second stresses the similarity. The three meanings are so radically different that they cannot be gathered up into a coherent whole, 'even under the rubric of "ambiguity" or "polysemy"':[156] because each represents a dimension of the text, the text cannot be totalized, and 'works against' or deconstructs itself.

The Parergon: The Frame as Frame-Up and the Undecideability of Borders

> Every analytic of aesthetic judgement presupposes that we can rigorously distinguish between the intrinsic and the extrinsic. Aesthetic judgement must concern intrinsic beauty and not the around and about. It is therefore necessary to know, and this is the fundamental presupposition, the presupposition of the fundamental—how to define the intrinsic, the frame, and what to exclude as frame, and as beyond the frame.[157]

Derrida practises the perverse logic of supplementarity by concentrating on marginal features of texts: the subliminal imagery of the *pharmakon*;

---

155. The academic convention by which we use 'Rousseau says' as a synonym for 'Rousseau writes' blurs the traditional distinction that Rousseau is trying to employ. Even Derrida confuses them, 'saying/writing' in a footnote to the Exergue in *Of Grammatology*, 'I shall *speak* of this later' (Derrida, *Of Grammatology*, p. 4 n. 3).

156. Hart, *The Trespass of the Sign*, p. 50.

157. Derrida, 'The Parergon', *October* 9 (1979), pp. 3-40 (26).

the obscure discussion of writing in the subtext of Rousseau. He focuses on elements that have been discarded by the canon of commentary, and his disproportionate concentration on the peripheral subverts the distinction between essential and inessential, inside and outside. Derrida does not argue that the seemingly marginal is really central; rather, he writes in such a way as to forestall the illusion that the marginal is being established as a new centre. In his discussion of Kant's *Critique of Judgement*[158] he focuses on a marginal discussion of *parerga*, which are marginal, liminal items such as picture frames, which border and enhance the aesthetic object but are ultimately detachable from it.[159]

In his 'Analytic of the Beautiful' Kant tries to establish the idea of pure form or essential beauty. There is, he argues, something intrinsic about a work of art that is separable from its 'parergon', its frame, 'accessory', or 'supplement'. The irony of his position is that even as he tries to separate the frame from the intrinsic object, he is himself writing a frame, or definition, for what constitutes a pure aesthetic. He defines intrinsic beauty as something that can be distinguished from the frame or adjunct, but in the act of definition he shows that the frame or boundary is essential (intrinsic) to establishing the notion of intrinsic beauty. The inside is defined over and against the outside: there can be no inside without an outside and the frame is necessitated by a 'lack—a certain "internal" indeterminacy, within that which it comes to frame'.[160]

The *parergon* disrupts the concept of boundary, the distinction between inside and outside, because it is, aporistically, 'an outside which is called inside the inside to constitute it as an inside'.[161] Since it is neither intrinsic, nor extraneous, nor 'half-and-half', it inhabits the binary opposition inside–outside, necessary–superfluous, and undecideably 'resist[s] and disorganise[s] it without ever constituting a third term'.[162]

158. Derrida, 'The Parergon'.

159. A further pun is at work here because *Kant* in German means 'edge' or 'border'. By taking the proper name from outside the text and setting it to work as a common noun within the text, Derrida is problematizing borders using the word *Kant*, or border. Kant is no longer simply the figure outside the text, the ultimate extratextual referent, but is also a force at work within the text. The discussion of borders extends the borders of the text, so that, potentially, 'there is nothing outside the text' (not even the author).

160. Derrida, 'The Parergon', p. 33.

161. Derrida, 'The Parergon', p. 26.

162. Derrida, 'Positions', p. 36.

The deconstruction of boundaries constantly spills over into Derrida's own work as he practises his own distinct brand of intertextuality. In 'Living On: *Border Lines*',[163] he suggests that a text has no borders that separate it from infinite con-text by reading Maurice Blanchot's *La folie du jour* (*The Madness of the Day*) and *L'arrêt du mort* (*Death Sentence*) as, in effect, interpretations of Shelley's *The Triumph of Life*. To compound the point that a text has no limits, his own intertextual commentary, 'Living On', is bordered by another text, 'Border Lines', which is separated from the main text by a line at the bottom of the page, but which constantly defies this line and mingles with the main text. Derrida shows how 'no context is saturable any more' and 'no border is guaranteed inside or out',[164] since a text always overruns its conceptualized edges, despite 'endless efforts to dam up, resist, rebuild the old partitions'.[165]

Defying the conventional borders of interpretation, Derrida suggests that a text should be read as at once referring only to itself and as referring to another piece of writing, and he constantly stages 'the question of relation between texts once their limits or borders can no longer be rigorously determined'.[166] His desire to demonstrate a 'sort of overrun, (*débordement*) that spoils all these boundaries and divisions', leads to texts like *Glas*, in which the philosophical ideas of Hegel, and the literary motifs of Genet, are played off against each other in two parallel columns. In *Glas*[167] Derrida overruns the border between literature and philosophy, and shows how even the most antipathetic ideas cannot be rigorously delineated. The boundaries for context can never be set, and a text can interact with any number of texts, including its seeming philosophical 'opposite'.

3. *Reactions to Derrida in Biblical Studies*

In biblical studies, deconstruction seems to be less an issue of undecideability (as in the heated debate over Derrida's honorary degree) than a phenomenon of *différance*, a study endlessly deferred. In 1982 a volume

---

163. Derrida, 'Living On: *Border Lines*', in H. Bloom (ed.), *Deconstruction and Criticism* (New York: Seabury Press, 1979), pp. 75-176.
164. Derrida, 'Living On', p. 78.
165. Derrida, 'Living On', p. 84.
166. Kamuf, in Kamuf (ed.), *A Derrida Reader*, p. 255.
167. Derrida, *Glas* (Paris: Galilée, 1974).

of *Semeia* was devoted to *Derrida and Biblical Studies*,[168] and H.N. Schneidau predicted that 'As he becomes better known, Derrida will have his day, even among the biblical texts'.[169] At the end of the decade in 1989, Edward L. Greenstein accurately observed that 'Little has been published as yet on the applications of deconstruction to the Hebrew Bible, and I have seen virtually no purely deconstructive readings of it.'[170] Of the few articles published the majority are theoretical,[171] arousing a sense of dialogue perpetually deferred between Derrida and biblical texts. Even more strangely, critics who studiously avoid Derrida or denounce deconstruction, still use deconstruction as a term: domesticised as a buzz word and separated from Derrida's anti-orthodoxy, it is increasingly misused as a synonym for taking a text apart (that is, conventional 'analysis').

Although deconstruction is one of the most prominent literary move-ments of the late twentieth century, biblical scholars often give it a mere cursory glance before excluding it from an ostensibly literary, and plural, perspective. Robert Alter and Frank Kermode, in their *Literary Guide*

---

168. R. Detweiler (ed.), *Derrida and Biblical Studies* (Semeia, 23; Atlanta: Scholars Press, 1982).

169. H.N. Schneidau, 'The Word Against the Word: Derrida on Textuality', in Detweiler (ed.), *Derrida and Biblical Studies*, pp. 5-28 (6).

170. E.L. Greenstein, 'Deconstruction and Biblical Narrative', *Prooftexts* 9 (1989), pp. 43-71 (44). Notable exceptions are David Clines's readings of Job ('Deconstructing the Book of Job', in *What Does Eve Do to Help and Other Readerly Questions to the Old Testament* [JSOTSup, 94; Sheffield: JSOT Press, 1990], pp. 106-23) and Haggai ('Haggai's Temple: Constructed, Deconstructed and Reconstructed', in T.C. Eskenazi and K.H. Richards [eds.], *Second Temple Studies: Temple and Community in the Persian Period* [JSOTSup, 175; Sheffield: JSOT Press, 1993], pp. 51-78), and David Jobling's as yet unpublished, 'Decon-structive Reading of Hosea 1–3', which I am grateful to him for allowing me to see.

171. All of the articles in *Derrida and Biblical Studies* are theoretical. Biblical studies seems to be following the same pattern as English Literature in its concentra-tion on theoretical aspects of deconstruction. In 1979 Paul de Man prophesied that the application of deconstruction would be the 'test of literary criticism in the coming years' (*Allegories of Reading*, pp. 16-17), but in 1989 J. Hillis Miller disappointedly observed, 'There has been more talk about deconstruction as a 'theory' or 'method', attempts to applaud it or to deplore it, than there has been an attempt to do it, to show that it is 'applicable' to Milton or to Dante or to Hölderlin, or to Anthony Trollope and Virginia Woolf' (J. Hillis Miller, 'The Function of Literary Theory at the Present Time', in R. Cohen [ed.], *The Future of Literary Theory* [London: Routledge, 1989], pp. 103-11 [103]).

to the Bible, are selectively 'pluralist' in their approach: in the same paragraph, Alter claims, 'Our own notion of criticism is pluralist, and the label that best fits most of our contributors is eclectic', *and* proposes to outlaw 'deconstructionists and some feminist critics who seek to demonstrate that the text is necessarily divided against itself' on the grounds that such criticism does not 'provide illumination'.[172] With a similarly dismissive attitude, Kath Filmer polemically argues that deconstruction is not for the 'person in the real world' and consigns Derrida to a 'philosophical cloud cuckoo land',[173] while D.S. Greenwood declares deconstruction a heretic pursuit that is 'virulently anti-Christian, with its assault on the Logos-idea'.[174] The New Testament scholar William Kurtz similarly argues that deconstruction should be dismissed without question as it represents 'a total scepticism denying any metaphysics or God behind words'.[175]

If deconstruction is being dismissed for not arguing within the Anglo-American pragmatist tradition, I would argue that its opponents are similarly belying that tradition by not providing a rigorous or convincing response. What is often being attacked is a crude parody of deconstruction as a pernicious opponent of God, ontology and the Johannine logos—an 'atheistic acid', as Vincent B. Leitch puts it,[176] that dissolves all orthodox stabilities. In response to these reactions I would argue that a defensive polarization of antipathy against Derrida seems to confirm the inadequacies of binary thinking which Derrida aims to subvert. For scholars to think they must be either solely for or against Derrida seems to be crudely simplistic: Derrida is not offering a competing system of thought which must be staunchly rejected, but he is offering a novel critique of the frameworks in which critics traditionally operate. One of the first points that Christopher Norris makes about deconstruction is that it does not proffer itself as an alternative creed or life philosophy:

172. R. Alter and F. Kermode (eds.), *The Literary Guide to the Bible* (London: Fontana Press, 1987), p. 6.

173. K. Filmer, 'Of Lunacy and Laundry Trucks: Deconstruction and Mythopoesis', *LB* (1989), pp. 55-64 (55).

174. D.S. Greenwood, 'Poststructuralism and Biblical Studies: Frank Kermode's The Genesis of Secrecy', in R.T. France and D. Wenham (eds.), *Studies in Midrash and Historiography* (Gospel Perspectives, 3; Sheffield: JSOT Press, 1983), pp. 263-88 (78).

175. W.S. Kurtz, 'Narrative Approaches to Luke–Acts', *Bib* 68 (1987), pp. 195-220 (198 n. 10).

176. Leitch, *Deconstructive Criticism*, p. 116.

'Deconstruction is...an activity of thought which cannot be consistently acted upon—that way madness lies—but which yet possesses an inescapable rigour of its own'.[177]

If deconstruction has often been condemned by an associative logic that sees deconstruction as synonymous with destruction and destruction as negative, then deconstruction in biblical studies is stereotyped as an act of desecration. In this next section I want to suggest that far from being incompatible with the Hebrew Bible, deconstruction is an appropriate strategy for analysing texts that appear, so often, to work against themselves. I want to demonstrate how the liaison is being anticipated in increasing acknowledgment of self-contradiction in the Hebrew Bible, and in the analogy between Derrida and 'prophecy'. I shall also investigate Derrida's Jewishness and his own 'exegesis' of biblical narratives, to counteract the reductive view that Derrida and the Bible are incompatible, simply because he subverts the concept of logos.

3.1. *New Paradigms for the Hebrew Bible: Images of Incompatibility and Self-Contradiction*

Ironically, alongside a large-scale, almost superstitious exclusion of deconstruction, a new view of the Hebrew Bible is emerging which, like Derrida, finds binary categories an inadequate framework of analysis. Robert Alter, who excludes 'unilluminating' deconstructive strategies in the introduction to his *Guide*, writes elsewhere that the 'biblical outlook is informed...by a sense of stubborn contradiction, of a profound and ineradicable untidiness in the nature of things', and that the reader 'repeatedly has to make sense of the intersection of incompatibles'.[178] Such a description comes very close to J. Hillis Miller's (deconstructive) view of language as a 'clash of incompatibles which grates, twists or bifurcates the mind'.[179] If incompatibles are ineradicable, as Alter acknowledges, then to exclude Derrida is to exclude one of the most thorough analyses of the inadequacies of dichotomy as a framework for texts.

177. Norris, *Deconstruction: Theory and Practice*, p. xii.

178. R. Alter, *The Art of Biblical Narrative* (New York: Basic Books, 1981), p. 154. The statement that incompatibles are ineradicable contradicts the *Guide*, which conforms to New Critical principles in its aim to 'integrate' the complex diversity of texts (Alter and Kermode [eds.], *The Literary Guide*, p. 5).

179. J. Hillis Miller, 'Ariachne's Broken Woof', *Georgia Review* 9 (1977), pp. 31-59 (56).

Alter is by no means the only scholar to draw the reader's attention to incompatibles in the Hebrew Bible. In an analysis of 1 Samuel 15 and the conflicting statements of Yhwh, Robert Carroll describes the text as on a collision course with 'Western Logic' and the 'law of the excluded middle'.[180] Shimon Bakon also notes the inconsistency of 1 Samuel 15 when read intertextually with Hosea 11.[181] In 1 Sam. 15.29 Yhwh maintains that he 'does not deceive or change his mind, for he is not human'; in Hos. 11.9 he argues that he has 'had a change of heart', for he is 'God and not man'. 'Different strands' come into 'direct conflict',[182] and the non-humanity of Yhwh is seen as a basis for changing, and not changing, his mind. In contrast to the traditional view of Yhwh as a faithful adherent of the law of binary opposition, Bakon describes a deity with little respect for mutual exclusives, and concludes that:

> The Bible is not a Greek book on logic, developing ideas along clearly defined categories. It is a record of the relationship between God and man, together with reversals and seemingly conflicting values.[183]

The Hebrew Bible tends to violate the rules by which we are accustomed to operate: the texts resist resolution, 'refuse...a pattern',[184] and are being redefined by many scholars as a 'compendium of questions' rather than, as traditionally, 'an anthology of answers'.[185] In his book *The Great Code*, Northrop Frye argues that the biblical texts have been hemmed in by 'anxiety structures' which set the parameter of our questions, and adds provocatively that:

> If Milton's view of the Bible as a manifesto for human freedom has anything to be said for it, one would expect it to be written in a language that would smash these (anxiety) structures beyond repair and let some genuine air and light in.[186]

---

180. R.P. Carroll, *Wolf in the Sheepfold: The Bible as a Problem for Christianity* (London: SPCK, 1991), p. 42.

181. S. Bakon, 'For I am God and not Man', *Dor le Dor* 17 (1988), pp. 243-49.

182. Bakon, 'For I am God and not Man', p. 243.

183. Bakon, 'For I am God and not Man', p. 245. I am not sure about the implications of the word 'seemingly' here. Perhaps even Bakon's more radical article is ultimately shying away from, or modifying, the idea that the two sayings collide and potentially deconstruct.

184. G. Josipovici, *The Book of God: A Response to the Bible* (New Haven: Yale University Press, 1988), p. 47.

185. S.C. Walker, 'Deconstructing the Bible', *LB* (1989), pp. 8-17 (9).

186. N. Frye, *The Great Code: The Bible and Literature* (New York: Harcourt

Frye's approach is interesting because, although by no means an advocate of deconstruction, he argues that in the very act of constructing edifices around it, the explainer of texts can conceal, obfuscate, and tame the text. From this realization it is but a short step to Derrida's contention that criticism need not always be holistic but can trace the inconsistencies and contradictions of a text. Derrida unremittingly opposes any symbols of closure and self-contained completeness: he questions 'the idea of the book as the idea of totality'[187] and one of his first moves in *Of Grammatology* is from 'The End of the Book' to 'The Beginning of Writing' (chapter 1). Biblical criticism, which has been so constrained by the sense of the Bible as totality and the need to fit each text into an overall system, might be liberated by a similar treatment of the 'book of books' and a critical attitude that will potentially liberate the play of *différance* in and between texts.

The effects of linking the self-subversion of biblical texts and deconstruction have been brilliantly foreshadowed in an article by Stephen C. Walker. Walker is the only critic, to my knowledge, to draw specific analogies between Derrida's deconstructive strategies and motifs and the habit of the Hebrew Bible to contradict, comment on and subvert itself. Walker argues:

> Although they have not been so applied, such deconstructive strategies as Derrida's production of 'undecideables' all strike me as eminently applicable reading approaches to the Bible.[188]

The self-commentative style of the texts (the way in which Chronicles comments on Samuel–Kings, Ruth on Ezra–Nehemiah, and texts comment on themselves) even leads Walker to declare that:

> 'Split-level texts', a hallmark of deconstructive style and deconstructionist concerns, appear so frequently in the Bible that it ought to have been their presence there that focused deconstructionists on the phenomena in the first place.[189]

Although Walker's claim that the Bible should be the primary text of deconstructionists is enthusiastically overstated, it does make the point that deconstruction is not an erudite imposition on the text from the ever-developing realm of literary theory, but rather a process that, to use

Brace Jovanovich, 1982), p. 233 (author's parentheses).
   187. Derrida, *Of Grammatology*, p. 18.
   188. Walker, 'Deconstructing the Bible', p. 10.
   189. Walker, 'Deconstructing the Bible', p. 14.

Derrida's phrase, is 'always already' occurring in the texts. If texts in the Hebrew Bible are prone to contradict and subvert themselves, it is, I suggest, one of the most pertinent approaches, and one that might yield particularly interesting results with reference to prophetic texts.

3.2. *Derrida: A Prophet among the Prophets*

Much has been written about Derrida as a prophet (who tries to describe the cataclysmic collapse of society and thought)[190] but the analogy has yet to be reversed. If the strategy of the prophets is interesting for understanding Derrida, deconstruction might provide useful insights into the strategy of the biblical prophets; however, their intersection is something as yet only anticipated. H.N. Schneidau tantalizingly broaches the possibility when he equates the prophets and the deconstructionists in his study, *Sacred Discontent*. His thesis is that far from being antipathetic, the self-criticizing scepticism of modern Western society is a near relation of the self-subverting style of the Hebrew Bible, and that the prophets, in particular, 'gave voice to a sceptical, often mocking spirit that has long since pervaded the intellectual life of the Western world'.[191]

Schneidau's study is largely abstract and theoretical, but he gives occasional hints as to how his thesis may be applied to texts. Examining Isaiah's disturbing commission—'Go, say to this people, "Hear and hear again, but do not understand; see and see again, but do not perceive"'—Schneidau observes that this statement 'has nothing for those who share the positivist creed that everything that can be expressed can be expressed clearly'.[192] He anticipates the reversal of the analogy between Derrida and the prophets when he describes Isaiah's elusive roles in terms borrowed from Alexander Gelley's description of the arch-deconstructionist. According to Gelley,

> Derrida represents a position that stresses the dearth of meaning, the occlusion of truth. He engages the interpreter in a labour of deciphering, of transcription that could refuse no refuge of historical empathy in the

190. For example, Derrida is included in A. Megill's study, *Prophets of Extremity: Nietzsche, Heidegger, Foucault, Derrida* (Berkeley: University of California Press, 1985).

191. H.N. Schneidau, *Sacred Discontent: The Bible and Western Tradition* (Baton Rouge: Louisiana State University Press, 1976), p. 12.

192. Schneidau, *Sacred Discontent*, p. 254.

manner of *Geistgeschichte,* to no act of participation and communion as intimated by certain phenomenological approaches.[193]

'So', adds Schneidau, 'does Isaiah'.[194]

3.3. *'Reb Rida': Derrida among the Rabbis*

Although Derrida's system cannot be said to derive in Hebraism... the resemblance between his thematics of the trace and certain Hebraic structures is startling.[195]

In a critical environment accustomed to Western principles and the tradition of Christian commentary, deconstruction can look like an alien imposition upon the biblical text. In fact, Derrida often evokes images and strategies from rabbinic discourse and Kabbalah, which he uses to disturb and displace logocentric assumptions. In the midrashic idea that the Torah was created two thousand years before heaven and earth, and that God 'looked into the Torah and created the world',[196] Derrida finds an image for the idea for writing that precedes all speech. In *Of Grammatology* he describes the idea of a primordial and inexhaustible writing using the words of Rabbi Eliezer:

If all the seas were of ink, and all ponds planted with reeds, if the sky and earth were parchments, and if all human beings practised the art of writing—they would not exhaust the Torah I have learned, just as the Torah itself would not be diminished any more than is the sea by the water removed by a paint brush dipped in it.[197]

In Derrida's texts midrashic motifs are not established as the new master-system but are used to deconstruct the logocentricism of Christianity. For Derrida, Christianity is logocentricism incarnate: it is based on ideas of origin, presence, representation, unity, communion and the transcendental signified. Theology and semiology are founded on the

193. A. Gelley, 'Form as Force', *Diacritics* 2 (1972), pp. 9-13 (13).

194. Schneidau, *Sacred Discontent,* p. 256.

195. S. Wolosky, 'Derrida, Jabès, Levinas: Sign-Theory as Ethical Discourse', *Prooftexts* 2 (1982), pp. 283-302 (290). (The following account is greatly influenced by Wolosky's article, though it is rarely quoted directly.)

196. *Gen. R.* 1.1, trans. L. Ginzberg, *The Legends of the Jews,* I (Philadelphia: Jewish Publication Society of America, 1968), p. 3.

197. Derrida, *Of Grammatology,* p. 16. For similar reasons he is also fascinated with Edmond Jabès, for Jabès situates himself firmly within the gigantic and all-embracing 'book': 'The book is my universe, my country, my roof and my enigma' (E. Jabès, *Livre des questions* [Paris: Gallimard, 1963], p. 32).

same assumptions: Derrida sees the relationship between God and Christ as the root and culmination of the idea that there is a visible signifier and an unseen signified, or truth which it/he represents. Christ as Logos promises 'the passage of the infinite to the finite, the finite to the infinite':[198] the Father *is* the Son, the Son *is* the Father and 'Truth comes into the world in the designation of the filial rapport'.[199]

Into these images of union and presence Derrida interposes ('grafts') Jewish motifs of difference. In *Of Grammatology* Rabbi Eliezer's expansive concept of the book immediately precedes, and comments upon, the Pauline philosophy that 'the letter kills, but the spirit gives life'.[200] Paul joins the ranks of philosophers like Plato and Rousseau by creating violent hierarchies (spirit–law, faith–works) in which the second term is 'unredeemed' and represents 'stain and sin'.[201] Derrida as exegete provides his own distinctive gloss: 'There is a good and bad writing; the good and natural is the divine inscription on the heart and soul; the perverse and artful is technique, exiled in the exteriority of the body'.[202]

As the logocentric bias against writing is displaced by Jewish concepts of the book, so the belief in origin as presence is disrupted with esoteric motifs from Lurianic Kabbalah. Since 'Mystical experience permits complementary and apparently contradictory modes of expression',[203] it is fertile ground for images of undecideability and difference. Derrida finds an 'image' for absence that precedes presence in *zimzum*, the mystical idea that it is 'God's withdrawal into himself that first creates a primordial space...and makes possible the existence of something other

198. Derrida, *Glas*, p. 39.

199. Derrida, *Glas*, p. 92. Susan Handelman provides a useful gloss of Judaism and Christianity as motifs in Derrida's texts when she contrasts Christian incarnation with Jewish interpretation. Christianity replaces the Jewish 'intense concentration on the text' with the Christ, or Logos, the 'true predicate of all statements', who 'resolves all tensions, stabilizes meaning, provides ultimate identity and collapses differentiation' (S. Handelman, 'Jacques Derrida and the Heretic Hermeneutic', in M. Krupnick (ed.), *Displacement: Derrida and After* [Bloomington: Indiana University Press, 1983], pp. 98-129 [106]).

200. 2 Cor. 3.6.

201. Derrida, *Of Grammatology*, p. 34.

202. Derrida, *Of Grammatology*, p. 17.

203. S. Ghose, 'Mysticism', *Encyclopaedia Britannica Macropaedia*, XII (15th edn), 786-93.

than God'.[204] Derrida is appealing to Kabbalistic ideas of negativity, separation and occultation when he writes, 'God separated himself from himself, in order to let us speak, in order to astonish and interrogate us'.[205]

Derrida's fascination with images from the *Zohar* is complemented by his interest in Edmond Jabès and Emmanuel Levinas[206] and a concept of God 'in perpetual revolt against God':[207] a God who, as Levinas puts it, turns his back to Moses and does not show himself except by his absence, or the 'trace' of his presence.[208] As well as Jewish philosophy and religious tradition, Derrida also uses the image of 'the Jew' as a potentially deconstructive force and a symbol of open-endedness, and evokes images of a Jewish community in which 'all affirmations and negations, all contradictory questions are welcomed',[209] a community which, in contrast to the Christian community, waits for a homeland ever elsewhere and a future always deferred.[210] Language itself is given specifically Jewish characteristics: Derrida writes of 'the *diaspora* of institutes and languages'[211] and 'the anxiety and the wandering of the language always richer than knowledge, the language always capable of the movement which takes it further than peaceful and sedentary certitude'.[212] Writing and Jewishness coincide in motifs of difference and deferral, and as Jabès puts it, the 'difficulty of being a Jew...coincides

204. G. Scholem, *On the Kabbalah and its Symbolism* (New York: Schocken Books, 1965), p. 111.

205. Derrida, 'Edmond Jabès and the Question of the Book', in *Writing and Difference*, p. 67.

206. See Derrida, 'Edmond Jabès and the Question of the Book', pp. 64-78; 'Violence and Metaphysics: An Essay on the Thought of Emmanuel Levinas', in *Writing and Difference*, pp. 79-153.

207. Jabès, *Livre des questions*, p. 177, cited in Derrida, 'Edmond Jabès and the Question of the Book', p. 68.

208. Derrida, 'Violence and Metaphysics', p. 108.

209. Derrida, 'Edmond Jabès and the Question of the Book', p. 76.

210. Derrida's descriptions of Judaism and Christianity in *Glas* are also revealing. He quotes from Moses Mendelssohn's description of Judaism, 'God does not manifest Himself, He is not truth, total presence or parousia' (*Glas*, p. 62), and argues that 'The Christian God manifests a concrete spirit which remains veiled and abstract in Judaism' (*Glas*, p. 39).

211. Derrida, 'Violence and Metaphysics', p. 79.

212. Derrida, 'Edmond Jabès and the Question of the Book', p. 72.

with the difficulty of writing; for Judaism and writing are but the same waiting, the same hope, the same depletion'.[213] As Jew and writing merge in the same motif, the writing of the Jew also shows some potentially deconstructive characteristics, for the Hebrew language has no form of the verb 'to be' in the present tense. Though Derrida makes no reference to this, it is intriguing to compare the way in which Hebrew— the 'wandering' language of the Jew—juxtaposes nominal forms, with Derrida's protest against the language of logocentrism and the 'binding, agglutinating, linamenting position of the copula *is* [that] conciliates the subject and predicate, and interlaces one around the other to form a sole being'.[214]

At the end of his essay on Jabès, Derrida provides a final quotation from 'Reb Rida' and numbers himself among the rabbis.[215] Explicitly, in his own quotations, and implicitly, Derrida's writing is influenced by his cultural and religious heritage as an Algerian Jew. In *Glas* he refers to the Torah and synagogue of his past,[216] but he also evokes a sense of the Babylonian Talmud by assembling different and contradictory voices on the same page. Implicitly, in the subtext of his writing, he evokes midrashic ideas and strategies and a style of biblical criticism which has been marginalized by logocentric ideals of empiricism and rationality. When he advocates reading *d'une certaine manière* ('in a certain way')[217] he seems to place himself among the rabbis who urged *'al tiqre*: that is, 'do not read it' (i.e., in its conventional form).[218] His

213. Jabès, *Livre des questions,* p. 132, cited in Derrida, 'Edmond Jabès and the Question of the Book', p. 65.

214. Derrida, *Glas*, p. 67.

215. Derrida, 'Edmond Jabès and the Question of the Book', p. 78.

216. Derrida, *Glas,* pp. 268-69.

217. Derrida refers twice to the project of deconstruction as reading *d'une certaine manière*, ('in a certain way'): 'What I want to emphasise is simply that the passage beyond philosophy does not consist in turning the page of philosophy (which usually amounts to philosophising badly) but in continuing to read philosophers in a certain way' ('Structure, Sign and Play', p. 288); 'The movements of deconstruction do not destroy (*sollicitent*) structures from the outside. They are not possible and effective, nor can they take accurate aim, except by inhabiting those structures. Inhabiting them *in a certain way*, because one always inhabits, and all the more when one does not suspect it' (*Of Grammatology*, p. 24).

218. The phrase *'al tiqre* ('do not read it') applied to private reading of the scriptures. Alluding to this level of reading, R. Joshua (first and second centuries) asked his younger colleague R. Ishmael (second century), 'How do *you* read [a passage in the Song of Songs]?' *'Abod. Zar.* II.5 (see J. Faur, *Golden Doves With Silver Dots:*

particular way of reading is also closely related to certain strands in Midrash in which opposite readings are upheld (as in the case of Hillel and Shammai),[219] and gaps are filled 'in incompatible ways'.[220]

Deconstruction may not have been pre-empted, but it is certainly related to the strand of midrashic interpretation that entertains antitheses and establishes endless obscure interconnections within the text. Although it has been used to support a general equation between pluralist theories of reading and Midrash, the rabbinic idea that all possible interpretations were contained within the original text given at Sinai[221] has more in common with deconstruction than with the reader-response theories of Wolfgang Iser and Stanley Fish, because Jewish interpretation and deconstruction are both based on the premise *il n'y a pas de hors-texte* ('there is nothing outside the text'). Comparing two opposite interpretations by the same *tanna*, Daniel Boyarin shows how, in contrast to an exegetical tradition that tends to resolve antitheses, Midrash 'doubles' the antithetical voices in the text.[222] James Kugel describes Midrash as a kind of writing that is relatively unthreatened by the possibility of undermining its own arguments: 'if the precise wording of a verse suggested an interpretative tack that would violate the overall allegorical frame, the midrashist sometimes picked up the suggestion nonetheless'.[223]

Deconstruction is a potentially productive enterprise in biblical studies because it reminds the academic institution that the 'Old Testament' leads to the Talmud and rabbinic discourse as much as to the New Testament and Christian interpretation, and addresses the critical violent hierarchy that subordinates rabbinic commentary to modern Western exegesis. Although it is most commonly described in terms of its philosophical background, deconstruction is also, as Susan Handelman suggests, a displaced re-emergence of rabbinic hermeneutics, and the 'heretic hermeneutic' that emphasizes writing (*écriture*) is reminiscent of an older 'heretic hermeneutic' that also refused transcendent solutions

Semiotics and Textuality in Rabbinic Tradition [Bloomington: Indiana University Press, 1986], p. xxi).

219. *B. 'Erub.* 13b.

220. D. Boyarin, *Intertextuality and the Reading of Midrash* (Bloomington: Indiana University Press, 1990), p. 48.

221. *Exod. R.* 47.1.

222. Boyarin, *Intertextuality and the Reading of Midrash*, p. 48.

223. J.L. Kugel, 'Two Introductions to Midrash', in G.H. Hartman and S. Budick (eds.), *Midrash and Literature* (New York: Yale University Press, 1986), pp. 77-103 (94).

and focused stubbornly and rigorously on scripture (*écriture*).[224] However, although the affinities between deconstruction and Midrash are numerous, it is important that they are not overstressed,[225] and that rabbinic commentary is not seen as the ultimate Hebraic 'other' that can replace the deficient and outmoded Hellenistic framework.[226] Derrida himself makes no such claims, and merely uses Midrash as a counter-commentary to destabilize logocentric icons of system, univocality and consistency.

3.4. *The Tower of Babel: An Example of Derrida's 'Biblical Exegesis'*

Derrida's essay on 'The Tower of Babel', acclaimed as 'the most elegant and most accessible of Derrida's excavations of the Bible',[227]

224. Handelman, 'Jacques Derrida and the Heretic Hermeneutic', p. 111.

225. This has been one of the dangers in the more general comparison between pluralist literary theory and Midrash, in which similarities have often been over-stressed and differences ignored. As Betty Roitman observes, while 'none of the games, reversals and anagrams of contemporary criticism are foreign to [Midrash]', it presupposes a 'standard of truth, in the logical and metaphysical sense of the term, which is alien to modern theories of interpretation' (B. Roitman, 'Sacred Language and Open Text', in Hartman and Budick [eds.], *Midrash and Literature*, pp. 159-75 [159]). A comparison between deconstruction and Midrash should show even more respect for the principle of difference. As Richard Rorty suggests, 'it is more inter-esting when one system cannot fit neatly into the code of another' (*Consequences of Pragmatism [Essays: 1972–1980]* [Minneapolis: University of Minnesota Press, 1982], p. xxvii).

226. José Faur makes this mistake by promoting Judaism as the ultimate philoso-phy which *pre-empted* Derrida: 'Jacques Derrida indicated the need to find the "dreamt of word" capable of designating both "difference and articulation". Long ago the Hebrews located such a word' (*Golden Doves With Silver Dots*, p. 3). He over-looks the interrelationship between Hebraism and Hellenism when he describes rabbinic tradition as 'the only intellectual and cultural movement to have continued developing since antiquity without a primeval rupture—an inaugural split—resulting in an endless series of hierarchical oppositions' (*Golden Doves With Silver Dots*, p. xxvi). As David Stern observes, 'No attempt will ever be sufficient that presents midrash and its hermeneutics in simple opposition to logocentrism, with the latter being characterised as a Greco-Christian development and the former as a Jewish one', because 'historically, Rabbinic Judaism arose in late antiquity out of the fusion between ancient Near Eastern Israelite tradition, and Hellenism' (D. Stern, 'Midrash and Indeterminacy', *CI* 15 [1988], pp 132-61, [134]).

227. J.F. Graham, 'Translator's Preface' to Derrida, 'Des Tours de Babel', in S.D. Moore and D. Jobling (eds.) *Poststructuralism as Exegesis* (Semeia 54; Atlanta: Scholars Press, 1991), pp. 3-34 (3).

challenges the idea that Derrida, as arch-enemy of onto-theology and the Logos could have nothing useful to say to the field of biblical studies. While his resistance to the idea of God as transcendental signified poses a challenge to theology,[228] it does not prevent him making some interesting points about Yhwh *as a character in a biblical text*, and the publication of the essay in a recent edition of *Semeia*[229] suggests that Derrida has an important part to play in biblical interpretation in the 1990s. Derrida treats Yhwh, as most literary critics do, not as an entity but as a construct of the text. His detachment from the systematic, univocal tradition of exegesis, in which Yhwh's actions are typically rationalized and defended, enables him to present an alternative picture of a character who is himself resistant to univocality and union. In stark contrast to the Yhwh who, in many Old Testament commentaries, is seen tying the strands of the narrative together into all-embracing, aphoristic meanings, Derrida's Yhwh is God of Babel, master of dispersal and confusion. He is the one who gives himself an unpronounceable, untranslatable name—interpreted by Derrida as 'I am the One who says I am the one who am'[230]—and who 'interrupts' the 'structures'[231] erected by men (which might be analogous to Frye's anxiety structures).

Derrida reads the story of Babel as a war between names. The sons of Shem, the sons of the name, want to make a name for themselves lest they be scattered abroad (that is 'disseminated'): they want univocality, one people and one lip (שָׂפָה אֶחָת, Gen. 11.6), a universal idiom. God in reaction (in jealousy, Derrida suggests)[232] intervenes and deconstructs the structure: he 'annuls the gift [of language], sows confusion among his sons, and poisons the present'.[233] In direct retaliation against those who want to establish the univocal name, he utters his own name, 'Babel'. Yhwh brings in the 'name of the versus, the adverse or

228. For a theological response to deconstruction see, for example, T.J. Altizer (ed.), *Deconstruction and Theology* (New York: The Crossroad Publishing Company, 1982).

229. Moore and Jobling (eds.), *Poststructuralism as Exegesis*; page references in this section are to the same translation in Kamuf (ed.), *A Derrida Reader*, pp. 243-53; I shall also be referring to Derrida's earlier comments on Babel in Derrida, *The Ear of The Other*, pp. 98-104.

230. Derrida, 'Des Tours de Babel', p. 249.

231. Derrida, 'Des Tours de Babel', p. 245.

232. Derrida, *The Ear of the Other*, p. 101.

233. Derrida, 'Des Tours de Babel', p. 246. Derrida puns on the German and English senses of *Gift* ('poison/present').

countername', and calls 'combat...between two names'.[234] The conflict, Derrida writes, becomes 'a war between two proper names and the one that will carry the day is the one that either imposes its law or in any case prevents the other from imposing its own'.[235]

In retaliation against Shem, the idea of the univocal name, Yhwh imposes 'Babel', a word that is 'divided, bifid, ambivalent, polysemic'.[236] Babel is a 'proper name' and a 'common noun': it is 'a pure signifier' that refers to a specific place or meaning (the city of god, or Babylon),[237] *and* a signifier that evokes multiple meanings and creates a state of confusion. The biblical text links בבל and בלל, so that Babel, in Derrida's words, is 'confusedly understood as confusion'.[238] Babel is linked to confusion and has created etymological confusion: thus, as Derrida notes, Voltaire claimed in *Le Dictionnaire Philosophioque* that '*Ba* signifies father in the oriental tongues and *Bel* signifies God'.[239]

'Babel', the word uttered by Yhwh, is poised between a proper (specific) meaning, and 'confusion' and confused etymologies: in Derrida's terms, it is a proper name (that refers to a single referent, a geographical site) *and* a common noun (or 'improper name'), that evokes multiple referents. In reply to Shem, the univocal name, Yhwh utters a word that is undecideably suspended between univocality and plurality. Derrida paraphrases Yhwh's act of intervention thus: 'You will not impose your meaning or your tongue, and I, God, therefore oblige you to submit to the plurality of languages which you will never get out of'.[240] He wins by restricting language's capacity for unity and coherence and by imposing the 'necessity' and 'impossibility' of translation.[241] Yhwh's victory over Shem is punningly interpreted by Derrida as an act of 'disschemination' which is at once 'dissemination or scattering', 'de-*Shem*itizing', or unnaming, de-schematization, the resistance to structure and schemes, and a diversion from the path, 'de-*chemin*ization'. He interprets the narrative allegorically, as a battle between the

234. Derrida, *The Ear of the Other*, p. 11.
235. Derrida, *The Ear of the Other*, p. 101.
236. Derrida, 'Des Tours de Babel', p. 249.
237. Derrida, 'Des Tours de Babel', p. 245.
238. Derrida, *The Ear of the Other*, p. 101.
239. Voltaire, cited in Derrida, 'Des Tours de Babel', p. 245. In Hebrew, which is the 'oriental language' which counts in this context, father is *ab* rather than *ba*, and the only god that approximates the sound 'Bel' is 'Baal.'
240. Derrida, *The Ear of the Other*, p. 103.
241. Derrida, *The Ear of the Other*, p. 102.

forces of reason (both communicating and repressive) and the nihilistic force of deconstruction (alienating, yet subverting oppressive power structures):

> The Semites want to bring the world to reason, and this reason can signify simultaneously a colonial violence (since they would thus universalise their idiom) and a peaceful transparency of the human idiom. Inversely, when God imposes... his name he ruptures the rational transparency but interrupts also the colonial violence or the linguistic imperialism.[242]

The idea of disrupting colonial violence and linguistic imperialism puts God in a heroic light. When Derrida allies himself with God by calling Yhwh the 'deconstructor of the Tower of Babel',[243] the reader might begin to wonder if this is not some kind of promotion of, or divine justification for, deconstruction. However, given Derrida's scepticism about transcendental signifieds, it is unlikely that he is looking for divine justification. Rather, his analogy between Yhwh and himself suggests a provocative new image of the deity as master-deconstructor, punster and dismantler of stories who speaks confusingly and refuses to conform to the ideal of univocality with which he has been traditionally associated.

Derrida's deconstruction of The Tower of Babel offers a provocative model for rereading biblical texts. In the next part of this analysis I want to ask whether Yhwh, as depicted in Hosea 1–3, might also be considered an arch-deconstructor and dismantler of stories, and to ask how, and in what ways, the text can be deconstructed.

My analysis of the text is divided into two major sections. In the first section I consider similarities between Derrida's writing and prophetic style, and in the second I propose three specific 'violent hierarchies' that are deconstructed in this text: I show how the hierarchy between innocence and deviation is deconstructed; I examine the undecideable relationship between Yhwh and Baal; and I consider the tense relationship between 'love' and 'hate'. In the final section these observations are drawn together and I comment on my overall impression of the text.

---

242. Derrida, 'Des Tours de Babel', p. 253. In *The Ear of the Other* Derrida gives another allegorical interpretation of Babel, in which the half-finished tower is seen as a symbol of deconstruction: 'The deconstruction of the tower of Babel, moreover, gives a good idea what deconstruction is: an unfinished edifice whose half-completed structures are visible, letting one guess at the scaffolding behind them' (Derrida, *The Ear of the Other*, p. 102).

243. Derrida, *The Ear of the Other*, p. 102.

4. *Deconstructing Hosea 1–3*

4.1. *White Mythology: Metaphor in the Text of Theology*

Derrida's work demonstrates how philosophy, even as it attempts to transcend language, is deconstructed by its use of language. In this reading of Hosea 1–3 I want to show how prophecy, and the theologizations that are derived from it, are not immune to the twists and bifurcations of the metaphors and images that they use.

Before proceeding to look at the violent hierarchies the text endorses and how they are vulnerable to deconstruction, a few preliminary words about the style of the text are necessary. For although readers are accustomed to reading the text through the filter of systematized, theological precepts (for example, 'God shows his enduring love for faithless Israel'), the text itself is not unlike an extract from Derrida's own writing. The style is punning and allusive, the metaphors overtly sexual, and the text seems to take delight in turning its own precepts around. As Harold Fisch provocatively observes, 'Hosea might have said with Feste in *Twelfth Night*, "A sentence is but a chevril glove to a good wit. How quickly the wrong side may be turned outward".'[244]

Fisch's comment is taken from his essay 'Hosea: A Poetics of Violence', in which, intriguingly, he does not quote Derrida directly, but describes Hosea in terms that are strongly reminiscent of deconstruction. When he comments on how the text defies the structural principles of Aristotelian order,[245] Fisch implies that the text resists logocentric expectations about plot and causality; when he observes that the text demonstrates the 'inadequacy' of words,[246] he comes close to Derrida's essay on Babel and the idea of language straining against its own limitations. Fisch's comment on the movement of language in Hosea is hardly distinguishable from Derrida's own comments on the *logos*: 'We are at a great distance here from the Greek *logos*, for the words...often lack a rational form or *telos*; they are to be found in isolation from one another with great gaps in between, their meanings undermined, discontinuous wandering signifiers...'[247] The idea that Hosea is not written 'with

---

244. H. Fisch, 'Hosea: A Poetics of Violence', in *Poetry With a Purpose: Biblical Poetics and Interpretation* (Bloomington and Indianapolis: Indiana University Press, 1990), pp. 136-57 (146).

245. Fisch, 'Hosea: A Poetics of Violence', p. 138.

246. Fisch, 'Hosea: A Poetics of Violence', p. 143.

247. Fisch, 'Hosea: A Poetics of Violence', p. 144.

systematic, linear logic' emerges in some unexpected sources, and leads to the suggestion that perhaps the book should be read in 'another way' that accounts for the 'fragmented feeling'[248] experienced by its readers.

Though he does not explicitly use the phrase 'the deconstruction of logocentricism', Fisch's essay seems to endorse the idea that this Hebrew text escapes from, and resists, the rationalizations of Western theological systems, and suggests that there might be some substance to the analogy between Derrida and the prophets. His essay is a general one and summarizes principles in the book as a whole, but his description of the antithetical, self-subverting movements of language can equally be supported by a close reading of Hosea 1–3. Fisch's general comment that 'throughout Hosea words re-echo, the second occurrence often providing an antithesis',[249] is amply demonstrated in the children's names given in 1.4-9 and converted into their opposite in 2.3 and 2.25. If words, as Fisch observes, are frequently turned inside out like a chevril glove, they become, in Derrida's terms, undecideables, which support both negative and positive premises.

Often cryptic and highly intertextual, Hosea 1–3 is full of references to other times and texts, including the Exodus and the histories of Achan and Jezreel. Like Derrida's own texts, it makes punning associations with other texts and plays erudite games at the level of the signifier, punning for example on וְהִשְׁבַּתִּי ('and I will put an end to') and וְשַׁבַּתָּה ('her sabbath', 2.13). The associative play of the signifier takes precedence over the signified, and the valley of Achor (itself a pun on Achan) seems to be introduced purely for the satisfaction of overturning it and transforming it into a 'door of hope' (2.17). The text appears to be less a presentation of a univocal message than a sustained attempt at punning, and the retraction and affirmation of various words and ideas suggests that the text deconstructs itself at a deeper, ideological level.

Fisch observes how 'seemingly disconnected sentences, cryptic

248. W.L. Doorly, *Prophet of Love: Understanding the Book of Hosea* (New York: Paulist Press, 1991), p. 40. Doorly's rather vague and simplistic suggestion is that the text be read according to 'the logic of a work of art', or a piece of music, in which 'themes are placed back-to-back in contrast to each other' (*Prophet of Love*, p. 40). Identifying what the 'logic of a work of art' might be creates a whole new set of problems, but interestingly, the same analogy is made by H.D. Beeby, who describes the text as a 'room in an art gallery in which we are shown panoramas of the same scene from different viewpoints' (*Grace Abounding: A Commentary on the Book of Hosea* [Grand Rapids: Eerdmans, 1989], p. 5.)

249. Fisch, 'Hosea: A Poetics of Violence', p. 139.

expressions, [and] words that stand out jaggedly from their context'[250] have presented enormous problems to biblical critics. I suggest that the conflict may be even more fundamental than that, and that the eighth-century text is so fundamentally distinct from the conventions of academic discourse that it refuses to succumb to its rigorous demands. Tracing the use of לָכֵן, usually translated 'therefore', shows how the text defies Western models of deductive logic and causation (or what Fisch terms 'Aristotelian order') by connecting opposite rather than complementary statements. In vv. 8 and 11 the use of לָכֵן suggests that sexual immorality leads to punishment ('Therefore I will hedge up her way with thorns'; 'Therefore I will take back my grain...and my wine...') but in vv. 13-14, לָכֵן introduces an opposite consequence of sexual immorality: forgiveness and renewal, expressed, ironically, in the language of seduction ('Therefore, behold I will allure her, and bring her into the wilderness...'). Sexual immorality leads to deprivation, and to forgiveness in an overtly sexual act. The translation 'therefore' is misleading for readers accustomed to logocentric logic, because it suggests that the text is advancing an argument and building upon it, whereas in fact the text retracts its own proposals and recoils upon itself, undecideably proposing punishment and reconciliation. 'Therefore', a word that establishes connection and continuity, becomes in this poem a pivot between antitheses and a sign of discontinuity. It does not further one argument but undecideably supports irreconcilable arguments and associates indiscriminately with threat and with promise.

The prophet's text, like Derrida's, is overtly written, punning, and metaphorical; it is also overtly sexual. Like Derrida's writing, it is 'more allusive' and 'sexier'[251] than might be expected from a biblical text, and challenges conventional distinctions between propriety and impropriety in academia and in theology. Significantly, this aspect of the text is not mentioned by Fisch, and is generally underplayed by commentators, but it is one of the major reasons why the text resists easy interpretation. Overtly sexual imagery is incompatible with dignified, logocentric discourse,[252] and just as few introductions to Derrida focus on his

250. Fisch, 'Hosea: A Poetics of Violence', p. 138.
251. Rorty, 'Philosophy as a Kind of Writing', p. 144.
252. The dignity of academic logocentricism is reflected, I think, in the divide between French avant-garde theorists like Barthes, Kristeva and Cixous, and Anglo-American pragmatism. Barthes also offers a challenge to the conventions of academic discourse when he describes reading in the language of *jouissance* ('orgasm'), but

flamboyant use of images of masturbation, so commentators on Hosea tend to omit discreetly or to dilute the association between Yhwh and sexuality.

As well as using masturbation as an instance of supplementarity, Derrida uses dissemination as a play on *Shem* and the language of the name, and on semen and the sowing (or scattering) of the seed of the father. The prophetic text evokes similar word play in the image of Jezreel, a word that stands for sowing and scattering, and which is associated with conception and the new-born child. The sexual connotation of seed and the link between terrestrial and human fecundity is reinforced by a puzzling change of gender in 2.24-25 in which Jezreel (the male child) becomes female:

> ... and the earth shall answer the grain, the wine and the oil,
> and they shall answer Jezreel;
> and I will sow her for myself in the land (2.24-25).

Although the text insistently links woman and land[253] and the sexual metaphor is attested by extra-biblical sources,[254] critics tend to translate the suffix וּזְרַעְתִּיהָ as 'and I will sow him'[255] and coyly avoid the

Anglo-American commentators on Barthes seem to make little mention of this fact. Even the Yale deconstructionists (Paul de Man, Geoffrey Hartman, J. Hillis Miller and Harold Bloom) seem to use sexual imagery significantly less than Derrida himself.

253. The analogy between woman and land is an extended metaphor: Gomer gives birth in quick succession, and her fertility is emphasized, but conception is ascribed to her lovers, just as the land's fertility is accredited to Baal. Yhwh threatens to 'strip her naked... and set her like a parched land' (Hos. 2.3), and equates the demise of the woman with terrestrial aridity. Threats to punish the oversexed female merge with threats to cut off material provision and to 'lay waste her vines and her fig trees' (2.13), and in 9.14 the threat is repeated in terms of female sterility and miscarrying wombs and dry breasts.

254. Incidentally, historical evidence seems to support the link between female and agricultural fertility: in a famous proverbial saying in the Armana letters, Rib-Addi of Byblos complains that 'My field is like a wife without a husband, on account of its lack of cultivation' (J.A. Knudtzon, *Die El-Armana-Tafeln* [Leipzig: Heinrichs, 1915], pp. 74, 75, 90 and J.B. Pritchard [ed.], *Ancient Near Eastern Texts Relating to the Old Testament* [trans. W.F. Albright; Princeton: Princeton University Press, 2nd edn 1955], p. 486).

255. The convention of emending the feminine suffix to the masculine was originally established by Wellhausen, and is supported, for example, by the RSV. The REB 'solves' the problem in a different way, by circumnavigating gender distinctions and translating, 'Israel will be my new sowing in the land'.

description of the woman as fertile 'ground' for insemination. A further textual embarrassment is implied because the connection between sexuality and fertility is traditionally associated with Baal religion, which the text explicitly denounces.

The possible allusion to Baal, even as Baal is rejected, is an example of a stylistic device that threatens to embarrass the text's own polemic. In this next section I want to move beyond an analysis of rhetorical devices such as puns, sexual language and intertextual allusions, and look at how seemingly innocuous rhetorical devices can deconstruct the text's rhetorical strategy.

4.2. *Three Violent Hierarchies: Their Establishment and Deconstruction*
The rhetorical strategy of Hosea 1–2, designed to secure Israel's conviction and repentance, can be reduced to three essential premises:

1.   Israel was initially pure but departed from the Lord.
2.   The specific nature of her betrayal was a pursuit of the false god Baal.
3.   Yhwh threatened Israel with rejection, but ultimately love triumphed and Israel was restored to favour.

In each statement, there is an implicit violent hierarchy, in which the first term is promoted as stronger, prior, superior and triumphant:

1.   Innocence–Deviance (the pattern of 'The Fall')
2.   Yhwh–Baal
3.   Love–Hate (Acceptance–Rejection)

Traditionally, each hierarchy has been affirmed not only by the text but by the critical tradition that seeks to uphold it, although the detailed defences constructed by critics suggest that they have been aware of points at which the text would potentially embarrass, or deconstruct itself. This reading does not seek to explain points of contradiction or potential embarrassment, but rather investigates how each hierarchy functions in the text, how it is reinforced by critical apologetic, but also how it inevitably deconstructs, because in this, as in all texts, what the author sees is systematically related to what he does not see.

4.2.1. *Innocence–Deviance: The Impossibility of an Unadulterated Story of Beginnings*
The text of Hosea begins with memories of a beginning. Yhwh declares that Israel has forsaken him, and so appeals to memories of a beginning

before the beginning of the text in which the relationship between God and nation was pure and reciprocal. As the text progresses the idea of a pure origin becomes the linchpin of the text's rhetoric: it is the reason why Yhwh has a prior claim to Israel's affections; it is the point to which Yhwh wants to 'turn the clock back' and 'begin...history...all over again';[256] it is used as an emotional lever to persuade Israel to return.

By appealing to an ideal past, Yhwh offers escape from the sordidness of the tainted present. In Hos. 2.5 Yhwh equates the woman Israel with a naked baby and infantile innocence, and in Hos. 2.16-17 he talks in terms of a second honeymoon in the wilderness, where he will bewitch Israel with memories of the past and entice her to answer him 'as in the days of her youth'. In the image of 'wilderness', the pure origin is identified with a particular historical moment: 'the time when [Israel] came out of the land of Egypt' (2.17). As J.L. Mays observes, the wilderness becomes a symbol of a 'time and situation in which the pristine relation between God and his people was untarnished and depended utterly on Yhwh'.[257]

Like Rousseau's 'Essay on the Origin of Languages', Hosea 1–3 is a manifesto against debasement which is concerned not with the fall from speech to writing, but with the fall from innocence and faithfulness to sexual promiscuity. In the attempt to persuade Israel that she has lost sight of her true priorities, the text repeats what Derrida sees as the most inevitable 'metaphysical gesture': 'the return, in idealisation, to an origin or to a "priority" seen as simple, intact, pure, standard...in order then to conceive of derivation...deterioration'.[258] Evil, expressed as harlotry, is depicted as supervening upon a good origin; it is seen as unnecessary, superfluous, regrettable. But, as in Rousseau's text, a subterranean logic of the supplement is at work, showing that 'degeneration' is 'prescribed in the genesis',[259] and that there can be no beginning without harlotry and no innocence without knowledge.

Extending Saussure's theory of language, Derrida shows how 'the

---

256. D.J.A. Clines, 'Hosea 2: Structure and Interpretation', in E.A. Livingstone (ed.), *Studia Biblica 1978*. I. *Papers on Old Testament and Related Themes* (Sixth International Congress on Biblical Studies, Oxford, 3-7 April 1978; JSOTSup, 11; Sheffield: JSOT Press, 1979), pp. 83-103 (86).

257. J.L. Mays, *Hosea: A Commentary* (OTL; London: SCM Press, 1969), p. 44.

258. Derrida, 'Limited Inc.', p. 236.

259. Derrida, *Of Grammatology*, p. 199.

play of differences...prevent[s] there from being at any moment, or in any way, a simple element that is present in and of itself and refers only to itself'.[260] There is no pure original word or concept that exists prior to, or independently of, its so-called derivations. In Hos. 1.2 Yhwh wants to demonstrate his message, that the people have fallen from a pure origin (innocence) into sin ('harlotry'). But to convey his message, a call to purity, he needs Hosea to marry a woman of harlotry. The implication is that the people will not understand purity unless it is defined against impurity, since 'purity' as a linguistic term or concept is only brought into being by an effect of difference. God himself is bound by the inexorable logic of *différance*, and the ideal he wants to create is deconstructed by the limits of language in which he operates. Ideologically, the text strives to construct a perfect and innocent beginning, but the rules of language insist that purity and impurity are interdependent, and that the 'derivation' is as necessary and original as the 'origin'.

One of the reasons critics find Hosea a problematic text is, I suggest, because of the uncomfortable subliminal effect created by the deconstruction of origins. Even as it begins, the text thwarts our Western, logocentric expectations: it does not begin 'once upon a time', but splits the notion of time and oneness by giving two time frames and two locations to the text. The text 'begins' in the reign of Uzziah and the reign of Hezekiah, and is set in a Judaean time frame (c. 783–687 BCE) and an Israelite time frame (c. 786–746 BCE).[261] The effect is to deny the reader a single original con-text, just as it denies her a pure ethical beginning.

If the deconstruction of origins generally hinges on subtle linguistic effects, it moves to the surface of the text in Hosea's marriage to a 'wife of harlotry' (1.2). The marriage, which every critic has instantly recognized as a problem, is a clue that points to the deconstructive conflicts that take place beneath the surface of the text. On the most obvious level (the level that I investigated in Chapter 1) Hos. 1.2 presents a problem because God initiates an improper marriage, but perhaps critics resist this detail for another, more fundamental reason. The marriage is not merely an offence against morality, but an image that deconstructs

260. Derrida, 'Semiology and Grammatology', p. 26.

261. Though these differences can be explained by redaction, this does not solve the problem, for as David Clines observes, understanding a discrepancy does not eradicate it and 'bring about a new state of affairs in which it is as if the discrepancy did not exist' (Clines, 'Deconstructing the Book of Job', p. 113).

God's own argument, for if Yhwh is claiming that Israel loved him and then betrayed him, this logical sequence is subverted by a metaphor in which the wife is already harlotrous at the point of marriage.

Yhwh's marriage metaphor, which is presumably designed to reinforce his position, also works against him. Again the limits of language deconstruct his position, but this time the deconstruction is graphic and explicit. The virginal ideal is snatched away; for Hosea, there is no pure origin and no virgin bride. To use Derrida's phrase, marriage is 'always already' contaminated by promiscuity, and deviation is prescribed in the beginning. Even as it struggles to affirm that evil has supervened upon a good origin, the text foregrounds an image in which the 'virginity of a story of beginnings' is denied. (Whereas for Derrida, the association of 'virginity' with 'beginning' is a metaphorical flourish, in this text the two ideas are inseparable, because beginning *is* virginity, and deviation *is* harlotry.)

In the overtly sexual image of harlotry which coincides with marriage, Hos. 1.2 deconstructs the convention of an unadulterated story of beginnings. The particular kind of solutions that commentators have offered suggests that the discomfort they have experienced is at least partly attributable to the way in which the marriage deconstructs the main argument.[262] The many critics who argue that Gomer *became* harlotrous are effectively attempting to preserve Yhwh's ideal of a pure beginning, and to prevent the discomforting countermove by which his own metaphor subverts his own position. Interestingly, the human level has always been adjusted to fit the divine: critics have never openly confessed that there is a conflict, and have resisted the possibility that the contradiction could in some way jeopardize Yhwh's claims.

In ch. 2 the text provides two images of regression or return to origin, 'nakedness' and 'wilderness'. But, like the *pharmakon* in Plato's *Phaedrus*, they are used in the text in such a way that they acquire a hinged, double and opposite meaning. Both refer to a time of innocence and beginnings but also to corruption and endings. Like the *pharmakon*, which is both a cure and a poison, they are images of hope, and threats,

---

262. David Clines makes a similar point about the epilogue to Job: 'The epilogue has often made readers uncomfortable. I suspect that the discomfort they have experienced has been the psychological registering of the deconstruction that was in progress. Until recently, we did not have this name for the process, however, and so did not perhaps properly appreciate its character' (Clines, 'Deconstructing the Book of Job', p. 112).

that simultaneously proffer and retract the possibility of reconciliation. In Hos. 2.5 Yhwh speaks of returning the woman to the nakedness of infancy, but the image, which has undertones of recovering the lost innocence of the past, occurs in the context of a threat. Unless the woman removes the marks of harlotry from her breasts and face, her aggrieved husband will 'strip her naked and make her as the day she was born' (כְּיוֹם הִוָּלְדָהּ). The act of stripping (פָּשַׁט) implies sexual violence and rape,[263] yet the nakedness uncovered is comparable to infant vulnerability. Nakedness is both sexual innocence, and intense eroticism, and like the harlotrous marriage, it points undecideably to virginal purity and adult knowledge.

Being stripped and being an infant involve mutually exclusive and mutually repellent attitudes of abuse and of tenderness. In the same action the male speaker expresses two irreconcilable aims, to expose and to erase the woman's sexuality. Punishment in its most extreme form (rape and deprivation) confronts restoration in its most extreme form (a return to the moment of birth). The undecideable dramatizes a psychological impasse, and the moment of beginning is marked with images of sex, violence and abuse.

The undecideable, according to Derrida's definition, is any term or motif that 'escapes from inclusion in the philosophical (binary) opposition and which nonetheless inhabit[s] it, resist[s] it and disorganise[s] it but without ever constituting a third term, without ever occasioning a solution'.[264] The undecideable 'produces a sense of indefinite fluctuation between two possibilities', but the two 'poles of reading' are not 'equally obvious'.[265] In the motif of nakedness, the innocence of beginning is the covert sense that is practically engulfed in the idea of nakedness as titillation, cruelty, pornography. Hosea 2 strips the female three times, and keeps returning, compulsively, pathologically, to the image of the naked woman. In 2.11 the male speaker threatens to take back his wool and his flax, which were to cover her genitalia (לְכַסּוֹת אֶת עֶרְוָתָהּ),[266]

---

263. Not unexpectedly, critics tend to underplay this obvious reference to sexual violence, and attempt to dilute it by providing excuses for the deity. H.W. Wolff, for example, civilizes the story by emphasizing Yhwh's reluctance: 'Yhwh himself must take severe measures against her; he would rather not!' (*A Commentary on the Book of Hosea* [trans. G. Stansell; Herm; Philadelphia: Fortress Press, 1974] p. 34).

264. Derrida, 'Positions', in *Positions*, p. 43.

265. Derrida, *Dissemination*, p. 225.

266. The phrase 'my flax' (וּפִשְׁתִּי) is itself a pun on פשׁט, 'to strip'.

and in 2.12 he threatens to 'uncover her lewdness in the sight of her lovers' (וְעַתָּה אֲגַלֶּה אֶת-נַבְלֻתָהּ לְעֵינֵי מְאַהֲבֶיהָ). The *hapax legomenon* נַבְלֻתָהּ is derived from נָבֵל (to be foolish) and/or נָבֵל (to wither), and refers to her genitalia (her foolishness or shame) and her degeneration.[267] As Saul Olyan observes, the sense of 'degeneration' has been largely forgotten by commentators, but in fact both derivations are plausible.[268] If naked-ness refers to infant purity and degeneration, then the text literalizes another Derridean metaphor and 'degeneration' is, quite literally, 'prescribed in the genesis'.[269]

From the moment that Yhwh threatens to strip the woman as in the day of her birth, and connects birth and destruction, 'nakedness' escapes from and disorganizes the related binary oppositions beginning–ending, innocence–knowingness, tenderness–cruelty. When the naked woman is paraded in front of her lovers, the undecideability is compounded: the act implies (moral) disapproval and (sexual) approval, because her judge is also her voyeur. Denunciation and titillation collide: the mutually exclusive reactions mirror contemporary attitudes towards the prostitute. The female is pitied, abused, lusted after and condemned; she is a naked baby and an object of lust. The provocative idea of woman gives rise to conflicting emotions and becomes, in this text, the linchpin of undecide-ability, the focus of the tension between restoration and punishment, endings and beginnings. As undecideable the woman marks the point of that which can 'never be mediated, mastered, sublated or dialecti-cized':[270] she is, in other words, the chief element that causes the text to equivocate, flounder and turn back on its own rhetoric.

The movement of the image of nakedness in ch. 2 can only be reduc-tively described in terms or word play, ambiguity or polysemy. The word play on the surface of the text is only a clue to a deeper, decon-structive conflict. Polysemy takes place at the level of semantics, when a word has several senses: undecideability involves two competing senses, which radically oppose one another and generate two incompatible paradigms for interpreting the text. If we believe the text is about

267. נַבְלֻת is not undecideable, merely ambiguous, since the two possible mean-ings fit into a generally negative context of destruction and humiliation but nuance it in a slightly different way.

268. S.M. Olyan, ' "In the Sight of Her Lovers": On the Interpretation of *nablút* in Hos. 2.12', *BZ* 36 (1992), pp. 255-61.

269. Derrida, *Of Grammatology*, p. 199.

270. Derrida, *Dissemination*, p. 221.

restoration and return to beginnings, this view is deconstructed. If we assume the opposite position, that the text is 'all about' destruction and endings, this view is also deconstructed. The image of nakedness perversely resists all binary reductions and participates in the deconstructive logic of the 'neither/nor' that is also 'either/or'.[271] The only thing that can be said about this text with any certainty is that it undermines its own certainties and snatches the ground from beneath the reader's feet.

In a subtle interweaving of imagery, woman is equated with land, and 'nakedness' with the denudation of the land, expressed in the motif of wilderness. Yhwh's first threat, that he will strip the woman as on the day of her birth, continues: 'and [I will] make her like a wilderness/and change her into an arid land/and kill her with thirst'.[272] As nakedness and wilderness are linked on the surface of the text, so they join forces to deconstruct crucial binary distinctions. Like nakedness, הַמִּדְבָּר is a motif that escapes and disorganizes the distinctions beginning–ending, tenderness–cruelty, and that 'enters the dialectic from both sides at once...and threatens the philosophical process from within'.[273]

Just as nakedness gestures to innocence and abuse, הַמִּדְבָּר is an image of extreme cruelty (abandonment and death by thirst) *and* the site for the glorious reunion of God and nation in which Yhwh will speak (tenderly) to the woman's heart (וְדִבַּרְתִּי עַל לִבָּהּ)[274] and she will speak lovingly to him 'as in the days of her youth' (כִּימֵי נְעוּרֶיהָ, 2.16-17). 'Wilderness' is the setting for a nightmare and for a second honeymoon; it is a scene of murder and of seduction, and because it speaks doubly it is a hypocrite word, an undecideable, a word never to be trusted in a simple univocal sense. Any suspicious reader, without any knowledge of deconstruction, might be expected to distrust a reconciliation scene which is set against exactly the same backdrop that has been associated with torture and threats. Indeed, it seems as if the text is virtually trying

271. Derrida, 'Positions', in *Positions*, p. 43.

272. Hos. 2.5, trans. R.J. Weems, 'Gomer: Victim of Violence or Victim of Metaphor?', in K. Geneva Cannon and E. Schüssler Fiorenza (eds.), *Interpretation for Liberation* (Semeia 47; Atlanta: Scholars Press, 1989), pp. 87-104 (91).

273. Kamuf, in Kamuf (ed.), *A Derrida Reader*, p. 113.

274. Speaking to the heart belongs to the language of courtship and has some interesting intertextual resonances. Shechem 'spoke to the heart 'of Dinah, since his 'soul was drawn to her and he loved her' (Gen. 34.3); Boaz 'spoke to the heart of Ruth' in an act of confidence (Ruth 2.13). The Levite also 'spoke to the heart' of his estranged wife (Judg. 19.3): his emotions, like those of Hosea/Yhwh, were a peculiar cocktail of tenderness and violence.

to encourage this suspicion, because if it wanted to preserve wilderness as a pure ideal, it would underplay, and not exaggerate, connotations of sterility, isolation and death. As trained readers of Hollywood films, we know we should be suspicious when a man who threatened murder suddenly offers love, but we do not generally extend the same deconstructive suspicion towards the biblical text. Reading deconstructively (suspiciously), I would suggest that the text seriously jeopardizes its own claim that the woman will respond, as scripted, with responses of love, because the previous wilderness scenario has led her (and the reader) to profoundly mistrust her male aggressor/lover.[275]

A conventional rhetorical reading of this text might suggest that the negative image in 2.5 is an attempt to enhance the glory of the reconciliation scene by contrast; a deconstructive reading shows how this risky rhetorical ploy works against itself. If the concept of beginnings is questionable, the idea of new beginnings is even more dubious, and the text hides within itself the tools for its own deconstruction. Reading deconstructively, the reader can no longer see the 'wilderness' simply as a symbol of the time in which the 'pristine relation between God and his people was untarnished',[276] because it is the site for the most dismal ending (death by thirst and deprivation) as well as the most promising of beginnings (a love affair). The collision of redemption and punishment in the undecideables nakedness and wilderness suggests that Yhwh himself turns into an undecideable, who nurtures and abuses, strips and restores, seduces and deprives.

4.2.2. *Baal and Yhwh*
The rhetorical linchpin of Hosea's argument is the claim that Yhwh has chronological and ethical priority over Baal. The text insists that Yhwh is Israel's 'first husband' אִישִׁי הָרִאשׁוֹן (2.9), that she has deserted him for other lovers (the Baalim, 2.7, 9, 15, 18, 19), and that she has mistakenly

---

275. Disturbingly, by presenting an outburst of violence followed by tenderness, this text conforms to a familiar pattern of marital violence. Contemporary sociological studies show that 'wife-battering' often involves a three stage cycle of violence: the 'tension building stage' (which corresponds to the dispute of the 'court scene') the acute battering incident (which corresponds to the threat to kill by deprivation and the stripping of the woman in ch. 2) and the 'kindness and contrite loving behaviour' stage (which corresponds with Hosea/Yhwh's plans to lead his wife, tenderly and seductively, into the desert) (see L. Walker, *The Battered Woman* [New York: Harper & Row, 1979], pp. 55-70).

276. Mays, *Hosea*, p. 44.

perceived Baal as the true provider (2.10, 11, 14). The purpose of the text is to teach Israel to differentiate between true and false gods, and restoration is described as the removal of the name of Baal from Israel's lips (2.19). The text relentlessly promotes (markets) Yhwh and systematically discredits Baal; when Israel learned to call Yhwh 'my husband' instead of 'my baal' (2.18), she will, commentators argue, have learnt the crucial distinction between a religion of mastery and a religion of love.

The rhetoric of the text depends on establishing and maintaining a violent hierarchy in which Yhwh is perceived as origin and true provider, and Baal worship is seen as a deviation from or perversion of the truth. Yahwism is autonomous and independent; Baalism is parasitic: the text implies that the Baalim are impostors and usurpers who have appropriated the role of provider for themselves and stolen one of Yhwh's best lines. The conviction with which commentators have upheld the distinction made by Hosea 1–3 fits into a general pattern in biblical scholarship in which Baalism is vigorously subordinated to Yahwism as true religion. Baalism has been depicted, variously, as a religion of nature as opposed to a superior religion of history and an 'orgiastic' fertility cult that inevitably proved inferior to the 'pastoral simplicity' and 'purity' of Israel, and its 'severe code' of monothesitic 'ethics'.[277] Although the discovery of the Ras Shamra tablets pointed to cultural overlap between Canaanite and Israelite religion, critics have, until recently, generally enforced the independence of the Israelites. T. Worden, like Albright, typifies the scholarship of the 1950s by enforcing a dubious distinction between 'style' and 'content' and arguing for the 'literary dependence of the Israelites upon their neighbours and their "dogmatic" independence'.[278] In Hosea scholarship this thesis has lingered, so that Hosea becomes a radical stylist who knows what he wants to say but uses the language of Baalism to give it contemporary impact.[279] Words are seen as receptacles for content—the text merely uses 'Canaanite literature' to express 'the true doctrine'[280]—and once

---

277. W.F. Albright, *From the Stone Age to Christianity: Monotheism and the Historical Process* (New York: Doubleday, 1957), p. 281.

278. T. Worden, 'The Literary Influence of the Ugarit Fertility Myth on the Old Testament', *VT* 3 (1953), pp. 273-97 (286).

279. Mays, for example, argues that '[Hosea] achieves a fresh modernism that plunges into the contemporaneity of his audience' (Mays, *Hosea*, p. 10).

280. Worden, 'The Literary Influence', p. 297.

all imported imagery has been removed, the reader will, the critics imply, find a doctrinal centre that is purely Yahwistic.

The hierarchy between Yhwh and Baal, whether it is cast in terms of history versus nature or a belief in Israel's dogmatic independence, has recently been challenged from several quarters. An erosion of confidence in the paradigm of 'conquest', and the proposal of several alternatives,[281] suggested that the ideological as well as the geographical struggle between Israel and its enemies was far more complex than scholarship had thus far acknowledged. As early as 1956, scholars were observing that the Ras Shamra tablets force us to see Baalism not only 'through Yahwistic spectacles',[282] and by 1986, Guy Couturier observed that now that Baalism could, as it were, speak for itself, 'the authority of the Old Testament must be itself tested if not criticised'.[283] The challenge to interrogate the authority and ideology of the Old Testament has been provocatively taken up by Robert Oden, who sees polemical attacks on the Baal cult as a device for maintaining 'ethnic boundary markings'.[284] Oden reinterprets accusations that the worshippers of Baal were 'voluptuous and dissolute'[285] or 'sensuous' and 'gross'[286] in the light of a statement by the anthropologist Rodney Needham, that 'any group can appreciate their own existence more meaningfully by conjuring up others as categorical opposites'.[287]

Ideological criticism of the biblical text (which could also be extended

---

281. Norman Gottwald's radical proposal, for example, is that 'Israel was emergent from a fundamental breach within Canaanite society and not an invasion or immigration from without' (N.K. Gottwald, *The Tribes of Yahweh: A Sociology of the Religion of Liberated Israel,* 1250–1050 BCE [London: SCM Press, 1979], p. xxiii).

282. G. Östborn, *Yahweh and Baal: Studies in the Book of Hosea and Related Documents* (LUÅ, 51; Lund: Hakan Ohlssons Boktryokeri, 1956), p. 3.

283. G. Couturier, 'Rapports culturels et religieux entre Israël et Canaan d'après Osée 2, 4-25', in M. Gourgues and G.D. Mailhick (eds.), *L'alterité vivre* (Montreal: Recherches, 1986), pp. 159-210 (183).

284. R.A. Oden, *The Bible Without Theology: The Theological Tradition and Alternatives to It* (San Francisco: Harper & Row, 1987), p. 134.

285. K. Budde, *Religion of Israel to the Exile* (American Lectures on the History of Religions 4; New York: Putnam's, 1899), p. 70.

286. Albright, *From the Stone Age to Christianity*, p. 281. The close correspondance between Albright's description and Budde's shows how little views had changed in the course of half a century.

287. R. Needham, review of W. Arens, 'The Man-Eating Myth', *TLS* (25 January 1980), p. 75.

to the critical text) has led critics to be slightly more circumspect and subtle in enforcing the hierarchy Yhwh–Baal. In the 1950s Albright could state boldly that: '[Yhwh's] coming is like the rising sun dispelling the darkness of Canaanite superstition',[288] but Andersen and Freedman, writing in 1980, use subtler tones of 'light' and 'darkness' to shade their argument, and maintain that 'There is no confrontation or trial of strength between Yhwh and Baal' because 'Baal is entirely in the background, a shadow'.[289] As they confine the rival deity to the shadow-lands of the text, so they deduce from the text's polemic that the attractions of Baal are purely materialistic, and that Israel is attracted to Baal by 'base motives', rather than being converted to a 'rival theology that could be stated in sophisticated terms'.[290] (What they do not consider is that the case for Yhwh is also based upon provision, and that the sophisticated theology they ascribe to Yahwism is the product of centuries of commentary and reflection and is not a 'given' of the text.)

One of the most popular and sophisticated ways of reconciling the idea of cultural borrowing with an affirmation of Yhwh's supremacy is to argue that Yahwism overturns the falsehoods of Canaanite religion by 'destroy(ing) the myth from the inside'.[291] Borrowing is seen not as evidence of dependence, but of skill and courage: J.L. Mays describes how Hosea appropriates the 'language and thought of Canaanite religion' 'with daring skill',[292] and H.D. Beeby describes the poem as 'the boldest example of cultural borrowing in the Old Testament'.[293] Gloriously, in his 'battle against polytheism, sexuality in heavenly places and debauchery on earth', the prophet 'turn(s) the weapons of the enemy against the spiritual host' and 'baptizes' Canaanite symbolism into 'a crusade against the Canaanite religion'.[294] Like the mythology of the Trojan

---

288. Albright, cited in U. Oldenberg, *The Conflict Between El and Baal in Canaanite Religion* (Leiden: Brill, 1969), preface (no precise reference is given).

289. F.I. Andersen and D.N. Freedman, *Hosea: A New Translation with Introduction* (AB; New York: Doubleday, 1980), p. 245. Andersen and Freedman reinforce Baal's confinement to the shadows by not mentioning the Ras Shamra texts or images from the Baal cult. In such an exhaustive study, it is surprising to find references only to one Ugaritic text 'Nikkal and the Moon' (p. 273) and the absence of the Ras Shamra texts suggests a defensive strategy of repression.

290. Andersen and Freedman, *Hosea*, p. 232.

291. Wolff, *Hosea*, p. 44.

292. Mays, *Hosea*, p. 8.

293. Beeby, *Grace Abounding*, p. 3.

294. Beeby, *Grace Abounding*, p. 3. Beeby's description is more dependent on

horse, this cult of criticism praises military sabotage; however, it also acknowledges an element of risk and 'daring' in the argument, even as it affirms the argument's rhetorical success.[295]

As criticism has progressed, it has found more sophisticated ways of acknowledging the evidence of Canaanite acculturation in the text, while at the same time maintaining that this does not undermine the text's main argument and its ideological resistance to Baal. In the latest and perhaps most refined way of dealing with the problem, acculturation and resistance are *harmonized*, and their opposing implications hastily passed over. E. Jacob creatively reconciles the desire for 'purification and a deepening of ancestral religion' and the annexing of Baal imagery in the image of *homeopathy*, which uses evil to cure evil and has a purgatorial effect.[296] More recently, Anton Wessels explained the inconsistency with an appeal to Hegelian philosophy. Opposing a simplistic interpretation in which 'one faith [in Yhwh] overcomes another [Canaanism]',[297] he problematized this naive idea of 'overcoming' by comparison with its German equivalent *aufheben*. The ambiguities of *aufheben*, which is 'used in describing interaction and has the dual meaning of "to raise to a

images from Paul than from Hosea, and draws on New Testament and Christian images of spiritual warfare, cosmic battles in heavenly places, 'baptisms' and 'crusades'.

295. At first glance it may appear that critics like Wolff, Beeby and Mays are describing Hosea's tactics in terms not dissimilar to deconstruction. The idea of destroying a myth from within is not very far from Derrida's own strategy, but the vital difference is that deconstruction entertains no illusions about *destroying* the prevalent myth. Like Derrida, Hosea uses his enemy's own language and images against them, and could feasibly be described as using Canaanite imagery 'under erasure': that is, with the utmost scepticism about its truth-content. But where Wolff, Beeby and Mays depart from deconstruction is in the triumphalist assertion that, by undermining the dominant system, Yahwism usurps it, destroys it and improves on it. Deconstruction must always acknowledge its difference from destruction: to deconstruct a myth is to subvert it *and* to affirm its pervasiveness, its success, and its ineradicability. There are no 'winners' and no 'losers' in deconstruction: Baalism does not conquer Yahwism or vice versa, but rather the two sides of a hierarchy are interminably played off against one another, in a mutually deconstructing play of *différance*.

296. E. Jacob, 'L'héritage cananéen dans le livre du prophète Osée', *RHPR* 43 (1963), pp. 250-59 (250).

297. A. Wessels, 'Biblical Presuppositions For and Against Syncretism', in J. Gort, H. Vroom, R. Ferhout and A. Wessels (eds.), *Dialogue and Syncretism: An Interdisciplinary Approach* (Grand Rapids: Eerdmans, 1989), pp. 52-65 (54).

higher level" and "to abolish"',[298] allow him to maintain that 'on the one hand [Hosea] delivered criticism of the cult, but on the other, he conserved and reappraised ('overcame') positive elements'.[299]

Wessels's article begins with the potentially deconstructive insight that 'He who was so opposed to illegitimate syncretism [that is, Hosea] himself participated in Canaanizing in a certain sense',[300] but the ambiguities of *aufheben* allow him to preserve a sense of hierarchy. As Spivak observes, Hegelian *Aufhebung* is a 'hierarchical concept', 'a relationship between two terms where the second at once annuls the first and lifts it up into a higher sphere of existence'.[301] The inferior term in a hierarchy is successfully *aufgehoben* if it is elevated and erased by the superior term: thus, according to Wessels, the weaker and less perfect form (Baal) is annulled and assimilated by the stronger force (Yhwh). Although it is more philosophically refined, Wessels's argument is not essentially different from Jacob's (whom he quotes)[302] and is simply another creative way of affirming that Yhwh is triumphant, and that the text capitulates to Baal only on the level of imagery.

The Hegelian concept of *Aufhebung* is ultimately more reassuring than Derrida's deconstruction. The deconstruction of a violent hierarchy leads to the irresistible temptation to reconstruct, particularly if the hierarchy is as theologically significant as the hierarchy Baal–Yhwh. Harold Fisch, who goes one step further than Wessels and argues that 'The Canaanite myth...is affirmed and dissolved at the same time' and 'is, so to speak, deconstructed',[303] also falls back on Jacob's argument, maintaining that where Baal and Anat are 'imprisoned in nature', Israel is made free from nature as a consequence of her 'divine marriage'.[304] The precariousness of the distinction suggests that, having described the deconstruction of the hierarchy, the critic has to find reasons why it is,

---

298. Wessels, 'Biblical Presuppositions', p. 54.

299. Wessels, 'Biblical Presuppositions', p. 61. Although he does not directly invoke the idea of Hegelian *Aufhebung,* Guy Couturier also implies that Baalism is absorbed and transformed in Yahwism when he suggests that the '*language* and *structure* of the Canaanite religion' were 'adapt[ed]...to a new meaning', to 'accommodat[e] a new religious experience' ('Rapports culturels et religieux', pp. 162-63).

300. Wessels, 'Biblical Presuppositions', p. 60

301. Spivak, 'Translator's Preface' to *Of Grammatology*, p. xi.

302. Wessels, 'Biblical Presuppositions', p. 63.

303. Fisch, 'Hosea: A Poetics of Violence', p. 148.

304. Fisch, 'Hosea: A Poetics of Violence', p. 149.

nevertheless, still tenable, and although he uses 'deconstruction' as a buzzword, he is unable to accept the consequences of his own observation.

Like Wessels and Jacobs, Fisch ultimately relapses into the safer observation that 'the [Canaanite] myth is overcome by being transcended'.[305] The use of *Aufhebung* to suggest that Israelite religion is superior ('transcendent') contrasts with Derrida's general avoidance of the term, specifically because it attempts to *harmonize* the hierarchy and *protect* the dominance of the superior term.[306] Derrida 'relaunches...the reading of the Hegelian *Aufhebung*...beyond what Hegel, inscribing it, understood himself to say or intended to mean'.[307] In the same way, this reading attempts to push Fisch and Wessels's observations beyond the theological/philosophical limits that they set for them, and to show how the violent hierarchy Yhwh–Baal is deconstructed, without resorting to the luxury of reconstruction.

According to Peggy L. Day, Canaanite religion has been virulently subordinated by biblical critics, precisely because Baal is Yhwh's 'closest and most persistent rival in the Hebrew Bible'.[308] The very enthusiasm with which critics affirm Yhwh's supremacy, and reinforce Hosea's main thesis, suggests that there are elements in Hosea 1–3 that threaten to subvert it. The description of Hosea's cultural borrowing as 'daring' is revealing: it suggests that critics are only too aware of a rival and a threat. Because a project is only 'daring' if it involves the possibility of failure, they are effectively admitting that the tools for the text's deconstruction are dangerously inscribed within the prophet's own rhetoric.

Reading commentary alongside the text of Hosea 1–3 suggests that critics are attempting to bolster up the text's argument where it appears to flounder. The way in which they unequivocally subordinate Baal and confine him to the 'shadows' implies a sense of dissatisfaction with the text's own polemic. Like Satan in Milton's *Paradise Lost*, Baal is all too present in the text and threatens to eclipse God. Commentary is an

---

305. Fisch, 'Hosea: A Poetics of Violence', p. 149.

306. Derrida conveys his scepticism about this practice by translating *Aufhebung* as *la relève,* which also parodically means 'the relief' of tension ('Tympan', in Kamuf (ed.), *A Derrida Reader*, pp. 149-68 [149]).

307. Derrida, 'Tympan', p. 150.

308. P.L. Day, 'Why is Anat a Warrior and a Hunter?', in D. Jobling, P.L. Day and G.T. Sheppard (eds.), *The Bible and the Politics of Exegesis: Essays in Honour of Norman K. Gottwald on his Sixty-Fifth Birthday* (Cleveland: Pilgrim Press, 1991), pp. 141-46 (141).

attempt to eradicate the sense of Baal as rival, which betrays, even as it denies, a strong sense of doubt in the text's own effectiveness.

Hosea's argument presents the case for a completely uncompromising expulsion of Baal, in which all traces of the false god, and even mention of his name, are to be obliterated from the life of Israel. Yet even before this argument has been clearly expounded, it is put in jeopardy by an undecideable reference to Jehu and the blood of Jezreel. Yhwh's declaration וּפָקַדְתִּי אֶת דְּמֵי־יִזְרְעֶאל עַל־בֵּית יֵהוּא is habitually translated 'and I will punish the house of Jehu for the blood of Jezreel' (1.4), but as Thomas McComiskey points out, this does not do justice to the ambiguity of the phrase פָּקַד עַל. Supporting his claim with a detailed word study, McComiskey shows how retributive justice is not necessarily implied and that פָּקַד עַל can equally mean simply 'visit upon' in the sense that the blood of Israel's past will 'reappear hauntingly' in the future.[309] Though McComiskey uses words like 'ambiguity' and 'irony' to describe the conflict between the two senses, פָּקַד עַל can also be termed 'undecideable', because it lends support to equal and opposite judgments of Jehu's actions. Yhwh may be establishing a causal link (Israel will be punished because of the blood of Jezreel), but he 'does not clearly affirm that Jehu's bloody purge is the real basis for punishment'[310] and might simply be saying that the dynasty will ironically end, as it began, in blood. The undecideability of Yhwh's response to Jehu has implications for attitudes towards Baal in the text. For according to 2 Kings 9–10 Jehu shed blood, under Yhwh's instruction, to purge the land of Baal.

Critics might expect that a text that is virulently anti-Baal (for so they describe Hosea) might express approval for Jehu's zealous purgation of the land. Instead, they are confronted with a Hebrew text that expresses an undecideable verdict, and English translations that have affirmed Jehu's culpability. The idea that Hosea was anti-Jehu, who was anti-Baal, is an uncomfortable aporia that threatens to deconstruct the text's rhetoric from within. Sensing the discrepancy, critics have worked to solve the 'problem' and to explain (and hence eradicate) the inconsistency in Hosea's position. Some have argued that Jehu did too much, and was over-zealous in his slaughter; others that he did too little, because he did not 'turn aside from the sins of Jeroboam the son of

---

309. T.E. McComiskey, 'Prophetic Irony in Hosea 1–4: A Study of the Collocation פָּקַד עַל and its Implications for the Fall of Jehu's Dynasty', *JSOT* 58 (1993), pp. 93-101 (100).

310. McComiskey, 'Prophetic Irony in Hosea 1–4', p. 101.

Nebat...the golden calves that were in Bethel and in Dan'.[311] Andersen and Freedman imply that Jehu's actions are not repudiated but *aufgehoben* in Hosea's 'higher and morally more sensitive standard of evaluation',[312] but to do this they have studiously to ignore the way in which Hosea 2 seems to endorse violence. 'Perhaps it is not the reform itself that is under suspicion', muses Michael Catlett, since 'Hosea would not oppose a resurgence of devotion to Yhwh'.[313] The conviction that Hosea 'would not oppose a resurgence of devotion to Yhwh' stems from a belief that the prophet must be consistent, and that the text, like all good logocentric texts, must obey the law of mutual exclusivity.

In its undecideable stance towards Israel's history, Hos. 1.4 hints, but only hints, at potential opposition to the complete eradication of Baal. Unfortunately for critics who wish to solve or eradicate this subversive strand in the text, it proves not to be a momentary lapse, or Freudian slip, but the first in a series of inconsistencies. In its attempt to establish the violent hierarchy Yhwh–Baal, and to convince apostate Israel that Yhwh will expel Baal and emerge as her victorious first love once again, the text gives the reader cause to doubt (1) Yhwh's supremacy, and (2) the possibility of Baal's complete eradication. It deconstructs the idea of a victorious first husband returning to claim his bride with an image of a rejected and desperate cuckold, and profoundly questions the possibility of Baal's eradication by founding its own argument on images from Canaanite religion.

In a text that presents itself as devised by Yhwh and written by one of his prophets, it is surprising that there is so much evidence of the power of Baal. Baal is the reason for the text being written, and Yhwh's polemic is, on one level, a testimony to his rival's power of seduction. Even as the text claims that Israel's 'first husband' was 'better' (2.9), it expresses fear that Israel is irrevocably 'captivated' by Baal. Alongside the picture of a self-assured deity who knows that Israel will return to him, the text presents a jealous and insecure husband who turns to violence in desperation. The tensions of the divine–human metaphor lead to a bizarre situation in which the deity who confidently asserts his

---

311. D.A. Hubbard, *Hosea: An Introduction and Commentary* (TOTC; Leicester: Inter-Varsity Press, 1989), p. 62.

312. Andersen and Freedman, *Hosea*, p. 178.

313. M.L. Catlett, *Reversals in Hosea: A Literary Analysis* (unpublished PhD dissertation, Emory University, 1988; Ann Arbor: University Microfilms International, no. 88-16934), p. 50.

superiority is also a rather pathetic figure who lashes out in anger and threatens to strip, to slay (2.5), to deprive his wife of clothes and sustenance (2.11), to set wild beasts on her vines and fig trees (2.14), and to block her way (2.8). The divine hope (that Israel will return when she sees sense) is deconstructed by a poignantly human hopelessness in which the husband seems to acknowledge that the only way he can keep the heroine is by physically trapping her and threatening, like the villain of Victorian melodrama, that 'no-one shall rescue her out of [his] hand' (2.12). 'Block[ing] her path' (2.8) and locking her away is not the action of a man assured of his attractive powers, but of a man who realises that he cannot emotionally captivate his wife, and can only physically capture her. Yhwh's own metaphor militates against him, and his rhetoric is deconstructed by the inadequacies of the male figure with whom he is identified.

Though the text never admits it, and is at pains to repress the negative implications of Israel's betrayal, the fact that his 'wife' has left him suggests inadequacies in Yhwh's character as well as in her own. According to the surface rhetoric, desertion is purely an indication of Israel's depravity, and Yhwh is faultless, but the fact that Israel has left him for another lover implies a fundamental lack in Yhwh's character, at least from the wife's perspective. The rhetoric of the text unequivocally asserts that Yhwh is 'better' than Baal, but the woman has already cast her vote by pursuing other lovers. Even though the text is effectively propaganda on Yhwh's behalf, there is evidence of another repressed perspective, the woman's point of view, which deconstructs the assertion that Yhwh is preferable to Baal. The woman's point of view is a 'repressed but articulate' language that deconstructs the main text by suggesting inadequacies in Yhwh. The psychologically convincing image of the enraged husband enforces this perspective, because indiscriminate violence seems to be an obvious symptom of rejection, insecurity and self-doubt. The limits of the divine–human metaphor lead to a peculiar impasse in which Yhwh is in control (even to the extent that he can seduce Israel, and script/predict her response, 2.17-18), but is also manifestly out of control. Even the text's climatic distinction between Baal (master) and Yhwh (husband) in 2.18 is deconstructed by the erratic husband's conduct, for this 'husband' traps, deprives and despotically 'masters' his wife.[314]

---

314. Though commentators are prepared to concede that the reference to Jehu is problematic, and that the use of Canaanite imagery is risky, few dare to comment on

The way in which Yhwh attempts to distinguish himself from Baal as 'husband', but describes himself in precisely the same terms as Baal as 'master', is symptomatic of one of the main 'problems' of the text. The text's argument depends on the premise that Yhwh is original, in both senses of the word—he is Israel's 'first husband' and he can be clearly distinguished from his rival—yet far from emphasizing Yhwh's autonomy and individuality, the text remakes him in the image of Baal. Baal is perceived by the woman as lover and provider, and to reclaim her affections, Yhwh describes himself in precisely the same terms. He depicts himself as giver of grain, wine and oil (precisely the same items attributed to Baal) and pledges to 'seduce' the woman and to become, effectively, no longer stern husband but rival lover. Although the author advances a 'finders keepers theology'[315] and urges Israel to return to the religion of the past, it is difficult to see what fundamental changes he is proposing. The pledge to remove Baal's name from Israel's mouth (2.19) seems to imply a quibbling over detail rather than a fundamental disagreement, and suggests an alteration as cosmetic as the removal of the signs of adultery from the harlot's breast. The text rejects Baal's name but not his function: in 2.14 Yhwh pledges to lay waste her lovers' vines and fig trees, and in 2.17 he promises to give her his own. Ironically, before he can give, Yhwh must clear the ground of the previous giving, and the god who claims he is original promises to repeat Baal's act of provision under a different name.

Yhwh's promise to uproot Baal's vineyards and plant his own is only one of the 'literary symptoms' which, as David Jobling puts it, suggest a 'situation in which Yhwh religion is confronting Baal religion on ground favourable to the latter'.[316] Yhwh's claim to originality is deconstructed

the potential risk of the metaphor God as husband. The tendency is to praise the image for 'provid[ing] a better understanding of the character of God—especially [his] faithful, forgiving and unconditional love' (M. Paolantonio, 'God as Husband', *The Bible Today* 27 [1989], pp. 299-303 [303]), and to explain the unfortunate association of God with violence as regrettable but inevitable. Critics bolster the main argument of the text, and eliminate or 'explain' aspects of the text that would jeopardize it, but the fact that they feel the need to explain violence shows that they have recognized its potential to disturb (or, as I would argue, deconstruct) the argument they enforce. Defences built against subversive effects can be as revealing about aporiae in the text as self-consciously deconstructive readings: both recognize the same potential embarrassments to the text, but one explains while the other explores.

315. Jobling, 'A Deconstructive Reading of Hosea 1–3', p. 8.
316. Jobling, 'A Deconstructive Reading of Hosea 1–3', p. 8.

by his tendency to plagiarize, and, like the image of the violent husband, creates a strong subliminal impression of lack and insecurity. It is not necessary to know that, historically, Yhwh 'was probably an "immigrant" who reached Canaan from the south',[317] to get a strong sense that the text is attempting to re-market Yhwh, in a new milieu, to meet the demands of a different religious consumer. Yhwh, the God of the Exodus and a nomadic tribe, must acquire new features if he is to adapt to the demands of an agricultural economy:[318] there is a new job description which he must fill.

The supreme deconstructive irony of this text is that Israel is not the only character striving to follow other gods. Like the Deuteronomist, the author criticizes those who ask 'How do these nations serve their gods?—that I may do likewise',[319] but deconstructs his own polemic by suggesting that Yhwh himself has responded to peer pressure to produce a new self-definition. Hosea 2.18 implies that the text is opposing a situation in which Yhwh and Baal had blurred 'to the point at which Yhwh differed in no way (even in name) from Baal',[320] but the alternative it proposes is precariously based on the system it seeks to supplant. The syncretism of the imagery threatens the argument for separatism, and, as Jobling observes, the text gives itself 'the (impossible) task in mediating...between an approach which merely affirms the ancient priority of Yhwh...and an approach which equates Yhwh structurally with Baal'.[321]

As the extent of the text's borrowing is uncovered, the idea that Baalism is merely a frame for Yahwism becomes inadequate. Even the terms that scholars use—Yahw*ism* and Baal*ism*—seem inappropriate, because they fit more easily into the logocentric language of scholarship than into a text which constantly defies proper distinctions and attempts illicit border crossings. Just as the prophet marries the prostitute with Yhwh's approval, and so mimics the trespass he attempts to eradicate,

317. T.N.D. Mettinger, 'The Elusive Essence: Yhwh, El and Baal and the Distinctiveness of Israelite Faith', in E. Blum (ed.), *Die hebräische Bibel und ihre zweifache Nachgeschichte* (Neukirchen–Vluyn: Neukirchener Verlag, 1990), pp. 393-417 (405).

318. In 1 Kgs 20.28, the Arameans taunt the Israelites with the saying, 'Yhwh is a god of the hills, but he is not a god of the valleys'. The meaning of the saying is unclear, but it may suggest a popular view of Yhwh as a god who lacks a reputation for agriculture, and who is unfamiliar with the terrain of the 'valleys'.

319. Deut. 12.30.

320. Couturier, 'Rapports culturels et religieux', p. 210.

321. Jobling, 'A Deconstructive Reading of Hosea 1–3', p. 8.

so the author of this text crosses the very cultural boundaries he is trying to enforce.

Baalism and Yahwism are inappropriate terms for this text because they suggest separate and self-contained theologies or systems. Yet while the surface polemic of the text enforces the assumption that there are two systems and they are mutually incompatible, it also treats them as Derrida treats philosophical systems: that is, as literary images that can be made to interact intertextually. There is no theology, or philosophy, that is not expressed in language, and even as the author upholds the boundaries, he blurs them by using identical imagery to constitute both. In so far as a theology is a literary construct, the concept of an antithetical battle between Yahwism and Baalism is deconstructed, because on another subversive level of the text, the imagery, and therefore the theologies, are not rivals but the same.

Conventionally, Baalism has been seen as a frame for Yahwism in this text, in that it is extraneous to it but helps to set the boundaries of pure religion. Baalism enhances the text's argument but is totally detachable from it, and because it is simply a stylistic frame, it does not threaten the intrinsic message of the text with 'syncretistic modification'.[322] The way in which 'the standard textbooks' struggle 'to tell a story of discontinuity'[323] is reminiscent of Derrida's description of 'endless efforts to dam up, resist, rebuild the old partitions'.[324] However, the attempt to reinstate boundaries merely highlights the text's tendency to overrun its conceptual boundaries, to mix the proper and the improper, and 'spoil all...divisions'.[325]

To describe how Baalism enhances Yahwism, without being in any way necessary to its self-definition, critics use a logic similar to Kant's logic of the parergon. However, defining pure religion, like defining a pure aesthetic, 'presupposes that we can rigorously distinguish between the intrinsic and the extrinsic',[326] and assumes that Yahwism can be distinguished from the Canaanite frame or adjunct. Just as a supra-rational pure aesthetic can only be realized when it is framed by rational definition, so Yahwism, which is 'above' Baalism, can only be defined in the context of a Canaanite frame. Canaanite religion is effectively 'an

---

322. Mays, *Hosea*, p. 10.
323. Mettinger, 'The Elusive Essence', p. 409.
324. Derrida, 'Living On', p. 84.
325. Derrida, 'Living On', p. 83.
326. Derrida, 'The Parergon', p. 26.

outside which is called inside the inside to constitute it as an inside'[327] and Baal becomes undecideably problematic, neither inside or outside, at once incorporated and rejected.

The central aporia of Hosea 1–3 (repressed by conventional criticism, but explored in deconstructive readings) is that that which is excluded is necessary to the definition of the pure centre. The so-called 'stylistic' frame cannot be removed without the whole edifice of Yahwism falling down, and the use of Baal imagery is necessitated by a 'lack—a certain "internal" indeterminacy, within that which it comes to frame'.[328] Just as parerga facilitate the very distinctions, pure–impure, inside–outside, that expel them as extraneous, so Baalism is intrinsically necessary to the polemic by which it is repudiated. The prophet deconstructs his argument that Israel should become separate by demonstrating that the inside, pure religion, cannot be detached from its Canaanite frame, and by using syncretistic imagery that suggests that Yahwism lacks the capacity to be autonomously self-defining.

In Hosea 1–3 Baal is invoked as rival and contrast, against whom Yhwh is defined, but is also used as the resource by which Yhwh is defined. The way in which images from Canaanite religion constantly spill over into the text suggests that Hosea 1–3 is, as Derrida would put it, a text written on the brink. As Derrida writes

> When a text quotes and requotes, with or without quotation marks, when it is written on the brink, you start, or indeed have already started, to lose your footing. You lose sight of any line of demarcation between a text, and what is outside it.[329]

If a synchronic reading of the text suggests an impression of living on border lines, this appears to reflect, to some extent, a historical reality. The crossing of borders in intertextual allusion seems appropriate to a context in which physical boundaries were crossed, and metaphorical liminality betrays geographical and cultural liminality. J.L. Mays provides a provocative emphasis in his commentary on Hos. 9.10. '*At the land's very edge*,' he writes, 'at the shrine of Baal-Peor, Israel began a flirtation with Baal'.[330] The capacity of the text to topple over its own borders reflects a transgression of borders, both religious/cultural and geographical, that took place at Baal-Peor, at the very edges of the land.

---

327. Derrida, 'The Parergon', p. 26.
328. Derrida, 'The Parergon', p. 33.
329. Derrida, 'Living On', pp. 81-82.
330. Mays, *Hosea*, p. 10 (my italics).

Reading Hosea 2 against the Ras Shamra Texts. 'One text reads another. How can a reading be settled on?'[331] I want to conclude this study of the deconstruction of the hierarchy Yhwh–Baal by reading Hosea 2, or Yhwh's text, against the major extra-biblical source for Baal religion, the Ras Shamra texts. I shall investigate how, as A. Deem puts it, 'this chapter is saturated with mythological motifs in its imagery and word play'[332] by inserting the echoes of one text, as Derrida does, into another. Though this study is synchronic, it may have historical implications: just as cultural borrowing seems to accurately reflect historical, geographical and cultural liminality, so the close affinities between Hosea 2 and Baal mythology may suggest that, as Guy Couturier claims, 'Hosea was well-acquainted with the structure and meaning' of a religion very similar to that at Ugarit.[333] In the absence of firm evidence to link the Baal religion of fourteenth-century Ugarit and the Canaanite religion of the eighth century BCE,[334] this study is on one level like Derrida's comparison of Blanchot with Shelley, an exercise in intertextual play. However, unlike 'Living On: *Border Lines*', it is haunted by the historical question, because as B.F. Batto observes, the 'similarities of language' are so suggestive that they indicate a link that is more than 'accidental'.[335]

Reading Hosea 2 against the Ras Shamra texts reinforces the deconstruction of the violent hierarchy Yhwh–Baal, because Yhwh's strategy for the expulsion of Baal is strongly evocative of images from Baal's own myth. The way in which Yhwh threatens to deprive the woman-

---

331. Derrida, 'Living On', p. 107.

332. A. Deem, 'The Goddess Anath and some Biblical Hebrew Cruces', *JSS* 23 (1978), pp. 25-30 (25).

333. Couturier, 'Rapports culturels et religieux', p. 192.

334. The only archaeological discovery that I am aware of that might be a significant testimony to the similarity of Ugaritic and Canaanite religion is an inscription at Tell Fahariyeh, dating from the second half of the ninth century, which is engraved on a statue of the king Had-Yit 'i, in the temple of Hadad de Sikanu, and describes Baal-Hadad in very similar terms to Baal at Ugarit (see S.A. Kaufman, 'Reflections on the Assyrian Aramaic Bilingual from Tell Fakhariyeh', *Maarav* 3 [1982], pp. 137-38).

335. B.F. Batto, 'The Covenant of Peace: A Neglected Ancient Near Eastern Motif', *CBQ* 49 (1987), pp. 187-211 (200). Though Hos. 2 appears to be strong evidence for the historical connection between the Baal of Ugarit and Canaan, it cannot be taken in isolation as evidence for completely ignoring the geographical and chronological divide.

land of her lovers, the Baalim, by hedging up her way with thorns (2.8) suggests an affinity with the role of Mot (Death), who also threatens to deprive the land of Baal by extending his huge mouth between earth and heaven[336] and swallowing him 'like a lamb'.[337] Like Mot, who 'scorch[es] the olives, the produce of the earth and the fruit of the trees',[338] Yhwh acts as an agent of drought, thirst and famine, and threatens to 'make [the woman/land] like a wilderness, and set her like a parched land, and slay her with thirst' (2.5).[339] The aridity and heat of the desert scenario seems to mimic the consequences of Baal's capture by Mot, in which dryness conquers fertility, the 'lamp of the gods, Shapsh, blaze[s] hot', and 'the heavens [are] wearied by the hand of divine Mot'.[340]

In the Baal cycle, following his capture by Mot, Baal is pursued by the woman Anat. In Hosea 2 causality is slightly adjusted, and Yhwh deprives the woman-land of Baal *because* he is pursued by her. Anat's agitated search, in which she wanders for 'days' and 'months' and searches 'every rock to the heart of the earth',[341] is paralleled in the woman Israel's determination to pursue her lovers. As Guy Couturier observes, 'with vehemence she [Israel] launches into pursuit (רדף), sustains her search (בקש), but without managing to find him (מצא) or to seize him (נשג); the vocabulary is deliberate and quite clearly defines a psychological state of intense emotion'.[342]

As Anat and Israel share in a 'breathless and anguished search' ('une

336. A. Herdner (ed.), *Corpus des tablettes en cunéiformes alphabétiques* (Paris: Imprimerie Nationale, 1963; hereafter CTA), 5.i.2-5. The numeration of the tablets in this edition (which is also adopted in the *KTU*) is used throughout unless otherwise specified. The translation, unless otherwise stated, is from J.C.L. Gibson, *Canaanite Myths and Legends* (Edinburgh: T. & T. Clark, 1977).

337. CTA 6.ii.22.

338. CTA 5.ii.5-6.

339. This analogy is also made by Mettinger, 'The Elusive Essence', p. 401.

340. CTA 6.ii.24-25, trans. N.H. Walls, *The Goddess Anat in Ugaritic Myth* (SBL Dissertation; Atlanta: Scholars Press, 1992), p. 182.

341. CTA 5.vi.27.

342. Couturier, 'Rapports culturels et religieux', p. 190: 'C'est avec vehemence qu'il se lance a la suite (*radaf*), qu'il maintient sa recherche (*biqqes*), mais sans réussir à le trouver (*masa*) ni à le saisir (*nasag*); le vocabulaire est choisis et definit clairement un état psychologique nourri d'emotions intenses'. I have taken the liberty of changing the masculine pronoun for Israel to the feminine, to correspond more closely to the Hebrew text and to emphasize that, like Anat, Israel is a woman in pursuit.

recherche haletante et angoisée')[343] for Baal, so their motives for the search also intersect. Anat is motivated by emotional tenderness, and 'the heart of Anat for Baal' is compared to 'the heart of a heifer for her calf';[344] she is also motivated by agricultural crisis because Baal's disappearance puts life in jeopardy: 'Baal is dead!—What becomes of the people?/Dagon's son!—What of the masses?'[345] Like Anat, Israel pursues Baal because she sees him as a source of agricultural plenty, of bread and water, wool and flax, oil and drink, vines and fig trees (2.7, 14), and like Anat she sees the recovery of the inaccessible deity as the recovery of terrestrial fecundity in which 'The heavens rain oil' and 'The ravines flow with honey.'[346] The sexual motive behind Israel's pursuit, made explicit in the description of the Baalim as her lovers (מְאַהֲבֶיהָ, 2.9), may also reflect Baal's relationship with Anat in the disputed text RS 319, which, according to one translation, reads 'He seizes and holds [her] womb/ [She] seizes and holds [his] stones/ Baal.../ the mai[den] Anat/[...] to conceive and bear'.[347]

The most powerful deconstructive ironies of an intertextual reading follow directly after Yhwh's declaration that he will remove the name of Baal from Israel's mouth. Having removed Baal from the woman's mouth, he seemingly cannot remove him from his, and states his vision of renewal in terms that powerfully echo images from the Baal cycle. Yhwh pledges to remove the 'bow, the sword and war from the land' and 'make [the nation] lie down in safety' (Hos. 2.20). Reading this promise against the Ras Shamra texts reveals a curious correspondence in which Yhwh's terms of peace echo Baal's command to Anat to desist from carnage: 'Remove war from the earth; set mandrakes [or love] in the ground/ Pour peace into the heart of the earth; rain down love into the heart of the fields'.[348] The speeches are similar in the images that

343. Couturier, 'Rapports culturels et religieux', p. 190.

344. CTA 6.ii.6-9; 28-31.

345. CTA 5.vi.23-24; 6.i.6-7.

346. CTA 6.iii.12-13.

347. RS 319, *ANET*, p. 142 (trans. H.L. Ginsberg). The simplistic caricature of Anat as a fertility goddess is currently disputed, for example by Peggy L. Day ('Why is Anat a Warrior and a Hunter?'). However, although critics contend with the judgmental descriptions of Baal religion as a fertility religion, and are less ready to assume, for example, that the calf that Baal copulates with is Anat, this does not mean that sexuality has to be eradicated from the Ras Shamra texts, and the sexuality of this passage, in particular, is hard to deny.

348. CTA 3.iii.11-14, trans. Batto, 'The Covenant of Peace', p. 198. Batto

they use, the sentiments they express, and in the circumstances in which they are uttered. As Baal seeks to discourage Anat from her bloodthirsty campaign, in which she plunges her skirts in the 'gore' of warriors,[349] so Yhwh speaks of peace to check his own violent acts of reprisal. The tension between war and peace, which is divided between the two deities Baal and Anat, is condensed in Hosea into one single, split divinity. The 'mood' of the poem is one of 'divine indecision',[350] and the way in which Yhwh speaks for and against violence is itself a deconstructive aporia.

Yhwh's vision of renewal culminates in what David Clines has termed a 'virtual orgy of responsiveness':[351]

> And in that day, says the Lord,
> I will answer the heavens
> and they shall answer the earth;
> And the earth shall answer the grain,
> the wine and the oil,
> and they shall answer Jezreel;
> and I will sow [her] for myself in the land (Hos. 2.23-25).

When read intertextually, this cosmic chain of communication suggests another response: the response of Yhwh to Baal mythology. Amid the cacophony of voices answering one another, Baal's voice can be heard telling Anat of the cosmic fertility that will be achieved when he builds his palace on Mount Sapan:

> For I have a word I will tell you,
> A message I will recount to you,
> A word of trees and a whisper of stone
> Converse of heaven with Earth,

translates Ugaritic *ddym*, which has received a variety of interpretations, as 'mandrakes' on the basis of the Egyptian parallel *ddyt*. This translation not only preserves the agricultural metaphor, but also seems appropriate, because mandrakes were thought to have love-producing qualities, and here *ddym* are watered by love and peace.

349. CTA 3B.ii.4-41 (28).

350. Clines, 'Hosea 2', p. 87. In his structuralist analysis Clines suggests that the mood is one of divine indecision, and adds, 'One would hardly imagine so were it not for other glimpses Hosea gives us of "struggling with himself" [6.4; 11.8]', ('Hosea 2', p. 87). In this deconstructive reading, I want to show how struggle is implicit in Hos. 1–3 in imagery that is at odds with itself and that deconstructs its own assertions.

351. Clines, 'Hosea 2', p. 90.

Of Deeps with Stars...
The word humans do not know.[352]

The scope of communication, from earth to heaven, and the response of inanimate nature suggests that Hos. 2.23-25 is Yhwh's answer to Baal as much as to Jezreel. Unlike Derrida's texts, which insert antithetical voices into the same text and find erudite metaphorical links between them, the insertion of Baal into this text seems to suggest plagiarism and indebtedness on the part of the later author. The affinity is noted by, among others, Andersen and Freedman[353] and Mark Smith,[354] but is also affirmed by commentators' anxiety to stress discontinuity at this point. The way in which H.W. Wolff argues that this passage is 'quite unlike the sapiental studies of nature found in the miracle stories of the Orient'[355] because it is wiser and genuinely scientific suggests that he is only too aware of the blurring of boundaries and is anxiously trying to drive a wedge between the two religions. In an attempt to escape the deconstruction of the hierarchy Yhwh–Baal, he tries to enforce it with a new hierarchy wise–foolish, but to do so he has to use the ridiculous argument that 'Only the listing of objects in a series derives immediately from wisdom'.[356] Yahwism is promoted by associating it with the ideals of humanistic scholarship and science: 'It is instructive to note', he observes, 'how Israel's *liberation* from the nature myths of Baal permitted the free study of nature to flourish'.[357]

Several commentators have noticed more discrete intertextual illusions in this passage.[358] The verb ענה, which refers to sexual response[359] as well as verbal answering, creates an impression of an 'orgy of responsiveness', but also suggests a pun on 'Anat' emphasized by frequent repetition. E. Jacob and A. Deem[360] find subtle intertextual echoes of

---

352. CTA 3.iii.18-24, trans. M.S. Smith, *The Early History of God: Yahweh and the Other Deities in Ancient Israel* (San Francisco: Harper & Row, 1990), p. 46.

353. Andersen and Freedman, *Hosea*, p. 287.

354. Smith, *The Early History of God*, p. 46.

355. Wolff, *Hosea*, p. 53.

356. Wolff, *Hosea*, p. 53.

357. Wolff, *Hosea*, p. 54.

358. See, for example, M. Fishbane, 'Israel and the "Mothers" ', in P.L. Berger (ed.), *The Other Side of God: A Polarity in World Religions* (New York: Doubleday, 1981), pp. 28-47 (38).

359. Cf. Hos. 2.14-15, where male seduction results in female answering.

360. Jacob, 'L'héritage cananéen', pp. 250-59; Deem, 'The Goddess Anath', p. 27.

another epithet for Anat, *rhm ʿnt*,[361] in the frequent use of the verb רחם
(1.6; 2.3, 6, 25) and suggest a possible reference to the mysterious goddess *rhmy*,[362] whom some critics have also associated with Anat.[363] The
phrase הַדָּגָן וְהַתִּירוֹשׁ וְהַיִּצְהָר ('the grain, the wine and the oil', 2.10, 24) is
doubly evocative, because the noun דָּגָן echoes one of the common epi-
thets for Baal, 'Dagon's Son', and because exactly the same triad is
attributed to Baal in Ugaritic literature. In 'The Legend of Keret' the
ploughmen and the farmers turn their heads upwards in anticipation of
Baal's sweet rain for 'The *grain* had failed [in] their bins, the *wine* had
failed in their skins, the *oil* had failed in their [cruses]'.[364] The items and
the order is the same, which suggests that Yhwh not only competes with
Baal for the role of provider, but competes using the same lexis.[365]

The undecideable 'Jezreel', which can mean sowing or scattering,
renewal or destruction, repeats the undecideability of Anat's sowing of
Mot. Anat 'splits' Mot with a 'blade', 'winnows' him with a 'sieve',
'grinds' him with 'millstones', and 'sows' him in the field,[366] and commentators are divided as to whether this passage refers to the 'complete
destruction of a hated enemy',[367] or the sowing of Mot as grain and sea-
sonal preparations for planting.[368] As in the image of Jezreel, both senses
collide: Mot is sown (with millstones), and destruction and renewal
compete in the same image. Though the critical tendency is to select one
option and exclude the other, the passage encourages a myth-ritual
interpretation *and* a literal interpretation, and, like Jezreel, suspends the

361. CTA 6.ii.27.
362. This name is mentioned four times, in CTA 15.ii.6 and 23.13, 16, 28.
363. See, for example, Gibson, *Canaanite Myths and Legends*, p. 77. For a fuller
discussion and bibliography see A.S. Kapelrud, *The Violent Goddess: Anat in the
Ras Shamra Texts* (Oslo: Scandinavian University Books, 1969), pp. 34-37.
364. CTA 16.iii.14-16 (my italics).
365. Historically, the evidence suggests that the triad is a 'traditional and stereotyped formula for the land's bounty' (Mays, *Hosea*, p. 41; cf. Couturier 'Rapports
culturels et religieux', p. 194). Yhwh and Baal are either sharing the same language,
or Yhwh is assimilating a Canaanite phrase, but the relatively late biblical occurrences
of the phrase (Num. 18.12; Deut. 7.13; 11.14; 12.17; 14.23; 18.4; 28.51; 2 Chron.
31.5; 32.28) tend to suggest the latter.
366. CTA 6.ii.31-35.
367. Walls, *The Goddess Anat*, p. 183.
368. See, for example, J.C. de Moor, *An Anthology of Religious Texts from
Ugarit* (Leiden: Brill, 1987), pp. 86-90. The image of a female deity sowing a male
deity appears to reverse the image of the woman sown; cf. the more conventional
sowing of the woman Jezreel by a male speaker in Hos. 2.23.

reader between the mutually exclusive senses of sowing and annihilation.

Reading Hosea 2 alongside the Ras Shamra texts suggests that as Yhwh enters the realm of Canaanite religion, he is becoming yet another contender in the battle for divine kingship. As Baal contends with Yam and Mot in a struggle for supremacy, so Yhwh seeks to overthrow Baal, and his attempt at usurpation is described in terms of sexual competition. The way in which Yhwh becomes a lover who contends with Israel's other lovers has been largely overlooked, because commentators tend to overplay the sexuality of the Baal cult and underplay the sexuality of Yhwh. The critical imagination has run riot in descriptions of the Baal cult: critics have alluded to 'orgies'[369] and 'Bacchanalian celebration',[370] and have even argued on the basis of Hos. 7.4, 6 that 'At times the feeling ran so high that only the symbolism of the oven at its hottest could adequately express the fervour of the cult exercises'.[371] At the same time they have underlined the non-sexuality and difference of Yhwh, staunchly maintaining that 'the sexual aspect, so important in Canaanite thinking, was excluded with respect to Yhwh' and that 'the marriage imagery...describes Yhwh's relation to Israel only insofar as it is the expression of the historically and legally orientated covenant relationship'.[372]

The very attempt to make Yhwh asexual suggests that sexuality is implied. In fact, as in the Ras Shamra texts, references to sex are graphic, even pornographic, and the text testifies to a powerful erotic imagination, a collective male consciousness composed of Yhwh and his prophet, that strips the woman to expose breasts (2.4) and genitalia (2.11). Though the verb *pty* is demurely translated 'allure' by the RSV,[373] it is a verb that has sexual designs on its object, and is applied to Yhwh's designs upon Israel. Significantly, in Ugaritic the verb *pty* is less bashfully translated: in its one occurrence it is taken to describe the sex act, or at the very least the seduction preceding intercourse.[374]

Though critics dispute the simplistic reduction of the Ras Shamra texts

369. H.G. May, 'The Fertility Cult in Hosea', *AJSL* 48 (1932), pp. 73-98 (93).

370. Mays, *Hosea*, p. 11.

371. May, 'The Fertility Cult in Hosea', p. 94.

372. Wolff, *Hosea,* p. 16.

373. Wolff also translates *pty* as 'allure' (*Hosea*, p. 31), but other commentators offer the less euphemistic translations, 'entice' (Andersen and Freedman, *Hosea*, p. 215) and 'seduce' (Weems, 'Gomer: Victim of Violence', p. 92).

374. The one occurrence is in 'Shachar and Shalim and the Gracious Gods' (CTA 23.39), translated by Gibson as 'Surely El seduced (*pt*) the two women'.

to fertility religion involving sexual rites,[375] the sexuality of Baal is beyond dispute. He copulates with a heifer seven and seventy times, and 'mounts' her eight and eighty times;[376] Keret sacrifices to him to obtain a child, and in a graphically sexual encounter he 'holds [Anat's] womb' and she 'holds his stones'. Yhwh also functions in Hosea 2 as a graphically sexual deity, but just as commentators attempt to gloss over this fact by repressing sex and violence in the text, so the text itself attempts to deny its parasitical status. The interpretation of the text on the level of theological abstraction, marriage and covenant, is encouraged by the surface rhetoric of the text, which claims a vital distinction between Baal as master and Yhwh as husband (Hos. 2.18), and which encourages the reader to supply reasons for this distinction. Yet while this declaration leads inevitably to conclusions that Yhwh is a 'warmer, more intimate'[377] god than Baal, it also leads, equally inevitably to its own deconstruction. Read deconstructively, Hos. 2.18 appears to be a smokescreen in that by ascribing to Yhwh the more sexual role as husband, it recasts Baal as relatively detached, a mere master. The text is trying to claim that intimacy is Yhwh's invention, and critics who argue that Yhwh invents intimacy with the divinity are accurately following the text but are also dupes of its all-too-convincing rhetoric. For on another level, Yhwh's new role as 'husband' highlights his mimicry of Baal's sexuality and emphasizes the deconstructive irony that the God who condemns the woman and her lovers (2.7, 9, 12, 15), ends by seducing Israel in the desert and playing the lover himself.

4.2.3. *Love–Hate (Acceptance–Rejection)*

In Hos. 1.4-6 Yhwh instructs Hosea to give his children the negative names יִזְרְעֶאל (Jezreel), לֹא רֻחָמָה (Not Pitied), and לֹא עַמִּי (Not-My-People). In Hos. 2.1 he promises that 'in the place where it was said to them "You are not my people", it shall be said to them, "Sons of the Living God"', and in 2.3 the text urges, 'Say to your brothers, "My People", and to your sisters, "She has obtained pity"'.[378] To accompany the

---

375. For a critique of the assumption that Baalism is exclusively a fertility religion, see J.W. Rogerson, *Myth in Old Testament Research* (Berlin: de Gruyter, 1974); R.A. Oden, 'Theoretical Assumptions in the Study of Ugaritic Myths', *Maarav* 2 (1979), pp. 43-63.

376. CTA 5.v.18-21.

377. Hubbard, *Hosea*, p. 85.

378. The RSV translation amends 'brothers' and 'sisters' to the singular, but I have retained the plural forms of the MT.

vision of restoration and cosmic communication, ch. 2 culminates in the promise, 'And I will have pity on Not Pitied, and I will say to Not My People, "You are my people"' (2.25). The conversion of the children's names is generally taken as an indication that love is stronger than hate, and that threats of annihilation give way to promises of acceptance.

'Call me but love', says Shakespeare's Romeo, 'and I'll be new baptized'.[379] The current critical tendency is to perceive Hosea's children, hence the nation of Israel, as 'new baptized' with names of love, in a way that completely eradicates their former shame. In contrast to earlier redaction critics, who insisted that same text could not be responsible for 'thunderbolts' and 'roses', critics such as M.J. Buss, Michael Catlett, Andersen and Freedman, and E.M. Good subscribe to a New Critical ideal[380] and stress reversal as an integrating motif and a 'technique[ ] of linkage'.[381] From a redactional approach that dealt with dichotomy by eradicating one of the conflicting perspectives, criticism has progressed to an approach that controls the shifting moods of the text by balancing them in a neat antithesis. The quest for unity remains the same, but the New Critical commentators argue more subtly and attempt to soothe the abrasive mood swings of the text by stressing continuity, balance, and appropriateness. M.J. Buss shows how 'The negative structure of man's direction and the positive word of God's purpose are ultimately connected with each other and are not to be considered as separate',[382] and Michael Catlett shows how reversals smooth the text rather than disturbing it, by creating 'relationships...between various and dissimilar portions of the text'.[383]

The art of New Critical readings is to transform Yhwh's schizoid utterances from something that may potentially disturb the reader into something that will reassure her. The image of reversal is rhetorically reassuring, showing how the opposite emotions are completely under the writer's and Yhwh's control, and it is also theologically reassuring, because, reading chronologically, blessing is Yhwh's 'last word'.

---

379. Shakespeare, *Romeo and Juliet*, II.ii, l. 50.

380. Though Catlett is the only critic to acknowledge the influence of I.A. Richards and M.H. Abrams, I refer to each of these critics as a 'New Critical Commentator' because they share the primary assumption of New Critics, that all texts are essentially unities (for a fuller discussion see the conclusion to this book).

381. E.M. Good, 'The Composition of Hosea', *SEÅ* 31 (1966), pp. 21-63 (25).

382. M.J. Buss, *The Prophetic Word of Hosea: A Morphological Study* (BZAW, III; Berlin: de Gruyter, 1969), p. 129.

383. Catlett, *Reversals in Hosea*, Abstract.

Michael Catlett argues that 'Theologically, the reversals point to the power of Yhwh who transforms judgement into salvation',[384] while Andersen and Freedman maintain that 'The names of the children, which symbolised the destruction of the relationship between God and his people, will be reversed so that at the end of days they will symbolise the reparation of the relationship, and the realisation of an Edenic existence on earth'.[385] The inconsistencies in their position is revealing, for while they express a belief in the priority of beginnings in their use of the Eden image, they ascribe no authority whatsoever to the beginning of this text and its discomforting message of alienation.

Andersen and Freedman are not alone in their repudiation of Yhwh's opening, negative message. The impression enforced by all New Critical commentators is that the symbolic curses are completely negated by Yhwh's later assertions, and that they are not at all representative of Yhwh's 'true' feelings. From 2.1 onwards, the text wakes up from its nightmare of annihilation to discover that it was, thankfully, only a bad dream. In the hierarchy love–hate the truth of Yhwh's indefatigable love unequivocally triumphs, and hate and annihilation are erased by the operation of grace.

Though his essay has many affinities with Derrida's observations, Harold Fisch supports the New Critical commentators on this point. His description of the reversal of the children's names is worth quoting at length, both for its astute literary observations, and the way in which it evades the full consequences of its own argument:

> The naming of names is the very matter of Hosea's prophecy. It is the act with which the book begins. But all these names (*Jezreel, Lo-Ruhamah, Lo-Ammi*) contain their own antitheses. In fact they are themselves antitheses, names that exist only by virtue of that which is denied. We are haunted by their contraries just as God in his anger is haunted by his own unsuppressed and inexpressible love... Already in the second chapter *Lo-Ammi* and *Lo-Ruhamah* have slipped into their opposites: 'Say to your brothers, *Ammi*/ And to your sisters, *Ruhamah*' (Hos. 2.1)... Paradoxically, we discover God's unconditioned love only through the negating of it... In the sign *Lo-Ammi* we discover the trace of its opposite. Negation is itself negated. Through the language of denial, God's overmastering love is manifested. It cannot be overcome, nor can the name *Ammi* be eradicated. The attempt to eradicate it simply establishes it and

---

384. Catlett, *Reversals in Hosea*, Abstract.
385. Andersen and Freedman, *Hosea*, p. 117.

confirms it...*Ammi*, we may say, proves to be more powerful than its opposite.[386]

Fisch's argument falls short of deconstruction because he enforces the violent hierarchy love–hate. Hate is seen as a 'supplement', or 'parergon' in Rousseau and Kant's sense of the words, and falls short of Derrida's radical redescriptions. The opening curses are a mere ornament, a rhetorical device, and are somehow less real than the overwhelming reality of love which inevitably asserts itself. In Fisch's terms, the first names given are unstable and inevitably collapse, or slip, into their stronger antitheses.

Though the New Critical commentators are anxious to emphasize the difference between their readings and redaction criticism,[387] both are attempts to control the oscillations of the text, and both stress one aspect of the dichotomy at the expense of the other. Though they do not elide the curses, in order to make Hosea an optimistic prophet, they handle the opposition in such a way that it becomes fundamentally positive. It becomes positive in a stylistic sense because, according to New Critical ideals, 'the bringing in of the opposite, the *complementary* impulses' is a 'character of poetry of the highest order'.[388] It is also positive in that the positive message takes precedence over the negative, even though the latter precedes the former.

386. Fisch, 'Hosea: A Poetics of Violence', pp. 143-45.

387. Catlett distinguishes himself from the redaction critics on the basis that he is 'more concerned with making sense of what exists rather than changing what exists to make sense' (*Reversals in Hosea*, p. 9), while Andersen and Freedman claim that final form critics differ from their predecessors because they regard the text as 'the work of serious people' (*Hosea*, p. 60).

388. I.A. Richards, *Principles of Literary Criticism* (New York: Harcourt Brace Jovanovich, 1925), p. 250, cited in Catlett, *Reversals in Hosea*, p. 31 (my italics). Compare Cleanth Brooks's statement that good poetry uses paradox and 'welds together the discordant and the contradictory' ('The Language of Paradox', in D. Lodge (ed.), *Twentieth Century Literary Criticism: A Reader* [London: Longman, 1972], pp. 292-304 [301]; repr. from C. Brooks, *The Well-Wrought Urn: Studies in the Structure of Poetry* [New York, 1947], ch. 1). New Criticism is a popular resource for critics who want to extol the worth of a biblical text on the basis of its literary techniques. Catlett, for example, uses Richards to define superlative literature, shows how the biblical text fits the definition, and argues for its position at the very centre of culture, in a way that is reminiscent of Meir Sternberg's *The Poetics of Biblical Narrative: Ideological Literature and the Drama of Reading* (Bloomington: Indiana University Press, 1985).

As deconstruction is not synonymous with destruction, the result of a deconstructive reading is not the opposite of conventional reading: that is, it does not emphasise hate and annihilation at the expense of love and reconciliation. The process of reversal itself must be brought into question, since as Derrida observes, 'To remain content with reversal is of course to operate within the system to be destroyed'.[389] Derrida advocates a reading that 'intervenes' in the 'established equilibrium':[390] that is, in this case, within the neat antitheses that the New Critical commentators have established. A deconstructive reading questions the violent hierarchy which promotes love as the ultimate message, and more than this, deconstructs the assumptions behind the idea of reversal and the belief that the second utterance effectively cancels out the first.

Appropriately, the tools for deconstructing the violent hierarchy love–hate are found within the commentators' own texts. Michael Catlett describes the children's names in terms more appropriate to a definition of the undecideable than to his own thesis when he observes that 'Judgement and salvation share the same vocabulary', and 'the children's names become vehicles of the negative and positive responses of Yhwh'.[391] Even more provocatively, Harold Fisch claims that each name contains the '*trace*' of its opposite and sees names in this text as two-edged, unstable signs that are liable to disintegration (or 'slipping' into their opposites). Although he maintains that the slippage happens in one direction only, and that only the negative name threatens to disintegrate, he opens up the possibility that the positive name, like the negative one, is always already 'haunted by its contrary'.

Just as contemporary readings suggest that the model of reversal can be pushed towards the brink of undecideability, so alternatives to reversal can be found in older, rabbinic commentaries on the text. Though he does not deal directly with the problem of the children's names, Rab Kahana confronts the potentially disconcerting effect of opposites in collision:

> The Holy One said to the Prophets: 'Go, comfort Jerusalem'. Thus Hosea came to comfort her saying: 'The Holy One sent me to comfort thee'. Jerusalem asked: 'What comfort do you bring me?' Hosea replied: '[The Holy One said through me] *Henceforth I will be as the dew unto Israel*' [Hos. 14.6]. Jerusalem retorted: 'Yesterday you reported as saying

389. Derrida, *Dissemination*, p. 6.
390. Derrida, *Dissemination*, p. 6.
391. Catlett, *Reversals in Hosea*, p. 27.

Ephraim is smitten, their root is dried up, they shall bear no fruit
[Hos. 9.16]. And now you claim that he will be as the dew unto Israel.
Which words am I to believe, yesterday's or today's?'[392]

The discomfort expressed in Jerusalem's retort is also reflected in the
Midrash: since Hosea utters blessings and curses, he is ranked between
Balaam, who hated Israel, and Moses, who loved her.[393] The idea that
Hosea 2 resists the binary structure love–hate is also reflected in a contemporary reading of the text: in attempting a structuralist, hence essentially binary reading, David Clines introduces an intermediate category,
'belonging wrongly', between the antithetical positions of 'belonging'
and 'not belonging'.[394] By interpolating a third term, Clines suggests
that the text resists binary categories, and intriguingly he concludes that
a structuralist approach is limited because it focuses on the 'way the
poem is' rather than 'how the poem moves'.[395] The idea that Hosea 2 is
a 'literary work with a dynamic'[396] that somehow resists binary structures through its own elusive movement is a proleptically poststructuralist observation and anticipates a deconstructive reading of the
text.

*Which Words am I to Believe, Yesterday's or Today's? Palaeonymy In
Hosea 1–3*

> In naming have we divided what
> unnaming will not undivide.[397]

Yhwh in Hosea 1–3, like Derrida's God of Babel, names, unnames and
renames, or as Derrida puts it, dis-shem-inates. The first names that he
utters, Jezreel, Lo-Ruhamah and Lo-Ammi, suggest that he is deconstructing previous assumptions, that Israel is loved and that she is a
people. 'Abandoned' and 'Alien' would convey the same meaning as
Lo-Ruhamah and Lo-Ammi, but the text deliberately chooses to negate
the positive term with the prefix לֹא. Because the new names both retain

---

392. *Pes. K.*, trans. W.G. Braude and I.J. Kapstein, in *Peskita de-Rab Kahana:
R. Kahana's Compilation of Discourses for Sabbaths and Festal Days* (Philadelphia:
Jewish Publication Society of America, 1975), p. 295.

393. Num. R. 2.17.

394. Clines, 'Hosea 2', p. 89.

395. Clines, 'Hosea 2', p. 99.

396. Clines, 'Hosea 2', p. 99.

397. A.R. Ammons, 'Two Motions', in *Northfield Poems* (Ithaca, NY: Cornell
University Press, 1966), p. 26.

the old (positive) meanings and invert them, the use of the לא prefix functions like Derrida's palaeonymy, or the art of placing a word under erasure.

According to Derrida, palaeonymy puts an old term to serve a new perspective, in a way that avoids the extremes of (1) allowing the old meaning to dominate, and (2) eradicating it completely. Fisch's description of the negative names, which retain the traces of their opposite even as they seek to invert them, suggests that the addition of the prefix לא functions similarly to Derrida's 'sign of crossing out'. The terms Ruhamah and Ammi are negated by their prefix, yet they are still visible. Meaning is subverted *and* preserved intact, and Yhwh, like the divine arch-deconstructor of Babel, begins to show some peculiar affinities with Derrida.

Reading the verb to be under erasure in Derrida's writing suggests a vast ontological and metaphysical background to the text that is being invoked but also subjected to interrogation. Reading the names Lo-Ammi and Lo-Ruhamah suggests a vast theological background in which love and belonging are at the heart of Israel's theology. By issuing negative names, Yhwh strikes to the core of Israel's history and identity, and challenges the violent hierarchy which places love above rejection. Critics who assert that love is the dominant theme of this text repress this act of deconstruction, and prove the inevitability by which, as Derrida argues, violent hierarchies will always reconstitute themselves.

Ironically, even as they castigate Israel for 'departing from the Lord', critics ignore, and even repeat, another of her faults: the complacent assumption that the people of God are loved.[398] Even as they attempt to comment on the text from a superior vantage point, the text comments on them, because they persist in an assumption that is deconstructed by the text. Stephen D. Moore notes a similar effect in commentaries on John 4, and shows how commentators effectively 'trade places with the woman',[399] because they are guilty of the interpretative naïveté of which they accuse her. As Moore writes, deconstruction shows how the 'literary text is capable of turning the tables on the critic who sets out to

398. The Talmud is also determinedly optimistic, and rewrites the story to salvage Israel's reputation and to demonstrate that Yhwh always loved her.

399. S.D. Moore, 'Are There Impurities in the Living Water that the Johannine Jesus Dispenses? Deconstruction, Feminism and the Samaritan Woman', *BI* 1 (1993), pp. 207-27 (212).

master it',[400] as well as how it is capable of turning the tables on itself.

Yhwh turns the tables on Israel's (and the critics') assumptions, by deconstructing the violent hierarchy love–hate. Although it is not simply reversal, deconstruction does involve a shocking act of inversion, because 'to take an attitude of neutralising indifference with respect to the classical oppositions would be to give free rein to the existing forces that have historically dominated the field'.[401] The ascendancy of positive terms such as love and presence over rejection and absence seems to be as pervasive in theology as in philosophy. Language itself seems to enforce this fundamental optimism, since it begins with what *is*, and can only talk of absence, or what *is not*, by derivation from the positive term. Both the Hebrew original and English translations struggle to express absence, and can only do so, ironically, by adding to the positive term: *Lo*-Ruhamah, *Not*-loved. The priority of the positive is inscribed in the very language structures, and is a 'violent', irrepressible hierarchy that can only be interrogated by an equally violent act.

With a shocking act of linguistic violence, and a disturbing triad of curses, Yhwh begins with the negative, and deconstructs his audience's assumptions. The effect is like the opening scene of *King Lear*, in which Cordelia is asked for a testimony of love and defies convention by replying 'Nothing, my Lord'.[402] Whereas Cordelia persists in her denial of love and resists her father's command to 'speak again',[403] Yhwh does speak again, several times, to supply a rival message. In *Lear* the heroine is consistent and retains her integrity; in *Hosea*, Yhwh doubly confounds his audience and deconstructs all expectations of textual integrity by issuing mutually exclusive statements.

Other words may shift and change, but a name might be expected to be a constant factor. In his commentary on Isaiah, Otto Kaiser describes the name of the prophet's son, Maher-Shalal-Hash-Baz, as a name 'inscribed in indelible ink',[404] but although M.J. Buss tries to extract a similar principle from Hosea, arguing that 'Every time the child's name

400. Moore, 'Deconstruction, Feminism and the Samaritan Woman', p. 211.
401. Derrida, *Dissemination*, p. 6.
402. Shakespeare, *King Lear*, I.i, l. 86.
403. Shakespeare, *King Lear*, I.i, l. 89.
404. O. Kaiser, *Isaiah 1–12: A Commentary* (trans. R.A. Wilson; OTL; London: SCM Press, 1972), p. 110. In the completely revised second edition, Kaiser rejects the reading 'indelible' and argues that, 'though it would fit well into the context', there is 'no good philological foundation' for this insertion (O. Kaiser, *Isaiah 1–12: A Commentary* [trans. J. Bowden; London: SCM Press, 1983, rev. edn], p. 178).

was called it would serve as an oracle of the unconcern of Yhwh for his people',[405] the naming of Hosea's children achieves an entirely different effect. The same names are used, undecideably, as oracles of concern and unconcern, and every time the names are called there is no guarantee that they will be the same. Slippages in meaning suggest that the names are written not in indelible ink, but in ink that can be erased (like Derrida's 'white ink') and the division of names suggests that there is no element of language that does not have the capacity to become 'divided, bifid'[406] and undecideable.

The giving of the names Lo-Ruhamah and Lo-Ammi is an exercise in 'split writing'. The names are delicately poised between the affirmations Ruhamah and Ammi, and the negating prefix Lo: they are the first, and the original names given by Yhwh in this text, and yet they appear to be dependent and parasitic on previous affirmations. As in Derrida's analysis of Babel, the names are also split between the 'proper' and the 'common' name, and refer specifically to a single child, and generally, to a nation. As the text progresses, these tensions are not resolved but multiplied, and the names pass through a chain of displacements.

In Hos. 2.1 Yhwh promises that 'in the place where it was said to them, "You are not my people", it shall be said to them, "Sons of the Living God" '. This can only be reductively described as reversal, for the text appears to be deliberately staging a battle between competing senses. The two opposite meanings are to converge *in the same place*, and the speaking of the new name is to be subverted by memories of the old. Today's words are, as Rab Kahana suggested, haunted by yesterday's, and just as the negative names were inscribed with the positive, so these new blessings cannot escape from their attachment to curse.

As reversal this passage is unconvincing, because the old name is not repudiated or eradicated, but retained. Again this is an act of palaeonymy, because the curse, Not My People, is neither erased, nor allowed to dominate. As the first act of palaeonymy put positive assumptions under erasure, so this new act of palaeonymy puts negative assumptions under erasure. The implied former term, My People, is not triumphantly re-established, as New Critical commentators suggest, but is displaced in another term, 'Sons of the Living God'. The effect of displacement, as in Derrida's texts, is to deny any perspective privilege, and to allow no single name to achieve permanent unequivocal status,

405. Buss, *The Prophetic Word*, p. 29.
406. Derrida, 'Des Tours de Babel', p. 249.

and to 'rise up as the master word or master concept'.[407] There is no
name that cannot be deconstructed by a rival name in the text, for, as
the image of convergence in one place might suggest, the text constantly
brings in 'the name of the versus, the adverse or the countername', and
calls 'combat...between two names.'[408]

Whereas the names Lo-Ruhamah and Lo-Ammi operate on a split
level, and have a common and proper referent, the 'reversed' names are
only given as common names. Hos. 2.1 is unequivocally addressed to
the nation, who have been a people (plural) and are to become sons, and
Hos. 2.3 similarly urges 'Say to your brothers, "My People" and to
your sisters, "She has obtained pity" '. The tendency of translators to
amend לַאֲחֵיכֶם and לַאֲחוֹתֵיכֶם to 'to your brother' and 'to your sister'
suggests that they are aware that the so-called reversal is neither neat
nor complete. To further confound the reversal theorists, the giver of the
names has changed, and the masculine plural imperative אִמְרוּ implies that
the new names are to be given by the nation to the nation. The act of
naming is authoritative, initiated by Yhwh and spoken through the voice
of his prophet; the act of re-naming, in contrast, is to be spoken by the
nation, to themselves. Even Catlett, an advocate of the reversal theory,
has to admit that this change is significant enough to make the reversal
'partial', and his qualification suggests that the idea of reversal is too
systematic to describe the shifts in meaning in this text.

As the children's names shift in meaning, so the children themselves
show a strange predilection for changing sides. In 1.2 the children of
harlotry are firmly equated with their mother, but in 2.4 they stand with
their father on the other side of the court and contend (plead) with her.
In 2.6 they become victims of their father's rhetoric once again: 'Upon
her children also I will have no pity, because they are children of
harlotry'. The children function as undecideables, because they enter the
dialectic of the court from both sides. They are aligned with the speaker
(2.4) but are also maligned by the speaker (2.6): they co-operate with the
text's rhetoric, and attack the woman, and are victims of the text's
rhetoric, and are attacked with the woman. Because they stand on the
side of the innocent and the guilty, the blessed and the cursed, they participate in binary oppositions but also destabilise them from within. Like
Derrida, who adopts 'positions' rather than one position, they shift
alliances and support mutually exclusive perspectives in a way that

---

407. Derrida, 'Positions', p. 35.
408. Derrida, *The Ear of the Other*, p. 11.

resists logocentric ideas of consistency, system or univocality.

Gomer's children deconstruct foundational binary oppositions, such as love–hate, inside–outside, legitimate–illegitimate, guilt–innocence. As their names endorse mutually exclusive judgments, so they move between the dichotomies represented by their parents, and deconstruct the text's foundational assumption that the woman-land is the guilty party, and that God-man is the victim of her behaviour. The distinction harlotry–marriage, legitimacy–illegitimacy, is also resisted by the children, since it is questionable whether they were born in or out of wedlock, and it is possible that Hosea is, and is not, their father. In the same way that they affirm the text's rhetoric (stand with the father) and deconstruct the text's rhetoric (stand with the mother), so the children affirm and deconstruct the text's affirmation of the woman's guilt, because they are undecideably legitimate and illegitimate, and refuse to corroborate unequivocally, or unequivocally resist, Hosea–God's accusation that his wife has been faithless.

The undecideability of the children is most audaciously exhibited by 'Jezreel', the ultimate pharmakon, that participates in and resists the distinctions Jezreel–Israel, place–time, sowing–scattering, affirmation–rejection, male–female. Like Derrida, Yhwh speaks punningly and gives a name/term that necessitates a split reading. His utterance of the name 'Jezreel' is an act of dis-Shem-ination and de-schematization, because, like *antre-entre* or *différance*, it defiantly evokes the rival meanings יִשְׂרָאֵל/יִזְרְעֶאל. As the signifier bifurcates into synonyms, so it splits to signify a time and a place, a point in history and a valley plain, and to evoke the opposite senses of sowing and of scattering seed, of blessing and curse. The historical event elicited opposite reactions from the prophets—Elisha sanctioned it, but Hosea associated it with 'blood'— though both claimed to speak in the name of Yhwh. The opposite semantic possibilities of sowing and scattering repeat this impasse in the mind of the reader, who, like Elisha-Hosea, is caught between blessing and curse, affirmation and rejection.

Jezreel, the historical site of battle, stages a war between competing senses. The tensions are never resolved; on the contrary, Jezreel becomes the site on which more and more puns are overlaid and in which antithetical meanings congregate. As Yhwh perversely brings together the incompatibles prophet and prostitute, so he leads opposite terms to converge 'in the same place': 'And in the place where it was said to them, "You are not my people", it shall be said to them, "Sons of the Living God"' (2.1). Since Jezreel is the only place mentioned, it appears to be the site of this collision,[409] just as in 2.2 it becomes the point of convergence for North and South, Judah and Israel, who are to congregate under the strange ambiguous banner Jezreel: 'And the people of Judah and the people of Israel shall be gathered together, and they shall appoint for themselves one head; and they shall go up from the land, for great shall be the day of Jezreel'.[410] Jezreel as a motif of a glorious future vies with Jezreel as a symbol of a dubious past. The eschatological vision of the anticipated 'great day' introduces a new temporal dichotomy, past–future, which Jezreel participates in and resists. Even in Hos. 2.24, the climax of Yhwh's vision of renewal, Jezreel does not come to rest in an unequivocally positive meaning, but continues to find new associations and new possibilities for ambiguation. Formerly associated with a male, it suddenly acquires a female gender, and the displacement suggests that even the most fundamental metaphor of the text's rhetoric, the gendered metaphor of man and wife, is not immune to the forces of deconstruction.

Hosea 1–3, like Plato's *Republic*, is a text that is radically disturbed by the riddle of the children. It involves a girl who is loved, and not; a boy who does and does not belong; and their brother Jezreel whose name is negative, and positive. Like Plato, critics have tried to tame the conflict of opposites to a paradox—that is, an aporia of meaning which is under the rhetorician's control—and to convince the reader that 'Paradoxically, we discover God's unconditioned love only through the negating of it'.[411] They base their argument on the fact that the positive names are triumphantly reiterated at the end of the text: 'And I will have pity (וְרִחַמְתִּי) on Not Pitied, and I will say to Not my People, "You are my people (עַמִּי-אַתָּה)"' (Hos. 2.25), but their attempt to convert the undecideable love–hate into 'the most reassuring of its poles' is deconstructed by the text itself, which begins by resisting the naive and simple affirmations Ruhamah and Ammi in Hos. 1.6 and 1.9. As Moore puts it, 'the critic, while appearing to grasp the meaning of the text from a position safely outside or above it, has unknowingly been grasped by the

---

409. This is the opinion of most commentators, for example J.L. Mays: 'The unnamed "place" where the names will be reversed must be Jezreel', *Hosea*, p. 32.

410. The one head or leader is, in an oblique way, a term *sous rature*. The leader is the non-king—another system that the prophet subverts is the monarchical system.

411. Fisch, 'Hosea: A Poetics of Violence', p. 145.

text and pulled into it'.[412] To assert that Israel is unequivocally, positively, loved and pitied, is to repeat the naive complacency of Israel,
which the text sets itself against and determinedly deconstructs.

By punning and playing on names, and linking the same name with
opposite concepts, Hosea 1–3 'radically suspends logic and opens up
vertiginous possibilities of referential aberration'.[413] As Rab Kahana
suggests, this makes it impossible to believe that the constantly shifting
names can ever be reconciled to a single, positive referent, or, as he puts
it, that a voice that speaks optimistically and pessimistically can ever
be trusted. Critics who try to reinstate the violent hierarchy negative–
positive (by arguing that curse is derived from, and always anticipates,
blessing, but that blessing is independent of, and effectively erases, curse)
find their position deconstructed by their own tortuous logic but also by
the text. For Yhwh's promise וְרִחַמְתִּי אֶת־לֹא רֻחָמָה וְאָמַרְתִּי לְלֹא־עַמִּי עַמִּי־אַתָּה is
not an unequivocal re-instatement of the positive, but an awkward sen-
tence in which opposites collide and the negative is repeated rather than
erased.

Hosea 1–3 'begins' with an act of palaeonymy that resists and retains
the names Ruhamah and Ammi by adding the prefix לֹא, and it 'ends'
with another act of palaeonymy that resists and retains the names Lo-
Ruhamah and Lo-Ammi. Both meanings, positive and negative, are
treated as 'old' names, which are deconstructively reinscribed in a way
that does not allow them to dominate but does not erase them completely. The text begins with a shocking *reversal* of the violent hierarchy
love–hate (in which Yhwh declares his alienation from Israel) and keeps
the hierarchy open, and prevents it from reforming, by an ongoing
(potentially infinite) chain of displacement. The effect of the text is circu-
lar rather than linear: the positive is deconstructed in Hos. 1.4-9, the
negative is deconstructed in 2.1, 3, 25, but any attempts to re-establish
the positive as the unequivocally dominant meaning lead back, inevitably, to the deconstruction of blessing in Hos. 1.4-9. The myopia of criticism in describing the text in terms of 'naming and renaming'[414] has
been to ignore the rules of *writing*. A double negative is not simply equivalent to a positive statement; similarly, according to the grammar or
logic of this text, calling a child Not-Not-Loved or Not-Not-My-People is

---

412. Moore, 'Deconstruction, Feminism and the Samaritan Woman', p. 211.
413. De Man, 'Semiology and Rhetoric' (1988), p. 129 (I have been unable to
trace further details for this reference).
414. Andersen and Freedman, *Hosea*, p. 142.

not the same as calling them Loved or My People. Ruhamah and Ammi as they emerge in Hos. 2.25 are not simple assertions but denials of a previous denial. As the poet A.R. Ammons suggests (see the quotation at the head of this section), in 'naming' we may 'have divided' what 'unnaming' will not 'undivide', because naming and unnaming are not equal and opposite actions but 'Two Motions' that bring into play the ineradicable operation of *différance*.

Like the Yhwh of Babel, Yhwh in Hosea 1–3 is an 'impish'[415] deconstructor. Like the God of Genesis 11 he seems to oppose the imposition of the univocal name and sets up a 'war between two...names',[416] between hate and love. The text leads to 'a set of assertions that radically exclude each other'[417] and leaves the reader wondering 'which words [he or she is] to believe', while at the same time 'destroying the foundations of any choice'.[418] The problem posed by this text is the problem of Babel, in that Yhwh de-schematizes and resists any system that can be deduced from the text.

Yhwh's Tour de Force: The Deconstruction of the Divine Name. By exploiting the undecideable 'Jezreel', and by repeatedly reinscribing Ruhamah and Ammi in mutually subverting acts of palaeonymy, Hosea 1–3 achieves its own kind of split writing. Yet by far the most radical deconstructive effect is Yhwh's negation of 'Yhwh' in Hos. 1.9, which deconstructs the most fundamental of hierarchies, between being and non-being, presence and absence. The divine name as it appears in the MT already states, as Derrida would put it, the 'impossibility of translation', and because it can be written but not spoken, it challenges the most fundamental logocentric hierarchy between writing and speech. As Derrida demonstrates, speech is associated with presence and writing with absence, but Yhwh is present in writing but absent in speech.

Yhwh's declaration in Hos. 1.8 resists the hierarchy presence–absence, being–non-being, in a way that is even more explicit. יְהוָה, the God whose name is a predicate of being, pronounces לֹא־אֶהְיֶה לָכֶם. Being and non-being collide as the speaker, introduced as 'Yhwh', pronounces his own non-existence and the negation of 'Yhwh'. The speech of Yhwh is

---

415. H. Bloom, *Ruin the Sacred Truths: Poetry and Belief from the Bible to the Present* (Cambridge, MA: Harvard University Press, 1989), p. 6.

416. Derrida, *The Ear of the Other*, p. 101.

417. De Man, *Allegories of Reading*, p. 245.

418. De Man, *Allegories of Reading*, p. 245.

a guarantee of presence, but presence is deconstructed in a statement that places presence and being under erasure and opens out, as Harold Fisch puts it, into an 'abyss of absence'.[419] Like the syllogism 'all my statements are lies', Yhwh's statement about the non-existence of Yhwh defies the principles of Western logic. The effect is similar to the naming of the prophet's third son as Not-My-People, in which a person is called a non-person, in a flagrant transgression of logical possibility. As Yhwh is present in writing, but absent in speech, so the declaration לֹא־אֶהְיֶה לָכֶם makes לֹא־אֶהְיֶה—יְהֹוָה an absent presence to Israel. By speaking and negating himself, Yhwh denies the possibility of the two most common transcendental signifieds—the speaking subject, and the divinity—who in this text are united in a single voice.

Like Yhwh, לֹא אֶהְיֶה demonstrates the impossibility of translation: commentators have variously suggested 'I am not your God', 'I am not *I Am* to you' or 'I will not be'.[420] The first translation (from the RSV) effectively dilutes the deconstructive force of the statement by emphasizing לָכֶם (to you) at the expense of the pun on the copula, and misses the point that the statement is also a punning act of palaeonymy and a play on Yhwh's self-identification in Exod. 3.14, אֶהְיֶה אֲשֶׁר אֶהְיֶה. Even the 'original' name opens up the hierarchy between identity and non-identity, because it is at once a definition and an evasion of definition, a name and no name at all. Yhwh's self-definition recoils back on himself, and if he will be who he will be, the divine 'name' is a cue for a series of infinite displacements.

The text of Hosea exploits this potential for displacement, and the logical problems implicit in the concept of self-definition. The statement לֹא אֶהְיֶה is an act of reversal and displacement that inverts the hierarchy being–non-being *and* keeps the hierarchy open. Absence and negation are foregrounded in a shocking linguistic act in which being is neither eliminated, nor allowed to dominate. לֹא אֶהְיֶה, like the names Lo-Ruhamah and Lo-Ammi, retains the old name even as it reverses it, and being is always a possibility (albeit repressed), because even as Yhwh declares his non-existence, he speaks. The text destroys confidence in the 'I' that speaks by opening up the gap between being and non-being. Though the narrator persists in calling the deity 'Yhwh', Yhwh never refers to himself with the positive statement of being, I AM. Unlike Ruhamah and Ammi, the name אֶהְיֶה אֲשֶׁר אֶהְיֶה is only implied through its

419. Fisch, 'Hosea: A Poetics of Violence', p. 144.
420. Fisch, 'Hosea: A Poetics of Violence', p. 144.

negation and is never spoken by Yhwh in reference to himself. The way
in which Yhwh speaks of himself deconstructs the simple faith of the
narrator, who refers to the deity constantly as 'Yhwh', or 'He who will
be', 'He who *is*'.

Against the narrative convention that gives 'Yhwh' a constant name
and identity, God presents (and absents) himself in a chain of bizarre
signifiers that deny the possibility of a stable signified. The narrator
affirms the constancy of God's being and invokes the copula every time
he uses the divine name, but in v. 2.1 'Yhwh' renames himself אֱלֹהָי in a
name based not on the copula הָיָה but on the virtual synonym חָיָה. The
verb 'to be' is displaced and reinscribed, and this is only the first in a
long chain of displacements in which God 'is', variously, pus and infection (5.12), lion (5.14), bear (13.7-8), trapper (7.12), vulture (8.1), farmer
(10.11), husband (2.16-25), parent (11.8-9), lover (14.3-7), and tree
(14.8). As in the case of 'wilderness' or 'nakedness', the senses are not
merely diverse but mutually exclusive and God 'presents' himself,
undecideably, as hunter and hunted, man and animal, infection and
protection, pus and parent.

'I was not one man only', says the narrator of Proust's *A la
recherche du temps perdu*, 'but the steady advance hour after hour of
an army in close formation, in which there appeared, according to the
moment, impassioned men, indifferent men, jealous men'.[421] Like
Proust's narrator, Hosea's Yhwh is impossible to 'conceive of as a single
person',[422] and denies the reader a stable centre, or as Gayatari Spivak
puts it, a 'sovereign subject who is the origin of the book'.[423]
'Problematic' and 'difficult' are in fact incredibly restrained adjectives
for a text that shockingly subverts the most fundamental logocentric
conventions. As the text deconstructs its own ideals of pure unadulterated origins, of Yhwh's supremacy over Baal, and the ascendancy of the
positive over the negative, so it also deconstructs the voice behind the
text, the transcendental certainty that is Yhwh himself. The text not only
resists the ideal of the book, the unified and systematic whole which the
reader can somehow master, but also the idea of the author and origin
of the book. As deity and speaker of the text Yhwh is the ultimate transcendental signified, but, like the text itself, he is impossible to conceive

---

421. M. Proust, 'The Fugitive', *A la recherche du temps perdu* (trans.
C.K.S. Moncrieff; New York: Vintage Books, 1970), p. 54.

422. Proust, 'The Fugitive', p. 54.

423. Spivak, 'Translator's Preface', *Of Grammatology*, p. xi.

of as a single entity and is fragmented, even to the extent that his very existence is at one point (1.9) placed 'under erasure'.

5. *Concluding Comments*

Hosea opens with the most logocentric of promises: דְּבַר־יְהוָה אֲשֶׁר הָיָה אֶל־הוֹשֵׁעַ בֶּן־בְּאֵרִי. The 'word' (the noun is singular) seems to be a unified communicative 'package' that has come to the prophet from God himself, and presumably, can just as easily be transferred to the reader. Like the words in Hos. 14.2 that the prophet urges the people to 'take with [them]', this word appears to be a solid, definable entity that can, as it were, be picked up and transferred to the audience. In Derrida's terms, the 'word' is the ultimate symbol of logocentrism, the promise of a self-contained meaning, like the 'book'; it is also a promise that the text cannot keep, as it traps the reader in an endless series of competing and mutually subverting statements.

All texts can be deconstructed, but Hosea 1–3, almost perversely, seems to lay bare the basis of its deconstruction. To deconstruct this text it is not necessary to make the same kind of subtle and erudite linkages that Derrida makes within the texts of Rousseau, Kant or Plato; significantly, whereas no one prior to Derrida had noted the tendency of these texts to subvert their own arguments, several biblical critics, such as Harold Fisch or Michael Catlett, have already noted the tendency of Hosea 1–3 to, as Catlett puts it, 'turn on its axis'. The undecideable tensions, between innocence and deviance, Yhwh and Baal, love and hate, are not concealed deep within the text's structure; they are not marginal, like Kant's parerga, but are central, and essential, to the text. The way in which the text seems audaciously to contradict its main theses suggests that it is surprisingly unconstrained by ideals of consistency, coherence and foolproof argumentation, and this raises the question, '(How) does a text, originating from the Near East in the eighth century BCE, fit into the category of "Western Metaphysics"'?

The processes of describing the 'nature' of a text or the 'intentions' of its author are, as I have already argued, hazardous critical activities; similarly, in the wake of Barr's *The Semantics of Biblical Language*,[424] it is extremely difficult to extrapolate from the structure of the language of the text to its philosophical context, and to make easy distinctions

424. J. Barr, *The Semantics of Biblical Language* (Oxford: Oxford University Press, 1961).

between 'Hebraic' and 'Hellenistic' modes of thought. However, without using reductive labels such as 'Hellenistic' or 'Hebraic', or making (in a strongly Hellenistic manner) distinctions between 'the diversive, distinction-forming analytic type of Greek thought' and 'the totality type of Hebrew thought',[425] I nevertheless want to fight my way through qualifying clauses and suggest that there is dissonance and difference between Western scholarly expectations of a text and the standards by which this particular text operates. Hosea 1–3 does, quite clearly, make distinctions (for example between harlotry and fidelity, curse and blessing, Yhwh and Baal), but at the same time it does not seem overtly concerned about subverting those distinctions, or contravening the 'law of the excluded middle'. The assumption that to support the thesis, one must disprove or denounce the antithesis, is not reflected in this text: thus Yhwh is delineated from Baal and described in terms associated with Baal, and the text simultaneously pursues one kind of action (blessing, reconciliation) and its opposite (denunciation, violence, imprisonment and curse).

Like Borges encountering the classic Chinese novel,[426] I want to underline the otherness of this text, which seems so audaciously to move in different directions at once. I do not want to conclude, however, that as an ancient Near Eastern text Hosea 1–3 somehow precedes or transcends the category 'Western metaphysics', for although the term is confusing, Derrida uses it to refer to all texts based on the idea of a pure first term (such as 'goodness' or 'purity') and a secondary derivation or corruption (such as 'impurity' or 'evil'). As a text that describes the people's 'fall' into apostasy and that calls them back to a pure relation to Yhwh, Hosea 1–3 can hardly be classed as outside the category of 'Western metaphysics', but at the same time it embodies an attitude to coherence and unity that does not quite fit with the totality that we also expect from a 'Western metaphysical' text. One of the 'problems' with this text may be that it does not correspond to the criteria conventionally used to analyse it, for whereas Western texts 'choose one [alternative] at the expense of the others', this text 'chooses—

425. Barr, *The Semantics of Biblical Language*, p. 10.
426. I am referring to Borges's 'The Garden of Forking Paths', in which he analyses the distinctive features of *Ts' ui pen,* the classical Chinese novel (see J.L. Borges, 'The Garden of Forking Paths', in *Ficciones* [trans. A. Kerrigan; New York: Grove Press, 1962]).

simultaneously, all of them', and 'creates various futures', 'branches', 'bifurcations', and so, inevitably, 'contradictions'.[427]

427. Borges, 'The Garden of Forking Paths', p. 98.

Chapter 4

GOMER'S MARRIAGE: A FEMINIST ANALYSIS OF HOSEA 1–3

In this chapter I want to draw together and develop themes and ideas from preceding chapters in a feminist reading of Hosea 1–3. Such a reading has already been hinted at: I have already considered reactions to (or against) the 'wife of harlotry', and suggested that Gomer represents a subversive counter-voice who weans (and presumably suckles) the children that Hosea rejects, and who intimates a certain lack in Yhwh/Hosea that leads her to desert him for other lovers. Though she has generally been characterized as 'provocative' in a merely sexual sense, I have suggested that she is provocative in more ways than one, and that her character suggests some thought-provoking tensions which have led me to describe her as the 'ultimate undecideable' of the text. In this chapter I want to explore in more detail the tensions of Gomer's role, and the tensions of my reaction, as a feminist, to this ideologically 'problematic' narrative.

The first stage of this analysis is, as the inverted title implies, a reconsideration of issues raised in Chapter 1. In this chapter I meta-commentate from a different angle, from feminist premises, and investigate whether the presentation of woman in these texts supports the feminist commonplace that women in androcentric texts are not entities in their own right, with their own feelings and desires, but a looking-glass for patriarchal ideology. 'Woman' as 'looking-glass' is a recurrent motif in feminist criticism, from Virginia Woolf's famous statement that women in fiction function as 'looking-glasses possessing the magic and delicious power of reflecting the figure of man at twice its natural size'[1] to Luce Irigaray's and Josette Féral's theory of 'specularization', in which 'Woman' is an image in the sense of phantom, 'a pure *ungraspable* reflection', the '*virtual* other side of the

1. V. Woolf, *A Room of One's Own* (New York: Harcourt Brace & World, 1929), p. 35.

mirror' who 'reflects back to man the inverse image of what he...wants himself to be'.[2] In the first section of this chapter I want to consider how the woman is represented, and to scrutinize, and problematize, the issue of solidarity between androcentric texts and readers.

If 'woman' in patriarchal texts is a looking-glass for the dominant ideology, then the task of feminist criticism is to step through the looking glass, like Alice, and to retrieve the female character from her 'virtual'[3] and reflective role. In the second section I go on to meta-commentate on responses to this text from female scholars, and to investigate the tensions between seeing through one's own eyes from a female point of view, and seeing oneself and representations of women as the object of the male gaze and the subject of androcentric definitions. Having explored possibilities for a feminist 'method' (§3), I attempt my own lateral inversion of critical tradition in the reading 'Gomer's Marriage', which inverts the critical obsession with Hosea's Marriage and emphasizes what the text represses: that the marriage is Gomer's as well as Hosea's, and that it is extremely problematic from a woman's point of view. Inverting a text and a tradition that has always presented the woman as a problem for patriarchy, I take the woman as a standard of judgment and explore how the premises of patriarchy are a problem for her.

1. *Comments on Metacommentary: A Feminist Reappraisal*

That which you are, that only can you read.[4]

According to Adrienne Munich, 'canonical texts' pass into culture 'tagged with a patriarchal interpretation and validated by what the Institution of Reading has understood'.[5] Munich suggests that readings and texts are canonized, but I would take this further: my analysis of

---

2.   J. Féral, 'Towards a Theory of Displacement', *Substance* 32 (1981), pp. 52-64 (55). For a discussion of Luce Irigaray's theory of specularization, see T. Moi, 'Patriarchal Reflections: Luce Irigaray's Looking-Glass', in *Sexual/Textual Politics: Feminist Literary Theory* (London: Methuen, 1985), pp. 127-49.

3.   In biblical narratives women's roles are often 'virtual' in another sense: they are partial roles, bit parts in stories enacted by male protagonists.

4.   H. Bloom, *Kabbalah and Criticism* (New York: Seabury, 1975), p. 96.

5.   A. Munich, 'Notorious Signs: Feminist Criticism and Literary Criticism', in G. Greene and C. Kahn (eds.), *Making a Difference: Feminist Literary Criticism* (London: Methuen, 1985), pp. 238-59 (251).

commentary in Chapter 1 suggested that readers make texts, and thus, that the reading is not only canonical like 'the text', but that it becomes, effectively, synonymous with it. Inevitably, where the dominant interpretative community has always been male, a male reading is fully equated with 'the text', and this interpretation passes into popular culture. Thus when Daphne Hampson tried to suggest, in a recent article in *The Independent*, that she found the text of Hosea 'pornographic',[6] her reading met with accusations that she had misread and had not done 'the great Israelite prophet Hosea' justice, by failing to make clear that 'he loved his fickle wife and could not bear to see her destroyed by the inevitable results of her wayward behaviour'.[7] Though her critic's reading was itself dependent on a romanticized interpretation promoted by commentators such as T.K. Cheyne, George Farr and G.A.F. Knight, he accused Hampson of her 'failure' to 'make clear' and her 'failure' to 'notice', as if his reading were implicit within, or actually constituted, the text. The pervasive optical illusion that has allowed an affinity between a reading and a dominant interpretative community to be interpreted as an affinity between the reading and 'the text' results in a critical double standard whereby the traditional androcentric reading is authorized as legitimate and objective, and the feminist reading is perceived as subjective excursion into fantasy and a departure from 'the text'.

The hierarchy between objective androcentric readings and subjective feminist readings is another variation on the archetypal prejudice that men are rational and women emotional, and that men 'deduce' while women 'feel'. The male is the standard and the woman the deviant; the man possesses the text and the woman is banished or strays beyond/outside it. I am concerned that the way that some feminist scholars describe their experience of biblical texts actually redefines, rather than challenges, this hierarchy. Phrases like 'reading against the grain'[8] or the idea that feminist readings take place within the silences and lacunae of the text are helpful but need to be qualified, because they may inadvertently suggest that androcentric readings by default read with the grain and are somehow exempt from the subjective business of gap-filling. The commentator who sees his own readings as dictated by

---

6. D. Hampson, 'Christianity will always be a male religion', letter in *The Independent*, 15 November 1992.

7. Letter from A.A. Macintosh, *The Independent*, 16 November 1992.

8. J.C. Exum, *Fragmented Women: Feminist (Sub)versions of Biblical Narratives* (JSOTSup, 163; Sheffield: JSOT Press, 1993), p. 11.

the text and who regards feminism as the subjective 'other' or a 'sect'[9] finds his stereotypes confirmed when feminist critics foreground their rebelliousness or the inventiveness of their readings. As Elizabeth Meese points out, a feminist critique that leaves 'oppositional logic in place...as the unquestioned ground and limit of thought' merely proposes 'cosmetic modifications on the face of humanism and its institutions' and 'reproduces the structure of woman's exclusion in the same code which has been extended to include her'.[10]

If traditional power structures reinforce the marginalization of feminist critics by establishing an illusion of 'choral harmony' between 'authoritative narrators' and 'objective critics', father texts and faithful sons,[11] then a feminist critique needs to confront this sense of mutual affirmation and the 'objective phallacy' (as Esther Fuchs wryly puts it) on which it is founded. The sense that objectivity is an illusion evolves from Cady Stanton's exasperated accusation that 'men have read their own selfish theories into the book'[12] into Cheryl Exum's claim that 'neutral reading' is merely a synonym for 'androcentric reading',[13] but unlike Cady Stanton's complaint, contemporary feminist critiques of the politics of 'objectivity' fit into a wider context of reader-response.[14]

9.   Joan W. Scott cites an instance of an eminent historian who asked a graduate student to delete a reference to 'feminist historians' from her thesis, as she was 'writing for all historians, not for a sect' (in B. Christian *et al.*, 'Conference Call: Notes From The Beehive: Feminism and the Institution', *Differences* 2 [1990], pp. 52-109 [83]).

10.   E.A. Meese, *Crossing the Double Cross: The Practice of Feminist Criticism* (Chapel Hill, NC: University of North Carolina Press, 1986), p. 143.

11.   E. Fuchs, 'The Objective Phallacy', in V.L. Tollers and J. Maier (eds.), *Mappings of the Biblical Terrain: The Bible as Text* (Toronto: Bucknell University Press, 1990), pp. 134-42 (138).

12.   E. Cady Stanton (ed.), *The Original Feminist Attack on the Bible: The Woman's Bible* (New York: Allo, 1974), p. 8.

13.   Exum, *Fragmented Women*, p. 12.

14.   The intersection of feminism and reader-response theory also suggests a reply to feminists such as Marian Lowe and Margaret Lowe Benston, who argue that feminists must detach themselves from the objectivity of the academy if they are to preserve the 'radical goals of feminist scholarship' (M. Lowe and M. Lowe Benston, 'The Uneasy Alliance of Feminism and Academia', in S. Gunew [ed.], *A Reader In Feminist Knowledge* [London: Routledge, 1991], pp. 48-60 [48]). Their thesis depends on a parody of scholarship as 'unemotional and uninvolved' (p. 52), and ascribes to feminists alone the 'recognition of the way personal bias can affect scholarly work' (p. 49), but this view of academia is itself biased and antiquated, and

From David Bleich's statement that readers invoke 'the text' to support their 'moralistic claim[s]...that one's own objectification is more authoritative than someone else's',[15] it is a short step to the recognition that objectivity is a political tool that has legitimated and naturalized androcentric readings. The relative power of interpretative communities has not been the concern of a largely male guild of reader-response theorists,[16] and it has been the task of feminist critics such as Annette Kolodny and Patricinio Schweickhart[17] to point out that theories of misreading call attention to, in Kolodny's words, 'interpretative strategies that are learned, historically determined, and thereby necessarily gender-inflected'.[18]

Kolodny's observation comes from a re-reading of Bloom's study of re-reading and his investigation of the relation between critics and texts. Writing from an androcentric point of view, Bloom assumes that the critical inheritance passes through the white male line, but also intriguingly describes misreading in Oedipal terms in which the critic son is made anxious by, and seeks to modify or displace, the father text. Since he describes the act of misreading in specifically male terms, Bloom suggests that men as well as women are 'resisting readers'.[19] Bloom assigns disobedience, transgression and subjectivity specifically to the male reader, and problematizes from outside the realm of women's studies the hierarchies set up between objective and subjective, obedient

selectively ignores the crisis of authority posed by the self-conscious subjectivity of reader-response theories and poststructuralism.

15. D. Bleich, *Subjective Criticism* (Baltimore: Johns Hopkins University Press, 1978), p. 112.

16. Jonathan Culler is one of the few critics who raises the question, 'If the meaning of a work is in the experience of a reader, what difference does it make if the reader is a woman?' (*On Deconstruction: Theory and Criticism after Structuralism* [London: Routledge, 1993], p. 42).

17. P. Patricinio Schweickhart, 'Reading Ourselves: Towards a Feminist Theory of Reading', in E. Showalter (ed.), *Speaking of Gender* (New York: Routledge, 1989), pp. 17-44.

18. A. Kolodny, 'A Map for Rereading: Gender and the Interpretation of Literary Texts', in E. Showalter (ed.), *The New Feminist Criticism: Essays on Women, Literature and Theory* (London: Virago, 1986), pp. 46-62 (47).

19. Bloom is not a feminist and his relationship to feminism is ambiguous. In *The Book of J* he argues that 'J' is a female author, but in *A Map of Misreading* he writes, dismissively if not disparagingly, that he has very little to say about what he vaguely terms 'the literature of women's liberation' (H. Bloom, *A Map of Misreading* [Oxford: Oxford University Press, 1975], p. 36).

and disobedient, and by implication androcentric and feminist (mis)readings.

Like Bloom's analysis of misreading, my own readings of commentary in Chapter 1 challenged the subjective–objective division and the borders between commentary and fiction, and problematized the assumption that the imagination is a specifically female domain or that rebellion is an exclusively feminist quality. If misreading is an inevitability rather than a crime, there is effectively no difference between radical feminist readings of the text and traditional commentaries; the difference lies not in their inventiveness or their relation to 'the text', but in their self-consciousness about that inventiveness[20] and their status. Because the human is eclipsed by the divine, and both Hosea and Gomer are merely puppets in Yhwh's cosmic morality play, there is no domestic detail from a male or female perspective[21] and no more evidence to support the idea of 'a man wounded in his deepest feelings through an ill-fated marriage that saddened his life and coloured his thought'[22] than to identify Gomer, as some feminist critics are beginning to do, with the subversive power of female Canaanite deities.[23] Even commentators themselves concede that 'the book...has extremely little help to give us about the prophet himself'[24] and so covertly admit, as the feminist

20. The tendency of feminist criticism to problematize 'truth' and to foreground 'the role of the reader in determining meaning' (Exum, *Fragmented Women*, p. 12) predates the influence of reader-response criticism. As early as 1929 Virginia Woolf wrote, 'when a subject is highly controversial—and any question about sex is that— one cannot hope to tell the truth. One can only show how one came to hold whatever opinion one does hold' (*A Room of One's Own*, p. 4).

21. In claiming that as much information is given about Gomer as about Hosea, I am not trying to covertly redeem Hosea as a non-patriarchal text, or to displace all culpability from text to interpretation. To say that a text sides with one character and that a text gives more information about one character is to say two completely different things: one is a statement about ideology and the other a statement about detail. Gomer and Hosea are 'equal' in one sense only, in the scanty information that is given about them.

22. C.H. Toy, 'Note on Hosea 1–3', *JBL* 32 (1913), pp. 75-79 (77).

23. For examples of this type of approach see H. Balz-Cochois, 'Gomer oder die Macht der Astarte: Versuch einer feministischen Interpretation von Hos. 1–4', *EvT* 42 (1982), pp. 37-65; M. Wacker, 'Frau–Sexus–Macht: Eine feministische Relecture des Hoseabuches', in Wacker, *Der Gott der Männer und der Frauen* (Theologie zur Zeit, 2; Düsseldorf: Patmos, 1987), pp. 101-25.

24. G. von Rad, *Old Testament Theology*. II. *The Theology of Israel's Prophetic Traditions* (trans. D.M.G. Stalker; Edinburgh: Oliver & Boyd, 1965), p. 138.

overtly admits, that they are reading 'between the lines'. J. Paterson, for example, admits that 'the one fact the prophet tells us concerning himself is that he married Gomer bat Diblayim who bore him three children and was guilty of marital infidelity'. Ironically, he then goes on to describe how Hosea sublimated his sex instinct into love for God and man, how he married a woman who disappointed him, and how he 'discovered the gospel buried deep in...his suffering' and so became 'essentially an evangelist, a prophet of grace'.[25]

Though the commentaries I analysed in Chapter 1 are chronologically and culturally diverse, they are ideologically united in their reaction against the 'wife of harlotry'. The verdict is that the unclean woman, the shrew, the טְמֵאָה, must be tamed, and though the boundaries are by no means distinct, four major strategies for controlling her begin to emerge. Ibn Ezra and Maimonides attempt to *contain* her by enclosing her in the realm of dream; Luther confines her to the quasi-reality of the stage; and later commentators, such as Keil and Delitzsch, confine her to the internal psychological world of the prophet. Critics such as Rudolph or Cheyne *humiliate* her by underlining the analogy between her name and 'shame' or describing her as a 'lily torn and trodden in the mire',[26] yet at the same time seem to savour the image of the fallen woman and revel in the contemplation of, as Cheyne puts it, the 'rustic beauty of Northern Israel'.[27] The targumist and Calvin *erase* her altogether, preferring to use fig leaves or figs as an innocuous substitute. Most commonly critics seek to *improve* the promiscuous woman, to work some kind of critical redemption by, for example, diluting her offence from 'wife of harlotry' to 'wife of lethargy', elevating her to the status of saint, or erasing her 'harlotry' by redaction.

The ideology of commentary that interprets the woman as a threat to be mitigated reinforces the assumptions of the text. Moreover, the strategies used to control her—restriction, humiliation, erasure and improvement—imitate the strategies of control described in the text. As commentary consigns Gomer to a dream, a play or a parenthesis, Yhwh/Hosea threaten to contain her by 'hedg[ing] up her way with thorns and build[ing] a wall against her' (Hos. 2.6). Both attempt to box

---

25. J. Paterson, 'Hosea', in F.C. Grant and H.H. Rowley (eds.), *A Dictionary of the Bible* (Edinburgh: T. & T. Clark, 2nd edn, 1963), p. 397.

26. T.K. Cheyne, *Hosea: With Notes and Introduction* (Cambridge Bible Commentary; Cambridge: Cambridge University Press, 1887), p. 20.

27. Cheyne, *Hosea*, p. 15.

her in or restrict her influence: one by a subtle use of words, and the other, more graphically, by hemming her in with walls and thorn bushes. The rhetoric of the text, like that of the commentaries, is extreme, and most extremely threatens to erase the woman altogether. As her male controllers outside the text attempt to eliminate the pernicious woman from it, so her male controllers within the text threaten to remove her by slaying her with thirst (Hos. 2.3). However, the reaction to the promiscuous woman is not without its tensions, as the ambiguous reaction of Cheyne might suggest. As condemnation and fascination mingle in Cheyne's response, so the text, far more graphically, combines titillation and humiliation in the threat to strip the promiscuous wife in the sight of her lovers (Hos. 2.10).

A comparison between commentary and text suggests that commentators are, like henchmen, carrying out the threats of the text issued against the unco-operative woman in Hosea 2. 'Objectivity' is an illusion created by ideological mimicry: the androcentric commentator is the 'faithful son' of the father text in the sense that he carries out and extends the father's wishes. Male commentators also follow the impulse of the male protagonist Yhwh/Hosea when they seek to 'redeem' the errant woman: just as the text demands an impossible return to innocence in which she will be made to respond 'as in the days of her youth' (Hos. 2.3; 15), so commentators strain at the very limits of possibility to redeem her reputation and bestow on her her 'long overdue halo'.[28] Critics not only empathize with Yhwh/Hosea's insistence that the woman must be pressed into moral conformity, but can be even more forceful than the text in their demands for reformation. L. Bouyer, for example, not only sympathizes with a love that 'would not tolerate any stain in his beloved', but reinforces Hosea's convictions with his own when he writes, emphatically, that Hosea wanted her 'pure, as on the first day of her marriage' and needed to give her a 'new and unalterable virginity'.[29]

As Hosea is said to enter into the consciousness of God,[30] so commentators enter into the consciousness of the prophet, creating a trinity of sympathy that unites against the female. However, although the tendency for commentators to side with the male characters reinforces the

28. L.W. Batten, 'Hosea's Marriage and Message', *JBL* 48 (1929), pp. 257-73 (257).

29. L. Bouyer, *La Bible et l'évangile* (Paris, 1951), p. 66.

30. Von Rad, *Old Testament Theology*, II, p. 140.

ideological link between commentator and text, it has some peculiar consequences for the text's symbolic structure. On the one hand, text and commentator unite in the desire to reshape the woman according to the desires of a stringent and sometimes violent purism, and the commentator's refusal to give Gomer a voice, or to empathise with her in any way, effectively duplicates the ideology of a text that allows her no voice of her own and filters her opinions through reported speech. On the other hand, by refusing to identify himself with Gomer, the commentator becomes a 'resisting'[31] rather than an acquiescent reader because he resists the symbolic role assigned to readers of the text. The symbolic structure of the text equates Gomer with the people of God, and Hosea with Yhwh, yet male commentators align themselves without exception with the prophet and the deity. This may be explained by a desire to stand on the side of right, to present oneself as censor rather than censored, but comparison with reactions to the Parable of the Prodigal suggest a more complex explanation.[32] Even as they criticize a 'heart swayed by licentious appetites', critics such as F. Godet are quite prepared to offer excuses on the prodigal's behalf:

> Two things impel him to act thus: the air of his father's home oppresses him, he feels the constraint of his father's presence; then the world without attracts him, he hopes to enjoy himself[33]

31. I use the term 'resisting reader' here quite deliberately, because since the term was first used by Judith Fetterly, it has been associated exclusively with feminist criticism (see J. Fetterly, *The Resisting Reader: A Feminist Approach to American Fiction* [Bloomington: Indiana University Press, 1978]).

32. The story of Gomer has often been shaped by comparison with the story of the prodigal son. G.W. Anderson, for example, reads Hosea in the light of the Lukan parable and sees Gomer's story as another variation on the plot 'sick of home; homesick; home' ('Hosea and Yahweh: God's Love Story', *RevExp* 72 [1975], pp. 425-36 [425]).

33. F. Godet, *Commentary on St Luke's Gospel*, II (trans. M.D. Cusin; Edinburgh: T. & T. Clark, 1957), p. 150. Although, like Gomer's return, the return of the prodigal is attributed to pragmatic and materialistic reasoning (the prodigal reasons, 'How many of my father's hired servants have bread enough and to spare, but I perish here with hunger' [Lk. 15.17], while Gomer 'says', 'I will go and return to my first husband for it was better with me then than now' [Hos. 2.7]), Godet makes much of the prodigal's faith and courage, observing, 'Here is faith in all its fulness, actually arising, going to God' (p. 153). There is no equivalent praise of Gomer.

or to express sympathy for one who has made 'foolish choices' but 'learnt in the school of hard knocks'.[34] This tendency to empathize with the prodigal son is markedly different from attempts to soften Gomer's offence: one approach enters into the consciousness of the offender and tries to see the text from his point of view, while the other focuses on improving Gomer's status in order to dilute the moral offence of the text and solve the problem of guilt by association.

To call the people of God 'woman', and even more disturbingly 'promiscuous woman', is, in a patriarchal context, to give offence. Mary Joan Winn Leith makes this point from a historical perspective: following Phyllis Bird she argues that the prophet was likely to be addressing a largely male audience and suggests, therefore, that the text is 'playing on male fears of the woman as "other" '.[35] Citing ancient Near Eastern curses in which men are threatened with the prospect of becoming 'women', or even worse 'prostitutes',[36] she gestures, almost super-fluously, to a historical context in which 'woman' was perceived as a term of denigration. What she does not say is that similar principles apply in a contemporary context: as Dale Spender's analysis in *Man Made Language* shows, 'woman' is still a term of abuse when applied to men,[37] and male readers of the text still take offence and resist the textual audacity that equates all people with the humiliating role of the female.

34. J. Nolland, *Luke 9.21–18.34* (WBC; Dallas: Word Books, 1993), p. 789.

35. M.J. Winn Leith, 'Verse and Reverse: The Transformation of the Woman Israel in Hosea 1–3', in P.L. Day (ed.), *Gender and Difference in Ancient Israel* (Minneapolis: Fortress Press, 1989), pp. 95-108 (98).

36. Winn Leith cites a curse from a vassal treaty of Esarhaddon—'May [the gods] spin you like a spindle whorl, may they use you like a woman in the sight of your enemy' (J.B. Pritchard [ed.], *Ancient Near Eastern Texts Relating to the Old Testament* [trans. E. Reiner; Princeton: Princeton University Press, 2nd edn 1955], p. 533)—and a treaty between Ashnurnirari V of Assyria and Mati'ilu of Arpad—'If Mati'ilu sins against this treaty with Ashnurnirari...may Mati'ilu become a prosti-tute, his soldiers women, may they receive [a gift] in the square of their cities (i.e. publicly) like any prostitute' (*ANET*, p. 540, trans. D.J. Wiseman).

37. While I do not agree with feminists who argue that language is an irredeem-ably male construct, I agree with Dale Spender that 'The relationship between sex and semantics is not occasional'. 'Mistress' and 'courtesan', for example, have become tainted, while 'master' and 'courtier' have retained their status; as Spender comments, 'Woman does not share equal status with man (linguistically or other-wise) because woman has become pejorated while man has remained pure and untainted' (*Man Made Language* [London: Pandora Press, 1990], p. 17).

In resisting identification with the woman, androcentric commentators support the ideology of the text but resist its symbolic roles. A similar tension emerges in the treatment of Hos. 1.2 and the statement that the prophet married an אֵשֶׁת זְנוּנִים. Critical refusal to tolerate such a woman reinforces the text's ideology—that men can issue ultimatums about how their brides must look/ behave—but paradoxically, the critics reinforce this ideology specifically by denying the text's detail. Like the prophet, they find themselves unable to resign themselves to the wife of harlotry, but this leads them to resist the text in its offensive declaration that the prophet deliberately took for his wife a promiscuous woman.

A close reading of commentary suggests that there is a vital difference between ideological affinity and objective fidelity to the text. Neither feminist nor androcentric readings diligently follow all textual detail, and both types of readers are forced by the text's sparseness to read between the lines. In terms of the technicalities of the text such as its symbolism and detail, there are cases in which the feminist reader may read more 'with the grain' than her androcentric predecessors. The feminist project of identifying oneself with the female in the text affirms the text's symbolic structure, and in this case feminist readers are the acquiescent readers and their androcentric predecessors the opposing countervoice.

Where the feminist reader cannot be acquiescent, and where it is dangerous for her to be so, is in her response to the text's ideology. She can recount women's victimization but not perpetuate it, and must read cunningly, and tactically, to avoid a situation in which women are complicit in the degradation of their sex. As Jonathan Culler puts it, feminist criticism is an attempt to alter conditions of reading and of culture so that 'women will not be led to co-operate in making women scapegoats'.[38] The task is to create an ideological space of their own and to avoid a looking-glass mentality in which 'identity is what you say you are according to what they say you can be'.[39]

As male critics have automatically empathized with 'poor dejected, spurned and broken-hearted Hosea',[40] and have faithfully imitated in their commentaries the actions and attitudes of the male characters in

---

38. Culler, *On Deconstruction*, p. 54.

39. J. Johnston, *Lesbian Nation: The Feminist Solution* (New York: Simon & Schuster, 1973), p. 68.

40. G.A.F. Knight, *Hosea: Introduction and Commentary* (London: SCM Press, 1960), p. 25.

the text, so feminist criticism, in reply, might extrapolate from Gomer's actions in the text in an act of counter-criticism. Gomer's role is to pose a problem for patriarchy, as the land poses a problem for Yhwh: her function in the text is to be so difficult and defiant that she has, ultimately, to be hemmed in and locked away (Hos. 2.8; 3.3). She runs away from male coercion and control, and threatens to bring the ideological edifice down (by consorting with Canaanite lovers and by placing the guarantee of paternity in jeopardy). Similarly, the feminist critic might work against the text not by resisting the text's description of the woman's function, but by following it stubbornly to the letter. As Alice Bach has noted, the task of feminist criticism is to form an 'alliance with the female character[s] in the text':[41] the resisting reader joins with the resisting character to consolidate a strategy of resistance and to explore, as Mary Jacobus puts it, the 'difference of view'.[42]

2. 'A "Right Strawy Epistle" for the Women's Bible':[43] Some Women's Responses to Hosea 1–3

There is no haven of the mind, no art is pure of ideology and politics, books are powerful weapons because they transform our sense of reality, how we read is a political self-declaration.[44]

In the background of patriarchal texts are women trying to escape into readability.[45]

The rise of the feminist movement, which has provided a context for women to critique their positions in society and in texts, has meant that Hosea has become 'problematic' in a way that Jerome could never have anticipated. The problem for the feminist scholar is not the fragmented nature of the text, its shifting sign-language, nor its potential threat to the

---

41. A. Bach, 'Good to the Last Drop: Viewing the Sotah (Numbers 5.11-31) as the Glass Half Empty and Wondering How to View it Half Full', in J.C. Exum and D.J.A. Clines (eds.), *The New Literary Criticism and the Hebrew Bible* (JSOTSup, 143: JSOT Press, 1993), pp. 26-54 (30).

42. M. Jacobus, 'The Difference of View', in Jacobus (ed.), *Women Writing and Writing About Women* (London: Croom Helm, 1979), pp. 10-21.

43. This phrase is borrowed from M. Wacker, 'Frau–Sexus–Macht', p. 102.

44. N. Auerbach, 'Engorging the Patriarchy', in S. Benstock (ed.), *Feminist Issues in Literary Scholarship* (Bloomington: Indiana University Press, 1987), pp. 150-60 (154).

45. A. Munich, 'Notorious Signs', p. 257.

prophet's morality, but rather the asymmetrical marriage metaphor which clearly casts the wife as transgressor and the husband as divine representative. The metaphor is not only 'extended' in the technical sense, but also pushed to its most extreme limits when the punishment of the land is expressed in threats of physical violence against the female.

In this section I want to investigate the responses of female readers to this text as represented by critics such as Fokkelien van Dijk-Hemmes, T. Drorah Setel, Marie-Theres Wacker, Helgard Balz-Cochois, Renita J. Weems, and Gale A. Yee.[46] The proliferation of women's reactions (at

---

46. I shall not be exploring Mary Joan Winn Leith's article 'Verse and Reverse' in detail here, since the main focus of her article is the inversion of the nation's mythical self-perception and the creation of a 'looking-glass world' ('Verse and Reverse', p. 97). Her analysis of the rhetorical device of addressing men as women, and the way in which it plays upon male fears of the woman as 'other' has already been considered (see p. 263). I would also like to direct the reader to two excellent studies which I have not been able to examine in detail here. Rut Törnkvist's *The Use and Abuse of Female Sexual Imagery in the Book of Hosea: A Feminist Critical Approach to Hos 1–3* (PhD dissertation, Uppsala University, 1994), was completed at the same time as this manuscript, and provides an uncompromising exploration of the political and ideological interests served by the marriage metaphor. Törnkvist's study is an extremely helpful companion to my own, for she extends the boundaries intertextually and looks at the social and legal context of the marriage metaphor and the biblical connotations of *znh*, as well as situating the rhetoric of the minor prophet within the context of the major prophets. Though I have not quoted directly from her analysis, the influence of our conversations can be seen throughout this book and I would like to take the opportunity of thanking Rut for our spirited discussions. Naomi Graetz also goes beyond the boundaries of this study in an article which I unfortunately discovered too late for inclusion in this manuscript. Graetz, like Törnkvist asks many of the questions that I criticize other feminist critics for not asking, and her conclusions suggest some provocative overlaps with my own. In an examination of the function of the 'wife-battering' metaphor in Jewish liturgical and exegetical tradition, she shows how 'despite the potential glimpse of a compassionate God, [Hosea's God] is accessible to His people only on His own terms' ('The Haftarah Tradition and the Metaphoric Battering of Hosea's Wife', *Conservative Judaism* 45 (1992), pp. 29-42 [33]) Tracing the equation of women with national sinfulness from the biblical text to ancient and contemporary midrashim, she shows how the 'ancient metaphor—God as male and the sinning people as female—is alive and well in present day rabbinical thinking' (just as it is in mainstream biblical scholarship), and how, even in an interpretation as recent as 1990, the sinning nation is depicted as a woman 'smothered in perfume', her arms and fingers 'dripping with cold cream and Chanel No. 5' (R. Shlomo Ruskin, *The Jerusalem Post* [Friday, 13 April 1990], cited in Graetz, 'The Haftarah Tradition', p. 35). Reading a midrash

least six have been published during the late 1980s and early 1990s) might suggest a cacophony of divergent voices, but surprisingly, apart from brief references in footnotes, very few critics make reference to other feminist articles and they never engage in dispute.[47] The situation would provide an apt illustration for Alice Bach's recent article on 'Feminist Criticism Approaching the Millennium' in which she attacks the illusion of homogeneity that pervades biblical feminist scholarship and that creates the impression of a 'monolithic viewpoint, an essentialist feminist approach to reading the Bible'.[48] Ironically, as biblical feminists, like all feminists, try to counter the idea of woman as the eternal feminine, or 'a universal unified simplistic abstract',[49] they inadvertently create another seeming monolith called Feminist Biblical Criticism.

Bach advocates that, following the example of critics like Ilana Pardes,[50] feminist biblical critics might increasingly sacrifice the illusion

from Numbers Rabbah that attempts to connect the Torah reading from Numbers with the Hosea haftarah, Graetz attacks the concept of God's 'overmastering love' (p. 35). R. Hanina explains God's statement 'I will not be to you' as meaning 'in spite of yourselves you will be my people' and 'with a mighty hand and with an outstretched hand and with fury poured out I will be king over you' (Ezek. 20.33), but Graetz retorts that this is symptomatic of denial, even 'mental illness' on God's part, for 'there has been no discussion, no ending of mutual recriminations' (p. 35). In a response that is similar to my own analysis of Hosea 2, she turns the text around and powerfully describes the woman/Israel's point of view: 'She doesn't want him, she's sick of him; sick of his mighty hand, outstreched arm and fury. She decides to leave him but he refuses to face facts. He doesn't recognise the writing on the wall' (p. 35).

47. I find it surprising, for example, that Renita J. Weems only makes a passing reference to an earlier article by T. Drorah Setel even though they consider strikingly similar themes. Van Dijk-Hemmes, who refers to Setel and Balz-Cochois, only makes reference to aspects she approves of: she welcomes Balz-Cochois's investigation of Asherah and Astarte, but I would be intrigued to know how she responded to the rest of the article.

48. A. Bach, 'Reading Allowed: Feminist Criticism Approaching the Millenium', *Currents in Research: Biblical Studies* 1 (1993), pp. 191-215 (192).

49. B. Christian *et al.*, 'Conference Call: Notes from the Beehive: Feminism and the Institution', *Differences* 2 (1990), p. 63.

50. Pardes believes, as I do, that feminist critics should not only critique the presuppositions of patriarchal belief systems but also their own 'feminist theories and assumptions' (I. Pardes, *Countertraditions in the Bible: A Feminist Approach* [Cambridge, MA: Harvard University Press, 1992], p. 155). She puts this into practice in her chapter 'Creation according to Eve', in which she sets up a polylogue

of 'bland harmony'[51] to achieve a 'more dissonant buzz'.[52] The image of 'a dissonant buzz' is both a response to Derrida's warning that feminism is in danger of enforcing its own marginality and of becoming 'just another cell in the university beehive',[53] and a way of locating Bach's own response to feminist biblical criticism within the larger context of women's studies, of which she is also a part. In a lively and contentious debate entitled, appropriately, 'Voices from the Beehive',[54] feminist critics discuss the possibility that by excluding or understating difference, they are in danger of 'reifying the homogeneous discourse they desire to decentre',[55] and of promoting 'woman' as monolith rather than as a 'complex and contradictory category'.[56] Differing on many points and with many diverse emphases, the critics illustrate their one point of intersection that, as Elaine Marks put it, 'we will have to do more than acknowledge or cite differences: we may have to see the intersection of our many differences as central to the quality of our work'.[57]

As feminism matures, it becomes like all fields in which 'various theoretical and ideological strands work side by side, contradicting each other, competing with each other'.[58] In presenting the beginnings of feminist criticism on Hosea, I want to create the sense of a dissonant buzz by juxtaposing one voice with another and highlighting points of difference among the critics, and ultimately between those critics and myself. My reactions are generally mixed: like the 'younger' scholar Ann DuCille responding to Barbara Christian, I find myself 'agreeing with [them] on one page, disagreeing on the next'.[59] By imagining one critic's response to another critic's claims and inserting interrogative footnotes, I want to create an atmosphere of lively debate, and show how feminist responses, like all responses, are conditioned by the commitments of the reader.

between critics as diverse as Kate Millet, Simone de Beauvoir, Elizabeth Cady Stanton, Phyllis Trible, Esther Fuchs and Mieke Bal.

51. Bach, 'Reading Allowed', p. 193.
52. Bach, 'Reading Allowed', p. 192.
53. Derrida, cited in Bach, 'Reading Allowed', p. 191.
54. Christian *et al.*, 'Conference Call: Notes from the Beehive'..
55. E. Marks, 'Notes from the Beehive', p. 65.
56. A. DuCille, 'Notes from the Beehive', p. 91.
57. Marks, 'Notes from the Beehive', p. 65.
58. Marks, 'Notes from the Beehive', p. 71.
59. DuCille, 'Notes from the Beehive', p. 90.

2.1. *Fokkelien van Dijk-Hemmes and T. Drorah Setel: Prophets, Pornography and Imaginative Power*[60]

By comparing Hosea 1–3 with the Song of Songs (in van Dijk-Hemmes's case) and sociological critiques of pornography (in Setel's) both critics explore the objectification of female sexuality in Hosea 1–3. Van Dijk-Hemmes list the contrasts: in the Song the woman is an 'active subject-lover', in Hosea she is a 'passive object';[61] desires which are cast positively in the Song are condemned by the prophet as 'harlotry';[62] the woman is denied all positive attributes, including the power of speech[63] and the power of provision;[64] and her autonomy and freedom to seek her lovers are negated as walls are built against her.[65] In comparing the text with contemporary pornography, Setel finds more points of intersection than differences. The analogy between woman and land is comparable to the way in which women in pornography are associated with 'nature in general and the land in particular', and, when considered

60. T. Drorah Setel, 'Prophets and Pornography: Female Sexual Imagery in Hosea', in L.M. Russell (ed.), *Feminist Interpretation of the Bible* (Oxford: Basil Blackwell, 1985), pp. 86-95. F. van Dijk-Hemmes, 'The Imagination of Power and the Power of Imagination: An Intertextual Analysis of Two Biblical Love Songs: The Song of Songs and Hosea 2', *JSOT* 44 (1989), pp. 75-88.

61. Van Dijk-Hemmes, 'The Imagination of Power', p. 84.

62. Dijk-Hemmes notes how the woman's 'words of love and longing for the beloved are deleted' and 'negative qualifications of her behaviour are added' ('The Imagination of Power', p. 82); Setel notes how the minor prophets seem to be 'the first to use objectified female sexuality as a symbol of evil' ('Prophets and Pornography', p. 86).

63. Van Dijk-Hemmes, 'The Imagination of Power', p. 80.

64. In reference to Hos. 2.7 van Dijk-Hemmes notes how the 'male speaker makes the woman ironically ignore the female role in the provision of food and clothing' ('The Imagination of Power', p. 82); abdicating from the positive roles of sustenance and nurture, the woman 'says', 'I will go after my lovers, who give me my bread and my water, my wool and my flax, my oil and my drink'. Setel also notes an emphasis on 'female passivity and dependence', and cites as an example Hos. 2.10-11, in which Yhwh asserts himself as true provider: 'For she did not know that it was I who gave her the grain, the wine, and the oil, and who lavished upon her the silver and the gold which they used for Baal' ('Prophets and Pornography', p. 92).

65. Van Dijk-Hemmes, 'The Imagination of Power', pp. 80-81. For another comparison of female eroticism in Hosea (and Ezekiel) and the Song, see Pardes, *Countertraditions in the Bible*, pp. 133-35.

alongside the sexual violence of ch. 2, suggests a similar pattern of 'conquest' and 'male domination'.[66]

While both critics see the woman in this text as defined by powerless-ness, they also suggest a subtext of women's power. Reading inter-textually, van Dijk-Hemmes can insert into this otherwise bleak text the language of women's desires and discover a countervoice which can never, she claims, be entirely eradicated.[67] She hints at, but does not develop, a project of feminist deconstruction; for since Hosea's vision of justice is constructed from an unjust metaphor, and 'the stones with which he constructs his vision seem to be the wall within which the woman-mother-lover is imprisoned',[68] his ideal is undermined by his own myopia. The beginnings of a counter-reading are also to be found in her title and in her comment that, though related to a particular social context, 'the text is seen...not so much as a window but rather as a figuration of and a response to the reality that brought it forth'.[69]

Van Dijk-Hemmes's observation that the relationship between text and reality is not necessarily 'straightforwardly reflective'[70] implies, by extension, that Gomer is not a mirror of patriarchal reality but a reflection of patriarchal ideals. Similarly, the title implies that the patri-archal violence of Hosea 2 is a fantasy of authority, an imaginative con-struct that counters the threat of female power.[71] The theme is picked up independently by Setel, who argues on the basis of contemporary psychology that pornography is the result of a 'psychological need for a sense of power and superiority as a proof of manhood', the corollary to which is the 'denial of individual or group powerlessness'.[72] For if God holds the power of life and death, then women, who have the power to

66. Setel, 'Prophets and Pornography', p. 87.
67. Van Dijk-Hemmes, 'The Imagination of Power', p. 86.
68. Van Dijk-Hemmes, 'The Imagination of Power', p. 86.
69. Van Dijk-Hemmes, 'The Imagination of Power', p. 78.
70. Van Dijk-Hemmes, 'The Imagination of Power', p. 78.
71. As the twist in van Dijk-Hemmes's title suggests, the imagination of power constitutes power, for the imagination is itself a powerful force. Texts can re-style reality. Van Dijk-Hemmes's title seems to encapsulate perfectly the tensions of femi-nist criticism: men are not all-powerful, and their texts conceal fear of female power, and yet paradoxically, they are all-powerful because imagination has redescriptive power and the texts are on their side.
72. The thesis is Andrea Dworkin's (see Chapter 1, 'Power', in *Pornography: Men Possessing Women* [London: The Women's Press, 1981]) but the corollary is Setel's ('Prophets and Pornography', p. 88).

give birth, are implicitly associated with the power of the divine, and patriarchy needs to 'diminish—or even negate—the power of female human beings in the life process'.[73]

Though both Setel and van Dijk-Hemmes are tantalisingly brief about evidence of male insecurity in this text,[74] their analyses suggest avenues for future study. For example, if Hosea 1–3 is a reaction against the association of the female and the divine, it is important that the text uses a metaphor which firmly equates the man with the divine and the female with the sordid realm of humanity.[75] It is also possible that 'harlotry', or the female potential to escape male control, is not simply a metaphor for the *real* anxiety, which is the loss of divine approval, but rather that the two anxieties are mysteriously intertwined. Both the tenor of the metaphor (loss of divine approval) and the vehicle (loss of sexual control) betray a fear of male powerlessness and may be displaced images of the same essential insecurity.

2.2. *Marie-Theres Wacker: Woman, Sex, and Power*[76]

In calling Hosea a 'right strawy epistle for *The Women's Bible*',[77] Marie-Theres Wacker borrows Luther's phrase about the Epistle of James, but not his absolutism: her relationship to the book of Hosea is ambiguous and fraught with tensions. On one level her rejection of such a book for the feminist canon is as unequivocal as Luther's objection to James's canonization, since it aligns the woman with the negative in the marriage metaphor, enforces the perception of woman as male property and suggests that she can, according to ch. 3, be purchased, locked away

73. Setel, 'Prophets and Pornography', p. 89.

74. Van Dijk-Hemmes, for example, makes the provocative suggestion that 'the metaphorical language reveals more than its user might realise or intend', but only hints at what it might reveal ('The Imagination of Power', p. 86.)

75. Van Dijk-Hemmes raises the question, 'Why is Israel, first the land, but then also the nation, represented in the image of a faithless wife, a harlot and not in the image of, e.g. a rapist?', which would have been far more appropriate to 'Israel's misdeeds' ('The Imagination of Power', p. 85). Her answer, that the text is anxious to establish the 'authority of the father', can be extended using Setel's observation that the link between the female and the divine must be broken if patriarchy is to establish undisputed power.

76. M. Wacker, 'Frau–Sexus–Macht: Eine feministische Relecture des Hoseabuches', *Der Gott der Männer und der Frauen* (Theologie zur Zeit, 2; Düsseldorf: Patmos, 1987), pp. 101-25 (I shall be using my own translations).

77. Wacker, 'Frau–Sexus–Macht', p. 102.

and denied sexual gratification.[78] The parameters of female behaviour are set by men: sociologically, the text implies a double standard where a man can commit adultery only with a married woman but a woman becomes culpable on the basis of *any* pre- or extra-marital sex.[79] At its most obvious level the text endorses 'Frauendiskrimierung und -unterdruckung' ('discrimination and repression of women'), and presents Yhwh as 'ein Mann-bestimmter Gott' ('a male-determined God').[80] Yet reading between the lines of its misogynistic polemic, Wacker finds that woman is presented not only as the personification of transgression but also as 'das Opfer männlicher Verfuhlungen' ('the sacrifice/victim of men's sins'),[81] and that Hosea, paradoxically, becomes 'ein Anwalt der Frauen' ('an acting attorney for the female cause')[82] even as he so relentlessly enforces the case for the prosecution.

Though Wacker's reading goes beyond the scope of this thesis and considers the book of Hosea as a whole, it has important methodological implications for this study. For although Wacker does not describe her approach as 'deconstructive', her reading seems to draw implicitly on Phyllis Trible's description of 'depatriarchalization', which itself strangely coincides with the language of deconstruction. Like Derrida, Trible maintains that 'Depatriarchalizing is not an operation which the exegete performs on the text' and that 'We expose it; we do not impose it'.[83] The reader's own preferences recede into the background; the text alone is responsible for the self-resistance it stages, although just as Derrida maintains that Western metaphysics is always a more dominant force than its potential subversion, Trible concedes (in a later qualifying statement) that the 'countervoices' hidden in the text do not equal and cancel out 'the male dominated character of scripture'.[84] A similar position is adopted by Wacker when she argues that *in* the book of Hosea ('im Hoseabuch')[85] there are 'two opposing tendencies' which simultaneously critique and affirm patriarchal concepts. Her concluding section

---

78. Wacker, 'Frau–Sexus–Macht', p. 112.

79. Wacker, 'Frau–Sexus–Macht', p. 112.

80. Wacker, 'Frau–Sexus–Macht', p. 101.

81. Wacker, 'Frau–Sexus–Macht', p. 107.

82. Wacker, 'Frau–Sexus–Macht', p. 110.

83. P. Trible, 'Depatriarchalization in Biblical Interpretation', *JAAR* 41 (1973), pp. 30-49 (49).

84. P. Trible, *God and the Rhetoric of Sexuality* (Philadelphia: Fortress Press, 1978), p. 203.

85. Wacker, 'Frau–Sexus–Macht', p. 121.

is entitled 'Hosea—Prophet of the Patriarchs?' and the implication is that the question mark in Hosea's relation to patriarchy is not inserted by contemporary feminists but is written in the text itself.[86]

Wacker's deconstructive/depatriarchalizing reading begins with Hos. 4.14,[87] in which Hosea deflects guilt from promiscuous women towards their male guardians/abusers, and so defends women, as Wacker puts it, against 'die Willkür der Männer' ('men's arbitrary judgments').[88] The prophet's apparent qualification of his own analogy (between women and the guilt of Israel) introduces an element of undecideability between Hosea's politically correct intention, which is to accuse *men* of political and religious transgression, and his politically incorrect metaphor.[89] Women are the image but not the substance of the problem: they are not the active partners in the covenant nor the addressees of Hosea's prophecies, since they are not responsible for their own actions (*selbstverantwortlich*).[90] In my opinion this argument is highly problematic: if women are exempt on the basis that they are not full members of society, patriarchy is not being subverted but only varied, and patriarchy in the form of misogyny and the identification of the woman as evil is merely being displaced by patriarchy in the form of social subordination.[91]

86. Wacker, 'Frau–Sexus–Macht', p. 102.

87. 'I will not punish your daughters when they play the harlot, nor your brides when they commit adultery; for the men themselves go aside with harlots, and sacrifice with cult prostitutes, and a people without understanding shall come to ruin.' Wacker's argument overlaps with Winn Leith's at this point as she shows how Hosea addresses himself to a male audience (the tenor of his argument) using 'woman' as vehicle.

88. Wacker, 'Frau–Sexus–Macht', p. 110.

89. Wacker, 'Frau–Sexus–Macht', p. 121. Compare Renita Weems's reading of the marriage metaphor in which the tenor is seen as correct but the vehicle inappropriate (R.J. Weems, 'Gomer: Victim of Violence or Victim of Metaphor?', in K. Geneva Cannon and E. Schüssler Fiorenza [eds.], *Interpretation for Liberation* [Semeia 47; Atlanta: Scholars Press, 1989], pp. 87-104).

90. Wacker, 'Frau–Sexus–Macht', p. 107. Wacker contrasts the rhetoric of Hosea with that of his contemporary, Amos, who directs his polemic specifically against women in his denunciation of the luxuriant 'cows of Bashan' (Amos 4.1-3).

91. Though Louise Foster, like Wacker, sees Hos. 4.14 as a statement of women's irresponsibility, she does not idealize this verse as a break with patriarchy, but rather sees it as the ultimate statement of female objectification. Her interpretation, that women cannot sin 'any more than a chair or a table may be said "to sin" '

A positive message for women based on female negligibility is highly dubious: ironically, in trying to exonerate Hosea from unmitigated misogyny, Wacker inadvertently draws attention to his myopic perspective that excludes half the nation in his attempts to address it. For many feminists, the idea that the dismissal of women constitutes some kind of anti-patriarchal gesture would be highly problematic; similarly, they might have problems with Wacker's argument that Hosea is not opposed to 'die Frauen als solche' ('women as such') but to women 'in ihrer biologischen Besonderheit als (potentielle) Gebärinnen' ('in their special biological capacity as potential childbearers').[92] While she explores the patriarchal fear of the potentially anarchic power of female reproduction, Wacker's emphasis ultimately is not on the hidden power (*Macht*) of women, as the title promises, but on the way this improves the prophet's standing from a feminist perspective.[93] The distinction between misogyny directed at women's bodies and at women themselves is impossible to sustain; more disturbingly, it suggests that the primary concern of this critic, like that of her androcentric predecessors, is to redeem Hosea's reputation.

The problem with Wacker's reading is not that she produces a positive reading for women, but that she ascribes this reading to 'the text'. Counter-readings are located at the level of the text's conception, rather than the text's reception, in a way that implies that Hosea, and by implication the deity, were in some respects proto-feminists. Unlike deconstruction, which claims that the author's argument is undercut by what he did not see in the language and concepts that he used, depatriarchalizing readings like those of Trible and Wacker tend to ascribe the counter

is double-edged, for the equation of women and chairs and tables hardly suggests liberation (L. Foster, ' "I Will Not Punish Your Daughters For Being Prostitutes": Reading Hosea 1.2–4.14 as a Prostitute' [version of a paper presented to the SBL, New Orleans, 1990], p. 77).

92. Wacker, 'Frau–Sexus–Macht', p. 113.

93. Compare explorations of a similar theme by, for example, Esther Fuchs and Carol Meyers, who see the potential power of reproduction as a subtext of female power in patriarchal texts (E. Fuchs, 'The Literary Characterisation of Mothers and Sexual Politics in the Hebrew Bible', in M. Amihai, G.W. Coats and A.M. Solomon [eds.], *Narrative Research on the Hebrew Bible* [Semeia 46; Atlanta: Scholars Press, 1989], pp. 151-66; C.L. Meyers, 'The Roots of Restriction', in N.K. Gottwald [ed.], *The Bible and Liberation* [New York: Maryknoll, 1983], pp. 289-306).

argument to the level of authorial intention.[94] The project is not merely to produce a redemptive reading of woman in this text, but to prove the value of the text itself[95] to a feminist audience that increasingly sees the Bible as, in the words of Margaret Atwood, 'powdery', antiquated, and 'exhausted'.[96]

Though Wacker draws attention to 'die Männerphantasien' ('male fantasies') of commentators and their 'risky speculation' about Gomer's 'unrestrained' and 'lustful' character,[97] the fact that she invokes the concept of 'risk' suggests that she subscribes to the ideal of objectivity in readings—an ideal which in feminist criticism is both difficult and dangerous to maintain.[98] She makes the vital point that these readings tell us more about the readers than 'the text', but fails to apply this observation to her own reading. Yet despite her attempts to conceal her own voice, it continually betrays itself, particularly in her attempts to amplify the countervoice in this text (which other feminist readers, including myself, find disturbingly faint). The feminist critic, no less than any other, manipulates the text so that it conforms to her desires: she highlights certain features and represses others, and, like androcentric

94. The text 'Hosea' and the person 'Hosea' are fully equated, and any inconsistencies found in the text are seen as evidence of the prophet's and Yhwh's uncertain relation to patriarchy.

95. I find it significant that Wacker's article ends with concern for the text, rather than for the woman described by it. Her ultimate concern, it seems, is: 'die Frage nach dem "Bleibenden" der Prophetie Hoseas' ('the question of the "lasting value" of Hosea's prophecies', 'Frau-Sexus-Macht', pp. 124-25).

96. The quotation comes from Atwood's powerful description of Gilead, a futuristic society built on biblical principles, in which women are subordinate and certain women are required to serve as 'handmaids' (or concubines). The Bible is read only by men, and yet even they seem 'bored' or 'reluctant' to read it: the book falls closed with an 'exhausted sound', the pages are 'thin' and 'oniony', and Atwood implies, through the antiquated state of the book, the antiquated and dangerous implications of its ideology (M. Atwood, *The Handmaid's Tale* [London: Virago, 1991], pp. 99-101).

97. Wacker, 'Frau–Sexus–Macht', p. 110.

98. It is difficult to maintain because there is very little evidence given about women in biblical texts; it is dangerous because, as Luce Irigaray warns, as long as women continue to subscribe to ideals of authority and objectivity, they 'will simply tell each other the same story that men have told or told about them for centuries' ('When Our Lips Speak Together', trans. C. Burke, *Signs* 6 [1980], pp. 69-79 [69]).

critics before her, she strives to mediate between the text and the potentially outraged reader. Wacker reads the image of 'miscarrying womb
and dry breasts' in Hos. 9.12 not as graphic misogyny but as an extension of the theme of woman as victim and an illustration of the fatal consequences of 'störrische...männliche Machtpolitik' ('a stubborn male
power politics');[99] and though she focuses on the equation between
woman and property and describes woman as 'das Opfer männlichen
Verfuhlungen' ('the victim of male transgression'),[100] she glosses over
the physical and sexual violence in ch. 2. Though her reading is
provocative, it loses a sense of women's suffering in its attempts to provide a positive message. A potential criticism is provided by Louise
Foster who insists that 'If we are ever to appreciate this particular piece
of Hebrew poetry, it will not be through any kind of reading which
misses the real terror it conveys to the woman reader'.[101] The tension
between positive and negative messages for women is described by
Wacker as an ambiguity or antithesis, but more realistically, it is an
undecideable relation in which the two elements are not equally represented, but in which one 'always lays hidden within the other as the sun
lies hidden within a shadow, or truth within an error.'[102]

2.3. *Helgard Balz-Cochois: Gomer or the Power of Astarte*[103]

> There is beneath the carved superstructure of every temple to God-the-
> Father, the dark cave or inner hall or cellar to Mary, mère, Mütter, pray
> for us.[104]

One of the most compelling features of Wacker's reading is her analysis
of Hosea 11: extending her observation that maternal and paternal
elements struggle for dominance in the description of the deity, it is

99. Wacker, 'Frau–Sexus–Macht', p. 109.
100. Wacker, 'Frau–Sexus–Macht', p. 107
101. Foster, 'I Will Not Punish Your Daughters For Being Prostitutes', p. 68.
102. P. de Man, *Blindness and Insight: Essays in the Rhetoric of Contemporary
Criticism* (New York: Oxford University Press, 1971), pp. 102-103.
103. H. Balz-Cochois, 'Gomer oder die Macht der Astarte: Versuch einer feministischen Interpretation von Hos. 1–4', *EvT* 42 (1982), pp. 37-65 (I shall be using my
own translation throughout). For a more detailed exposition of Balz-Cochois's
argument, see *Gomer: Der Höhencult Israels im Selbstverständnis der
Volksfrömmigkeit* (Frankfurt am Main: Peter Lang, 1982).
104. H.D.'s 'The Gift' (MS, Beinecke Library), Chapter 4, p. 10; quoted in
S. Friedman, *Penelope's Web: Gender, Modernity, H.D.'s Fiction* (Cambridge:
Cambridge University Press, 1990), p. 329.

possible to argue that a brief glimpse of the female face of God jeopardizes the absolutism of the God–man metaphor of Hosea 1–3.[105] The theme of a repressed association between the feminine and the deity is picked up by another German feminist, Helgard Balz-Cochois, who develops the theme on a level that Wacker only briefly touches on, and looks at this text as a reaction against the potentially anarchic power of female deities in the outlawed Canaanite religion. The two articles intersect in their provocative explorations of repressed female power, but also in their ambiguous relations to the question of female subordination. For as Wacker condemns the text but at the same time attempts to promote it, so Balz-Cochois writes in the shadow of androcentric scholarship and is intimidated by the force of a tradition which she ostensibly aims to resist.

In its introductory statements 'Gomer or the Power of Astarte' is anything but submissive. Defiantly Balz-Cochois lays down the terms of her reading's validity: she will be no more 'impertinent' to the standards of historical-critical exegesis than her androcentric predecessors, and her 'dichterisch Eheroman' ('poetic marriage story')[106] will only show as much sympathy towards Gomer as the 'romantic stories of the past' have traditionally shown towards her husband.[107] Dramatically, she announces her intention of 'blow[ing] up' (*sprengen*) scholarly theology[108] by 'redeeming [Gomer] from silence',[109] and if her deflation of androcentric objectivity can be taken as any indication, she shows every likelihood of fulfilling her promise. Yet curiously, when Gomer's story does emerge, it is flanked with methodological apologetic and anxious reflections on whether her reading is too 'risky' and whether it goes astray (*sich verirrt*) from historical critical exegesis in an act of 'overinterpretation'.[110]

---

105. Wacker, 'Frau–Sexus–Macht', p. 123 (see also Wacker, 'God as Mother? On the Meaning of a Biblical God-Symbol for Feminist Theology', *Concilium* 206 [1989], pp. 103-11). Many feminist critics have focused on the maternal imagery in ch. 11 to explore the association of the female and the deity (Wacker, 'Frau–Sexus–Macht'; H. Schüngel Straumann, 'Gott als Mutter in Hosea 11', *TQ* 166 [1986], pp. 119-34). Balz-Cochois's approach is particularly interesting because she explores the possibility of a female deity in relation to Hosea 1–4.

106. Balz-Cochois, 'Gomer', p. 51.

107. Balz-Cochois, 'Gomer', p. 54.

108. Balz-Cochois, 'Gomer', p. 38.

109. Balz-Cochois, 'Gomer', p. 51.

110. Balz-Cochois, 'Gomer', p. 58.

Balz-Cochois's choice of the verb *sich verirren* is telling. Rather than perceiving herself as going away in a neutral act, she sees herself going 'astray' in a verb that implies transgression. Since one can only transgress from a right path or the correct standard, this implies that the androcentric standard she denounces also haunts her, and that she incorporates its imagined voice into her own act of 'rebellion'. Even as she tries to imagine Gomer's voice and to bring to the surface a perspective that has long been repressed, Balz-Cochois cannot escape the dominant voice of her culture, and relativizes Gomer's story by anticipating and incorporating the voice of an androcentric critic. As the feminist critic tries to discover her own voice, she imagines herself in an act of reply, more commented on than commenting, and she addresses herself to the accusations of one who would perceive 'feministische Freiheit' ('feminist freedom') as 'methodische Schwäche' ('methodological weakness').[111] Though her reading is no more romantic than the excesses of Cheyne or Batten (as she herself concedes), it is far less authoritarian and more tentative, with the tone of one who is not only exploring uncharted territory but consciously trespassing onto forbidden paths.

Following the model of Hegelian dialectic, Balz-Cochois presents a thesis, which is Hosea's point of view, and an antithesis, which is Gomer's. Ostensibly, as she argues in her introduction, the two are equal, equally imaginative and non-objective (although one is supported by tradition), and are to be reconciled in a concluding 'synthesis'.[112] Yet as the term 'antithesis' suggests, even the feminist critic cannot always escape from the point of view that perceives Gomer's story as secondary and derivative, and although the feminist voice does not intrude into the thesis, the antithesis is marked by the presence of another, more dominant and implicitly judgmental voice. At one point in 'Gomer's story' the narrator breaks off to self-consciously renew her poetic licence or, as she puts it, 'take a particularly deep breath of poetic freedom'.[113] Her joke, in a reflex of self-deprecation, reinforces the

111. Balz-Cochois, 'Gomer', p. 46.

112. Compare the voice of another contributor to feminist criticism on Hosea, T. Drorah Setel, who argues that in the attempt to produce a new kind of feminist criticism that avoids the polarity of androcentric traditions, 'positing a combination of the dualistic opposites in a "balance" or "synthesis" of existing stereotypic polarities is insufficient' ('Feminist Insights and the Question of Method', in A. Yarbro Collins [ed.], *Feminist Perspectives on Biblical Scholarship* [Chico, CA: Scholars Press, 1985], p. 39).

113. Balz-Cochois, 'Gomer', p. 53.

perspective of androcentric readers who would see Gomer's point of view as less legitimate, less *serious*, than Hosea's.

Like the androcentric critics who preceded her, Balz-Cochois seems to confuse objectivity and standards of historical criticism with the exchange of ideological affirmation between the reader and the text. The woman's voice seems to fit so disjunctively with the text that even the feminist critic distances herself from it in a self-critical aside or joke, but though she apologizes on the level of 'methodological weakness', she is in fact responding to a sense of ideological disparity. As Balz-Cochois simultaneously proclaims and apologizes for Gomer's point of view, so her dramatization of Gomer affirms and deconstructs patriarchal structures. For if Gomer represents the disturbing power of female sexuality,[114] she also endorses the rational–emotional, male–female hierarchy, and affirms patriarchy's worst parodies of woman as irrational and trivial. On one level she represents the antithesis promised: she worships Astarte, counters biblical prejudices about Canaanite culture, and perceives Hosea as eccentric, and Yahwism as essentially uninteresting and irredeemably male. Yahwism, she complains, is 'not interesting enough' and Yhwh is 'only a god for men';[115] reversing the judgment of the text, which describes her 'promiscuity' in unequivocally negative terms, she describes the desire to escape from an Israelite context, in which her sexuality is perceived as a threat which must be controlled,[116] to the more affirming context of Canaanite religion which celebrates female sexual power as 'holy, right and good' ('heilig, gerecht, und gut').[117]

For Balz-Cochois, Gomer represents 'a primordial chaos' ('ein ursprunghaft Chaos')[118] and the power of 'the eternal feminine',[119] and though she makes no specific acknowledgment of the fact, her reading

114. Balz-Cochois, 'Gomer', p. 48.
115. Balz-Cochois, 'Gomer', p. 52.
116. Balz-Cochois, 'Gomer', p. 46.
117. Balz-Cochois, 'Gomer', p. 48. While Ugaritic texts suggest a role for feminine deities, I find Balz-Cochois's idealization of Canaanite religion as a celebration of female sexual power problematic. In the context of the ancient Near East it is impossible for me to imagine a situation in which female sexual power was completely liberated. T. Drorah Setel's comment that '*all* Ancient Near Eastern material. . . provides information concerning an extensive period in the formation of patriarchal societies' suggests that she would also disagree with Balz-Cochois on this point ('Prophets and Pornography', p. 86).
118. Balz-Cochois, 'Gomer', p. 50.
119. Balz-Cochois, 'Gomer', pp. 50-51.

fits into a much larger context of critics from Bachofen to Carol Christ, who explore the concept of mother religion or a primordial identification of the woman with the divine.[120] In particular, her reading suggests a background model of a split cultural psyche, put forward by psychologists such as Erich Neumann,[121] a disciple of Jung, in which the maternal and the feminine signify the lack in patriarchy and the dimension of a complete psyche that culture has repressed. In contrast to my own reading of ch. 2, which sees Yhwh as intimidated by, and commented on by the more successful deity Baal, Balz-Cochois imagines a situation in which Yhwh is less intimidated by Baal, whose function he can assimilate, than by female deities like Astarte,[122] whom he can never ultimately replace. Balz-Cochois's Yhwh, as an essentially male god, can imitate Baal's insemination of the ground with rain, but can never have access to the secret rhythms of growth and decline[123] controlled by the womb of the earth.

As Balz-Cochois's 'antithesis' is marked by the presence of an antagonistic voice, so her description of Gomer is notable for the way in which it succumbs to patriarchal definitions of 'woman'. On a symbolic level, Gomer represents a powerful feminine force who will inevitably break through the narrow limits of orthodox marriage,[124] but on a human level her character is reminiscent of the traditional androcentric

120. The idea of a matriarchal society that was replaced by patriarchy was introduced as early as 1861 in J. Bachofen's *Das Mutterrecht: Eine Untersuchung über die Gynaikokratie der alten Welt nach ihrer religiösen und rechtlichen Natur* (Basel, 1897), and was popularized by books such as E.G. Davis's *The First Sex* (New York: Putnam's Sons, 1971) and M. Stone's *When God Was a Woman* (New York: Harcourt Brace, 1978). How the myth is interpreted depends upon the writer's predilection towards chaos: Bachofen saw patriarchy as a superior culture that replaced the chaos of mother religion, but feminist critics, influenced by the language of Freud and psychoanalysis, see chaos as the expression of society's subconscious and patriarchy as the tool of repression.

121. Neumann wrote, '[T]his problem of the feminine has equal importance for the psychologists of culture, who realise that the peril of present day mankind springs in large part from the one-sidedly patriarchal development of the male intellectual consciousness, which is no longer kept in balance by the matriarchal world of the psyche' (E. Neumann, Introduction to *The Great Mother*, cited in A. Rich, *On Lies, Secrets and Silence: Selected Prose 1966–78* [London: Virago, 1986], p. 74).

122. Balz-Cochois argues that in the eighth century Anat was gradually being replaced by Astarte; she also speaks of Asherah and Astarte interchangeably.

123. Balz-Cochois, 'Gomer', p. 46.

124. Balz-Cochois, 'Gomer', p. 63.

view of Gertrude in *Hamlet* as a 'soft animal creature...very dull and very shallow...[who] loved to be happy in a good-humoured, sensual fashion'.[125] Without questioning the motives of her male predecessors, Balz-Cochois subordinates herself to the androcentric tradition that attempts to redeem Gomer, and, extrapolating from Wolff's dubious argument that Gomer is good but misled, she builds a character who is well-meaning, reliant on her senses and not given to serious thought. When Hosea forbids her to attend a cult festival, she does not go defiantly of her own accord but because the neighbours come to call for her. When Hosea pursues her and gives a sermon to the rebellious people, some laugh, some are vexed, but Gomer does not know what to think, and does not want to think at all but simply to enjoy the feast.[126] Characterized by ignorance, she knows nothing of her husband's religious context or history,[127] and interprets the name 'Jezreel' naively and romantically as 'a beautiful name' evocative of fertile plain and cornfields.[128] Even in 'prison' she does not experience sorrow and anger for the injustices of male authority, but rather a shallow regret that she will not be able to participate in the 'lovely festivals'.[129]

In a re-reading of a feminist reading of Eros and Psyche, Rachel Blau du Plessis acknowledges that female characters will be created according to different 'needs', but at the same time rejects a reading that argues that Psyche becomes truly feminine when she chooses beauty over knowledge.[130] Similarly, while I maintain that as Norman Snaith makes

125. A.C. Bradley, *Shakespearean Tragedy* (New York: Macmillan, 1949), p. 167. The traditional view of Gertrude as a sensuous animal was challenged by Carolyn Heilbrun as early as 1957 (see C.G. Heilbrun, 'The Character of Hamlet's Mother', in *Hamlet's Mother and Other Women: Feminist Essays on Literature* [London: The Women's Press, 1991], pp. 9-17). I find it both ironic and disturbing that, almost 40 years later, a feminist biblical critic can describe a sensuous biblical character in Bradleyan terms, as if female sexuality automatically indicates a soft and shallow nature.

126. Balz-Cochois, 'Gomer', p. 52.

127. Balz-Cochois, 'Gomer', p. 51.

128. Balz-Cochois, 'Gomer', p. 52. Balz-Cochois uses the naming of the first son creatively to demonstrate different cultures through different semantic fields. For Hosea 'Jezreel' is evocative of Israel's past, but for Gomer it is evocative of a fertile plain blessed by her gods. The effect of difference is powerful, but unfortunately the contrast is based on Gomer's ignorance.

129. Balz-Cochois, 'Gomer', p. 53.

130. R. Blau du Plessis, 'Psyche, or Wholeness', *Massachusetts Review* (Spring 1979), pp. 77-96.

Gomer from his need so it is the feminist critic's prerogative to make her from hers, I want to suggest that a feminist re-creation of Gomer that links passivity, ignorance and insipidity with the female should be seriously re-examined to see to whose needs, and to whose ideals, this version of Gomer is really subordinated. Balz-Cochois's Gomer is compliant, sensuous and relatively ignorant—everything that patriarchal society decrees a woman should be. The shallowness of Gomer's speech, as Balz-Cochois imagines it, is hardly preferable to the silence the text gives her; silence conveys a sense of mystery and dignity, but Balz-Cochois's Gomer, in contrast, lamely and repetitively describes her world as 'schön'.

2.4. *Renita J. Weems and Gale A. Yee: 'Gomer: Victim of Violence or Victim of Metaphor?'*[131]

If God is male, then the male is God.[132]

Like Wacker, who argues that Hosea simultaneously affirms and deconstructs patriarchal culture, and Balz-Cochois, who attempts to synthesize Gomer and Hosea's point of view, Renita J. Weems and Gale A. Yee both reject and embrace the assumptions of this text. The marriage metaphor in particular elicits a strained reaction: Weems accepts the theological tenor, 'the presumably sound theological notion that the deity has a right to punish the people',[133] but 'as a black and womanist scholar' rejects a motif which 'rel[ies] upon the physical and sexual abuse of a woman to develop its larger, presumably congenial, theological point'.[134] Caught in the double bind between her commitment as a

---

131. R.J. Weems, 'Gomer: Victim of Violence or Victim of Metaphor?', in K. Geneva Cannon and E. Schüssler Fiorenza (eds.), *Interpretation for Liberation* (Semeia 47; Atlanta: Scholars Press, 1989), pp. 87-104; G.A. Yee, 'Hosea', in C.A. Newsom and S.H. Ringe (eds.), *The Women's Bible Commentary* (London: SPCK, 1992), pp. 195-202. For another critique of Weems and Yee see Törnkvist, *The Use and Abuse of Female Sexual Imagery in the Book of Hosea*, pp. 63-73.

132. M. Daly, *Beyond God the Father*, cited in S. McFague, *Metaphorical Theology: Models of God in Religious Language* (London: SCM Press, 1983), p. 147.

133. Weems, 'Gomer', p. 87.

134. Weems, 'Gomer', p. 90 n. 10. Yee's article follows Weems in many respects: compare Yee's complaint that the text makes its point at the expense of real victims of sexual violence, and seems to stamp physical abuse with the seal of divine approval ('Hosea', p. 200).

womanist and her commitment as a theologian, she finds herself theologically committed to the text but experientially alienated from it. To explain this bifurcation, she identifies her double response with the two dimensions of metaphor, and argues that while the tenor (divine retribution) is acceptable, the vehicle (physical abuse) is repellent.

Weems's focus on the problems of the metaphor is innovative and intriguing. Together with T. Drorah Setel she breaks the bashful silence of critics who have never confronted 'Hosea's use of sexual imagery and gynomorphic language',[135] and she is not shy of detailed analysis of ch. 2 in which, as she comically observes, 'the metaphor and the historical situation of Israel come together and climax'.[136] Yet even as she confronts the association of God and sexual violence and the related theological problems,[137] her dual response, which criticizes the means of expression and yet keeps the referent intact, suggests a subtle manipulation of metaphorical theory to serve her own purposes. Whereas Eybers and Snaith work on a premise of complete identification of tenor and vehicle,[138] Weems's description of metaphor, though more sophisticated, goes too far in the other direction. Manipulating the theory that metaphor is a tension between similarity and dissimilarity, she uses it to drive a wedge between Yhwh and his all-too-human representative. Sexual violence, she insists, functions only 'to demonstrate the extent to which Hosea the betrayed husband will go to preserve his marriage' and to 'underscore the point that punishment precedes reconciliation'.[139] In her conclusion she separates the positive connotations from the negative, and insists that the only message is an unequivocally positive one. The statement that 'while the strength of the marriage metaphor is its ability to tell us about Yhwh's love, anguish, jealousy and forgiving nature, it is not capable of shedding any light on the question of divine retribution'[140] raises the question, if metaphor is a relation of similarities and dissimilarities, who decrees what is and is not transferable?

Weems's and Yee's attempts to assign the problems of the text to the human level, the bad taste of the marriage metaphor, the 'violent and

135. Weems, 'Gomer', p. 89.
136. Weems, 'Gomer', p. 97.
137. Weems, 'Gomer', p. 100.
138. See Chapter 1, §3.4, 'Escape by Metaphor'.
139. Weems, 'Gomer', p. 97.
140. Weems, 'Gomer', p. 100.

highly erratic'[141] imagination of the prophet, and ultimately to the limitations of language, have the effect of protecting Yhwh's reputation and retrieving a sanitized deity from a perilous text. Like Wacker, they attempt to distinguish between politically correct meaning and politically incorrect expression: though Weems begins with a discussion of literary appreciation of texts and the idea that 'meaning cannot be abstracted from form',[142] she goes on to enforce such a division between a theology of retribution and its unfortunate expression in abuse. Another anomaly in their treatment of metaphor is the way in which both Yee and Weems see the potential danger of the marriage metaphor only in terms of transference from tenor to vehicle. Weems seems to imply that the (only) consequence of 'over-simplification and rigid correspondence'[143] is that God will be seen to endorse the physical abuse of a wife by her husband, and Gale A. Yee is insistent on this point: 'it is the human behaviors of Israelite husbands towards their wives that are represented as God's actions, *not vice versa*'.[144]

As critics have traditionally attempted to prevent or dilute the dangerous liaison between Hosea and the 'wife of harlotry', so Weems and Yee try to prevent an equally awkward conjunction: the metaphorical association of Yhwh and the abusing husband. The representation of metaphor as the transference from tenor to vehicle not only goes against conventional theories (in which the vehicle describes the tenor) but ignores the claims of many contemporary theorists that tenor and vehicle are mutually modified by their co-existence.[145] In order to protect Yhwh from taint, the critics not only resist the consensus of metaphorical theorists but ignore other critics of Hosea who find that the human and the

141. Weems, 'Gomer', p. 96.
142. Weems, 'Gomer', p. 88.
143. Weems, 'Gomer', p. 100.
144. Yee, 'Hosea', p. 199 (my italics).
145. Though Weems quotes Sally McFague ('Gomer', p. 100), she chooses to ignore her description of metaphor as a 'two-way traffic in ideas'. For McFague, as for many contemporary theorists, a metaphor such as 'God is man' is 'interactive' and means 'that men not only model God but God, in return, bestows divine qualities on men'. McFague undercuts Weems's assumptions by showing that metaphor is a two-way process, and by claiming that the transference of divine qualities to man is only a secondary effect. The aspect that Weems chooses to ignore—the representation of God by man—is for McFague the *primary* effect of the metaphor (see McFague, *Metaphorical Theology*, p. 149).

divine strands of the male persona are impossible to disentangle.[146] Even as she tries to maintain the 'is not' in the relation between Hosea and Yhwh, Weems deconstructs her own argument by referring to the male protagonists as 'Hosea (Yhwh)'[147] and by demonstrating how sympathetic identification with Yhwh through theological commitment inevitably leads to empathy with the prophet.[148]

Though she makes a conscious effort to support Gomer, describing her as a 'sexually victimized woman' and a 'pawn in a match between Hosea (Yhwh) and her lovers (other gods)',[149] Weems ultimately relapses into the familiar dichotomy between 'Hosea the betrayed husband' and his 'stubborn and recalcitrant'[150] wife. Hosea's position is 'correct' (because Yhwh's must be) and Gomer in contrast is 'incorrect':[151] Hosea 'does not want to kill his wife, though, according to Deuteronomy 22.22 it is his prerogative as a wronged husband to do so, nor does he wish to humiliate her, but he will if he must'.[152] Weems's

146. Van Dijk-Hemmes, for example, speaks of the 'complex character which has been constructed in chapter 1 and which we could name Yhwh/Hosea' ('The Imagination of Power', p. 83).

147. Weems, 'Gomer', p. 97.

148. Although theological metaphors are famously described as a way of describing the unknown (the deity) by recourse to the known (see, for example, McFague, *Metaphorical Theology*, p. 15), Weems starts from the level of the divine relationship with Israel and shapes her description of the human relationship according to her knowledge about God. God is the 'known' from which her reading begins, and his love and infallibility dictate her understanding of Hosea. While theological responses to this text are not my main concern, I suggest that there must be more creative ways of reading this text as a feminist theologian than by automatically siding with the prophet and Yhwh. A Post-Enlightenment culture, and particularly the strong emphasis placed on individuality in Western democratic society, lead to a clash of interest, and twentieth-century readers are more likely to sympathize with Gomer's desire for freedom and autonomy than any theologian has thus far acknowledged. Theologians, and particularly feminist theologians, seem to me to be working in reverse: that is, like Weems they accept the divine prerogative to restrain and to punish, and then apply that principle in their response to the errant women. I find that my own culturally conditioned sympathy with a woman who desires independence, and my repulsion at ideas of imprisonment and restraint, lead me to question the principles of a religion that seems to deny reciprocity (the woman/land has no voice) and to advocate restraint of the defiant will.

149. Weems, 'Gomer', p. 97.

150. Weems, 'Gomer', p. 96.

151. Weems, 'Gomer', p. 96.

152. Weems, 'Gomer', p. 97.

desire to present Yhwh as a gracious deity leads not only to praise of the prophet's leniency, but to the ultimate anti-feminist gesture in which she argues that the stripping of the woman is the woman's fault. If only Gomer had 'taken off her brazen apparel, as Hosea had first ordered', she insists 'she could have been spared public stripping and humiliation'.[153] Disturbingly, she sides with the male even more emphatically than her androcentric predecessors,[154] and accuses Gomer, in the tones of a notorious twentieth-century judge, of 'contributory negligence'.[155]

2.5. *Postscript: Norman Nicholson's 'A Match For the Devil'*

An interesting postscript to characterizations of Gomer is provided by Norman Nicholson's play *A Match for the Devil*.[156] Odd man out in more ways than one, this text has a male author, predates 'feminist' readings of Hosea 1–3, and does not claim in any way to confront the problem of gender or dramatize the woman's point of view. On one level Nicholson's Gomer is a cliché of womanhood, and her most ambitious desire, poignantly, is not to be content but to be needed. On another level, however, she represents a twentieth-century voice that argues with the theological premises of the text: unlike many Old Testament critics she speaks out about her problems with her marriage,

---

153. Weems, 'Gomer', p. 98.

154. Compare, for example, Andersen and Freedman's analysis: 'Why the husband should now deliberately share this privilege (that is, the seeing and enjoying of his wife's naked body) with his rivals is not clear, although in view of the context of the former's courage, and legitimate demand for retribution, it is to be seen as a punishment appropriate to the crime. Just as in the past the errant wife has sought out her lovers and eagerly disrobed in their presence for the purpose of sexual gratification, so now she will be forcibly exposed to the same situation and publicly humiliated. The subtlety of the talion here is essentially that what she did secretly and for pleasure will now be done openly and for disgrace' (*Hosea*, p. 249). Although there are problems with this from a feminist perspective, Andersen and Freedman are at least bewildered by the public act of stripping (albeit for the wrong reasons, a sense that a man's woman is not to be shared). Weems, in contrast, acknowledges that the stripping is a violent and voyeuristic act and still tries to justify it.

155. Presumably, van Dijk-Hemmes, who attacked Andersen and Freedman's reading ('The Imagination of Power', p. 84), would have disagreed even more strongly with Weems's approach.

156. N. Nicholson, *A Match for the Devil* (London: Faber & Faber, 1953); see Chapter 1, §4.5.

which she sees as no more ethical than her role as a temple prostitute,[157] and she defiantly resists her husband's attempts to hem her in. Though the restraint imposed on her is more gentle than that of the original text—Hosea merely proposes to make her 'live like a queen/Eating grapes and pomegranates/Spitting the pips into rose leaves'[158]—she finds this oppression stultifying and returns to her life as a hierodule.

Significantly, Nicholson's Gomer returns to Hosea only after negotiations in which she sets her own terms and radically revises the antiquated concept of forgiveness he offers. She does not want to come back 'to be coddled like a pot plant' and 'sheltered even from the draught of a memory'; she does not regret her past and refuses to become a 'dirty cup to be rinsed out and set on the shelf again' while Hosea 'twiddles' his 'magnanimous thumbs'.[159] If his main concern is to protect her purity, she proposes that he buy himself a balloon and 'spend [his] nights watching that no-one bursts it';[160] Hosea in response revises his distorted concept of relationships and his realization that he has offered her 'the consciousness of guilt in part-exchange for love'[161] leads him to challenge the concept of divine forgiveness.

Although I am reluctant to let a male writer have the last word in a study of women's responses, Nicholson's play is worthy of mention because it represents a radical subversion of the text's ideology. Poetic licence seems to enable him to step outside the text's assumptions more thoroughly than some feminist critics who are restrained by their

157. In Nicholson's play the match between Gomer and Hosea is contrived by Gomer's son and grandmother using Gomer's dowry of thirty shekels as bait. Gomer protests that since the marriage is arranged and money is involved it cannot be morally superior to her work as a temple prostitute: the marriage, she suggests, is a tainted thing, motivated by contrivance rather than love. Though Nicholson inverts the circumstances of the original text, and the marriage is contrived by the bride's family rather than Yhwh and Hosea, Gomer's point about contrivance is a poignant comment on the original text. From a twentieth-century Western perspective, represented by Gomer's voice, a contrived marriage is inadequate, and there is something distasteful about using a marriage simply as a visual aid. Foster argues that religious zeal and the desire to educate Israel through symbolism may be laudable in itself, but is 'hardly a God-given reason for marriage' ('I will not punish your daughters', p. 64). Though not a feminist, Nicholson protests against 'ugly relationships' based simply on duty and, like Foster, he characterizes Gomer as an educating force.

158. Nicholson, *A Match for the Devil*, p. 31.

159. Nicholson, *A Match for the Devil*, p. 74.

160. Nicholson, *A Match for the Devil*, p. 76.

161. Nicholson, *A Match for the Devil*, p. 79.

commitment to the text's theology. In contrast to the passive and culpable Gomers of some feminist re-readings, Nicholson's Gomer is 'the most attractive character in the play', who plays the 'generous Canaanite'[162] and challenges the text's misperceptions of the 'other'.

Nicholson's strategy of re-reading is the reverse of Weems's: he does not begin with assumptions about the deity but with his reaction to the human situation, which he then allows to colour and adjust his perception of the relationship between Yhwh and Israel. The result is not theological pronouncements and a reiteration of God's love and infallibility, but a tense dialogue between the assumptions of the text and the twentieth century:

> But what does his forgiveness mean?
> It asks us to be what we don't want to be—
> We resent the presumption;
> We deny the right.
> How can God begin to forgive us
> Till we learn to forgive God?[163]

3. *Towards a Feminist Approach to Hosea*

3.1. *Critical Seductions*

> Few of us approach this text of Hosea without having first had it obscured by Christian theology, individual soteriology and romantic fiction; and all this conspires with the narrator to *seduce* us into reading the text from Hosea's point of view.[164]

The readings of Hosea by Wacker, Balz-Cochois, Weems and Yee represent the beginnings of a feminist response to this text but also provide some cautionary lessons. For in trying to 'find a way to talk about [a] female character in a text in which "there are no literary remains of women's voices"',[165] they relapse into the lexis and ideals of patriarchal discourse. The countervoice is not always clearly distinct from the voice of the text and of traditional critics: the antithesis, like the thesis, is marked by the androcentric point of view. As clearly as do male commentators' descriptions of 'haloes' and depravity, feminist recreations of

---

162. M. Roston, *Biblical Drama in England: From the Middle Ages to the Present Day* (London: Faber & Faber, 1968), p. 294.

163. Nicholson, *A Match for the Devil*, p. 79.

164. Foster, 'I Will Not Punish Your Daughters For Being Prostitutes', p. 68.

165. Bach, 'Reading Allowed', p. 195.

Gomer fall roughly into the categories of angel and whore: Balz-Cochois's Gomer is acquiescent and associated with 'holiness, righteousness and goodness', while Weems's Gomer is 'brazen' and provocative, and brings violence upon herself.

Problems arise for feminist critics when they try to move beyond 'Images of Women Criticism', like Setel's excellent critique of female *objec*tification, to an attempt to see the female character, and the female commentator, as *subject* and creators of their own identity. The transition is at once desirable (if feminist critics are not content to leave female victimization intact)[166] and problematic, for, as feminist critics have pointed out and as the above articles seem to testify, women's minds are 'masculinized'[167] or 'immasculated',[168] because they have assimilated values that are not their own. Commenting on this bizarre and disturbing phenomenon, Barbara Johnson has suggested that the way in which women have been socialized to see more than one point of view, and certainly more than their own perspective, has positive and negative implications. On the one hand, women have been well-trained as potential deconstructors, but on the other, the capacity to see more than one perspective often results in 'self-repression and ambiguation', and a deferential style[169] in which the feminist critic persistently promotes the

166. As Elisabeth A. Meese puts it, 'Images of Women' criticism is both necessary and inadequate, and while 'the catalogue of injustices, abuses, and misrepresentations... bears repeating, ritualistically, in the way of chants and evocations', it can merely perpetuate anger and depression if not complemented by another more positive approach (*Crossing the Double-Cross*, p. 5).

167. S. Snaider Lanser and E. Torton Beck, '[Why] Are There No Great Women Critics? And What Difference Does It Make?', in J.A. Sherman and E. Torton Beck (eds.), *The Prism of Sex: Essays in the Sociology of Knowledge* (Madison, WI: University of Wisconsin Press, 1979), p. 86, cited in J. Donovan, 'Towards a Women's Poetics', in Benstock (ed.), *Feminist Issues in Literary Scholarship*, pp. 95-122 (98).

168. Judith Fetterly famously replaces the androcentric stereotype of the castrating bitch (the emasculating woman) with the new feminist stereotype, the immasculated woman: 'Though one of the most persistent of literary stereotypes is the castrating bitch, the cultural reality is not the emasculation of men by women, but the *immasculation* of women by men. As readers and teachers and scholars, women are taught to think as men, to identify with a male point of view, and to accept as normal and legitimate a male system of values' (Fetterly, *The Resisting Reader*, p. xx).

169. B. Johnson, 'Interview', in I. Salusinszky (ed.), *Criticism in Society: Interviews with Jacques Derrida, Northrop Frye, Harold Bloom, Geoffrey Hartman, Frank Kermode, Edward Said, Barbara Johnson, Frank Lentricchia and J. Hillis*

other's point of view over and above her own.

As a description of Wacker and Balz-Cochois's articles, Johnson's thesis is too accurate to ignore. Both critics present a bifurcated point of view, a thesis and an antithesis, yet they ultimately defer to the dominant discourse and hedge the feminist counter-voice in apologetic. Like Monique Wittig, who represents the female subject as *j/e,* these articles express 'the implicit schizophrenic or split nature of any female who attempts to constitute herself as the subject of her own discourse.'[170] As Kathryn Allen Rabuzzi comments, 'To internalise otherness is almost definitionally to be unable to speak in the language of the self...To experience being an Other is often to feel so schizophrenically torn, that not even a clandestinely authentic "I" dares to speak.'[171]

Whereas Rabuzzi qualifies her description with words like 'almost' and 'often', there is another strain of feminist criticism, represented by critics like Jane Miller and Jane Gallop, who argue that patriarchy is internalised in women to such an extent that it is ultimately insurmountable. Both critics describe the capitulation of women to the patriarchal standard under the motif of 'seduction': Jane Miller argues in *Seductions* that women are not merely seduced by men, but that 'they are seduced as well by the stories men have told about these seductions and by the visions of women which may be derived from such stories',[172] while Jane Gallop, in *The Daughter's Seductions: Feminism and Psychoanalysis*, asks 'how [can] patriarchy be overthrown if it is necessarily internalized in everybody who could possibly act to overthrow it?'[173] Like Nina Baym I want to protest against the pessimism of these descriptions[174] and suggest that the ambiguities of androcentric

---

Miller (London: Methuen, 1987), pp. 169-70. Johnson does not characterize all feminist criticism as deferential, and wryly observes that some criticism is certainly not 'shy of ambiguity', but she does perceive a marked tendency in feminist criticism towards self-repression.

170. H. Wenzel, 'The Text as Body/Politics: An Appreciation of Monique Wittig's Writing in Context', *FS* 7 (1981), pp. 264-87 (267).

171. K. Allen Rabuzzi, *The Sacred and the Feminine: Toward a Theology of Housework* (New York: Seabury, 1982), p. 176.

172. J. Miller, *Seductions: Studies in Reading and Culture* (London: Virago, 1990), p. 1.

173. J. Gallop, *The Daughter's Seduction: Feminism and Psychoanalysis* (Ithaca, NY: Cornell University Press, 1982), p. 14.

174. Commenting on *The Daughter's Seduction*, Nina Baym argues that while many women become feminists because they recognise the 'abjectness of their

discourse allow for all kinds of creative possibilities. Patriarchy allows, for example (albeit from a misogynistic perspective), that women can be seducing as well as seduced, sexually powerful as well as sexually vulnerable, and by using the metaphor in one sense only, Miller and Gallop are making the choice only to replicate myths of female credulity and passivity.

Unlike Gallop and Miller, Hosea 1–3 retains all the ambiguities of seduction. The text begins with a woman, a 'wife of harlotry', who presumably plays a seductive role, and ends with a fantasy of a pliant woman who is the object of her husband's seduction.[175] Seduction in Hosea 1–3 also retains all the ambiguities of the chase, and the capitulation of the woman is not a *fait accompli*, but is something that the text struggles to achieve. Although the text presents the seduction of the woman as an ideal, it is by no means a foregone conclusion, and the dream of the submissive woman is flanked by images of binding and captivity (2.5, 8, 9; 3.3) which betray the fear that the reality may prove far more recalcitrant than the ideal.

While the text urges that submission is the best strategy for the woman-nation, it seems by no means certain that this is a strategy that she will accept. The woman in the text may or may not be seduced; similarly, the woman outside the text is given a choice as to which character she will follow and which point of view she will promote. Like the woman who leaves her husband, she can choose the extent of the master(text)'s power over her, but by departing from its ideology she becomes, by the text's own standards, transgressive. The fact that the feminist poet Leda Whitman can step outside the theological assumptions of Eden and create an Eve who laughs at and defies God's 'tree, his keep out/sign and electrical fence'[176] suggests that critics are not

---

attitudes towards men...a theory that valorises or prescribes abjectness seems to...confuse the starting point with the end' (N. Baym, 'The Madwoman and Her Languages: Why I Don't Do Feminist Literary Theory', in Benstock [ed.], *Feminist Issues in Literary Studies*, pp. 45-61 [60, n.13]).

175. Unlike the author of Proverbs 7, the male author sees himself not only as victim of seduction but as seducer, and imagines 'alluring' his wife and 'lead[ing] her into the wilderness' (Hos. 2.16).

176. Leda Whitman, cited in A.S. Ostriker, *Feminist Revision and the Bible* (The Bucknell Lectures in Literary Theory, 7; Oxford: Basil Blackwell, 1993), p. 82. The tendency of some feminist biblical critics to allow their commitment to the text to compete with, and occasionally eclipse, their commitment to feminism initially created a breach between secular and biblical feminist criticism. Looking from the

necessarily bound by patriarchal ideology, but are confronted with a conflict of interests—their commitment to feminism and their commitment to the (pervasively androcentric) theology of the text.

3.2. *Another Transgressive Coupling: Feminism and Deconstruction*

The quest for a method in feminist criticism has resulted in several categories of approach. Feminist critics can be either 'Images of Women' (or 'first wave') critics or 'Gyno-' (or 'second wave') critics; for biblical feminists the categories, as outlined by Carol Osiek, are extended to include 'rejectionist', 'loyalist', 'revisionist', 'sublimationist', or 'liberationist' approaches.[177] Categorization is useful because it defines and therefore foregrounds the difference between women's voices, but it is also restrictive because it denies the differences within a single voice. Many gynocritics working with women's writing see their work as superior and antithetical to 'Images of Women' criticism (which is parodied as a remnant from the relatively submissive first wave),[178] and similarly Osiek's positions deny the possibility that a rejectionist critic can also, on occasions, be liberationist in her approach.

However sophisticated the various positions appear, they each fall into

outside in, Gerda Lerner accused scholars such as Phyllis Trible, Phyllis Bird and John Otwell of trying to 'balance the overwhelming evidence of patriarchal domination by citing examples of a few female heroic figures' (G. Lerner, *The Creation of Patriarchy* [Oxford: Oxford University Press, 1986], pp. 176-77). The idea that feminist readings of the Bible are characterized by compromise and special pleading has been very influential: apart from Carol Christ and Mary Daly, criticism of the Bible is rarely included in general feminist readers. Yet what is excluded is a stereotype based on a misunderstanding; in fact, many biblical feminists start from the same assumptions as Lerner, and Cheryl Exum, for example, begins her book *Fragmented Women* with a quotation from *The Creation of Patriarchy*.

177. C. Osiek, 'The Feminist and the Bible: Hermeneutical Alternatives', in Collins (ed.), *Feminist Perspectives on Biblical Scholarship*, pp. 93-105. (To clarify the less transparent terms, a 'sublimationist' critic looks for and glorifies the eternal feminine in the text, and a 'liberationist' starts from the assumptions of liberation theology.)

178. Elaine Showalter, for example, characterizes the transition from feminist criticism of androcentric texts to the recovery of women's writing as a *progression*. She argues that although it is a necessary stage in the development of a feminist agenda, 'Images of Women' criticism compromises itself by engaging with male authors. Gynocriticsm is ideologically purer and 'genuinely independent' because 'woman-centred' ('Feminist Criticism in the Wilderness', in Showalter [ed.], *The New Feminist Criticism* [London: Virago, 1989], pp. 243-70 [247]).

an essential dichotomy between positive and negative images of women. A biblical critic *either* presents negative images of women and denounces the patriarchal text, *or* recuperates positive images of women and so redeems the text. The pattern is similar in 'secular' feminist criticism: 'Images of Women' criticism is cast as the *'negative* hermeneutic of ideological unmasking' as opposed to the *'positive* [act] of recovering and cultivating women's culture'[179]—using a biblical metaphor, 'Images of Women' criticism is even cast as the Old Testament of feminism that has not yet discovered the redemptive grace of the New (women's writing).[180] Categories that ostensibly describe 'method' in fact articulate ideological positions, and from the binary opposition between positive and negative, new and old, it is but a short step to the related opposition of 'right' and 'wrong'. The reduction of critical approaches to a diametrical opposition is detrimental to the feminist enterprise because it encourages feminist fundamentalism, or the type of criticism in which critics admonish other critics across an abyss of opposition in articles heavy with imperatives and exhortation.[181]

Recently, feminist scholars in the field of biblical studies have begun to strain against the restrictions imposed by binary opposition. In *Death and Dyssymetry*, Mieke Bal protests that the 'radical/conservative, biblical/post-biblical dichotomy is crudely reductive',[182] and Cheryl Exum proposes that we 'move beyond this kind of either–or approach to explore new and more suitable methods of feminist critique'.[183] A

179. Schweickart, 'Reading Ourselves', p. 35 (my italics).

180. C.G. Heilbrun and C.R. Stimpson, 'Theories of Feminist Criticism: A Dialogue', in J. Donovan (ed.), *Feminist Literary Criticism* (Lexington, KY: University Press of Kentucky, 1975), pp. 61-73 (64).

181. Like Nina Baym, I instinctively react against 'essays in feminist journals [that] are permeated with "musts" and "shoulds", with homily and exhortation' ('The Madwoman and her Languages', p. 59). Jane Marcus for example, tends to exhort and accuse her reader, only lightly diluting the accusation by putting it in the third person: 'She must...she must...she must' ('Storming the Toolshed', *Signs* 7 [1982], pp. 622-40 [626]). Reacting against Marcus's legalistic criticism, Baym protests 'If that *she* is *me*, somebody (once again) is telling me what I *"must"* do to be a true woman, and that somebody is asserting (not incidentally) her own monopoly on truth as she does so. I've been here before' ('The Madwoman and Her Languages', p. 61 n. 32).

182. M. Bal, *Death and Dyssymmetry: The Politics of Coherence in the Book of Judges* (Chicago: University of Chicago Press, 1988), p. 34.

183. Exum, *Fragmented Women*, p. 11.

new kind of feminist biblical criticism is emerging that both acknowledges woman's oppression *and* defies it, and in order to describe this
new approach critics are appealing to the language and motifs of deconstruction. Cheryl Exum proposes 'deconstructing the dominant male
voice, or phallogocentric ideology of [biblical] narratives',[184] while
David Jobling begins his feminist rereading of Hosea with an analogy
between a theory that exposes 'the limits of the text's ability to establish
its fiction' and the feminist project of exposing the flaws and limits of a
gendered, patriarchal perspective.[185] Alice Bach, in her rereading of the
Law of the Sotah, uses Derrida, or as she puts it, 'the general of the
French Resistance',[186] to break down the barrier between text and context. However, although critics have hinted at the potential for dialogue
between these two fugitive and notoriously radical approaches to texts,
the intersection has yet to be explored in detail. Biblical scholars have
only begun to probe the potential rewards of a feminist deconstructive
approach and have not yet begun to consider that, like the marriage of
the prophet and the prostitute, this may be a precarious and even
dangerous liaison.

   The deconstructive reader of classical texts and the feminist reader of
androcentric texts do in fact have much in common. Both deny the
control of authorial intention and yet both imply its existence, for
implicit in both reading strategies is a sense that these readings are
transgressive and subvert intended meanings. Both are conscious of
reading against the grain, of producing the one reading that definitely
was not intended, yet despite their similar status as outlaws, many feminist critics have been careful to highlight the differences. Some affirm
the independence of feminist criticism and warn against the dangers of
losing its distinctive individuality in the idiosyncrasies of Jacques Derrida;
others warn of the danger of submitting to another male literary guru;
and others point to the way in which Derrida and the Yale deconstructionists exclude women's writing from their enquiries, just like their
more orthodox predecessors. For some scholars there is an implicit
irony in Derrida's warning that feminists should not subscribe to male
ideals of 'truth, science and objectivity' and aspire to become like the

---

   184. Exum, *Fragmented Women*, p. 17.
   185. D. Jobling, 'Deconstructive Reading of Hosea 1–3' (unpublished paper),
p. 1.
   186. Bach, 'Good to the Last Drop', p. 26.

'masculine dogmatic philosopher',[187] for as I suggested in the previous chapter, deconstruction denies the particular situation of the reader, which is vital to a feminist perspective.

However, to use Derridean reading strategies does not necessarily involve submission to all of Derrida's premises, nor does it limit the reader to being bound by Derrida's oversights. Feminist criticism in particular is adept at being 'playfully pluralist' and 'responsive to all the critical schools and methods but captive of none',[188] and is accustomed to reading 'strategically' and taking risks, most recently the 'risk of essence'.[189] The question is not of submission but of *bricolage*: the feminist critic can choose elements from theory to supplement and enhance her own unique perspective. As with primary, so with secondary texts: women cannot be seduced without their consent, and it is the critic's choice to what extent she allows the text to master her.[190]

Although he consistently deconstructs the logocentric order, Derrida is less sensitive to androcentric biases in his writing, and in order to deconstruct what many feminists are now calling the 'phallogocentric' order, feminist critics have to extend and transform the deconstructive project. Derrida is concerned with the relegation of writing in Western philosophy, while feminist critics are more concerned with the equally systematic relegation of women; Derrida is concerned with difference on

187. J. Derrida, *Spurs: Nietzsche's Styles* (trans. B. Harlow; Chicago: University of Chicago Press, 1978), p. 65.

188. A. Kolodny, 'Dancing Through the Minefield: Some Observations on the Theory, Politics and Practice of a Feminist Criticism', *FS* 6 (1980), pp. 1-25 (19).

189. Trying to negotiate between the anti-essentialism of deconstruction and the importance of the reader's gender and situation in feminist criticism, Gayatri Chakravorty Spivak has advocated reading strategically, and taking the risk of using essentialism and deconstruction, as it suits the critic's purposes. 'A strategy suits a situation', and 'works through a persistent deconstructive critique of the theoretical': it does not claim to be 'universal' or 'disinterested', but is a battle metaphor, 'an artifice or trick designed to outwit the enemy' (Spivak, *Outside in the Teaching Machine* [London: Routledge, 1993], pp. 3-4).

190. P. Schweickart and E.A. Meese, working with reader-response criticism and deconstruction respectively, do not see their dialogue with theory as submissive, but interactive. Schweickart claims defiantly, 'To put the matter plainly, reader-response criticism needs feminist criticism. The two have yet to engage in a sustained and serious way, but if the promise of the former is to be fulfilled, such an encounter must soon occur' ('Reading Ourselves', p. 20). Meese, similarly, is a guardian of difference and insists that 'feminism must not compromise its goals in order to achieve a reconciliation with deconstruction' (*Crossing the Double-Cross*, p. xi).

a conceptual and abstract level, while feminism is concerned with the differences that structure society. Adapting Derrida's project to her own agenda, Hélène Cixous constructs her own series of pervasive hierarchies—activity–passivity, seed–ground, intelligible–sensitive, subject–object—which are all displaced forms of the central hierarchy male–female. Foregrounding a question that haunts Derrida's texts, she asks, '[I]s the fact that logocentrism subjects thought—all the concepts, the codes, the values—to a two-term system, related to "the" couple man/woman?'[191]

By adjusting 'binary opposition' to 'couple', Cixous transposes Derrida's argument from philosophical texts to the level of gender studies and human relationships.[192] This translation of Derridean motifs to the realm of social interaction and power relationships characterizes feminist deconstruction: Charlotte Guillaumin teases out the implications of 'difference' for women's studies and explores how it structures 'reality' as well as texts;[193] and E.A. Meese outlines ways in which it can be used to redescribe relationships between men and women in such a way that it threatens 'the efficacy of the dominant discourse to maintain social institutions that oppress women'.[194] In feminist deconstruction the political agenda that is always implicit in Derrida's work, though repeatedly denied, is brought to the fore,[195] and the critic explores ways in which 'the discourse of domination writes its own undoing in the

191. H. Cixous, 'Sorties', in D. Lodge (ed.), *Modern Criticism and Theory: A Reader* (London: Longman, 1988), pp. 287-93 (287); repr. from E. Marks and I. de Courtivron (eds.), *New French Feminisms: An Anthology* (Brighton: Harvester Press, 1981).

192. It is yet another testimony to the pervasiveness of logocentric philosophy that I find it impossible to describe Cixous's relation to Derrida without adopting the language of contrast and appealing to the dichotomy philosophical–physical (abstract–real).

193. 'There is a great realism hidden in the word "difference": the knowledge that there exists a source of evaluation, a point of reference, an origin of the definition. And if there is an origin of the definition, it means precisely that this definition is *not* "free". The definition is seen for what it is: a fact of dependence and a fact of domination' (C. Guillaumin, 'The Question of Difference' [trans. H.V. Wenzel], *Feminist Issues* 2 [1982], pp. 33-52 [45]).

194. Meese, *Crossing the Double-Cross*, p. 82.

195. In 'Positions' Derrida maintains that he has no Marxist agenda, although his approach lends itself to revolutionary interpretation. Similarly he maintains that he is neither a feminist nor an antifeminist, though the idea that the dominant discourse can be deconstructed inevitably lends itself to gender studies.

discourse of subordination'.[196] The course of feminist deconstruction draws attention to the role of the reader, which Derrida always represses, for as readings are radically transformed when the reader is a woman, so deconstruction is radically rewritten when approached from a woman's point of view.

For Derrida difference operates in and between words, but feminist deconstructionists extend difference, by analogy, to encompass the strained relationship that exists between the feminist reader and androcentric texts. Exploring what she terms the 'difference of view', Mary Jacobus proposes that 'Though necessarily working within male discourse, women's writing...would work ceaselessly to deconstruct it: to write what cannot be written'.[197] Her description is provocative because it implies that in feminist deconstruction 'Images of Women' criticism and 'Women's Writing' can be made to coincide. Reading deconstructively involves detailing *and* creatively displacing repressive hierarchies, and allows critics who operate exclusively within androcentric texts to do more than merely provide a dreary record of women's oppression. By reading cunningly and creatively, biblical feminists can elude the restrictive roles prescribed for woman by the text *and* by theory. In a genuinely '*double* gesture' they can show how the text constructs and deconstructs a particular image of woman, while at the same time eluding binary theoretical categories that would tend to label them *either* rejectionist *or* revisionist.

As Derrida retains the terms of Western metaphysics but interrogates their assumptions, so the feminist critic can adopt a similar strategy with Derridean motifs. When Derrida writes, for example, that 'In a given situation, which is ours, which is the European phallogocentric structure, the side of the woman is the side from which you start to dismantle the structure',[198] he seems to be making the same controversial claim as feminist critics, but this statement also betrays a controversy between feminism and deconstruction, and a use of the word 'woman' that needs to be regarded with suspicion. For Derrida, as for Nietzsche, 'woman' is like writing or undecideability: she is the signifier with no stable signified, and, as some feminists argue, the complete antithesis of the

196. Meese, *Crossing the Double-Cross,* p. 83.

197. Jacobus, 'The Difference of View', pp. 12-13.

198. 'Women in the Beehive: A Seminar with Jacques Derrida', in A. Jardine and P. Smith (eds.), *Men in Feminism* (New York: Methuen, 1987), pp. 189-203 (194).

idea that women have a distinct (though multiple) perspective and that 'reading as a woman' is somehow different from 'reading as a man'. Reading *sous rature*, or with extreme suspicion, I nevertheless want to take up the Derridean idea that 'woman' is 'the wild card, the joker in the pack, who upsets the logocentric and phallocentric stack of appellations',[199] and to look at how Gomer-bat-Diblayim disturbs Hosea 1–3 with undecideabilities and places the premises of patriarchy in jeopardy.

4. *Toppling the Pack: A Feminist Deconstructive Reading of Hosea 1–3*

> In biblical cosmology, the universe is seen rather like a house of cards; if the lines are not kept neat, the whole edifice will collapse.[200]

Hosea 1–3 is a doubly transgressive text. Not surprisingly, as an androcentric text from the eighth century BCE, it audaciously transgresses standards set by the feminist movement concerning the treatment and depiction of women, but more surprisingly, it transgresses feminist standards in a different sense by occasionally subverting feminist definitions of 'the androcentric text'. The second (muted) transgression does not cancel out the first, but the coexistence of the two transgressions shows the vulnerability of the text to deconstruction, and in a secondary sense, the vulnerability of feminist theorizations of androcentricism. Reading deconstructively primarily exposes the self-contradictions of patriarchal rhetoric, but also suggests that even the most 'misogynistic' and 'patriarchal' texts deconstruct, as well as conform to, feminist definitions.

'Texts trigger readings; that is what they are, the occasion of a reaction', writes Mieke Bal. The relationship between Hosea 1–3 and the feminist reader is inevitably an abrasive one: a reaction is 'triggered' or provoked, rather than 'elicited', because this text seems to violate all feminist principles and to actualize virtually every indictment against androcentric texts. The painful progress of the אֵשֶׁת זְנוּנִים through the text is like an allegory in which every complaint of feminist critics is symbolized and catalogued. The woman is denied the right to name, is appropriated as a symbol, and is literally stripped, trapped, and pressed into

199. E. Showalter, 'Critical Cross-Dressing: Male Feminist and the Woman of the Year', in Jardine and Smith (eds.), *Men in Feminism*, pp. 116-32 (124).

200. T. Frymer-Kensky, 'Law and Philosophy: The Case of Sex in the Bible', in D. Patrick (ed.), *Thinking Biblical Law* (Semeia 45; Atlanta: Scholars Press, 1989), pp. 89-101 (98).

conformity as the text dramatically visualizes the classic features of an androcentric text.

In its strategy of repression Hosea 1–3 becomes a prooftext for practically every keynote speech of feminist criticism. Carol Christ and Judith Plaskow's argument that 'men have reserved for themselves the right to name'[201] is questioned by some Old Testament texts, but justified by a text in which *she* conceives but *he* names, and which emphatically excludes the mother from the naming process. Similarly, Dworkin's and Munich's protest that women are always 'symbols of something other than themselves'[202] and are 'mythologized... interpreted',[203] is endorsed by a text in which a woman not only symbolizes 'the land' and 'transgression', but labours over the production of child-signs—who will also signify 'the land' and 'transgression'. The text not only suggests the woman's symbolic function but emphasizes it, for Gomer 'bears' Israel's sins in a double sense, as a marked woman, a walking sign of adultery, and as the mother of further meaning. The birth of three children in quick succession suggests that this text is laboured in more ways than one: the text not only uses woman as a symbol, but emphasizes how she is subordinated to, and labours over, the production of a meaning which is not her own.

Designed as an illustration of religious apostasy, Hosea 1–3 could also be used as the ultimate manifesto of patriarchy, for it supports even the most polemical and reductive feminist claims. The most extreme assertions, such as Susan Griffin's pronouncement that 'every shade of pornographic feeling has its origin in the church', could find a prooftext (if one were required) here.[204] Chapter 2 details violent misogyny that

---

201. C. Christ and J. Plaskow (eds.), *Womanspirit Rising: A Feminist Reader in Religion* (New York: Harper & Row, 1979), p. 7. The danger of generalization is demonstrated by the fact that in many Old Testament texts the mother is granted the power to name (see, for example, Gen. 4.1; Judg. 13.24; 1 Sam. 1.20).

202. See for example Dworkin, *Pornography*, p. 128.

203. Munich, 'Notorious Signs', p. 250.

204. S. Griffin, *Pornography and Silence: Culture's Revenge Against Women*, in M. Humm (ed.), *Feminisms: A Reader* (Hemel Hempstead: Harvester Wheatsheaf, 1992), pp. 80-81 (80). I find Griffin's statement unsatisfactory not only because it is authoritarian and mimics the absolutism that feminism tries to counteract, but also because it is a dangerous instance of replacing one scapegoat (woman) with another (religious institutions). A more measured approach to the Bible and Jewish and Christian religion is adopted by feminists such as Setel and Plaskow, who argue that while the Bible is a central document of patriarchy, no one single document or

would not look out of place in a novel by Norman Mailer: 'female eroticism' is made 'synonymous with abomination, promiscuity and infidelity',[205] and the text promotes, as contemporary pornography does, hostility, 'male power', and the 'graphic depiction of women as vile whores'.[206] The way to tame a woman, the text recommends, is to humiliate her: explicitly, by stripping her to reveal her 'shame' (genitalia),[207] but also implicitly by suggesting that whoredom is 'part and parcel of the female body'.[208] The command that the woman remove her harlotries (זְנוּנֶיהָ) from her face and adulteries (נַאֲפוּפֶיהָ) from between her breasts (Hos. 2.4) has been variously interpreted by commentators as a reference to jewellery, headbands, and even scratch marks on the breasts caused by ecstatic frenzy,[209] but it is also, more simply, a way of marking the woman's body with the words 'adultery' and 'harlotry'.[210] In a graphic literalisation of the feminist metaphor 'writing on the body', the woman's body is appropriated by her male observers and marked with their mis*interpretations*, which are themselves symbols of mis*use*.

The claim that patriarchy dispossesses women of language, speech and a voice is perfectly demonstrated in a text that obstinately refuses to allow woman the right to self-expression. There is a disjuncture in her characterization that makes the woman of Hosea 1–3 highly unbelievable, for even as she is characterized as an obstinate woman who runs

institution can be labelled as patriarchy's origin (Setel, 'Prophets and Pornography', p. 86; J. Plaskow, 'Blaming the Jews for the Birth of Patriarchy', in E.T. Beck [ed.], *Nice Jewish Girls: A Lesbian Anthology* [Watertown, MA: Persephone Press, 1982], pp. 250-54).

205. Pardes, *Countertraditions*, p. 134.

206. Dworkin, *Pornography*, pp. 199-202.

207. W.D. Whitt captures the implicit aggression of the text in his graphic translation of Hos. 2.12: 'Therefore I now expose her cunt in front of her lovers and none can save her from my hand' ('The Divorce of Yahweh and Asherah in Hos. 2.4-7; 12ff', *SJOT* 6 [1992], pp. 31-67 [52]).

208. Pardes, *Countertraditions*, p. 134.

209. H.W. Wolff, *A Commentary on the Book of Hosea* (trans. G. Stansell; Herm; Philadelphia: Fortress Press, 1974), p. 34.

210. In Ezek. 23.7 the woman Oholah is depicted bestowing her harlotries upon Assyria: an abstract noun 'harlotries' is metaphorically concretized, qualified by a female suffix, and described in terms of a gift that can be picked up and given. As promiscuous women can give their harlotries, so in Hosea they can wear them; in a text that denies female possession, 'harlotries' and 'adulteries' are two of the few items attributed to the woman.

away and resists the patriarchal will, she utters stylized and artificial speeches that reinforce patriarchy's case against her. In 2.7 and 2.14 she provides the evidence for her own conviction: in 2.7 she merely repeats the case against her established in 1.2 when she expresses her intention to go after her lovers; and in 2.14 she characterizes herself as a prostitute by terming basic provisions her 'hire'. The manipulation of the woman's speech described in 2.19, when Yhwh threatens to extract the names of Baal from her mouth, only foregrounds the manipulation of the woman's mouth/speech in the rest of the text. As she 'speaks' in perfect compliance with the text's accusations against her, so she conforms entirely to the text's project of improvement, saying, as scripted, 'I will go and return to my first husband because it was better for me then than now' (Hos. 2.9). As 2.18 makes clear, the woman is told what she will say, and she becomes, effectively, a puppet of patriarchal rhetoric.

As Hosea 1–3 traps the woman's voice in inverted commas and allows her to speak only within the parameters of (mis)quotation, so too it subjects the woman to physical imprisonment and literalizes metaphors of entrapment used in feminist descriptions of androcentric texts. In Hosea 1–3 'captivity' is not simply a figure of speech, as in Tania Modleski's protest that 'women have long been held prisoners of male texts',[211] but is a dominant motif *used by the text* as it describes in detail the purchase of a woman for 'fifteen shekels of silver, and a homer and a lethech of barley' (Hos. 3.2)—that is, the price of a slave.[212] The text's relentless project of confinement not only offends against feminist ethics, it jars with the most fundamental claims of the Suffragette movement that, as Sylvia Pankhurst put it, 'a husband might not imprison his wife to enforce conjugal rights'.[213] It violates not only radical and recent feminist claims, but principles which society has been growing

211. T. Modleski, 'Feminism and the Power of Interpretation: Some Critical Readings', in T. de Lauretis (ed.), *Feminist Studies/Critical Studies* (Bloomington: Indiana University Press, 1986), pp. 121-38 (121). Compare Monique Wittig's comment that 'The perenniality of the sexes and the perenniality of slaves and masters proceed from the same belief, and as there are no slaves without masters, there are no women without men' ('The Category of Sex', *Feminist Issues* 2 [1982], pp. 63-68).

212. Most commentators calculate that the price of the woman is thirty shekels, that is the price of a slave according to Exod. 21.32 (see, for example, Wolff, *Hosea*, p. 61).

213. S. Pankhurst, *The Suffragette Movement* (London: Virago, 1978), p. 95.

accustomed to over the last century: it appeals to motifs of slavery, which causes embarrassment within Western democratic society; and it contravenes one of our most cherished ideals, the ideal of personal autonomy.

4.1. *Dissension Against—and Within—the Text*

Though they have lacked the critical context in which to launch a sustained complaint against the text,[214] I find traces of discomfort in androcentric readings. Renaud, for example, makes a pointed comment about the 'great...cultural distance'[215] between reader and text, and commentating on 2.12 he notes how the woman is trapped by violence and constrained by 'une main de fer' ('a hand of iron').[216] Writing in a tradition which ideologically affirms the text, he inevitably feels the need to qualify his reaction: violence is the violence of love, and the hand of iron is also 'une main qui se veut éducatrice' ('a hand that desires to educate');[217] but these mediating explanations do not entirely eradicate his dissatisfaction with male despotism and control. This dissatisfaction is echoed by another androcentric critic, Henry McKeating, who protests in response to Hos. 2.8 that 'The talk about chasing lovers and being restrained by hedges and walls is more appropriate to an animal on heat than to a human being'.[218]

A conflict between reader and text may, as Jonathan Culler suggests,

---

214. In biblical studies feminist criticism has set a precedent for heated debate between the reader and the text that is largely unrepresented in earlier criticism. Feminist criticism represents a new departure in which the critic is no longer expected to comply with and endorse the text's assumptions, but can debate with those assumptions from the perspective of her own culture.

215. B. Renaud, 'Fidélité humaine et fidélité de Dieu', *Revue de droit canonique* 33 (1983), pp. 184-200 (184).

216. Renaud, 'Fidélité humaine et fidélité de Dieu', p. 197. Renaud's implied discomfort with this text suggests the possibility of men critiquing male as well as female roles in biblical texts. Like Alice Bach ('Reading Allowed', p. 192), I find it intriguing that male contributions to gender studies have thus far concentrated on images of women. To compound the paradox of 'critical cross-dressing', the expansion of women's studies to take in gender studies seems to be led by women (see, for example, A. Brenner and F. van Dijk-Hemmes, *On Gendering Texts: Female and Male Voices in the Hebrew Bible* [BI, 1; Leiden: Brill, 1993]).

217. Renaud, 'Fidélité humaine et fidélité de Dieu', p. 197.

218. H. McKeating, *The Books of Amos, Hosea and Micah* (Cambridge: Cambridge University Press, 1971), p. 83.

indicate a repressed point of disjuncture within the text:[219] Renaud's discomfort points to a textual moment in which Hosea 1–3 seems unsure about its own strategy of confinement. The source of unease is the verb נצל in the threat וְאִישׁ לֹא יַצִּילֶנָּה מִיָּדִי (Hos. 2.12), which can mean neutrally 'take', negatively 'snatch away', or positively 'rescue' or 'deliver'. The undecideability of the verb suggests censure *and* applause for the man who attempts to snatch or rescue Gomer, and casts him both as antagonist to God's purposes *and* potential hero. The translation 'rescue/ deliver', favoured by most translators, suggests that even the text itself mutinies against divine despotism by subtly and almost imperceptibly siding with Yhwh's imagined opponent rather than with Yhwh himself. In another possible reversal of the wilderness tradition, Yhwh, who moulds his reputation on his deliverance of Israel from 'the hand of the Egyptians' (Exod. 18.10), becomes liberator turned oppressor, and Renaud's reference to a 'hand of iron', like my analogy between Yhwh and the villain of Victorian melodrama,[220] begins the deconstructive process by pointing to a site of conflict that it is in the text's interests to repress.

More obliquely than Renaud, Fokkelien van Dijk-Hemmes points to a potential site of conflict in Hos. 2.12 when she asks, 'Why is Israel represented...in the image of a faithless wife, a harlot, and not in the image of, e.g., a rapist, which would have been far more appropriate to Israel's misdeeds?'[221] Van Dijk-Hemmes protests from a twentieth-century perspective against the metaphor's inappropriateness and the text's double standards, but reading deconstructively, a similar protest, though veiled, can be read in the tensions of Hos. 2.12. The verse presents a faithless woman and a rapist, and it is the rapist who wins the text's approval. Female infidelity is seen as the cause, the *provocation*, and 'rape' as the justified response, but the associations of the root נבל, like the undecideability of נצל, suggests a possible deconstruction of this position. Like נצל, נבל works both with and against the text's rhetoric: as the men strip her

219. Culler writes, 'texts thematise, with varying degrees of explicitness, interpretive options and their consequences and thus represent in advance the dramas that will give life to the tradition of their interpretation. Critical disputes about a text can frequently be identified as a displaced re-enactment of conflicts dramatised in the text, so that while the text assays the consequences of various forces it contains, critical readings transform this difference within into a difference between mutually exclusive positions' (*On Deconstruction*, pp. 214-15).

220. See Chapter 3, §4.2.

221. Van Dijk-Hemmes, 'The Imagination of Power', p. 85.

to reveal her shame (נַבְלָתָהּ) it functions as a confirmation of the woman's guilt, but at the same time it sets up embarrassing intertextual echoes which threaten to disturb the distribution of guilt and innocence. According to the dominant argument, women's sexual acts make them culpable but men are protected by divine approval, but נבל disturbs the equilibrium because it reminds the reader of sexual crimes perpetrated by men in the rest of the canon. In a verse that ascribes sexual shame to the female and underplays the male sexual violence involved in her 'exposure', the noun נבלוּת is an unfortunate choice, because it is reminiscent not only of sexual violence perpetrated by men but of the notorious rape scenes of Judg. 19.23 and 20.6, 2 Sam. 13.12 and Gen. 34.7.[222] Embarrassingly, in a text that implies rape but never names it, the noun נבלה reverberates with memories of biblical rape scenes and reminds the reader of men's crimes just when the text requires that he/she forget them.

Joining the dissonant voices against the text's desire to confine, which also includes a muted voice within the text itself, Wilhelm Rudolph expresses reservations about the use of the verb אהב in Hos. 3.1. Whereas most critics see this command as far less problematic than the command in 1.2, and comment simply that a command to love implies a far greater degree of intimacy than a command to take, Rudolph sees 3.1, like 1.2, as an awkward and impossible conjunction because love and entrapment are as uneasy bedfellows as a prophet and a prostitute. 'Love' when coupled with confinement suggests black, sardonic humour: for Rudolph, 'love' can only be ironic when it involves 'depriv[ing] Israel of all that was previously of value to her'.[223] He

---

222. For a full discussion of incidences of נבלוּת in the Hebrew Bible, see A.A. Keefe, 'Rapes of Women/Wars of Men', in C. Camp and C.R. Fontaine (eds.), *Women, War and Metaphor: Language and Society in the Study of the Hebrew Bible* (Semeia 61; Atlanta: Scholars Press, 1993), pp. 79-97 (82).

223. W. Rudolph, *Hosea* (KAT; Gütersloh: Gerd Mohn, 1966), p. 92, G.I. Davies, *Hosea* (OTG; Sheffield: JSOT Press, 1993), p. 84. Rudolph, unlike Renaud, does not offer to dilute his critique, and it is left to other androcentric critics to placate the reader. In response to Rudolph, G.I. Davies argues that 'It is best to take *'aheb* in its straightforward sense, and see the measures in vv. 3-4 as designed for punishment and correction, but not repudiation' (*Hosea*, p. 86). Since his argument for why this is critically preferable is in my opinion weak (he claims, for example, that Hosea could not have understood an ironic command, and that he does not usually employ this kind of irony) I suspect that Davies is rejecting Rudolph's argument for more fundamental reasons. The phrase 'it is best' may also imply that it

describes the tension in the only critical language available to him—the language of irony, which is attached to authorial intention—but it is more accurate to use the language of deconstruction, which allows for the possibility that the conflict may or may not occur according to the author's design. Critics' eulogies to Yhwh's 'indestructible love'[224] on the basis of this passage are over-optimistic, if not naive, for love is deconstructed, placed under erasure, by the outworking of that love, which is confinement.[225] It is reasonable to assume that resistance to confinement is not simply a modern sentiment: the Song of Songs, for example, sees confinement as the opponent of love, and casts those who build walls against the woman and seek to trap her as love's adversaries. In Hosea the lover is also the adversary, redemption is also a trap, and the woman's saviour is also her enemy. Rudolph's observation provides the corollary to Renaud's: as the imagined opponent of Yhwh/Hosea is both rescuer and adversary, so Yhwh/Hosea is both rescuer and adversary and the lines of delineation between Yhwh and his opponent become dangerously blurred.

As Rudolph resists the text's distorted concept of 'love', so Fokkelien van Dijk-Hemmes resists the offence of Hos. 2.7, 9, 14, 18, and the way in which the woman's voice becomes a mere echo of patriarchal ideology. In the phrase '*he* says that *she* says',[226] she seems to recall the petulance of childhood tale telling, and in response to the male misrepresentation of the female voice, to parody the male voice as that of a selfish child. Although she only mentions the distortion of the female

is best for the reader to make his peace with the text, as Davies reasserts the premises of traditional androcentric criticism that readers must read with, and not against, the ideological grain.

224. Wolff, *Hosea*, p. 60.

225. The tension between love and entrapment is addressed in a memorable quotation from George Bernard Shaw (the source of which I have been unable to trace). He observes that 'Those who talk most about the blessings of marriage and the constancy of its vows are the very people who declare that if the chain is broken and the prisoners left free to choose, the whole social fabric would fly asunder. You cannot have the argument both ways. If the prisoner is happy, why lock him up? If he is not, why pretend that he is?' Shaw's concern is obviously for the male victim of matrimony (the imprisoned 'he'), but his comments provide an interesting gloss on this text. If Gomer is a partner in a love relationship, why is she locked in? Like the people quoted by Shaw, this text works against itself and undercuts the love it professes.

226. Van Dijk-Hemmes, 'The Imagination of Power', p. 80.

voice in passing, this one phrase seems to gesture to the complex responses of the twentieth-century reader, who instinctively sees a refusal to acknowledge the perspective of the 'other' as symptomatic of psychological immaturity. Van Dijk-Hemmes begins a train of enquiry that has radical implications, because the text's anxiety to erase and exclude the woman's voice suggests fear of what she might say, and implies that the text is neither as easy about its actions against her nor as convinced of women's powerlessness as the text's surface rhetoric would like to suggest.

4.2. *Towards a Deconstructive Feminist Reading: Starting Points*
Although Renaud, Rudolph and van Dijk-Hemmes all draw attention to points of dissension within the text and highlight starting points for deconstructive readings, van Dijk-Hemmes's protest is particularly interesting because it suggests a radical new framework for re-reading the text. The idea that the main/male voice cannot tolerate a rival self and seeks to subjugate and eradicate it suggests that every sign of female powerlessness in this text, and every offence to the feminist reader, can be read deconstructively as evidence of women's power. From this perspective, the text is *suspiciously* anxious to censor the woman's voice and to create a passive woman who plays the part that is given her, speaks the words that are prescribed for her, and who quietly follows her husband into the desert. Attempts to control her by censoring her voice, trapping her, stripping her, buying her, and locking her away, are not merely offensive but are also symptomatic of a frenzied and inadequate response to a potentially anarchic force.

On a conscious level this text offers itself as an allegory of the religious life of Israel; on an unconscious level, I suggest, it is an allegory of the mechanisms of patriarchal control. The two levels are linked, since both betray a fear of the loss of power: the androcentric author fears the loss of order that results from alienation from Yhwh *and* the loss of power that results from female sexuality unrestricted by monogamy. Though on a conscious level the text places Yhwh and woman at opposite poles, by equating woman and land and God and man, an angry god and an errant woman are versions of the same fear. Both in some way are guarantors of male identity: Yhwh is not the only one who can make Israel into a 'non-people', for the perpetuation of the nation also depends on the co-operation, and fidelity, of its women.

Ostensibly, the symbolic structure of this text ascribes to God and woman a completely opposite relation to man. One must dominate, the other be dominated: the offence of the asymmetrical marriage metaphor, from a feminist perspective, is the assumption that man must submit to God as woman must submit to man. However, it is possible to read this metaphor, and the polarization of 'God' and 'woman', not as a confident statement but as an anxious (over-)reaction. As the names 'Not-Loved' and 'Not-My People' imply a context in which Israel perceived itself as 'Loved' and 'A People', so the polarization of God and woman suggest that women, like Yhwh, guard power that this text is at pains to appropriate.

As I argued in Chapter 2, conventional readings of Hosea 1–3 tend to focus on the level of the signified and see the signifier merely as a means to an end, but one of the 'problems' with this text is that the signifier has a life of its own. The signification breaks down because the signifier and the signified seem to develop in different directions; one theory that accounts for this is that both levels are important, and that they represent parallel but fundamentally different fears. If man's struggle with woman is merely a vehicle for a deeper meaning, why is it described in such agonizing detail, and if the author is not concerned with unrestrained female sexuality, why does he create a woman whose major functions are to conceive relentlessly and to pursue other lovers? One possible answer is that both woman and the deity represent the power of life, and that man must appropriate this power by recovering the deity's favour and 'returning', and by subjecting women to control. Read conventionally, the marriage metaphor suggests that man's submission to God and woman's submission to her husband are, by analogy, 'the same'. Reading between the lines suggests that both acts of submission are organized by men, and that both are governed by the same psychological motivation of appropriating power.

In the background of Derrida's deconstruction is a conspiracy theory, and the implication that writing was deliberately written out of philosophy because it posed a threat to authority and truth. Even as he suggests that speech–writing, like other hierarchies, was constituted at the level of the social unconscious, the word 'violent' seems to imply that some deliberate offence or crime has been committed. This feminist deconstructive reading of Hosea 1–3 preserves a similar undecideability: 'women', like 'writing', is a relegated term which cannot be tolerated because it poses a threat to (patriarchal) authority and truth. Whether the relegation is conscious or unconscious, it is, like the dismissal of writing, emphatic, and the text dramatizes the struggle to repress, entrap and systematically exclude the female will.

The violent hierarchies in Hosea 1–3 are, and are not, like the hierarchies described by Derrida. The violence of their formation is not merely metaphorical but is often graphically visible, and unlike the assimilated hierarchies of Derrida's 'Western metaphysics', they seem to lay bare the struggle of their formation. The impression is of patriarchy in process rather than patriarchy as an established and unassailable system, as if the dominant voice is aware of a countervoice that, if listened to, threatens to relativize and jeopardize the main/male perspective. Points of inconsistency and conflict in the text can also be read as points of anxiety, and in the following reading I want to focus on three such crises in the central hierarchy subject–object, and the related hierarchies accuser–accused and possessor–possession.

4.3. *The Fantasy of the Woman in Pursuit: Deconstructing the Subject–Object Dichotomy*
One of the fundamental premises of feminist criticism is that woman is objectified in androcentric texts. Women are never the focalizers of the narrative but rather the *object* of male contempt or desire; women are not the active participants in the text but the *abject* recipient of actions done to/against them. Hosea 1–3 is a special case that both endorses, and subliminally resists, the stereotype. Objectification is not a *fait accompli* but a struggle in progress, and in an unguarded moment the text suggests that a non-passive woman is also, ironically, something to be desired.

Hosea 1–3 is a tale of two women. These are not 'Gomer' and 'the other woman' of ch. 3, as several critics have argued,[227] but rather the

227. Criticism of Hosea has focused not only on the question of Hosea's marriage but on the related question, how many women are there in this text? (For a summary of the argument and the various positions see H.H. Rowley, 'The Marriage of Hosea', in his *Men of God: Studies in Old Testament History and Prophecy* [London: Nelson, 1963], pp. 66-97). The question must be revised before it can be useful to a feminist critic, because as it stands, it assumes the presence of real women and is also motivated by androcentric concerns. Like the preoccupation with Hosea's marriage to a 'wife of harlotry', the preoccupation with the question of whether the women in chs. 1 and 3 are the same person betrays concern for Hosea's moral reputation. If Hosea takes one promiscuous woman, that is morally problematic, but if he takes more than one he becomes promiscuous himself. As scholars ostensibly debate over whether the puzzling reference to 'a woman' in ch. 3 indicates a woman other

rebellious woman and a secondary figure, the submissive woman, who stars in the patriarchal fantasy of 2.16-25. One is a patriarchal nightmare of rebellion, the other is a dream of submission; one is 'woman as we perceive her', and the other 'woman as we desire her to be'.[228] Neither can be accurately called a female subject,[229] since both are focalized through male eyes, but the rebellious woman is, at least, the subject of her own verbs. Significantly, she does just four things: she 'conceives', 'gives birth', 'weans' and 'goes' after her lovers.

Gomer's power to conceive—unaided by the deity and even, by implication, by her husband—sets her apart from her assimilated sisters Sarah, Rebekah, Rachel and Hannah, who are denied natural reproductive powers, are restrained by marriage, and who require divine assistance in order to produce a child.[230] These women represent the ultimate feminist stereotype, woman as a 'colonised element of patriarchy':[231] they have lost their right to procreative power and have become infertile and dependent; but Gomer, in contrast, is a glimpse of

than Gomer, what is really at stake is Hosea's and hence God's moral integrity.

228. The male fantasy of submission in which the woman passively follows her husband into the desert is to my mind no more convincing than Gimpel's dream of a newly submissive Elka in Isaac Bashevis Singer's 'Gimpel the Fool'. Having acted the shrew throughout her married life, swearing at him, cursing him, and even wounding him Elka (Gomer) appears to her gullible husband after her death with her 'eyes as radiant as the eyes of a saint' ('Gimpel the Fool', in *Gimpel the Fool and Other Tales* [Harmondsworth: Penguin, 1981, p. 24) to stroke, kiss and comfort him. Unlike Thomas Hennings, who sees the dream as proof that the errant wife reaches perfection through love ('Singer's "Gimpel the Fool" and the Book of Hosea', *JNT* 13 [1983], pp. 11-19), I read it as highly ironic. Gimpel is described throughout the narrative as a character who will believe the most unbelievable things, and I find it more likely that his naive and endearing imaginings are a comment on the equally impossible imaginings of the prophet in the original text.

229. As Mieke Bal points out, one of the potential dangers of feminist biblical criticism is to overstress the subjectivity of biblical women in the attempt to retrieve a positive feminist reading. Critics tend, she argues, to 'subjectify the objectification' and use the slightest evidence to argue that the narrative is focalised through female eyes (M. Bal, 'Metaphors He Lives By', in Camp and Fontaine [eds.], *Women, War and Metaphor*, p. 196).

230. Fuchs, 'The Literary Characterisation of Mothers', pp. 151-66. Fuchs makes no mention of Gomer, although Hosea's 'wife of harlotry' provides an interesting exception to the thesis that the Hebrew Bible normally tries to dissociate women and the power of procreation.

231. Munich, 'Notorious Signs', p. 250.

woman *prior to* her colonialization, and a rare and frightening spectre of autonomous female sexuality. As Tikva Frymer-Kensky demonstrates, female sexuality in the Hebrew Bible is a 'volatile, creative and potentially chaotic force'[232] which threatens to blur divisions, but which is controlled by absolute dichotomies between one household and another, between wife and prostitute, mother and whore. Gomer, by these definitions, is the ultimate category mistake, patriarchy's worst case scenario, because like Daniel Defoe's outrageous Roxana, she participates in the 'opposite circumstances of a *Wife* and a *Whore*'.[233]

Gomer's freedom 'to go' is seen as the cause, and visual expression, of her ability to conceive. Reductively, the text diagnoses and treats the problem of her promiscuity at its most basic level and works on the premise that if she can no longer go after her lovers, she can no longer offend (Hos. 2.8-9). As 'going' is an emblem of Gomer's sexual freedom, so attempts to block her path with walls and thorn bushes (2.8) and finally, significantly, to contain her in a man's hands (2.12), are all symptoms of the patriarchal project of control. In 2.7, 9 and 15 the woman is the subject of the verb הלך in the qal form; in 2.16 she is the object of the verb in the hiphil. The transition from אֵלְכָה and וַתֵּלֶךְ to וְהֹלַכְתִּיהָ reflects, in subtle manipulations of the verb, the desire to change the woman from subject to object.[234]

The woman in Hosea 1–3 is, significantly, not merely an object, but an offensive woman who is gradually objectified and forced into conformity with the patriarchal ideal. As the male speaker implements his strategy of confinement, so the language and structure of the text becomes more and more restrictive: the woman is transformed from the subject to the object of verbs, and her voice is enclosed in reported speech. As in the film *The Stepford Wives*,[235] the autonomous woman with her own recalcitrant will is replaced by a woman who is merely the puppet of male rhetoric. I find it sinister that by Hos. 2.19 no resistance from the woman is anticipated, and that she is expected to act as scripted and to meekly follow her husband into the desert.

The depiction of the woman as subject of the verbs הרה ('to conceive'), ילד ('to give birth') גמל ('to wean') and הלך ('to go') gives rise to

---

232. T. Frymer-Kensky, 'Law and Philosophy', p. 89.

233. D. Defoe, *Roxana: The Fortunate Mistress* (Penguin: Harmondsworth, 1987), p. 14.

234. Bal, 'Metaphors He Lives By', p. 196.

235. Palomar/Fadsin, 1975.

two different, but not mutually exclusive, interpretations. It is possible to argue, as I have argued above, that this restricted 'subjectivity' distinguishes the rebellious woman from the passive 'ideal', but it is also possible that these occasional lapses from the subject–object, male–female hierarchy point to a hidden tension within the patriarchal psyche. Since only women can conceive, give birth and wean, the position of the woman as subject of the verbs הרה, ילד and גמל is not particularly significant, but the assertion that the woman goes after her lovers is both insistent (repeated three times) and revealing. Not only is 'woman' the subject of the verb, but man (in the form of her lovers) is the object: woman is the pursuer and man the pursued, and man replaces woman as the 'object of desire'.

The deconstruction of the subject–object dichotomy as the pursuer and the pursued change places constitutes a moment of resistance to the textual rhetoric. On one level this resistance is a way of characterizing the rebellious woman and of posing the problem that patriarchy then solves; but on another deeper level it is not only a description of a certain kind of woman that patriarchy cannot tolerate, but of repressed male desires that patriarchal structures also find undesirable. There are two sides to the inverted hierarchy, the female subject and the male object, and both are outlawed in patriarchal society. Yet the repeated description of men as object suggests that this role has subliminal appeal. On the most obvious level, man wants to be pursued because activity is linked to guilt, and the inversion of the subject–object dichotomy transfers the burden of adultery from the male (even the male Baalim) to the female. But on another level, the role of sexual object is *in itself* appealing, and there is a strong element of self-indulgence in the repetition of the image of the eager female lover who follows in a virtual frenzy of pursuit (Hos. 2.9). The role of object is in this case more desirable because it suggests physical attractiveness and the ability to arouse desire—attributes that are normally ascribed to women. The woman is allowed to pursue, I suspect, because this is the less flattering role that implies subordination to, and infatuation with, the object of one's desires.

The dynamics of this text, which objectifies women and yet betrays a covert desire for male objectification, is analogous to the paradoxes of contemporary pornography. Like most generalizations, the feminist commonplace that pornography objectifies women omits an important although minor detail, that even while it markets women as sexual objects to be consumed, the appeal of soft pornography in particular is that it also situates the male reader/consumer as the object of desire. As Joan Smith observes, though pornographic models are sexual objects, 'an essential part of the Page Three mythology is that the girls...are really panting for sex with the reader'[236]—they are desperate, just as the woman in Hosea 2 is desperate to find her Baalim. Women who are frantic with desire for their lovers are not antithetical to the male ideal but are another version of it, and the active woman and the passive woman can be seen as illegitimate and legitimate expressions of male desire.

Although the woman in Hosea 1–3 retains the power to conceive, the pattern of her characterization is, on another level, very similar to that of Sarah, Rebekah and Hannah. As women's power to give birth is transferred to the deity, so the traditional power of the woman to allure is, in the case of the אֵשֶׁת זְנוּנִים, transferred to her lovers and her husband, who in 2.16 dreams of enticing his wife into the desert. All qualities implying power (be it sexual power or simply the power of provision) are transferred to the male, but in its relentless enthusiasm to humiliate the woman, the text overreaches itself by stacking up too many negatives to be plausible, and ultimately by describing the woman in terms that are mutually exclusive. The woman is humiliated as an אֵשֶׁת זְנוּנִים and as a pursuer who is never pursued: separately the negatives are plausible, but when they are placed together, even the most credulous reader might begin to suspect that this is not a real woman at all but rather a misogynistic parody. Ironically, in attempting to eradicate the threat of the woman by systematically humiliating her, Hosea 1–3 creates the undecideable, the 'undesired whore', who poses a threat to the text's rhetoric. If Gomer lacks the power to seduce, it is far less likely that she is promiscuous, and the metaphor of harlotry, which is also the linchpin of the text, begins to look precariously unstable.

236. J. Smith, *Misogynies* (London: Faber & Faber, 1993), p. 27. As a male consumer of pornography makes clear, a successful pornographic model is able to create the illusion that 'she is looking directly at you and me' and that 'everything that's going through her head is with us in mind'. Although pornography is the epitome of male looking, it also expresses the desire to be looked at: 'just look at that face—those parted lips waiting to kiss the next man she sees, those eyes looking straight into yours' (*Daily Girls* 5 [London: Branch], cited in Smith, *Misogynies*, p. 27).

4.4. *Guilty as Charged?: Deconstructing the Hierarchy 'Accuser–Accused'*

Feminist responses to Hosea 1–3 are full of references to 'double standards', a common shorthand for the moral asymmetry of the text. The origin of these double standards is the 'double' hierarchy accuser–accused which decrees that man is to woman as God is to sin, and that casts woman as the scapegoat of the text. The phrase 'double standards', however, implies more than binarity: it also suggests hypocrisy and inequality. Exposing the double standards of the text implies that the hypocrisy of the hierarchies makes them vulnerable to critique, or to put it another way, to deconstruction.

The hierarchy accuser–accused represents an extreme and improbable distribution of guilt, but it can be deconstructed through at least three loopholes in the text. As I argued earlier and as Mary Joan Winn Leith has suggested, the stable equations between God and man, sin/Israel and woman are profoundly disturbed by the fact that man is also part of Israel and is implicated in the role of the errant wife. Alongside the identification of divine power and patriarchy stands the deconstructive challenge of the text that audaciously forces a male audience into identification not with God but with a promiscuous woman. Man condemns the woman from a godlike superiority but is also forced to identify with her as the text subtly weaves into its symbolism a challenge to 'double standards' that becomes more explicit in Hos. 4.14.

The second assault to the accuser–accused hierarchy comes from the undecideable verb רִיב in Hos. 2.4. Most commentators have observed that ch. 2 can be read as a court scene, but fewer have gone on to observe that it is impossible to discern who is accusing whom. Though the man's denunciation speech, 'She is not my wife, and I am not her husband' (Hos. 2.4), is usually taken as initiating divorce, this is not at all clear from the text, which confuses the issue by 'beginning' *in medias res*. The husband's case begins with the undecideable verb רִיב, which can be translated variously as 'plead with',[237] 'reason with',[238] and 'accuse'.[239]

The hierarchy accuser–accused is jeopardized in a scene which begins by suggesting a prior, vital but invisible context, and which uses the imperative רִיב, which means 'dispute' in a disputed sense and can

237. RSV.
238. Weems, 'Gomer', p. 91.
239. Wolff, *Hosea*, p. 30.

indicate any kind of confrontation from supplication to denunciation. The undecideability of the verb condenses in microcosm the undecideability of the man's and woman's respective positions: if the man accuses, he is bringing the lawsuit, but if he pleads, he is responding to his wife's initiative. The verb רִיב is undecideable because it supports both possibilities and quite literally enters the dispute on both sides. If the husband accuses, this supports the main/male perspective that his wife is culpable; if he pleads, this enforces the possibility explored in Chapter 3 of this book that beneath the text's surface rhetoric, which exclusively criticizes the woman, there is a strong implied criticism of her husband from the woman's point of view.

I find it intriguing that, like the relationship between Baal and Yhwh or the inversion of the children's names, this tension in ch. 2 has been noted by other commentators in a potentially deconstructive fashion. Like Wessels or Fisch, Beeby strongly suggests a more radical conclusion than he reaches when he asks, 'But which party did seek the divorce? Was it the mother or the father? The text may be read both ways so that one is tempted to ask whether it is not correct to say that it is a case of "both and" and not "either or".'[240] H.W. Wolff makes a similar suggestion, though it is based on the stripping of the woman rather than the ambiguity of the opening verses. 'By stripping her "naked"', he argues, '[the husband] indicates his freedom from the obligation to clothe [his wife], a legal obligation the man assumes with marriage', and he adds provocatively that 'The husband's right to do this is stipulated by ancient oriental law, *if the wife initiates divorce proceedings*'.[241]

When viewed in a historical context, stripping, which is ostensibly a manifestation of male power, hints subversively at male weakness and at female dissatisfaction with her partner. Recent research on contemporary pornography suggests a similar verdict: according to some sociologists, increase in pornography, and particularly violent pornography, is a reaction to the threat of female autonomy expressed in the increased

---

240. H.D. Beeby, *Grace Abounding: A Commentary on the Book of Hosea* (Grand Rapids: Eerdmans, 1989), p. 22.

241. Wolff, *Hosea*, p. 34 (my italics). Wolff's assertion is based on a marriage document from Hana which states that if a wife wishes to divorce her husband, she must be stripped, sent out of the house naked, and publicly exhibited (see C. Kuhl, 'Neue Dokumente zum Verständnis von Hosea 2,4-15', *ZAW* 52 [1934], pp. 102-109 [105]).

influence of the feminist movement. Attempting to account for the increased consumption of pornography in the Western world, theorists such as Irene Diamond, Diana Russell and Ellen Willis have reinterpreted pornography as 'misogynist society's answer to women's demand to be respected as people rather than exploited as objects'[242] and as a 'fantasy solution' which involves 'punishment for uppity females'.[243] Since pornography, and presumably the dynamics of pornography, are not unique to a particular historical period,[244] it is possible to read Hosea 1–3 as contemporary feminists read the current situation and to see the desire to strip and violently humiliate as male rhetoric that protests too much and betrays a subtext of female power.

Reading between the lines, the 'court case' can be seen not as one dominant voice presenting his case for separation, but as two colliding voices, both arguing for separation and both claiming the initiative. The way in which the husband's dismissal of his wife coincides with her initiative to leave prefigures the tensions of Hos. 8.8, 11, 13 and 9.1-3 in which Israel's decision not to be a peculiar people and to become one of the nations *coincides* with Yhwh's decision to send her back among the nations.[245] The question of initiative is open to dispute, and, in a very realistic picture of divorce, both man and wife assume the role of accuser and accused. The verb ריב strikes at the very foundations of the hierarchy accuser–accused by suggesting that the two roles are interchangeable.

Hos. 2.4 questions whether the husband is the only prosecutor in this case, and also demonstrates that his case, such as it is, is not completely watertight. The attribution of guilt to the female is vividly summed up in the accusation that her face is marked with harlotries and her breasts with adulteries (Hos. 2.4), but, reading deconstructively, this accusation implicates the male lovers that it tries to exonerate. The way in which the text marks the woman by and for sexual transgression is a graphic illustration of the double standards of the Hebrew Bible. The male partner in 'crime' is invisible and inculpable; her body, rather than her lover's, retains the marks of promiscuity, and the implication is that the

242. E. Willis, 'Sexual Counterrevolution I', *Rolling Stone* (24 March 1977), p. 29.

243. D. Russell, 'On Pornography', *Chrysalis* 4 (1977), p. 12.

244. I. Diamond, 'Pornography and Repression: A Reconsideration', *Signs* 5 (1980), pp. 686-701 (690).

245. For a similar collision of interest see Amos 9.7.

female body is guilty because it incites. Yet even as the text tries to write out the male partner, it reveals his presence in the focus of the description. The location of the offences on her face and on her breasts makes the reader aware of an otherwise invisible presence, the male author and his desires.

The male speaker's superior position as detached and innocent observer is deconstructed by his fascination with the female body. The focus of the male gaze betrays a guilty author who revels in female sexuality even as he condemns it, and who, like the author of Ezekiel 23, focuses lasciviously on the act of stripping and on the woman's breasts.[246] The text deconstructs its own double standards by exposing the presence of men just as it tries to erase them, and leave the woman alone on the textual stage. According to the rhetoric of the text, woman is the sole representative of adultery and guilt but, ironically, the accusation rebounds upon the accuser and underlines male complicity in her 'harlotries'.

4.5. *(In)dependence: The Woman Dispossessed*

> The specific difference that has determined the movement of history as a movement of property is articulated between two economies (masculine and feminine) that define themselves in relation to the problematics of giving.[247]

In order to establish patriarchal control, Hosea 1–3 forces the woman into a position of complete dependence. Control is established on an explicit level as the woman is forced into the position of a slave or prisoner (Hos. 3.1), but the text also enforces a more sinister, latent project of control which strips woman of her conventional roles of nurturing and sustenance just as it strips her of her clothes. The woman in this text is dispossessed: she needs men because she is unable to provide for herself. Her nakedness is a symbol of her destitution and need, which is useful to patriarchy because it leads to her subordination.

Hosea 1–3 controls the woman by casting man as provider and woman as need personified, but a close analysis of the distribution of need in this text (which is also the distribution of power) reveals cracks

---

246. Ezekiel 23 is even more explicit in its sexual imagery and focuses on 'the handling of virgin bosoms' (23.8); the pressing of young breasts (23.21); stripping (23.10, 26); and the woman's exhibition of her nakedness (23.18).
247. Cixous, 'Sorties', p. 289.

in the patriarchal rhetoric. While the dominant voice of the text insists that Israel needs God as a wife needs her husband, and maintains adamantly that life is better for her with him (2.9), the very existence of the text is a testimony to male desire, for the text is motivated by the assumption that Yhwh (man) desires Israel (woman) in some sense. As the content of the text is jeopardized by the fact of the text's existence, so the ideals of the text are undercut by the technicalities of the text's production. For even as it determinedly denies men's need of women, and especially promiscuous women, Hosea 1–3 demonstrates that it does need a woman, and particularly an אֵשֶׁת זְנוּנִים, for its message to be communicated. Even as it urges that Gomer remove her harlotries and implies that it would have been better if she had not adorned herself with them in the first place, the text *needs* her to be a woman of harlotry. Yhwh and the prophet make the ultimate deconstructive gesture when they argue for the eradication of harlotry, which is also the basis of their own argument.

The way in which the text denounces the promiscuous woman and yet needs her as metaphor can itself be taken as a metaphor for the ambiguous relations between the prostitute and patriarchal society. For just as Gomer is scripted and yet accused of playing the role assigned to her, so patriarchal societies accuse prostitutes for playing a part that is built into the very fabric of patriarchal ideology. The contemporary prostitute, like Gomer, is blamed for prostitution and yet plays a part that is created by male desire. Patriarchal societies, like Hosea 1–3, place the woman in an impasse, thus raising the rhetorical question, 'Is she expected to become the perfect wife or is she not?'[248]

By obfuscating male need, Hosea 1–3 creates a precarious fiction of a totally unreciprocal relationship—woman (Israel) needs man (God) but man has no need of woman. In order to establish this fiction, the text depicts Yhwh and Baal as the only possible contenders for the role of provider; the issue at stake is who will provide for the woman, and the dispute is based on the unquestioned assumption that she must be provided for. The way in which commentators describe provision as a contest suggests that Yhwh's power is still in the process of being constituted, but it assumes that the threat to this power comes from one quarter only. Generally, commentators ignore the fact that Baal's claims are presented through the reported speech of the woman (Hos. 2.17, 14) which, even though it is (mis)quoted from a male perspective, suggests

248. Foster, 'I Will Not Punish Your Daughters', p. 65.

ways in which the dominant male voice can be deconstructed.

Writing to promote Yhwh as provider, the author of Hosea 1–3 quotes the misled woman and the false god Baal only to denigrate them, yet even the presence of these repressed and misquoted voices in the text serves to jeopardize the main male voice. Even though they are contained in reported speech and parody, rival voices still have the power to relativize the dominant voice as only one perspective in three, suggesting that there is no ultimate truth in this text but only competing ideologies and three vying subject positions. The woman is quoted polemically—the text scripts her to say, 'I will go after my lovers who give me my bread and my water, my wool and my flax, my oil and my drink'—so that the male speaker can, quite literally, take her argument apart. In 2.10 he accuses her of lack of knowledge and strips the items of her possessive suffixes ('And she did not know that it was I who gave her the grain, the wine and the oil'), while in 2.11 he takes his parody one step further and not only replaces her suffix of possession with his but argues that when he takes away *his* wool and *his* flax all that will remain is *her* nakedness. The male speaker uses 'her' speech as a foil for his wit as, in a cruel joke, he parodies her claim to possession by suggesting that the only thing she has a right to is her nakedness (עֶרְוָתָהּ). The woman's claim that her possessions are hers is set up so that it can be mocked and repudiated, and many commentators take up the cue. David Hubbard, for example, repeats and enhances the text's misogyny: 'Graspingly she has claimed all this beneficence as her own, with the Hebrew suffix *my* attached to every noun. A two-fold error is this: credit to the wrong giver; possessiveness by a selfish recipient'.[249]

In parodying and denouncing the woman's selfishness, both text and commentators refuse to entertain the possibility that the woman's claim to ownership may be valid, but it is precisely this view that the text allows to slip through the interstices of its own rhetoric. The woman's claim to ownership may be mocked but it can never be fully exorcised from the text: it haunts, for example, the catalogue of provisions, which includes 'bread', 'wool' and 'flax'—items that are strongly associated with a domestic context and with the activities of women.[250] In trying to write women out of the process of sustenance and provision, the text

---

249. D.A. Hubbard, *Hosea: An Introduction and Commentary* (TOTC; Leicester: Inter-Varsity Press, 1989), p. 75.

250. The good wife of Prov. 31.10-31 is associated with wool, flax and also vineyards, which may suggest that women's work also provides the wine of Hos. 2.10.

betrays its own sleight of hand, for it cannot find staple items that are not strongly evocative of women's work. Moreover, it confuses the issue of provision to such an extent that it becomes impossible to see who is really giving what to whom, and who is the real beneficiary. In 2.17 Yhwh declares 'I will give her her vines and her fig trees'; most scholars attempt to erase the tension by appealing to a New Testament model of stewardship, but their concern to do so suggests that they sense an awkwardness here which is reflected in the awkwardness of the English syntax. Are the trees essentially hers or his?—the text suggests another voice, besides that of Yhwh and Baal, who perceives the vine-yards as her own, a voice that speaks more audibly in 2.14 when the woman 'says', 'These are my *wages*, which *my* lovers have *given* to me'. Beneath the foregrounded dispute between Yhwh and Baal another dispute is taking place in which the woman argues with the deities over the issue of her (in)dependence. In this dispute Yhwh and Baal are not antagonists; from the woman's perspective they serve a similar function, and the issue is not who is served but whether they are 'served' at all.

Hos. 2.14 and 2.17 are undecideable because they support the equal and opposite assumptions that the woman provides (the vines are hers, they are her wages) and that she is provided for (the vines are his, they are given). The woman's claim to ownership that is implicit in 2.17 is dramatized in 2.14 when a dissenting voice speaks possessively of 'my lovers' (מְאַהֲבַי), and talks of vineyards as her hire and prostitution as a roundabout way of going shopping. The countervoice is designed, I sus-pect, to support the text's rhetoric; read in the context of the text's ideology it is further proof that the woman is, as ideologically submissive critics put it, assertive, selfish and arrogant. Reading the woman's speech within the context of contemporary feminism recreates it, how-ever, as a force which no longer enhances the text's argument but deconstructs it. In so far as feminist criticism has created a semantic revolution in which words like 'arrogance' and 'defiance' are radically inverted and given a positive sense, it is possible to read Gomer's speech as evidence of, as Nickie Roberts approvingly puts it, the untamed, 'arrogant and rebellious spirit of the whore'.[251] Read in this context, the single word 'wages' seems to imply a surprisingly modern view of the economics of prostitution: the woman speaks in terms of contracts rather than subordination, and suggests that she strikes her own bargain

251. N. Roberts, *Whores in History: Prostitution in Western Society* (London: HarperCollins, 1992), p. 352.

with a society ruled by men and deities. Once it is no longer constrained by the safeguards of the text's ideology, the woman's voice becomes a threatening force: it represents a woman who is 'dangerously free' and whose 'financial and sexual autonomy strikes at the roots of patri-archy'.[252] Gomer is a thoroughly modern miss, but not in the way that Wolff argued; as she speaks of wages, her voice seems to merge with the voices of contemporary prostitutes: 'I have something they want and I give it to them for a price. It's a mutual thing, an agreement.'[253]

Gomer's actions can be variously construed, depending on which set of values the reader selects as a filter. The author's intention is irre-coverable and no readers can escape from the assumptions of their own historical context into the mindset of an original audience; as my study of androcentric and feminist readings shows, there are potentially many different texts and many different Gomers to be made. Traditionally, the text has been viewed through a standard that seems rather antiquated in the 1990s: the ideal of romantic love, of gallant husbands and 'rustic beauties'. By this standard, Gomer's view of relationships as a means of obtaining 'bread and water, wool and flax, oil and drink' (Hos. 2.7) appears materialistic and reductive in comparison to Yhwh's inde-fatigable love, and critics inveigh enthusiastically against her selfishness and greed. But how does the text look to a reader brought up in a capi-talist society and taught to admire entrepreneurial skill, or how does it look to a socialist aware of the links between ethics and economics, and prostitution and economic deprivation? A feminist Marxist reading might begin by pointing out Gomer's gains are not luxuries but necessi-ties, and by redefining her actions as a valid response to a society that discriminates against her.

The difference that most powerfully deconstructs this text is the dif-ference between the reader's values and those of the text. Whether they are androcentric critics disputing with the text's seeming immorality, or feminist critics disputing with the text's misogyny, commentators have focused on points where their ethical sensibilities jar and where they feel, to paraphrase L.P. Hartley, that '[this text] is a foreign country, and that they do things differently there'.[254] Points of dissension between the reader and the text suggest that although the hierarchies that structure this text have endured, they have been subverted and interrogated with

---

252. Roberts, *Whores in History*, p. 352.
253. Unnamed prostitute, cited in Roberts, *Whores in History,* p. 338.
254. L.P. Hartley, *The Go-Between* (Harmondsworth: Penguin, 1958), p. 1.

the passage of time. Although promiscuous women are still degraded, readers such as Renaud hesitate to sanction the double standard whereby violence is condoned but sex is condemned. The hierarchy is chronologically deconstructed: the twentieth century has offered its own reinscription, that it is 'violence, not sex [that] is truly obscene'.[255] Whether it is expressed in attempts to reassimilate or excuse the text, or in condemnation of the text's values, reservations about this text suggest that hierarchies might not be, as Derrida suggested, eternal, and that there is a chance that with the passage of time, and resistance, they might come undone.

5. *Concluding Comments*

In this chapter I have focused on the subject–object (male–female) dichotomy as it affects (1) contemporary criticism, and (2) the ancient text. Metacommentating on androcentric and feminist responses to Hosea 1–3, I have examined the gendering of criticism: feminist critics are considered 'subjective' and androcentric critics 'objective', and this is linked to the parallel observation that women are construed as objects in androcentric texts. One observation is the corollary of the other: if objectivity is defined as the ability to 'deal with what is external to the mind',[256] then it follows that only the defining subject can see himself as objective. If man is the centre of definition, then women will be 'objects' (tellingly defined as the 'non-ego' in the *OED*), and will be considered 'subjective' because their role is conventionally that of the observed rather than the observer.

Theoretically, this chapter represents an intersection between reader-response theory, deconstruction, and feminist criticism. Like deconstruction, both reader-response and feminist critics intervene in, and attempt to reinscribe, the subject–object dichotomy: both suggest that objectivity is sustained only by excluding a repressed term, which in the case of the reader-response critic is subjectivity, and which in the case of the feminist critic is the woman's point of view. Since a woman's viewpoint and subjectivity are traditionally seen as one and the same, reader-response and feminist critics are working to approximately the same end. As Derrida tries to establish that writing (distanciation) is the true condition of language, so feminist and reader-response critics argue that

255. Roberts, *Whores in History*, p. 352.
256. *Oxford Dictionary of English Etymology*.

objectivity, like speech, is a false ideal, and that subjectivity is the only reliable quality of criticism.

On one level a text from the eighth century BCE and the contemporary critical context are structured by the same hierarchy. However, like the perception of sex and violence, this hierarchy is both affirmed and deconstructed by current critical trends. The assumption that man perceives and defines his world neutrally and objectively is besieged not only by feminist criticism (the contrary views of the 'non-ego'), but by post-modern, materialist and psychoanalytic re-definitions of the thinking subject. The subject is redefined not as one who observes with detachment but as one who is *subjected* to the defining pressures of his or her environment.

Since their situations are in many ways the same, it is no accident that I have often drawn analogies between Gomer and feminist critics. In my critique of critical standards and the standards of the text, I have demonstrated the pervasiveness of the subject–object dichotomy by showing how feminist critics have found it difficult to re-locate themselves as subject, or by showing how the text excludes Gomer's voice and objectifies her as a mere cipher in a male-scripted play. In spite of its apparent naturalness, the subject–object dichotomy is vulnerable to deconstruction: men as well as women can be 'resisting readers', and the characterization of Gomer depends, paradoxically, on the idea of a defiant and subversive will. Within the text and within the field of criticism it is possible to intervene in and reinscribe the hierarchy; whether the 'shrew' is eventually tamed is open to debate, and whether the feminist critic co-operates in female objectification is ultimately up to her.

Conclusion

THE SENSE OF A (NON) ENDING

Whoever is wise, let him understand these things;
whoever is discerning, let him know them;
for the ways of the Lord are right,
and the upright walk in them,
but transgressors stumble in them (Hos. 14.9).

The book of Hosea, including Hosea 1–3, ends in this simplistic, epigrammatic conclusion. The binary distinctions between the 'upright' and the 'transgressors', the 'wise' and 'discerning' and (by implication) the 'foolish', are clearly demarcated, and a clear path is described which the reader can follow. The aphoristic conclusion contrasts sharply with the aporiae of Hosea 1–3, and the ideal of a direct path stands in ironic juxtaposition with a text which is more like Jorge Luis Borges's 'Garden of Forking Paths'. Unsatisfied with the author/redactor's conclusion, therefore, I would like to propose my own.

Hosea 1–3 is a text of tensions that exists primarily to 'contend' with and provoke a 'controversy'[1] with its implied audience, Israel. Throughout centuries of reading, this sense of friction between the reader and the text has been repeated, but with an ironic twist: the sense of displeasure has been mutual and, covertly or overtly, readers have taken issue with the text. Traditional readings by androcentric commentators have tended to repress their disagreement with the text, but at the same time, by altering it to suit their tastes, they have expressed their refusal to tolerate its shocking strategies. Recent feminist readings, in contrast, completely reverse the text's initiative: 'text' and 'audience' effectively change places as the reader takes the ethical high ground and perceives the text as a source of disappointment and displeasure.

The tension between the text and reader is mirrored in the internal tensions of the text. The audacious coupling of 'wife of harlotry' and

---

1.   רִיב Hos. 2.4 and 4.1.

man of God can be seen as the icon of all dysfunctional and abrasive relationships, and the tendency to produce strange pairings is repeated at the level of the sign-language of the text. As the prophet is paired with the prostitute, so signifiers are given outrageous signifieds: thus 'children' mean 'alienation', and abstinence from adultery is equated with abstinence from, among other things, Israelite religious practice. In the ultimate disjunctive relationship the text co-exists uneasily with itself: it recalls the nation to its pure beginnings, but at the same time deconstructs the ideal of a pure origin; it condemns Baal as a false god, and yet defines Yhwh in terms associated with Baal; and it deconstructs the possibility of a happy ending in which love triumphs, because curses linger subversively in the margins of the text.

It is indicative of deep critical assumptions that assertions that a text is 'fragmented' or at odds with itself are likely to be taken as negative statements against the text. This reflects a particular situation in biblical studies but also a bias in literary criticism generally. In Shakespeare studies, for example, the problem plays have habitually been regarded as an aberration in the canon and an embarrassment to the whole concept and reputation of 'Shakespeare': writing in the 1930s W.W. Lawrence saw the plays as distinctly second-rate,[2] while more recently Philip Edwards has argued that because the plays 'refuse to provide a pattern' they ultimately 'fail'.[3] The assumption that in order to be a 'great work' a text must be 'well-wrought'[4] is conventionally associated with Structuralism, Formalism, and New Criticism. However, the history of the reception of the problem plays suggests that the desire for unity and structure transcends literary critical categories and permeates the history of literary criticism in general.

In biblical studies the particular evolution of 'literary criticism' has conspired to reinforce the assumption that a text's value lies in its structural unity. The term 'literary criticism' has acquired distinctive meanings: writing in 1971, Amos Wilder recorded his astonishment that the term should have 'such different connotations for biblical scholars as for

2. W.W. Lawrence, *Shakespeare's Problem Comedies* (New York: Ungar, 1960; 1st edn 1931).

3. P. Edwards, *Shakespeare and the Confines of Art* (London: Methuen, 1972), p. 110.

4. This phrase is borrowed from Cleanth Brooks, *The Well-Wrought Urn: Studies in the Structure of Poetry* (New York: 1947), a central work of the so-called New Criticism.

students of literature generally', and that it should refer to an investigation of authorship, dates, source and purpose, as well as 'those appreciative and interpretative questions that are the goal of criticism everywhere else'.[5] In its first phase 'literary criticism' meant a type of analysis similar to 'dissection', in which texts were examined 'from the standpoint of lack of continuity, inconsistencies and different linguistic usages',[6] and the new literary criticism in biblical studies was seen as a reaction to this. As early as 1957 Northrop Frye made a distinction that, as Ryken and Longman observe, was to become 'axiomatic'[7] in the discipline when he prophesied that 'A purely literary criticism would see the Bible not as a scrapbook of corruptions, glosses, redactions, insertions, conflations, misplacings, and misunderstandings revealed by the analytic critic, but as a typological unity'.[8] Whereas the old literary criticism had been diachronic, the new literary criticism would be synchronic; whereas the old literary critics had stressed disunity, the New Critics would 'share the conviction that literature is the result of conscious composition, careful patterning, and an awareness of literary conventions prevalent at the time'.[9] The hierarchy in Frye's description is, I think, quite clearly inscribed: fragmentation is negative and unity is positive, and '*pure* literary criticism' is used to replace a 'scrapbook of *corruptions*'.[10]

The 'axiomatic' dichotomy between the 'old' literary criticism, with its emphasis on fragmentation, and the 'new' literary criticism, with its stress on unity and coherence, ultimately breaks down. As Andersen and Freedman concede, the quest of the older literary critics is not merely to highlight dissonance but also to explain it, and thus to attempt to 'repair the damaged text'.[11] The older literary critic explains apparent disunity

---

5. A. Wilder, *Early Christian Rhetoric: The Language of the Gospel* (Cambridge, MA: Harvard University Press, 1971), p. xxii.

6. K. Koch, *The Growth of the Biblical Tradition: The Form-Critical Method* (New York: Charles Schribner's Sons, 1969), p. 69.

7. L. Ryken and T. Longman III, *A Complete Literary Guide to the Bible* (Grand Rapids: Zondervan, 1993), p. 19.

8. N. Frye, *Anatomy of Criticism* (Princeton: Princeton University Press, 1957), p. 315.

9. Ryken and Longman, *A Complete Literary Guide to the Bible*, p. 18.

10. Ryken and Longman, *A Complete Literary Guide to the Bible*, p. 18 (my italics). The *OED* defines 'corruption' as 'The perversion of anything from an original state of purity'.

11. F.I. Andersen and D.N. Freedman, *Hosea: A New Translation with*

by dividing the text into smaller internal unities and ascribing these coherent segments to different sources. The new literary critic, similarly, seeks to explain apparent disunity by linking different portions of the text and describing them as thematic parallels or structural echoes. Both produce a (different) set of internal unities, a coherent patterning, but one set of critics interpret it diachronically and the other synchronically. Both show that on close reading, apparent disunity reveals a complex pattern, and attempt to describe a deeper structure behind the text.

Although the new literary criticism tends to conceive of itself as a 'paradigm shift'[12] and a departure from the assumptions of 'previous generations'[13] of scholars, it borrows one of the fundamental assumptions of the older literary criticism. As Gale A. Yee puts it in her analysis of Hosea, the older literary criticism takes 'aporiae', 'inconsistencies of thought' and 'the juxtaposition of contradictory themes'[14] as signs of different authors—the assumption being that a work of literature must be unified, and that a biblical author cannot knowingly contradict himself. The new literary criticism does not question this assumption, and so, in trying to prove that the text is a 'conscious composition',[15] it has to prove, sometimes against the odds, the integral unity of the whole. The starting point for this approach is, as Andersen and Freedman put it, that the text only appears 'amorphous, *on first sight*',[16] and that apparent disunity belies an underlying coherence.

Studies of Hosea 1–3 that have preceded this book generally reflect the rubric of the new literary criticism and reveal a preference for homogeneity over heterogeneity, patterning over disorder. Yet even as critics such as Andersen and Freedman attempt to demonstrate that the text is an 'intricate network of interwoven themes and verbal signals' and is 'unified by...architectonic arrangement[s]...which balance one another quantitatively',[17] their experience of the text is such that they are forced to concede that 'some of the connections' that they make are 'clearer than others'.[18] Unable to reconcile the text's 'turbulent

Introduction and Commentary (AB; New York: Doubleday, 1980), p. 67.

12. Ryken and Longman, *A Complete Literary Guide to the Bible*, p. 19.

13. Andersen and Freedman, *Hosea*, p. 67.

14. G.A. Yee, *Composition and Tradition in the Book of Hosea: A Redaction Critical Investigation* (Atlanta: Scholars Press, 1987), p. 49.

15. Ryken and Longman, *A Complete Literary Guide to the Bible*, p. 18.

16. Andersen and Freedman, *Hosea*, p. 69 (my italics).

17. Andersen and Freedman, *Hosea*, p. 141.

18. Andersen and Freedman, *Hosea*, p. 140.

vacillations' to the stringent ideal of unity, they devise the hypothesis that the text 'does not present us with finished oracular utterances, ready for public delivery', but offers 'preliminary reflections', 'material from an earlier stage in the process',[19] which cannot be expected to meet the standards of a finished text.[20] Most extremely, their observations about the text lead them from the familiar language of New Criticism to terms that are virtually postmodern: observing that 'God's will to punish and his will to pardon do not neutralize each other' but are 'expressed together in the strongest terms',[21] and they conclude that the text has 'reached the *limits of language* for talking about the goodness and the severity of God'.[22]

The concept of the 'limits of language' is, as Brain McHale observes, the starting point for postmodern theory. A world view that emphasizes the 'disparity between man's finite mind [or language] and the unfathomably vast, ungraspably complex universe [or God]'[23] sets the arena for a postmodern scepticism about language; similarly, the embarrassed asides in New Critical analyses explaining why Hosea 1–3 is not quite a unity, or is an unfinished unity, anticipate some of the arguments in this book. Andersen and Freedman's comment about opposites in tension or the limits of language has been developed in this book to a deconstructive analysis, while the theory that the text is unfinished has been developed into the suggestion that the text 'lays bare the device', like a Brechtian play or a postmodern novel. Both the postmodern and the New Critical analyses imply that the text is performed or exposed to the reader prematurely, but whereas Andersen and Freedman use this to explain why the text fails to meet the accepted literary criterion of unity, I have used different models of literature (such as Brecht's plays or Sterne's *Tristram Shandy*) to question the criterion by which the text is judged.

The way in which New Critical analyses of Hosea 1–3 occasionally (and I would argue, inevitably) move towards postmodern concepts

19. Andersen and Freedman, *Hosea*, p. 45.

20. This theory, Andersen and Freedman claim, 'liberat[es] readers from the impasses of form-critical studies' by making the text exempt from the exacting criterion of unity (*Hosea*, p. 45). What they do not realize, or certainly do not say, is that it is also a way of suspending, momentarily, the rigid assumptions of New Criticism on which their study is based.

21. Andersen and Freedman, *Hosea*, p. 51.

22. Andersen and Freedman, *Hosea*, p. 52.

23. B. McHale, *Postmodern Fiction* (London: Routledge, 1991), p. 29.

suggests that a new-er model of criticism is required when analysing the final form of this text. By reading the text in the con-text of 'new-er' criticisms such as deconstruction and reader-response, I have been able to bring to the centre of analysis observations that have long been repressed in margins and footnotes. The text's disjunctive style and its capacity to subvert itself are no longer seen as negative features outside the critical language but as features that can be accounted for within the critical language. Difficulties in the text are no longer seen negatively, but creatively, and tensions can be interpreted not as the frustration of meaning but as a way of suggesting different meanings.

Over the last 25 years the 'problem plays' of Shakespeare have become increasingly esteemed; their inconsistencies still remain, but because, rather than in spite of them, they are seen as 'astonishingly modern and full of resonances for contemporary society'.[24] Hosea 1–3 can similarly be reappraised in a postmodern context: it might have little in common with texts that adhere to the notion of unity (such as the Victorian novel) but it shows more than a casual resemblance to a relatively new mode of fiction which seeks deliberately to contravene the standards of the Western literary tradition. Like the novels of Thomas Pynchon, Donald Barthelme and Alain Robbe-Grillet, Hosea 1–3 seems to work on the principle that 'excluded middles are bad shit, to be avoided',[25] and asserts simultaneously that something did and did not happen.[26] If the text has nothing in common with the 'Dear Reader' tradition,[27] it has much in common with the postmodern tradition of 'Offending the Audience':[28] as the postmodern author tends to insult

24. V. Thomas, *The Moral Universe of Shakespeare's Problem Plays* (London: Croom Helm, 1987), p. 212.

25. T. Pynchon, *The Crying of Lot 49* (New York: Bantam, 1972), p. 136.

26. John Barth, for example, asserts, 'Naturally he didn't have enough nerve to ask Magda to go through the funhouse with him. With incredible nerve and to everyone's surprise he invited Magda, quietly and politely, to go through the funhouse with him' ('Lost in the Funhouse', in *Lost in the Funhouse: Fiction for Print, Tape, Live Voice* [New York: Bantam, 1969], p. 83).

27. I am referring here to the way in which writers such as George Eliot or Charlotte Brontë confidentially address the reader: thus Brontë in *Jane Eyre* invites us to 'Hear an illustration reader' (C. Brontë, *Jane Eyre* [Oxford: Oxford University Press, 1988], p. 429), and reveals, famously, 'Reader, I Married him' (p. 454).

28. *Offending the Audience* is the title of a play by Peter Handke which dramatizes the technique of offending the reader used in postmodern fiction. In postmodern fiction, as in Handke's play, the purpose of 'offending the audience' is to break

and threaten her readers,[29] so the prophet denounces the audience as 'harlotrous' (Hos. 1–3), liars, murderers and thieves (4.2), a 'stubborn heifer' (4.16), a 'band of drunkards' (4.18), and an 'oven' whose 'heart burns with intrigue' (7.6).

The analogy between prophecy and postmodernism constitutes a study in itself, which begins in, but ultimately goes beyond the bounds, of this book. Such a study might look at how, for example, the prophetic and postmodern authors confuse the boundary between the 'world' outside and inside the novel by inserting real names into an often fantastic fiction: thus Hosea begins its dream-like narrative with the names of historical kings (anachronistically confused) just as Pynchon imports 'Jack Kennedy' and 'Malcolm X' into the audacious fiction of *Gravity's Rainbow*. It might look at the distortion of temporal sequence and consider how 'there always comes a moment when the story breaks in half, turns back, or jumps ahead';[30] or it might choose to compare the distorted syntax of a text like Hosea with the postmodern 'back-broke sentence'.[31] Finally, it might look at how both prophecy and post-modernism employ 'lexically and sexually exhibitionistic' terms in order to 'get past the reader's hardworn armour',[32] and so end where this study began, with images of harlotry, and the unexpected, and an exploration of the text's capacity to shock.

down the barriers between characters inside and outside the fiction: as one of the actors puts it, 'We will insult you because insulting you is one way of speaking to you... the distance between us will no longer be infinite' (P. Handke, *Offending the Audience* [trans. M. Roloff; London: Methuen, 1971], p. 35).

29. John Barth, for example, subjects his reader to gratuitous abuse: 'The reader! You dogged, uninsultable, printoriented bastard, it's you I'm addressing, who else, from inside this monstrous fiction' ('Life-Story', in *Lost in the Funhouse*, p. 123), while William Gass corners and threatens the reader: 'Now that I've got you alone down here, you bastard, don't think I'm letting you get away easily, no sir, not you brother' (W.H. Gass, *Willie Masters' Lonesome Wife* [Evanston, IL: Northwestern University Press, 1968], unnumbered).

30. A. Robbe-Grillet, *Project for Revolution in New York* (trans. R. Howard; London: Caldar & Boyars, 1973), p. 132.

31. D. Barthelme, in T. LeClair and L. McCafferey (eds.), *Anything Can Happen: Interviews with American Novelists* (Chicago: University of Chicago Press, 1983), p. 34.

32. Barthelme, in LeClair and McCafferey (eds.), *Anything Can Happen*, p. 34.

BIBLIOGRAPHY

Abel, L., 'Jacques Derrida: His "Difference" with Metaphysics', *Salmagundi* 25 (Winter 1974), pp. 3-21.

Aichele, G., *Limits of Story* (Atlanta: Scholars Press, 1985).

Albrektson, B., *History and the Gods* (Lund: Gleerup, 1967).

Albright, W.F., *From the Stone Age to Christianity: Monotheism and the Historical Process* (New York: Doubleday, 1957).

Alexander, P. (ed.), *William Shakespeare: The Complete Works* (Glasgow and London: Collins, 1985).

Allen Rabuzzi, K., *The Sacred and the Feminine: Toward a Theology of Housework* (New York: Seabury, 1982).

Allwohn, A., *Die Ehe des Propheten Hosea in psychoanalytischer Beleuchtung* (BZAW, 44; Berlin: de Gruyter, 1926).

Alter, R., *The Art of Biblical Narrative* (New York: Basic Books, 1981).

Alter, R., and F. Kermode (eds.), *The Literary Guide to the Bible* (London: Fontana Press, 1987).

Althusser, L., 'Ideology and State Apparatuses' in *Lenin and Philosophy and Other Essays* (trans. B. Brewster; New York: Monthly Review Press, 1971).

Altizer, T.J. (ed.), *Deconstruction and Theology* (New York: The Crossroad Publishing Company, 1982).

Amichai, Y., *Selected Poems* (trans. A. Gutmann; London: Cape Goliard, 1967).

Amihai, M., G.W. Coats and A.M. Solomon (eds.), *Narrative Research on the Hebrew Bible* (Semeia 46; Atlanta: Scholars Press, 1989).

Ammons, A.R., 'Two Motions', in *Northfield Poems* (Ithaca, NY: Cornell University Press, 1966).

Andersen, F.I., and D.N. Freedman, *Hosea: A New Translation with Introduction and Commentary* (AB; New York: Doubleday, 1980).

Anderson, B.W. (ed.), 'The Problem and Promise of Commentary', *Interpretation* 36 (1982).

Anderson, G.W., 'Hosea and Yahweh: God's Love Story', *RevExp* 72 (1975), pp. 425-36.

Atwood, M., *The Handmaid's Tale* (London: Virago, 1991).

Auerbach, E., *Mimesis: The Representation of Reality in Western Literature* (trans. W. Trask; Princeton: Princeton University Press, 1953).

Auerbach, N., 'Engorging the Patriarchy', in Benstock (ed.), *Feminist Issues in Literary Scholarship*, pp. 150-60.

Austin, J.L., *How to Do Things with Words* (London: Oxford University Press, 1963).

Bach, A., 'Good to the Last Drop: Viewing the Sotah (Numbers 5.11-31) as the Glass Half Empty and Wondering How to View it Half Full', in J.C. Exum and

D.J.A. Clines (eds.), *The New Literary Criticism and the Hebrew Bible* (JSOTSup, 143; Sheffield: JSOT Press, 1993).

—'Reading Allowed: Feminist Criticism Approaching the Millenium', *Currents in Research: Biblical Studies* 1 (1993), pp. 191-215.

Bachofen, J., *Das Mutterrecht: Eine Untersuchung über die Gynaikokratie der alten Welt nach ihrer religiösen und rechtlichen Natur* (Basel, 1897).

Bakon, S., 'For I am God and not Man', *Dor le Dor* 17 (1988), pp. 243-49.

Bal, M., 'The Bible as Literature: A Critical Escape', *Diacritics* 16 (1986), pp. 71-79.

—*Death and Dyssymmetry: The Politics of Coherence in the Book of Judges* (Chicago: University of Chicago Press, 1988).

—*Lethal Love: Feminist Literary Readings of Biblical Love Stories* (Bloomington and Indianapolis: Indiana University Press, 1987).

—'Metaphors He Lives By', in Camp and Fontaine, (eds.), *Women, War and Metaphor*, pp. 185-207.

—*Reading 'Rembrandt': Beyond the Word–Image Opposition* (Cambridge: Cambridge University Press, 1991).

Balz-Cochois, H., *Gomer: Der Höhencult Israels im Selbstverständnis der Volksfrömmigkeit* (Frankfurt am Main: Peter Lang, 1982).

—'Gomer oder die Macht der Astarte: Versuch einer feministischen Interpretation von Hos. 1–4', *EvT* 42 (1982), pp. 37-65.

Barr, J., *The Semantics of Biblical Language* (Oxford: Oxford University Press, 1961).

Barth, J., *Lost in the Funhouse: Fiction for Print, Tape, Live Voice* (New York: Bantam, 1969).

Barthelme, D., in T. LeClair and L. McCafferey (eds.), *Anything Can Happen: Interviews with American Novelists* (Chicago: University of Chicago Press, 1983).

Barthes, R., 'The Death of the Author', in R. Barthes, *Image–Music–Text* (trans. S. Heath; London: Fontana, 1987), pp. 142-48.

—*Elements of Semiology* (trans. A. Lavers and C. Smith; New York: Hill & Wang, 1968).

—'Myth Today', in Barthes, *Mythologies* (trans. A. Lavers; London: Jonathan Cape, 1972), pp. 109-59.

—'Saussure, the Sign, Democracy', in Barthes, *The Semiotic Challenge* (trans. R. Howard; Oxford: Basil Blackwell, 1988), pp. 151-59.

—*S/Z* (trans. R. Miller; Oxford: Basil Blackwell, 1990).

—'Texte, Théorie du', in *Encyclopaedia Universalis* (Paris, 1968–82), XV, pp. 1013-17.

—*The Pleasure of the Text* (trans. R. Miller; New York: Hill & Wang, 1975).

Barton, J., 'Eisegesis', in Coggins and Houlden (eds.), *A Dictionary of Biblical Interpretation*, pp. 187-88 .

Batten, L.W., 'Hosea's Marriage and Message', *JBL* 48 (1929), pp. 257-73.

Batto, B.F., 'The Covenant of Peace: A Neglected Ancient Near Eastern Motif', *CBQ* 49 (1987), pp. 187-211.

Baym, N., 'The Madwoman and Her Languages: Why I Don't Do Feminist Literary Theory', in Benstock (ed.), *Feminist Issues in Literary Studies*, pp. 45-61.

Beeby, H.D., *Grace Abounding: A Commentary on the Book of Hosea* (Grand Rapids: Eerdmans, 1989).

Benstock, S. (ed.), *Feminist Issues in Literary Scholarship* (Bloomington: Indiana University Press, 1987).

Benveniste, E., 'Sémiologie de la langue', *Semiotica* 1 (1969), pp. 127-35.

Bird, P.A., 'The Harlot as Heroine: Narrative Art and Social Presupposition in Three Old Testament Texts', in Amihai, Coats and Solomon (eds.), *Narrative Research on the Hebrew Bible*, pp. 119-39.

—' " To Play the Harlot": An Enquiry into an Old Testament Metaphor', in Day (ed.), *Gender and Difference in Ancient Israel*, pp. 75-94.

Birkeland, H., *Zum hebräischen Traditionswesen: Die Komposition der prophetischen Bücher des Altes Testaments* (Oslo: Jacob Dybwad, 1938).

Bitter, S., *Die Ehe des Propheten Hosea: Eine auslegungsgeschichtliche Untersuchung* (Göttingen: Vandenhoeck und Ruprecht, 1975).

Bleich, D., *Subjective Criticism* (Baltimore: Johns Hopkins University Press, 1978).

Bloom, H., 'From J to K, or the Uncanniness of the Yahwist', in F. McConnell (ed.), *The Bible and the Narrative Tradition* (New York: Oxford University Press, 1986).

—*Kabbalah and Criticism* (New York: Seabury, 1975)

—*A Map of Misreading* (Oxford: Oxford University Press, 1975).

—*Ruin the Sacred Truths: Poetry and Belief from the Bible to the Present* (Cambridge, MA: Harvard University Press, 1989).

Boas, F.S., *Shakespere and His Predecessors* (London: Murray, 1896).

Bogatyrev, P., 'Les signes du théatre', *Poétique* 8 (1971), pp. 517-30.

—'Semiotics in the Folk Theatre', in L. Matjeka and I.R. Titunik (eds.), *Semiotics of Art: Prague School Contributions* (Cambridge, MA: MIT Press, 1976), pp. 33-49.

Booth, W., *Critical Understanding* (Chicago: University of Chicago Press, 1979).

Borges, J.L., 'The Garden of Forking Paths', in *Ficciones* (trans. A. Kerrigan; New York: Grove Press, 1962).

Bouyer, L., *La Bible et l'évangile* (Paris, 1951).

Boyarin, D., *Intertextuality and the Reading of Midrash* (Bloomington and Indianapolis: Indiana University Press, 1990).

Bradley, A.C., *Shakespearean Tragedy* (New York: Macmillan, 1949).

Braude, W.G., 'Open Thou My Eyes', in A. Corre (ed.), *Understanding the Talmud* (New York: Ktav Publishing House, 1975), pp. 55-61.

Braude, W.G. and I.J. Kapstein, *Peskita de-Rab Kahana: R. Kahana's Compilation of Discourses for Sabbaths and Festal Days* (Philadelphia: Jewish Publication Society of America, 1975).

Brecht, B., *Gesammelte Werke*, XVI (ed. E. Hauptmann; Frankfurt: Suhrkamp, 1967).

—'Kleines Organon für das Theater' (Potsdam, 1949); trans. J. Willett, in Willett (ed.), *Brecht on Theatre*.

Brenner, A. and F. van Dijk-Hemmes, *On Gendering Texts: Female and Male Voices in the Hebrew Bible* (BI, 1; Leiden: Brill, 1993).

Brett, M.G., 'Four or Five things to do with Texts: A Taxonomy of Interpretative Interests', in D.J.A. Clines, S.E. Fowl and S.E. Porter (eds.), *The Bible in Three Dimensions: Essays in Celebration of Forty Years of Biblical Studies in the University of Sheffield* (JSOTSup, 87; Sheffield: JSOT Press, 1990), pp. 357-77.

—'The Future of Reader Criticisms', in F. Watson (ed.), *The Open Text* (London: SCM Press, 1993), pp. 13-31.

Brillet, G., *Amos et Osée* (Paris: Editions du Cerf, 1958).

Bromiley, G.W. (ed.), *International Standard Bible Encyclopaedia* (Grand Rapids: Eerdmans, rev. edn, 1988).

Brontë, C., *Jane Eyre* (Oxford: Oxford University Press, 1988).

Brooks, C., 'The Language of Paradox', in Lodge (ed.), *Twentieth Century Literary Criticism: A Reader*, pp. 292-304 (repr. from C. Brooks, *The Well-Wrought Urn: Studies in the Structure of Poetry* [New York, 1947], ch. 1).

Brown, S.L., *The Book of Hosea with Introduction and Notes* (Westminster Commentaries; London: Methuen, 1932).

Brueggemann, W., *Tradition For Crisis: A Study in Hosea* (Richmond: John Knox Press, 1968).

Budde, K., *Religion of Israel to the Exile* (American Lectures on the History of Religions, 4; New York: Putnam's Sons, 1899).

Burroughs, J., *An Exposition of the Prophecy of Hosea* (Edinburgh: James Nichol, 1643).

Buss, M.J., *The Prophetic Word of Hosea: A Morphological Study* (BZAW, 111; Berlin: de Gruyter, 1969).

—'Tragedy and Comedy in Hosea', in Exum (ed.), *Tragedy and Comedy*, pp. 71-82.

Cady Stanton, E. (ed.), *The Original Feminist Attack on the Bible: The Woman's Bible* (New York: Allo, 1974).

Calvin, J., *Commentaries on the Twelve Minor Prophets. I. Hosea* (trans. J. Owen; Edinburgh: Edinburgh Printing Company, 1846).

Calvino, I., *If on a Winter's Night a Traveller* (London: Picador, 1982).

Camp, C., and C.R. Fontaine (ed.), *Women, War and Metaphor: Language and Society in the Study of the Hebrew Bible* (Semeia, 61; Atlanta: Scholars Press, 1993).

Carey, J., *John Donne: Life, Mind and Art* (London: Faber & Faber, 1981).

Carroll, R.P., 'Ideology', in Coggins and Houlden (eds.), *A Dictionary of Biblical Interpretation*, pp. 309-11.

—*Wolf in the Sheepfold: The Bible as a Problem for Christianity* (London: SPCK, 1991).

Cathcart, K.J., 'Targum Jonathan to Hos. 1–3', *IBS* 10 (1988), pp. 37-43.

Cathcart, K.J., and R.P. Gordon, *The Aramaic Bible. XIV. The Targum of the Minor Prophets* (Edinburgh: T. & T. Clark, 1989).

Catlett, M.L., 'Reversals in Hosea: A Literary Analysis' (unpublished PhD dissertation, Emory University, 1988; Ann Arbor: University Microfilms International, no. 88-16934).

Cheyne, T.K., *Founders of Old Testament Criticism: Biographical, Descriptive, Critical Studies* (Cambridge Bible Commentary; London: Methuen, 1893).

—*Hosea: With Notes and Introduction* (Cambridge Bible Commentary; Cambridge: Cambridge University Press, 1887).

Childs, B.S., *Introduction to the Old Testament as Scripture* (London: SCM Press, 1979).

Christ, C., and J. Plaskow (eds.), *Womanspirit Rising: A Feminist Reader in Religion* (New York: Harper & Row, 1979).

Christian, B., *et al.*, 'Conference Call: Notes From The Beehive: Feminism and the Institution', *Differences* 2 (1990), pp. 52-109.

Cixous, H., 'Sorties', in Lodge (ed.), *Modern Criticism and Theory: A Reader*, pp. 287-93 (repr. from E. Marks and I. de Courtivron [eds.], *New French Feminisms: An Anthology* [Brighton: Harvester Press, 1981]).

Clines, D.J.A., 'Deconstructing the Book of Job', in *What Does Eve Do to Help? and Other Readerly Questions to the Old Testament* (JSOTSup, 94; Sheffield: JSOT Press, 1990), pp. 106-23.

—'Haggai's Temple: Constructed, Deconstructed and Reconstructed', in T.C. Eskenazi and K.H. Richards (eds.), *Second Temple Studies: Temple and Community in the Persian Period* (JSOTSup, 175; Sheffield: JSOT Press, 1993), pp. 51-78.

—'Hosea 2: Structure and Interpretation,' in E.A. Livingstone (ed.), *Studia Biblica 1978. I. Papers on Old Testament and Related Themes* (Sixth International Congress on Biblical Studies, Oxford, 3-7 April 1978; JSOTSup, 11; Sheffield: JSOT Press, 1979), pp. 83-103.

Coggins, R.J., and J.L. Houlden (eds.), *A Dictionary of Biblical Interpretation* (London: SCM Press, 1990).

Cohen, R. (ed.), *The Future of Literary Theory* (London: Routledge, 1989).

Collini, S. (ed.), *Interpretation and Overinterpretation* (Cambridge: Cambridge University Press, 1992).

Collins, A.Y. (ed.), *Feminist Perspectives on Biblical Scholarship* (Chico, CA: Scholars Press, 1985).

Coppens, J., 'L'histoire matrimoniale d'Osée' (BBB, 1; Bonn: Peter Hanstein, 1950), pp. 38-45.

Couturier, G., 'Rapports culturels et religieux entre Israël et Canaan d'après Osée 2, 4-25', in M. Gourgues and G.D. Mailhick (eds.), *L'alterité vivre* (Montreal: Recherches, 1986), pp. 159-210.

Craghan, J.F., 'The Book of Hosea: A Survey of Recent Literature on the First of the Minor Prophets', *BTB* 1 (1971), pp. 81-170.

Crane, W.E., 'The Prophecy of Hosea', *BSac* 89 (1932), pp. 480-94.

Crossan, J.D. (ed.), *Polyvalent Narration* (Semeia, 9; Atlanta: Scholars Press, 1977).

Crowley, S., *A Teacher's Introduction to Deconstruction* (Illinois: National Council of Teachers of English, 1989).

Culler, J., *On Deconstruction: Theory and Criticism after Structuralism* (London: Routledge, 1993).

—*The Pursuit of Signs: Semiotics, Literature, Deconstruction* (London: Routledge & Kegan Paul, 1981), p. vii.

—*Saussure* (Glasgow: Collins, 1976).

Cunningham, V., *In the Reading Gaol: Postmodernity, Texts and History* (Oxford: Basil Blackwell, 1994).

Damian, P., 'Letter 59', in *The Fathers of the Church. II. Peter Damian, Letters 31-60* (trans. O.J. Blum; Washington, DC: Catholic University of America Press, 1990), pp. 394-403.

Davidson, A.B., 'Hosea', in J. Hastings (ed.), *A Dictionary of the Bible* (Edinburgh: T. & T. Clark, 1904), p. 421.

Davies, G.I., *Hosea* (OTG; Sheffield: JSOT Press, 1993).

Day, P.L. (ed.), *Gender and Difference in Ancient Israel* (Minneapolis: Fortress Press, 1989).

—'Why is Anat a Warrior and a Hunter?', in D. Jobling, P.L. Day and G.T. Sheppard (eds.), *The Bible and the Politics of Exegesis: Essays in Honour of Norman K. Gottwald on his Sixty-Fifth Birthday* (Cleveland: Pilgrim Press, 1991), pp. 141-46.

De Man, P., *Allegories of Reading: Figural Language in Rousseau, Nietzsche, Rilke and Proust* (New Haven: Yale University Press, 1979).

—*Blindness and Insight: Essays in the Rhetoric of Contemporary Criticism* (New York: Oxford University Press, 1971).

—*Semiology and Rhetoric* (1988).

Deem, A., 'The Goddess Anath and some Biblical Hebrew Cruces', *JSS* 23 (1978), pp. 25-30.

Defoe, D., *Roxana: The Fortunate Mistress* (Harmondsworth: Penguin, 1987).

Derrida, J., 'Deconstruction and the Other', in R. Kearney (ed.), *Dialogues with Contemporary Continental Thinkers* (Manchester: Manchester University Press, 1984), pp.107-25.

—'Des Tours de Babel', trans. J.F. Graham; in Moore and Jobling (eds.), *Poststructuralism as Exegesis*, pp. 3-34.

—*Dissemination* (trans. B. Johnson; Chicago: University of Chicago Press, 1982).

—*The Ear of the Other: Otobiography, Transference, Translation* (ed. C.V. McDonald; trans. P. Kamuf and A. Ronell; New York: Schocken Books, 1985).

—'Edmond Jabès and the Question of the Book', in Derrida, *Writing and Difference*, pp. 64-78.

—*Glas* (Paris: Galilée, 1974).

—'Interview with Alan Montefiore', in D. Jones and R. Stoneman (eds.), *Talking Liberties* (London: Channel 4 Television, 1992), pp. 6-9.

—'Interview with Jacques Derrida', in Salusinszky (ed.), *Criticism in Society*, pp. 8-26.

—'Letter to a Japanese Friend', in Kamuf (ed.), *A Derrida Reader*, pp. 270-76.

—'Limited Inc.', *Glyph* 2 (1977), pp. 162-254.

—'Living On: *Border Lines*', in H. Bloom (ed.), *Deconstruction and Criticism* (New York: Seabury Press, 1979), pp. 75-176.

—*Margins of Philosophy* (trans. A. Bass; Chicago: University of Chicago Press, 1982).

—*Of Grammatology* (trans. G. Chakravorty Spivak; Baltimore and London: Johns Hopkins University Press, 1976).

—'The Parergon', *October* 9 (1979), pp. 3-40.

—'Positions', *Diacritics* 2 (1972), pp. 35-43 (rev. edn in Derrida, *Positions*, pp. 37-96).

—*Positions* (trans. A. Bass; Chicago: University of Chicago Press, 1981).

—'Semiology and Grammatology', in Derrida, *Positions*, pp. 17-36.

—'Signature, Event, Context', *Glyph* 1 (1977), pp. 172-97.

—*Spurs: Nietzsche's Styles* (trans. B. Harlow; Chicago: University of Chicago Press, 1978).

—'Structure, Sign and Play in the Discourse of the Human Sciences', in Derrida, *Writing and Difference*, pp. 278-93.

—'The Time of a Thesis: Punctuations', in A. Montefiore (ed.), *Philosophy in France Today* (Cambridge: Cambridge University Press, 1983), pp. 34-50.

—'Tympan', in Kamuf (ed.), *A Derrida Reader*, pp. 149-68.

—'Violence and Metaphysics: An Essay on the Thought of Emmanuel Levinas', in Derrida, *Writing and Difference*, pp. 79-153.

—'White Mythology: Metaphor in the Text of Philosophy', *NLH* 6 (1974), pp. 7-74.

—*Writing and Difference* (trans. A. Bass; London: Routledge, 1990).

Detweiler, R. (ed.), *Derrida and Biblical Studies* (Semeia, 23; Atlanta: Scholars Press, 1982).

Diamond, I., 'Pornography and Repression: A Reconsideration', *Signs* 5 (1980), pp. 686-701.

Dijk-Hemmes, F. van, 'The Imagination of Power and the Power of Imagination: An Intertextual Analysis of Two Biblical Love Songs: The Song of Songs and Hosea 2', *JSOT* 44 (1989), pp. 75-88.

Donne, J., 'The Canonization', in C.A. Patrides (ed.), *The Complete Poems of John Donne* (London: Dent, 1985).

Donoghue, D., *Ferocious Alphabets* (London: Faber & Faber, 1981).

Donovan, J., 'Towards a Women's Poetics', in Benstock (ed.), *Feminist Issues in Literary Scholarship*, pp. 95-122.

Doorly, W.L., *Prophet of Love: Understanding the Book of Hosea* (New York: Paulist Press, 1991).

Du Plessis, R.B., 'Psyche, or Wholeness', *Massachusetts Review* (Spring 1979), pp. 77-96.

Dworkin,A., *Pornography: Men Possessing Women* (London: The Women's Press, 1981).

Eagleton, T., *Ideology: An Introduction* (London: Verso, 1991).

—'The Revolt of the Reader', *NLH* 13 (1982), pp. 439-52.

Eakin, F.E., 'Yahwism and Baalism before the Exile', *JBL* 84 (1965), pp. 407-14.

Eco, U., *A Theory of Semiotics* (Bloomington: Indiana University Press, 1976).

—'Interpretation and History', in Collini (ed.), *Interpretation and Overinterpretation*, pp. 23-43.

—*The Role of the Reader: Explorations in the Semiotics of Texts* (Bloomington: Indiana University Press, 1979).

Edwards, P., *Shakespeare and the Confines of Art* (London: Methuen, 1972).

Elam, K., *The Semiotics of Theatre and Drama* (London: Routledge, 1991).

Ellis, J.M., *Against Deconstruction* (Princeton: Princeton University Press, 1989).

Emmerson, G.I., *Hosea: An Israelite Prophet in Judaean Perspective* (JSOTSup, 28; Sheffield: JSOT Press, 1984).

Ewald, G.W., *Commentary on the Prophets of the Old Testament*. I. *Joel, Amos, Hosea and Zechariah* (trans. J.F. Smith; London: Williams & Norgate, 1875).

Exum, J.C., *Fragmented Women: Feminist (Sub)versions of Biblical Narratives* (JSOTSup, 163; Sheffield: JSOT Press, 1993).

— *Tragedy and Comedy in the Bible* (Semeia, 32; Atlanta: Scholars Press, 1985).

Eybers, I.H., 'The Matrimonial Life of Hosea', *Die Oud Testament werkgemeenskap in Suid-Afrika* 7-8 (1964–65), pp. 11-34.

Farr, G., 'The Concept of Grace in the Book of Hosea', *ZAW* 70 (1958) pp. 98-107.

Faur, J., *Golden Doves with Silver Dots: Semiotics and Textuality in Rabbinic Tradition* (Bloomington: Indiana University Press, 1986).

Felperin, H., *Beyond Deconstruction: The Uses and Abuses of Literary Theory* (Oxford: Clarendon Press, 1985).

Féral, J., 'Towards a Theory of Displacement', *Substance* 32 (1981), pp. 52-64.

Fetterly, J., *The Resisting Reader: A Feminist Approach to American Fiction* (Bloomington: Indiana University Press, 1978).

Filmer, K., 'Of Lunacy and Laundry Trucks: Deconstruction and Mythopoesis', *LB* (1989), pp. 55-64.

Fisch, H., 'Hosea: A Poetics of Violence', in H. Fisch (ed.), *Poetry with a Purpose: Biblical Poetics and Interpretation* (Bloomington: Indiana University Press, 1990), pp. 136-57.

Fish, S., *Is There a Text in this Class? The Authority of Interpretive Communities* (Cambridge, MA: Harvard University Press, 1980).

—'Normal Circumstances, Literal Language, Direct Speech Acts, the Ordinary, the Everyday, the Obvious, what Goes without Saying, and Other Special Cases', *Critical Inquiry* 4 (1978), pp. 625-44 .

—*Self-Consuming Artifacts: The Experience of Seventeenth Century Literature* (Berkeley: University of California Press, 1972).

—*Surprised by Sin: The Reader in Paradise Lost* (London: University of California Press, 1971).

—'Why No One's Afraid of Wolfgang Iser', *Diacritics* 11 (1981), pp. 2-13.

Fishbane, M., 'Israel and the "Mothers" ', in P.L. Berger (ed.), *The Other Side of God: A Polarity in World Religions* (New York: Doubleday, 1981), pp. 28-47.

Foster, L., '"I Will Not Punish Your Daughters For Being Prostitutes": Reading Hosea 1.2–4.14 as a Prostitute' (amended version of a paper presented to the SBL, New Orleans, 1990).

Foucault, M., *The Birth of the Clinic* (trans. A.M. Sheridan Smith; New York: Vintage Books, 1975).

Freedman, H., *The Babylonian Talmud: Seder Mo'ed* (London: Soncino Press, 1938).

Frei, H., *The Eclipse of Biblical Narrative* (London: Yale University Press, 1980).

Fretheim, T.E., 'Old Testament Commentaries: Their Selection and Use', *Interpretation* 36 (1982), pp. 356-71.

Freud, S., *Moses and Monotheism* (Harmondsworth: Penguin, 1985).

Freund, E., *The Return of the Reader: Reader-Response Criticism* (London: Methuen, 1987).

Friedman, S., *Penelope's Web: Gender, Modernity, H.D.'s Fiction* (Cambridge: Cambridge University Press, 1990).

Frye, N., *Anatomy of Criticism* (Princeton: Princeton University Press, 1957).

—*The Great Code: The Bible and Literature* (New York: Harcourt Brace Jovanovich, 1982).

Fuchs, E., 'The Literary Characterisation of Mothers and Sexual Politics in the Hebrew Bible', in Amihai, Coats and Solomon (eds.), *Narrative Research on the Hebrew Bible*, pp. 151-66.

—'The Objective Phallacy', in Tollers and Maier (eds.), *Mappings of the Biblical Terrain*, pp. 134-42.

Gallop, J., *The Daughter's Seduction: Feminism and Psychoanalysis* (Ithaca, NY: Cornell University Press, 1982).

Garver, N., 'Derrida on Rousseau on Writing', *Journal of Philosophy* 74 (1977), pp. 663-73.

Gasché, R., 'Deconstruction as Criticism', *Glyph* 6 (1979), pp. 177-215.

Gass, W.H., *Willie Masters' Lonesome Wife* (Evanston, IL: Northwestern University Press, 1968).

Gélin, A., 'Osée', in L. Pirot and F. Vigouroux (eds.), *Dictionnaire de la Bible, Supplément*, VI (Paris, 1960), pp. 926-40.

Gelley, A., 'Form as Force', *Diacritics* 2 (1972) pp. 9-13.

Geneva Cannon, K., and E. Schüssler Fiorenza (eds.), *Interpretation for Liberation* (Semeia, 47; Atlanta: Scholars Press, 1989).

Ghose, S., 'Mysticism', *Encyclopaedia Britannica Macropaedia* (15th edn), XII, pp. 786-93.

Gibson, J.C.L., *Canaanite Myths and Legends* (Edinburgh: T. & T. Clark, 1977).

Ginsberg, H.L., 'Hosea, Book of', in *EncJud*, XVIII, cols. 1010-25.

Ginzberg, L., *The Legends of the Jews* (Philadelphia: Jewish Publication Society of America, 1968), I.

Godet, F., *Commentary on St Luke's Gospel* (trans. M.D. Cusin; Edinburgh: T. & T. Clark, 1957), II.

Good, E.M., 'The Composition of Hosea', *SEÅ* 31 (1966), pp. 21-63.

Gordis, R., 'Hosea's Marriage and Message', *HUCA* 25 (1954), pp. 9-35.

Gordon, V.R., 'Sign', in *ISBE*, IV, p. 505.

Gottwald, N.K., *The Tribes of Yahweh: A Sociology of the Religion of Liberated Israel, 1250–1050 BCE* (London: SCM Press, 1979).

Graetz, N., 'The Haftarah Tradition and the Metaphoric Battering of Hosea's Wife', *Conservative Judaism* 45 (1992), pp. 29-42.

Graham, J.F., 'Translator's Preface' to Derrida, 'Des Tours de Babel', in Moore and Jobling (eds.), *Poststructuralism as Exegesis*, pp. 3-34.

Greenlee, D., *Peirce's Concept of Sign* (The Hague: Mouton, 1973).

Greenstein, E.L., 'Deconstruction and Biblical Narrative', *Prooftexts* 9 (1989), pp. 43-71.

Greenwood, D.S., 'Poststructuralism and Biblical Studies: Frank Kermode's The Genesis of Secrecy', in R.T. France and D. Wenham (eds.), *Studies in Midrash and Historiography* (Gospel Perspectives, 3; Sheffield: JSOT Press, 1983), pp. 263-88.

Griffin, S., *Pornography and Silence: Culture's Revenge Against Women*, in M. Humm (ed.), *Feminisms: A Reader* (Hemel Hempstead: Harvester Wheatsheaf, 1992), pp. 80-81.

Guillaumin, C., 'The Question of Difference', *Feminist Issues* 2 (1982), pp. 33-52.

Guiraud, P., *Semiology* (trans. G. Gross; London: Routledge & Kegan Paul, 1975).

Gunn, D.M., 'In Security: The David of Biblical Narrative', in J.C. Exum (ed.), *Signs and Wonders: Biblical Texts in Literary Focus* (Atlanta: Scholars Press, 1989), pp. 133-51.

Habermas, J., *The Philosophical Discourse of Modernity: Twelve Lectures* (trans. F. Lawrence; Cambridge: Polity Press, 1987).

Hampson, D., 'Christianity Will Always Be a Male Religion', letter in *The Independent* (15 November 1992).

Handelman, S., 'Jacques Derrida and the Heretic Hermeneutic', in M. Krupnick (ed.), *Displacement: Derrida and After* (Bloomington: Indiana University Press, 1983), pp. 98-129.

Handke, P., 'Nauseated by Language (Interview with Arthur Joseph)', *The Drama Review* 15 (1971), pp. 56-61.

—*Offending the Audience* (trans. M. Roloff; London: Methuen, 1971).

Hans, J.S., 'Derrida and Freeplay', *MLN* 94 (1979), pp. 809-10.

Harper, W.R., *A Critical and Exegetical Commentary on Amos and Hosea* (ICC; Edinburgh: T. & T. Clark, 1905).

Harrison, R.K., 'Teraphim', in *ISBE*, IV, p. 793.

Hart, K., *The Trespass of the Sign: Deconstruction, Theology and Philosophy* (Cambridge: Cambridge University Press, 1989).

Hartley, L.P., *The Go-Between* (Harmondsworth: Penguin, 1958).

Hartman, G.H., 'The State of the Art of Criticism', in Cohen (ed.), *The Future of Literary Theory*, pp. 86-101.

Hartman, G.H., and S. Budick (eds.), *Midrash and Literature* (New York: Yale University Press, 1986).

Hauptmann, E. (ed.), *Gesammelte Werke* (Frankfurt: Suhrkamp, 1967), XVI.

Hauret, C., *Amos et Osée: Un livret de famille originale* (Paris: Beauchesne, 1970).

Hawkes, T., *Structuralism and Semiotics* (New Accents; London: Routledge, 1989).

Hawthorne, N., *The Scarlet Letter* (New York: Norton, 1978).

Heerman, A., 'Ehe und Kinder des Propheten Hosea', *ZAW* 40 (1922), pp. 287-312.

Heidegger, M., *The Question of Being* (trans. W. Klauback and J.T. Wilde; New York, 1958).

Heilbrun, C.G., 'The Character of Hamlet's Mother', in *Hamlet's Mother and Other Women: Feminist Essays on Literature* (London: The Women's Press, 1991), pp. 9-17.

Heilbrun, C.G., and C.R. Stimpson, 'Theories of Feminist Criticism: A Dialogue', in J. Donovan (ed.), *Feminist Literary Criticism* (Lexington, KY: University Press of Kentucky, 1975), pp. 61-73.

Hengstenberg, E.W., *Christology of the Old Testament*, I (trans. T. Mayer; Edinburgh: 1954).

Hennings, T., 'Singer's "Gimpel the Fool" and the Book of Hosea', *JNT* 13 (1983), pp. 11-19.

Herdner, A., *Corpus des tablettes en cunéiformes alphabétiques* (Paris: Imprimerie Nationale, 1963).

Heschel, A.J., *The Prophets* (New York: Harper & Row, 1969).

Hillis Miller, J., 'Ariachne's Broken Woof', *Georgia Review* 9 (1977), pp. 31-59.

—'The Function of Literary Theory at the Present Time', in Cohen (ed.), *The Future of Literary Theory*, pp. 103-11.

—'The Still Heart: Poetic Form in Wordsworth', *NLH* 2 (1971), pp. 297-310.

Hjelmslev, L., *Prologemena to a Theory of Language* (trans. F.J. Whitfield; Madison, WI: University of Wisconsin Press, 1969).

Hubbard, D.A., *Hosea: An Introduction and Commentary* (TOTC; Leicester: Inter-Varsity Press, 1989).

Irigaray, L., 'When our Lips Speak Together', trans. C. Burke, *Signs* 6 (1980), pp. 69-79.

Iser, W., 'The Reading Process: A Phenomenological Approach', in Lodge (ed.), *Modern Criticism and Theory: A Reader*, pp. 212-28 (repr. from *NLH* 3 [1972]).

Izachak, *The Marriage of Hosea: A Passion Play in Three Acts* (New York: Halcyon, 1929).

Jabès, E., *Livre des questions* (Paris: Gallimard, 1963).

Jacob, E., 'L'héritage cananéen dans le livre du prophète Osée', *RHPR* 43 (1963), pp. 250-59.

—'Osée', in *Osée, Joël, Abdias, Jonas, Amos* (CAT; Neuchâtel: Delachaux et Niestlé, 1965).

Jacobus, M., 'The Difference of View', in M. Jacobus (ed.), *Women Writing and Writing about Women* (London: Croom Helm, 1979), pp. 10-21.

Jakobson, R., *Coup de l'oeil sur le développement de la sémiotique* (Bloomington: Indiana University Press, 1975).

—'Language in Relation to Other Communication Systems', in R. Jakobson (ed.), *Selected Writings*, III (The Hague: Mouton, 1971), pp. 697-708.

Jameson, F., 'Metacommentary', in *The Ideologies of Theory*. I. *Situations of Theory, Essays 1971–1986* (London: Routledge & Kegan Paul, 1988), pp. 3-16.

—*The Prison House of Language: A Critical Account of Structuralism and Russian Formalism* (Princeton: Princeton University Press, 1972).

Jardine, A., and P. Smith (eds.), *Men in Feminism* (New York: Methuen, 1987).

—'Women in the Beehive: A Seminar with Jacques Derrida', in Jardine and Smith (eds.), *Men in Feminism*, pp. 189-203.

Jerome, *Commentaria in Osee prophetam*, in J.P. Migne (ed.), *Divinae Bibliotheca Pars Prima: Hieronymi Opera*, 9 (Patrologia, Series Latina, XXV; Paris: Vrayet de Surcy, 1845).

Jobling, D., 'Deconstructive Reading of Hosea 1–3' (unpublished paper).

Johnson, B., 'The Critical Difference', *Diacritics* 8 (1978), pp. 2-9.

—'Interview', in Salusinszky (ed.), *Criticism in Society*, pp. 169-70.

—'Translator's Introduction', in J. Derrida, *Dissemination* (Chicago: University of Chicago Press, 1981).

Johnston, J., *Lesbian Nation: The Feminist Solution* (New York: Simon & Schuster, 1973).

Josipovici, G., *The Book of God: A Response to the Bible* (New Haven: Yale University Press, 1988).

Kaiser, O., *Isaiah 1–12: A Commentary* (trans. R.A. Wilson; OTL; London: SCM Press, 1972).

—*Isaiah 1–12: A Commentary* (rev. edn.; trans. J. Bowden; London, SCM Press, 1983).

Kamuf, P. (ed.), *A Derrida Reader: Between the Blinds* (Hemel Hempstead: Harvester Wheatsheaf, 1991).

Kapelrud, A.S., *The Violent Goddess: Anat in the Ras Shamra Texts* (Oslo: Scandinavian University Books, 1969).

Kaufman, S.A., 'Reflections on the Assyrian Aramaic Bilingual from Tell Fakhariyeh', *Maarav* 3 (1982), pp. 137-38.

Kaufmann, Y., *The Religion of Israel: From its Beginnings to the Babylonian Exile* (trans. M. Greenberg; London: George Allen & Unwin, 1961).

Keefe, A.A., 'Rapes of Women/Wars of Men', in Camp and Fontaine (eds.), *Women, War and Metaphor*, pp. 79-97.

Keiffer, R., 'Was heißt das, ein Text zu kommentieren?', *BZ* 20 (1976), pp. 212-16.

Keil, C.F., 'The Minor Prophets', in C.F. Keil and F. Delitzsch, *Biblical Commentary on the Old Testament* (trans. J. Martin; Edinburgh, 1880).

Kierkegaard, S., *Concluding Unscientific Postscript* (Princeton: Princeton University Press, 1941).

—*Fear and Trembling* (trans. H.V. Kong and E.H. Kong; Princeton: Princeton University Press, 1983).

Knight, G.A.F., *Hosea: Introduction and Commentary* (London: SCM Press, 1960).

Knudtzon, J.A., *Die El-Armana-Tafeln* (Leipzig: Heinrichs, 1915).

Koch, K., *The Growth of the Biblical Tradition: The Form-Critical Method* (New York: Charles Schribner's Sons, 1969).

Kolodny, A., 'Dancing through the Minefield: Some Observations on the Theory, Politics and Practice of a Feminist Criticism', *FS* 6 (1980), pp. 1-25.

—'A Map for Rereading: Gender and the Interpretation of Literary Texts', in Showalter (ed.), *The New Feminist Criticism*, pp. 46-62.

Koonthanam, G., 'Divine Love in the Prophet Hosea', *Jeedvahara* 13 (1983), pp. 130-39.

Kristeva, J., 'The Bounded Text', in *Desire in Language*, pp. 36-63.

—*Desire in Language: A Semiotic Approach to Literature and Art* (ed. L.S. Roudiez; Oxford: Basil Blackwell, 1980).

—'The Ethics of Linguistics', in *Desire in Language*, pp. 23-35.

—'From Symbol to Sign', in Moi (ed.), *The Kristeva Reader*, pp. 62-73.

—'Semiotics: A Critical Science and/or a Critique of Science', in Moi (ed.), *The Kristeva Reader*, pp. 75-87.

—'The System and the Speaking Subject', *TLS* (12 October 1973), pp. 1249-50.

Kugel, J.L., 'Two Introductions to Midrash', in Hartman and Budick (eds.), *Midrash and Literature*, pp. 77-103.

Kuhl, C., 'Neue Dokumente zum Verständnis von Hosea 2,4-15', *ZAW* 52 (1934), pp. 102-109.

Kurtz, W.S., 'Narrative Approaches to Luke–Acts', *Bib* 68 (1987), pp. 195-220.

La Bonnardière, A., 'Saint Augustine et le prophète Osée', *VSpir* 143 (1989), pp. 623-32.

Lawrence, W.W., *Shakespeare's Problem Comedies* (New York: Ungar, 1960 [1931]).

Leavey, J.P., 'Four Protocols: Derrida, his Deconstruction', in Detweiler (ed.), *Derrida and Biblical Studies*, pp. 43-57.

Leib, I.C. (ed.), *Charles Sanders Peirce's Letters to Lady Welby* (New Haven: Whitlock's, 1963).

Leitch, V.B., *Deconstructive Criticism: An Advanced Introduction* (New York: Columbia University Press, 1983).

Lerner, G., *The Creation of Patriarchy* (Oxford: Oxford University Press, 1986).

Levi-Strauss, C., *The Savage Mind* (Chicago: Chicago University Press, 1961).

Lippl, J., 'Der Prophet Osee übersetzt und erklärt', in F. Feldman and H. Herkeene (eds.), *Die heilige Schrift des Alten Testaments, übersetzt und erklärt in Verbindung mit Fachgelehrten* (Bonn: Peter Hanstein, 1937), pp. 7-84 .

Lipshitz, A., *The Commentary of Rabbi Abraham Ibn Ezra on Hosea* (New York: Sepher-Hermon Press, 1988).

Locke, J., *An Essay Concerning the Human Understanding* (London: J.M. Dent & Sons, 1947).

Lodge, D. (ed.), *Modern Criticism and Theory: A Reader* (London: Longman, 1988).

—*Twentieth Century Literary Criticism: A Reader* (London: Longman, 1972).

Lowe, M., and M. Lowe Benston, 'The Uneasy Alliance of Feminism and Academia', in S. Gunew (ed.), *A Reader In Feminist Knowledge* (London: Routledge, 1991), pp. 48-60.

Luther, M., *Lectures on the Minor Prophets* (trans. H.C. Oswald; St Louis: Concordia, 1975).

Lyotard, J., *The Postmodern Condition: A Report on Knowledge* (trans. G. Bennington and B. Massumi; Manchester: Manchester University Press, 1984).

Macherey, P., *A Theory of Literary Production* (London: Routledge, 1989).

Macintosh, A.A., letter in *The Independent*, 16 November 1992.

Maimonides, M., *The Guide of the Perplexed* (trans. S. Pines; Chicago: University Of Chicago Press, 1963), 98b.

Marcus, J., 'Storming the Toolshed', *Signs* 7 (1982), pp. 622-40.

May, H.G., 'The Fertility Cult in Hosea', *AJSL* 48 (1932), pp. 73-98.

Mays, J.L., *Hosea: A Commentary* (OTL; London: SCM Press, 1969).

McComiskey, T.E., 'Prophetic Irony in Hosea 1–4: A Study of the Collocation פקד על and its Implications for the Fall of Jehu's Dynasty', *JSOT* 58 (1993), pp. 93-101.

McCurdy, J.F., 'Hosea', in *The New Schaff-Herzog Encyclopaedia of Religious Knowledge*, V (Grand Rapids: Baker Book House, 1908), p. 371.

McFague, S., *Metaphorical Theology: Models of God in Religious Language* (London: SCM Press, 1983).

McGuire, M., 'Sympathy and Prophetic Consciousness in Hosea', *Review for Religious* 39 (1985), pp. 884-93.

McHale, B., *Postmodern Fiction* (London: Routledge, 1991).

McKeating, H., *The Books of Amos, Hosea and Micah* (Cambridge: Cambridge University Press, 1971).

Meese, E.A., *Crossing the Double Cross: The Practice of Feminist Criticism* (Chapel Hill, NC: University of North Carolina Press, 1986).

Megill, A., *Prophets of Extremity: Nietzsche, Heidegger, Foucault, Derrida* (Berkeley: University of California Press, 1985).

Mettinger, T.N.D., 'The Elusive Essence: Yhwh, El and Baal and the Distinctiveness of Israelite Faith', in E. Blum (ed.), *Die hebräische Bibel und ihre zweifache Nachgeschichte* (Neukirchen–Vluyn: Neukirchener Verlag, 1990), pp. 393-417.

Meyers, C., 'Ephod', in D.N. Freedman (ed.), *The Anchor Bible Dictionary*, II (New York: Doubleday, 1992), p. 550.

—'The Roots of Restriction', in N.K. Gottwald (ed.), *The Bible and Liberation* (New York: Maryknoll, 1983), pp. 289-306.

Miles, J.R., 'Radical Editing: *Redaktionsgeschichte* and the Aesthetic of Willed Confusion', in R.E. Friedman (ed.), *The Creation of Sacred Literature: Composition and Redaction of the Biblical Text* (Berkeley: University of California Press, 1981), pp. 85-98.

Miller, J., *Seductions: Studies in Reading and Culture* (London: Virago, 1990).

Miscall, P.D., 'Isaiah: The Labyrinth of Images', in Moore and Jobling (eds.), *Poststructuralism as Exegesis*, pp. 103-21.

Modleski, T., 'Feminism and the Power of Interpretation: Some Critical Readings', in T. de Lauretis (ed.), *Feminist Studies/Critical Studies* (Bloomington: Indiana University Press, 1986), pp. 121-38.

Moi, T. (ed.), *The Kristeva Reader* (Oxford: Basil Blackwell, 1986).

—'Patriarchal Reflections: Luce Irigaray's Looking-Glass', in *Sexual/Textual Politics: Feminist Literary Theory* (London: Methuen, 1985), pp. 127-49.

Moor, J.C. de, *An Anthology of Religious Texts from Ugarit* (Leiden: Brill, 1987).

Moore, S.D., 'Are there Impurities in the Living Water that the Johannine Jesus Dispenses? Deconstruction, Feminism and the Samaritan Woman', *BI* 1 (1993), pp. 207-27.

—*Literary Criticism and the Gospels: The Theoretical Challenge* (New Haven: Yale University Press, 1989).

Moore, S.D., and D. Jobling (eds.), *Poststructuralism as Exegesis* (Semeia, 54; Atlanta: Scholars Press, 1991).

Morrison, T., *Beloved* (London: Picador, 1988).

Munich, A., 'Notorious Signs: Feminist Criticism and Literary Criticism', in G. Greene and C. Kahn (eds.), *Making a Difference: Feminist Literary Criticism* (London: Methuen, 1985), pp. 238-59.

Needham, R., review of W. Arens, *The Man-Eating Myth*, *TLS* (25 January 1980), p. 75.

Nicholson, N., *A Match for the Devil* (London: Faber & Faber, 1953).

Nietzsche, F., 'On Truth and Falsity in their Ultramoral Sense', in O. Levey (ed.), *The Complete Works of Friedrich Nietzsche*, II (New York 1964).

—*Will to Power* (trans. W. Kaufmann; New York: Vintage Books, 1968).

Nolland, J., *Luke 9.21–18.34* (WBC; Dallas: Word Books, 1993).

Norris, C., *Deconstruction: Theory and Practice* (New Accents; London: Routledge, rev. edn 1991 [1982]).

—'Limited Think: How not to Read Derrida', in *What's Wrong with Postmodernism: Critical Theory and the Ends of Philosophy* (Hemel Hempstead: Harvester Wheatsheaf, 1990), pp. 134-63.

North, C.R., *The Second Isaiah: Introduction, Translation and Commentary to Chapters 40–55* (Oxford: Clarendon Press, 1964).

North, F., 'Solution of Hosea's Marital Problems by Critical Analysis', *JNES* 16 (1957), pp. 128-30.

Oden, R.A., *The Bible Without Theology: The Theological Tradition and Alternatives to it* (San Francisco: Harper & Row, 1987).

—'Theoretical Assumptions in the Study of Ugaritic Myths', *Maarav* 2 (1979), pp. 43-63.

Oldenberg, U., *The Conflict Between El and Baal in Canaanite Religion* (Leiden: Brill, 1969).

Olyan, S.M., ' "In the Sight of Her Lovers": On the Interpretation of *nablút* in Hos. 2.12', *BZ* 36 (1992), pp. 255-61.

Osiek, C., 'The Feminist and the Bible: Hermeneutical Alternatives', in Collins (ed.), *Feminist Perspectives on Biblical Scholarship*, pp. 93-105.

Östborn, G., *Yahweh and Baal: Studies in the Book of Hosea and Related Documents* (LUÅ, 51; Lund: Hakan Ohlssons Boktryokeri, 1956).

Ostriker, A.S., *Feminist Revision and the Bible* (The Bucknell Lectures in Literary Theory, 7; Oxford: Basil Blackwell, 1993).

Pankhurst, S., *The Suffragette Movement* (London: Virago, 1978).

Paolantonio, M., 'God as Husband', *The Bible Today* 27 (1989), pp. 299-303.

Pardes, I., *Countertraditions in the Bible: A Feminist Approach* (Cambridge, MA: Harvard University Press, 1992).

Paterson, J., 'Hosea', in F.C. Grant and H.H. Rowley (eds.), *A Dictionary of the Bible* (Edinburgh: T. & T. Clark, 2nd edn, 1963), p. 398.

Patrick, D. (ed.), *Thinking Biblical Law* (Semeia, 45; Atlanta: Scholars Press, 1989).

Patte, D. (ed.), *Semiology and Parables: An Exploration of the Possibilities Offered by Structuralism for Exegesis* (proceedings of the conference 'Semiology and Exegesis', Vanderbilt University, Nashville, 15-17 May 1975; Pittsburgh: The Pickwick Press, 1976).

Peirce, C.S., *Charles Sanders Peirce's Letters to Lady Welby* (ed. I.C. Leib; New Haven: Whitlock's, 1963).

—*The Writings of Charles Sanders Peirce*. II. *Collected Papers* (ed. C. Hartshorne, P. Weiss and A.W. Burks; 8 vols.; Cambridge, MA: Harvard University Press, 1931–58).

Pfeiffer, R.H., *Introduction to the Old Testament* (New York: Harper & Row, 1941).

Pirsig, R., *Zen and the Art of Motorcycle Maintenance* (London: Bodley Head, 1974).

Plank, K.A., 'The Scarred Countenance: Inconstancy in the Book of Hosea', *Judaism* 32 (1983), pp. 343-54.

Plaskow, J., 'Blaming the Jews for the Birth of Patriarchy', in E.T. Beck (ed.), *Nice Jewish Girls: A Lesbian Anthology* (Watertown, MA: Persephone Press, 1982), pp. 250-54.

Plato, *The Republic* (trans. D. Lee; Harmondsworth: Penguin, 1987).

Poovey, M., 'Feminism and Deconstruction', *FS* 14 (1988), pp. 51-65.

Powis Smith, J.M., 'The Marriage of Hosea', *BW* 42, pp. 94-101.

Proust, M., 'The Fugitive', in Proust, *A la recherche du temps perdu* (trans. C.K.S. Moncrieff; New York: Vintage Books, 1970).

Pynchon, T., *The Crying of Lot 49* (New York: Bantam, 1972).

Quine, W.V.O, *Word and Object* (Cambridge, MA: MIT Press, 1960).

Rad, G. von, *Old Testament Theology*. II. *The Theology of Israel's Prophetic Traditions* (trans. D.M.G. Stalker; Edinburgh: Oliver & Boyd, 1965).

Renaud, B., 'Fidélité humaine et fidélité de Dieu', *Revue de droit canonique* 33 (1983), pp. 184-200.

—'Osée 1–3: Analyse diachronique et lecture synchronique: problèmes de méthode', *RevScRel* 57 (1983), pp. 249-60.

Rich, A., *On Lies, Secrets and Silence: Selected Prose 1966–1978* (London: Virago, 1986).

Richards, I.A., *Principles of Literary Criticism* (New York: Harcourt Brace Jovanovich, 1925).

Robbe-Grillet, A., *Project for Revolution in New York* (trans. R. Howard; London: Caldar & Boyars, 1973).

Roberts, N., *Whores in History: Prostitution in Western Society* (London: HarperCollins, 1992).

Robinson, T.H., 'Hosea', in T.H. Robinson and F. Horst (eds.), *Die zwölf kleinen Propheten: Hosea bis Micha* (HAT; Tübingen: Mohr, 1954), pp. 1-54.

Rogerson, J.W., *Myth in Old Testament Research* (Berlin: de Gruyter, 1974).

Roitman, B., 'Sacred Language and Open Text', in Hartman and Budick (eds.) *Midrash and Literature*, pp. 159-75.

Rorty, R., *Consequences of Pragmatism (Essays: 1972–1980)* (Minneapolis: University of Minnesota Press, 1982).

— 'Philosophy as a Kind of Writing: An Essay on Derrida', *NLH* 10 (1978), pp. 141-60.

—'The Pragmatist's Progress', in Collini (ed.), *Interpretation and Overinterpretation*, pp. 89-108.

Rossiter, A.P., *Angel with Horns* (London: Longman, 1971).

Roston, M., *Biblical Drama in England: From the Middle Ages to the Present Day* (London: Faber & Faber, 1968).

Rousseau, J., *Essai sur l'origine des langues* (Bordeaux: Ducrois, 1968).

Rowley, H.H., 'The Marriage of Hosea', in Rowley, *Men of God: Studies in Old Testament History and Prophecy* (London: Nelson, 1963), pp. 66-97.

Rubin Suleiman, S., 'Pornography, Transgression and the Avant-Garde: Bataille's Story of the Eye', in N.K. Miller (ed.), *The Poetics of Gender* (New York: Columbia University Press, 1986), pp. 117-36.

Rudolph, W., *Hosea* (KAT; Gütersloh: Gerd Mohn, 1966).

Ruppert, L., 'Erwägungen zur Kompositions- und Redaktionsgeschichte von Osea 1–3', *BZ* 26 (1982), pp. 208-23.

Russell, D., 'On Pornography', *Chrysalis* 4 (1977).

Ryken, L., and T. Longman III, *A Complete Literary Guide to the Bible* (Grand Rapids: Zondervan, 1993).

Salusinszky, I. (ed.), *Criticism in Society: Interviews with Jacques Derrida, Northrop Frye, Harold Bloom, Geoffrey Hartman, Frank Kermode, Edward Said, Barbara Johnson, Frank Lentricchia and J. Hillis Miller* (London: Methuen, 1987).

Saussure, F. de, *Cours de linguistique générale* (ed. R. Engler; Wiesbaden: Otto Harrassowitz, 1967–74); ET *Course in General Linguistics* (ed. C. Bally and A. Sechehaye; trans. W. Baskin; Glasgow: Fontana/Collins, 1974; 1st edn, New York: Philosophical Library, 1959).

Schanzer, E., *The Problem Plays of Shakespeare: A Study of Julius Caesar, Measure for Measure, Antony and Cleopatra* (London: Routledge & Kegan Paul, 1963).

Schenk, W., 'Was ist ein Kommentar?', *BZ* 24 (1980), pp. 1-20.

Schlovsky, V., 'Art as Technique' and 'Sterne's Tristram Shandy: Stylistic Commentary', in T. Lemon and J. Reis (eds.), *Russian Formalist Criticism: Four Essays* (Lincoln, NB: University of Nebraska Press, 1965), pp. 3-57.

Schneidau, H.N., *Sacred Discontent: The Bible and Western Tradition* (Baton Rouge: Louisiana State University Press, 1976).

—'The Word against the Word: Derrida on Textuality', in Detweiler (ed.), *Derrida and Biblical Studies*, pp. 5-28.

Scholem, G., *On the Kabbalah and its Symbolism* (New York: Schocken Books, 1965).

Schweickhart, P.P., 'Reading Ourselves: Towards a Feminist Theory of Reading', in E. Showalter (ed.), *Speaking of Gender* (New York: Routledge, 1989), pp. 17-44.

Scott, M., *The Message of Hosea* (New York: Macmillan, 1921).

Searle, J., 'Reiterating the Differences: A Reply to Derrida', *Glyph* 1 (1977), pp. 198-208.

Selden, R., *A Reader's Guide to Contemporary Literary Theory* (Brighton: Harvester Press, 1985).

Sellers, O.R., 'Hosea's Motives', *AJSL* 41 (1924–25), pp. 243-47.

Setel, T.D., 'Feminist Insights and the Question of Method', in Collins (ed.), *Feminist Perspectives on Biblical Scholarship*, pp. 35-42.

—'Prophets and Pornography: Female Sexual Imagery in Hosea', in L.M. Russell (ed.), *Feminist Interpretation of the Bible* (Oxford: Basil Blackwell, 1985), pp. 86-95.

Showalter, E., 'Critical Cross-Dressing: Male Feminist and the Woman of the Year', in Jardine and Smith (eds.), *Men in Feminism*, pp. 116-32.

—'Feminist Criticism in the Wilderness', in Showalter (ed.), *The New Feminist Criticism*, pp. 243-70.

Showalter, E. (ed.), *The New Feminist Criticism: Essays on Women, Literature and Theory* (London: Virago, 1986).

Silverman, K., *The Subject of Semiotics* (Oxford: Oxford University Press, 1983).

Singer, I.B., 'Gimpel the Fool', in *Gimpel the Fool and Other Tales* (Harmondsworth: Penguin, 1981).

Sitterson, J.C., 'Will to Power in Biblical Interpretation', in Tollers and Maier (eds.), *Mappings of the Biblical Terrain*, pp. 134-41.

Smith, J., *Misogynies* (London: Faber & Faber, 1993).

Smith, M.S., *The Early History of God: Yahweh and the Other Deities in Ancient Israel* (San Francisco: Harper & Row, 1990).

Smolar, L., and M. Aberbach, *Studies in Targum Jonathan to the Prophets* (Baltimore: Ktav, 1983).

Snaith, N.H., *Amos, Hosea, and Micah* (London: Epworth Press, 1959).

Sontag, S., 'Against Interpretation', in Lodge (ed.), *Twentieth Century Literary Criticism: A Reader*, pp. 652-60 (repr. from *Evergreen Review* [1964]).

Sowerby, R. (ed.), *Alexander Pope: Selected Poetry and Prose* (London: Routledge & Kegan Paul, 1988).

Speirs, R., *Bertholt Brecht* (London: Macmillan, 1987).

Spender, D., *Man Made Language* (London: Pandora Press, 1990).

Spivak, G.C., *Outside in the Teaching Machine* (London: Routledge, 1993).

—'Translator's Preface', in Derrida, *Of Grammatology*.

Stern, D., 'Midrash and Indeterminacy', *CI* 15 (1988), pp 132-61.

Sternberg, M., *The Poetics of Biblical Narrative: Ideological Literature and the Drama of Reading* (Bloomington: Indiana University Press, 1985).

Sterne, L., *The Life and Opinions of Tristram Shandy* (Harmondsworth: Penguin, 1987).

Stibbe, M.W.G., 'Semiotics', in Coggins and Houlden (eds.), *A Dictionary of Biblical Interpretation*, p. 618.

Straumann, H.S., 'Gott als Mutter in Hosea 11', *TQ* 166 (1986), pp. 119-34.

Strauss, J., 'Hosea's Love: A Modern Interpretation', *Judaism* 19 (1970), pp. 226-33.

Taylor, M.C., 'Deconstruction: What's the Difference?', *Soundings: An Interdisciplinary Journal* 66 (1983), pp. 387-403.

Thomas, V., *The Moral Universe of Shakespeare's Problem Plays* (London: Croom Helm, 1987).

Tillyard, E.M.W., *Shakespeare's Problem Plays* (London: Chatto & Windus, 1950).

Tindal, M., *Christianity as Old as the Creation* (London, 1730).

Tollers, V.L., and J. Maier (eds.), *Mappings of the Biblical Terrain: The Bible as Text* (Toronto: Bucknell University Press, 1990).

Tompkins, J.P. (ed.), *Reader-Response Criticism: From Formalism to Poststructuralism* (Baltimore: Johns Hopkins University Press, 1980).

Törnkvist, R., 'The Use and Abuse of Female Sexual Imagery in the Book of Hosea: A Feminist Critical Approach to Hos 1–3' (PhD dissertation, Uppsala University, 1994).

Toy, C.H., 'Note on Hosea 1–3', *JBL* 32 (1913), pp. 75-79.

Trible, P,.'Depatriarchalization in Biblical Interpretation', *JAAR* 41 (1973), pp. 30-49.

—*God and the Rhetoric of Sexuality* (Philadelphia: Fortress Press, 1978).

Tushingham, A.D., 'A Reconsideration of Hosea Chapters 1–3', *JNES* 12 (1953), pp. 150-58.

Ure, P., *Shakespeare: The Problem Plays* (London: Longman, 1970).

Van Selms, A., 'Hosea and Canticles', *OTWSA* 7-8 (1964–65), pp. 85-90.

Veltrusky, J., 'Man and Object in the Theatre', in P.L. Garvin (ed.), *A Prague School Reader on Aesthetics: Literary Structure and Style* (Washington, DC: Georgetown University Press, 1964), pp. 83-91.

Verdiglione, A. (ed.), *Psychoanalyse et politique* (Paris: du Seuil, 1974).

Vogels, W., ' "Osée–Gomer": *car* et *comme* "Yahweh–Israël", Os 1–3', *NRT* 103 (1981), pp. 711-27.

Wacker, M., 'Frau–Sexus–Macht: Eine feministische Relecture des Hoseabuches', in *Der Gott der Männer und der Frauen* (Theologie zur Zeit, 2; Düsseldorf: Patmos, 1987), pp. 101-25.

—'God as Mother? On the Meaning of a Biblical God-Symbol for Feminist Theology', *Concilium* 206 (1989), pp. 103-11.

Walker, L., *The Battered Woman* (New York: Harper & Row, 1979).

Walker, S.C., 'Deconstructing the Bible', *LB* (1989), pp. 8-17.

Walls, N.H., *The Goddess Anat in Ugaritic Myth* (SBLDS; Atlanta: Scholars Press, 1992).

Waterman, L., 'The Marriage of Hosea', *JBL* 37 (1918), pp. 193-208.

Watts, C., *Shakespeare: Measure for Measure* (Harmondsworth: Penguin, 1986).

Waugh, P., *Metafiction: The Theory and Practice of Self-Conscious Fiction* (London: Methuen, 1984).

Weems, R.J., 'Gomer: Victim of Violence or Victim of Metaphor?', in Geneva Cannon and Schüssler Fiorenza (eds.), *Interperation for Liberation*, pp. 87-104.

Wenzel, H., 'The Text as Body/Politics: An Appreciation of Monique Wittig's Writing in Context', *FS* 7 (1981), pp. 264-87.

Wessels, A., 'Biblical Presuppositions for and against Syncretism', in J. Gort, H. Vroom, R. Ferhout and A. Wessels (eds.), *Dialogue and Syncretism: An Interdisciplinary Approach* (Grand Rapids: Eerdmans, 1989), pp. 52-65.

White, H., 'Conventional Conflicts', *NLH* 13 (1981), pp. 145-60.

Whitt, W.D. 'The Divorce of Yahweh and Asherah in Hos. 2.4-7; 12ff', *SJOT* 6 (1992), pp. 31-67.

Wilder, A., *Early Christian Rhetoric: The Language of the Gospel* (Cambridge, MA: Harvard University Press, 1971).

Willett, J., *The Theatre of Bertolt Brecht: A Study From Eight Aspects* (London: Eyre Methuen, 1977).

Willett, J. (ed.), *Brecht on Theatre* (London: Eyre Methuen, 1974).

Willis, E., 'Sexual Counterrevolution I', *Rolling Stone* (24 March 1977).

Winn Leith, M.J., 'Verse and Reverse: The Transformation of the Woman Israel in Hosea 1–3', in Day (ed.), *Gender and Difference in Ancient Israel*, pp. 95-108.

Winny, J.L., *A Preface to Donne* (London: Longman, 1981).

Wittig, M., 'The Category of Sex', *Feminist Issues* 2 (1982), pp. 63-68.

Wittig, S., 'A Theory of Multiple Meanings', in Crossan (ed.), *Polyvalent Narration*, pp. 75-103.

Wolfe, R.E., *Meet Amos and Hosea* (New York: Harper & Row, 1945).

Wolff, H.W., *A Commentary on the Book of Hosea* (trans. G. Stansell; Herm; Philadelphia: Fortress Press, 1974).

Wolosky, S., 'Derrida, Jabès, Levinas: Sign-Theory as Ethical Discourse', *Prooftexts* 2 (1982), pp. 283-302.

Woolf, V., *A Room of One's Own* (New York: Harcourt, Brace & World, 1929).

Worden, T., 'The Literary Influence of the Ugarit Fertility Myth on the Old Testament', *VT* 3 (1953), 273-97.

Wright, E., *Postmodern Brecht: A Re-Presentation* (London: Routledge, 1989).

Yee, G.A., *Composition and Tradition in the Book of Hosea: A Redaction Critical Investigation* (Atlanta: Scholars Press, 1987).

—'Hosea', in C.A. Newsom and S.H. Ringe (eds.), *The Women's Bible Commentary* (London: SPCK, 1992), pp. 195-202.

INDEXES

INDEX OF REFERENCES

OLD TESTAMENT

INDEX OF AUTHORS

JOURNAL FOR THE STUDY OF THE OLD TESTAMENT

Supplement Series